Essays on American Indian and Mormon History

Essays on American Indian and Mormon History

edited by
P. Jane Hafen and Brenden W. Rensink

The University of Utah Press   Salt Lake City

The Defiance House Man colophon is a registered trademark of The University of
Utah Press. It is based on a four-foot-tall Ancient Puebloan pictograph (late PIII)
near Glen Canyon, Utah.

Library of Congress Cataloging-in-Publication Data

Names: Hafen, P. Jane, 1955– editor. | Rensink, Brenden W., editor.
Title: American Indians and Mormons/P. Jane Hafen and Brenden W. Rensink, eds.
Description: Salt Lake City : The University of Utah Press, 2019. | Identifiers:
    LCCN 2018048204 (print) | LCCN 2018050416 (ebook) | ISBN 9781607816911 |
    ISBN 9781607816904 (cloth : alk. paper) | ISBN 9781647692100 (paperback : alk. paper)
Subjects: LCSH: Mormon Church—Relations. | Indians of North America—Religion. |
    Indians of North America—Cultural assimilation—History. | Mormon Church—
    Missions. | Indians of North America—Missions. | Church of Jesus Christ of Latter-day
    Saints. Northern Indian Mission. | Church of Jesus Christ of Latter-day Saints. Indian
    Student Placement Program.
Classification: LCC BX8643.I53 (ebook) | LCC BX8643.I53 A44 2019 (print) |
    DDC 289.3/08997—dc23
LC record available at https://lccn.loc.gov/2018048204

Permission acknowledgments
Tacey Atsitty, *Rain Scald* (Albuquerque: University of New Mexico Press, 2017). Excerpts on
pages xxi–xxviii are published with the permission of University of New Mexico Press.
From Buffalo to Bread, on pages xxxiii–xxxiv, was originally published on the *By Common
Consent* blog on November 28, 2017. Republished here with permission. See https://
bycommonconsent.com/2017/11/28/from-buffalo-to-bread/.

Errata and further information on this and other titles available online at UofUpress.com.

And it came to pass that there was no contention in the land, because of the love of God which did dwell in the hearts of the people.

And there were no envyings, nor strifes, nor tumults, nor whoredoms, nor lyings, nor murders, nor any manner of lasciviousness; and surely there could not be a happier people among all the people who had been created by the hand of God.

There were no robbers, nor murderers, neither were there Lamanites, nor any manner of -ites; but they were in one, the children of Christ, and heirs to the kingdom of God.

4 Nephi 1: 15–17
Book of Mormon

Contents

PART ONE

Native Experience with the Early LDS Church, Interpretation of Mormon Scripture, and Literary Representations

Figures and Table

Introduction

P. JANE HAFEN AND BRENDEN W. RENSINK

On Thursday, January 29, 1863, about 450 Northwestern Shoshone were in their winter encampment on the Bear River in what is now southern Idaho. In the early morning before dawn, troops of the United States Army, stationed at Fort Douglas, Utah, attacked the tribe in the largest massacre in United States Indian history. The army reported about 250 Shoshone were killed. The Shoshone say more than 400 were slaughtered. After the shooting ceased, members of the army continued to desecrate the bodies, rape survivors, burn the tepees, and steal horses and food resources. Mormon settlers in Cache Valley expressed their gratitude to the army. Some survivors of the massacre later accepted Mormonism and exercised its principles of faith in the atoning sacrifice of Jesus Christ by forgiving the perpetrators of the massacre. One hundred fifty years later, the Northwestern Shoshone Tribe has purchased the massacre site and is planning an interpretive memorial.[1]

However, on September 6, 2016, the town of Wellsville, Utah, gathered at their annual Founders' Day celebration to watch as groups of white residents, painted red and dressed as Indians, reenacted a supposed historical battle between Natives and white Mormon settlers. The "Sham Battle" has taken place for the last 100 years and reveals a great deal about historical and contemporary relations between American Indians and Mormons in Utah and elsewhere. Located in the Cache Valley about 75 miles north of Salt Lake City, Wellsville is emblematic of the archipelago of Mormon settlements that stretched far along the Wasatch Mountains and a Mormon corridor from Alberta to California after Mormon settlers arrived in (then) northern Mexico in 1847. Located in fertile valleys also frequented by various Indian groups, Wellsville's Mormon settlement created tension with Native inhabitants. There was, however, no historical battle that resembles the "Sham Battle" of the Wellsville Founders' Day celebration. The event narration mentions the 1863 Battle of Bear River, which is more commonly known as the Bear River Massacre. The "Sham Battle" is a fiction that has persisted for a century. Such fictions permeate the history of Indian-Mormon relations.[2]

This premise is peculiar, given that American Indians have an association with The Church of Jesus Christ of Latter-day Saints from the very origins of the Church. The Church was organized in 1830, and much of its early theology centered on Native Peoples. The Book of Mormon, a foundational book of scripture, claimed to be the record of ancient Israelites who migrated to the Americas and were "among the ancestors of the American Indians."[3] The title page of the Book of Mormon acknowledges that the scripture is "written to the Lamanites, who are a remnant of the house of Israel." Indeed, within seven months of the organization of the Church, Parley P. Pratt, Oliver Cowdery, Peter Whitmer Jr., and Ziba Peterson went to the Cattaraugus, then the Shawnee, Delaware, and Wyandot Indians as missionaries. The Indigenous Peoples of this hemisphere, who were on the receiving end of this and subsequent evangelizing, have histories and stories going back to their own creations. This collection of essays explores how these apparently diverse understandings intersect, overlap, sometimes conflict, engage, and often fail to engage each other.

This missionary effort established a pattern of seeing Indian Nations as objects that would fulfill Book of Mormon prophecies about Natives' presumed ancestors, the Lamanites. Much as the Wellsville "Sham Battle" engaged with fictitious Indians as objects of constructed historical memory, much of the literature concerning Mormon-Indian relations engages with Native Peoples as the objects of study, not subjects who exert their own agency, construct their own identities, and internalize their own perspectives of their Mormon experiences. What then of the Indigenous Nations themselves who were facing nineteenth-century settler colonialism, among which the Mormons were part? Reframing the narratives of encounter and association recognizes American Indians as citizens of sovereign nations with distinct cultures, histories, and languages.

Shifting emphasis and reframing historical and contemporary narratives demonstrate a process of academic research that represents Indigenous thought and asserts resistance. These decolonizing inquiries are necessary for the intellectual survivance of Native Peoples. Susan Miller (Seminole) and James Riding In (Pawnee) identify six principles of Indigenous thought: 1. Indian sovereignty; 2. Land and resources; 3. European claims of discovery based on racially based assumptions; 4. Language of racism-rationalized aggression against Indians;

5. Discourses of colonialism entrenched in historical narratives; and 6. Colonialism as a crime against humanity.[4] This essay collection, *Essays on American Indian and Mormon History,* identifies ways Indigenous thought interacts with Mormon histories, Mormon arts, and contemporary Mormon practices. Reframing familiar, traditional stories and assumptions to consider the elements of Indigenous thought can be challenging. Many histories acknowledge Native elements but then proceed to reaffirm colonialist discourses without regard to Native sovereignty, Native lands, and colonial relationships.

American Indians are distinct from other groups now categorized as Lamanites. Although the term *Lamanite* eventually extends to Indigenous Peoples throughout the Western Hemisphere and to Asian Pacific Islanders, the appellation initially was limited to the contact the early Saints had with local tribes. American Indians have unique characteristics that other ethnic groups do not have.[5] Their status as a group separate from domestic citizens was noted in the United States Constitution.[6] During the early years of LDS Church history, Native sovereignty was further enshrined by a series of Supreme Court decisions.[7] As the United States extended control over the continent in subsequent decades, Indigenous inhabitants were also recognized as members of distinct tribal nations. Currently there are more than 565 sovereign Indian Nations recognized by the federal government. Additional tribes not recognized by the federal government have state recognition. The political and governmental relationship of American Indian tribes with the United States differentiates Indigenous Peoples from other Lamanites.

Also, in order to be acknowledged as an American Indian, an individual must belong to a federally recognized tribal nation. The qualifications are established by each sovereign tribe. Many tribes base membership on blood quantum, or degree of Indian blood, a practice dating back to treaty enforcement. Some tribes, like the Cherokee Nation, have shifted to define tribal membership according to descendancy.[8] However, in most cases, the legal authority of the tribe determines who may belong and who does not. Unlike other categories of Lamanites where no proof is required, American Indians must prove their identities. Or, as the aphorism goes, only Indians, horses, and dogs are required to have a legal pedigree.

The westward movement of the Mormons engaged American Indians along the way. This essay collection cannot address all the encounters of Mormon settlers with tribal nations. The primary sources recording most of those encounters are not narrated by Indigenous Peoples and are told from a singular point of view, often intending to heroicize Mormon pioneers and their legacy. One exception that includes a Native point of view is a well-known story of a wandering cow from a Mormon immigrant train. Charles Eastman (Santee Dakota) narrates this account in his 1918 collection, *Indian Heroes and Great Chieftains*.

> In 1854, when [Man-Afraid-of-His-Horse] was barely thirty-five years old, the various bands were again encamped near Fort Laramie. A Mormon emigrant train, moving westward, left a footsore cow behind, and the young men killed her for food. The next day, to their astonishment, an officer with thirty men appeared at the Indian camp and demanded of old Conquering Bear that they be given up. The chief in vain protested that it was all a mistake and offered to make reparation. It would seem that either the officer was under the influence of liquor, or else had a mind to bully the Indians, for he would accept neither explanation nor payment, but demanded point-blank that the young men who had killed the cow be delivered up to summary punishment. The old chief refused to be intimidated and was shot dead on the spot. Not one soldier ever reached the gate of Fort Laramie! Here Red Cloud led the young Ogallalas, and so intense was the feeling that they even killed the half-breed interpreter.[9]

Obviously, Eastman's retelling of this conflict 50 years later relies on oral tradition and Eastman's own familiarity with Red Cloud's life story. Other narratives of the same event emphasize the deaths of the soldiers. The facts of the events are unchangeable; the motivations and responses depend on who is telling the story. Many of the stories of Indians and Mormons, as told by settler communities, were framed to protect the narrative of building the LDS Church kingdom of God without considering the complex relations of settler colonialism and Indigenous nations. The stories told by Native Peoples are often preserved in oral retellings or not recounted outside of Native communities at all.

For example, the infamous 1857 Mountain Meadows Massacre directly involved local Paiutes. Approximately 120 members of an immigrant train from Arkansas were murdered in southern Utah by local Mormons. The killings were kept under a code of silence by the perpetrators and their descendants until

Juanita Brooks exposed them in *The Mountain Meadows Massacre*, published in 1950.[10] Since then, a burgeoning publishing field, from popular history to serious scholarship to polemic, has attempted to understand the killings. Local Paiutes were politically and culturally implicated, first by Mormons blaming them for actions of local Church members, and second by engaging them in the aftermath. Yet none of these narratives consider the Paiute experience as primary. In *Massacre at Mountain Meadows*, Walker, Turley, and Leonard devote five pages in Appendix D to Indian issues.[11] The book refers readers to "additional information on the Indians" at mountainmeadowsmassacre.org. However, the website does not offer specific details regarding Indians but links back to the Walker, Turley, and Leonard volume, along with more recently published collected legal papers. The LDS Church has begun including the event in Church educational curriculum without addressing the Paiute complications.[12]

One hundred fifty years later, some Paiutes claim they were not involved according to oral tradition.[13] The Paiute version contradicts some Mormon accounts. Transcending the conflicting histories, the Church officially apologized to the Paiutes at the 2007 dedication of Mountain Meadows Massacre Monument. "Elder Eyring [of the LDS Church First Presidency] said that a separate expression of regret is owed the Paiute people, 'who have unjustly borne for too long the principal blame for what occurred during the massacre.'"

More recently, then LDS Church assistant Church historian Richard E. Turley Jr., helped dedicate a monument to the largely forgotten 1866 Circleville Massacre, where Mormon settlers killed 30 men, women, and children of the Koosharem band of Paiutes. Although 150 years late, the voices and historical memories of Paiutes were privileged in the monuments' text.[14]

In other cases, historical narratives purport to recount American Indian events. For example, *Sagwitch: Shoshone Chieftain, Mormon Elder, 1822–1887* by Scott R. Christensen tells of Sagwitch's life, but the point of view and the bulk of the story does not and cannot contain the voice of Sagwitch. Despite its title and its best efforts, it is still a story of the Mormons and the West, not the Shoshone experience. The Bear River Massacre interpretive center is a recovery of Indigenous traditions. However, in many cases, obtaining historical American Indian voices is beyond reach despite best practices and archival research. One methodology is to recenter the discourse as this collection attempts to do.

Recent discussion of race in American history has extended to the Mormon Church, but the implicit meaning is that *race* refers to African Americans or those of African descent. In 2006 Church president Gordon B. Hinckley decried continued racial strife within the Church following the 1978 lift of the priesthood ban. In broader terms, he continued:

> Now I am told that racial slurs and denigrating remarks are sometimes heard among us. I remind you that no man who makes disparaging remarks concerning those of another race can consider himself a true disciple of Christ. Nor can he consider himself to be in harmony with the teachings of the Church of Christ.... I have recognized and spoken a number of times on the diversity we see in our society. It is all about us, and we must make an effort to accommodate that diversity.... Brethren, there is no basis for racial hatred among the priesthood of this Church. If any within the sound of my voice is inclined to indulge in this, then let him go before the Lord and ask for forgiveness and be no more involved in such.[15]

Such unequivocal denunciation of racist attitudes in the Church is laudatory. The default conversation and framing, however, within and without the LDS Church, is often black-and-white—this despite the broader racial diversities and social constructs.[16] The unbalanced formula is white and the "other" or non-white, including any group that does not fall within the purity of white-ism. Even though current parlance renders race as white and black, and recent essays published by the Church have tried to ameliorate historic prejudices toward black peoples and the priesthood and temple ban, racist attitudes toward American Indians have yet to be addressed specifically and officially by the Church.[17] Yet, essays in this collection demonstrate the empowerment of white privilege in defining and developing doctrine and policy toward American Indians. That issue originates in discourse, the defining of and claiming identity of Indigenous Peoples through the Book of Mormon. Indigenous others are defined by the colors of their skin such as the Lamanites in 1 Nephi 12.23: "a dark, and loathsome, and a filthy people, full of idleness and all manner of abominations." Indigenous Peoples are unlikely to define themselves this way. Moreover, a hemispheric literalism is unsustainable. Scripturally, Natives are the objects of projected ideas, metaphors of good and evil used to cloak racism. Bifurcated colonization in the nobility of the Lamanites juxtaposes against the perceived savagery of the occupants of desired land resources. The discourses of doctrine and policy both ennoble Native Peoples while justifying colonization, racial discrimination, and sympathetic ownership. This reading of the foundational sacred text of Mormonism compromises the race and agency of a people.

Another aspect of colonization includes assumptions about traditional gender roles. Whereas European traditions are primarily patriarchal and patrilineal, many Native societies are matriarchal and/or matrilineal.[18] This social structure stems from origin stories where the primary deities and creators are women. Matriarchal societies also empower women. Unlike colonizing beliefs, gender definitions are complex; individuals outside the male/female binary are respected and often given places of honor in the tribe. Culturally, most Indigenous communities have linguistic terms for people who do not fall in the pattern of heteronormativity, and those terms are often imbued with sacredness. For example, the Zuni have *lhamana*, the Navajo use *nádleehí*, the Lakota *winktje*, and so on. In the Tiwa language of Taos Pueblo, from whence co-editor Hafen hails, the word is *lhunide*. The closest English term is "Two-Spirit."[19]

If the Church has institutionally patronized and colonized American Indians, the place of individual members becomes complicated. Telling a history that acknowledges those complexities respects the faith of those who have committed to the Church and respects those who have left for their own reasons. Listening to individual stories, and looking at local communities can reaffirm the fundamental principles of the Restored Gospel while still recognizing human errors. These stories need to be told and heard.

Additionally, non-Indigenous Peoples can ask some basic questions to help decolonize and to assist in understanding Native Peoples. On whose ancestral land do you live? Who are the local Indigenous Peoples? What is their history? Almost every tribal nation has a historical moment when their world changes forever, such as the Bear River Massacre for the Shoshone. What is that apocalyptic moment for local tribes? Who is telling the story and the history? What are individual relations with Mormonism?

In compiling the essays in this collection, we have tried to refocus the narrative to consider Indigenous methodology, to incorporate contemporary American Indian voices along with recognized and new scholars in American Indian Studies. We have tried to address the complicated questions of faith and analysis, history, colonization, and decolonization. A major challenge is acknowledging how a scholar presents a history of Indigenous experience that may conflict with personal beliefs held as absolute truths, how the individual fits in the communal discourse of indigeneity and the academy.

Throughout this volume, readers will encounter varied methodologies, approaches, and disciplines, including literary criticism, documentary analysis, history, ethnography, and religious studies. Terminologies will likewise vary, often interchanging *Native, Indian,* and *Indigenous,* and individual tribal identifications, as well as *Mormon* and *LDS* as context demands. Most of the chapters here were workshopped, along with a few additional pieces, at a seminar hosted by the Charles Redd Center for Western Studies at Brigham Young University in the summer of 2015. Our aim at that workshop was to avoid familiar narrative patterns of settler colonialism. Rather, participants sought to make American Indians the subjects rather than objects of discussion in relationships with Mormons by reframing critical and scholarly questions from an American Indian/ Indigenous point of view within a framework of truth-telling while increasing understanding, and without contention. We feel the endeavor has borne fruit, and this anthology demonstrates new ways to explore these themes further.

This volume begins with three pieces that foreground *personal* Native experience and voice. As much of the following essays are academic in tone, it is important to privilege these personal reflections, imbued with the humanity and intimacy that are too often lost under the apparatus of scholarly methodology and presentation. First, we begin with the words of acclaimed Navajo poet, Tacey Atsitty, excerpted from her recently published collection, *Rain Scald.*[20] Atsitty graced our 2015 seminar with a powerful reading of her poetry, and her words exert equal weight in print as well. Second, in a personal narrative, "Sovereignty and the Corn Soup Social," associate professor of law at Brigham Young University Michalyn Steele (Seneca) recalls the role of the LDS Church in establishing a social center in her childhood Cattaraugus community. This recollection underscores the complexity of lived Mormon-Indian experiences and the intimate level at which they unfold. Third, we include a recently published blog post, "From Buffalo to Bread," by the current chairman of the Northwestern Shoshone Nation, Darren Parry. In his short piece, Parry links the history of the 1863 Bear River Massacre to subsequent and current tribal relations with Mormonism—a powerful pondering on cultural, history, adaptation, and agency. Together, the words from Atsitty, Steele, and Parry establish a nuanced tone of Native perspectives and voices that can inform the following chapters.

This anthology is divided into two parts. Part One, "Native Experience with the Early LDS Church, Interpretation of Mormon Scripture, and Literary Representations" contains five chapters. Though diverse in content, they share common themes and chronologies. In Chapter 1, "The Book of Mormon as Mormon Settler Colonialism," Elise Boxer (Dakota, Fort Peck Assiniboine and Sioux Tribes) outlines the historic developments of the Indian racial other in the history of the LDS Church. Employing the framework of settler colonialism, Boxer reexamines the Book of Mormon's relation to Native Peoples. In Chapter 2, "Other Scriptures: Restoring Voices of Gantowisas to an Open Canon," Thomas W. Murphy offers a personal reflection on Native readings of the Book of Mormon, the idea of a more open canon of LDS scripture, and more openly multicultural possibilities for LDS belief and worship. In Chapter 3, "Joseph Smith in Iroquois Country: A Mormon Creation Story," Lori Elaine Taylor suggests a provocative connection between Joseph Smith and Seneca leader, Handsome Lake. This creative reimagining of the beginnings of the LDS Church centers Native Peoples in new ways. In Chapter 4, "When Wakara Wrote Back: The Creation and Contestation of the 'Paper Indian' in Early Mormon Utah," Max Perry Mueller examines a moment in early Utah history when Ute Chief Wakara created a physical document that illustrates Wakara's literacy and the agency he exerted by putting pen to paper. In Chapter 5, "In the Literature of the Lamanites: (Un)settling Mormonism in the Literary Record of Native North America, 1830–1930," Michael P. Taylor examines literary representations by Indians of Mormons and vice versa in provocative ways.

Part Two, "Native Mormon Experiences in the Twentieth Century," contains six additional essays, all employing historical methodology to understand twentieth-century experiences of Native Peoples with and within the LDS Church. In Chapter 6, "Mormonism and the Catawba Nation," Stan Thayne considers the unique case of the mass conversation of Catawbas to the LDS Church in the early twentieth century. Here, many Catawbas interviewed take a literal interpretation of their being Book of Mormon descendants. These are compelling interviews and Thayne's own positionality as an interviewer makes for complicated ground. Chapter 7, "Reclamation, Redemption, and Political Maneuvering in Diné Bikéyah, 1947–1980," Erika Bsumek explores the intersection of Navajo economic development, environmental politics, and Mormons surrounding Glen Canyon Dam. In Chapter 8, "Aloha in Diné Bikéyah: Mormon Hawaiians and Navajos, 1949 to 1990," Farina Noelani King (Navajo) highlights the history of Native Hawaiians who served in Navajo country as LDS missionaries and the cultural exchanges that occurred. In Chapter 9, "Grafting Indians and Mormons Together on Great Plains Reservations: A History of the

LDS Northern Indian Mission, 1964–1973" Jay H. Buckley, Kathryn Cochran, Taylor Brooks, and Kristen Hollist offer a history of the LDS Northern Indian Mission and Native experiences there, the first of its kind, and uncover valuable sources and experiences of missionaries and Native members on the Northern Great Plains. In Chapter 10, "The Indian Student Placement Program and Native Direction," Megan Stanton presents a history of the LDS Indian Student Placement Program that highlights Native contributions to and experiences with the program. The placement program is examined in context with federal government boarding schools whose purpose was to "kill the Indian, save the man." In Chapter 11, "'Which Side of the Line': American Indian Students and Programs at Brigham Young University, 1960–1983," Warren Metcalf uncovers the experiences of Native students attending Brigham Young University during a brief era when the university hosted one of the largest Native student populations in the country.

Finally, co-editor Brenden W. Rensink offers a conclusion of sorts, highlighting various issues raised by the preceding chapters, asking questions, and suggesting how they might provide foundations for future study.

These essays address a variety of important topics in discussing American Indians and Mormons. Yet, there is no shortage of other pressing topics in need of scholarly inquiry. In particular, we must consider the relationship between specific tribes and their interactions with Mormons. These would include the history of Lumbees and Mormons, Western Shoshone-Bannocks and Mormons, the relationship of Hopi tribal councils and Mormon lawyers, tribal water rights in Arizona and complications with Mormon settlers. Additionally, researchers could consider an examination of violence in San Juan County, New Mexico, civil rights violations in San Juan County, Utah, and elsewhere. The establishment of the Bears Ears National Monument and its reduction is an issue still in flux between a consortium of tribes in conflict with local non-Native (often Mormon) politicians. In short, there is a rich field of ideas to explore. Resulting work will surely satisfy scholarly interests, but the more pressing needs and concerns of Indigenous individuals and communities that could be met by such work holds even greater promise for understanding, reconciliation, and community.

Poetry Selections from *Rain Scald*

TACEY ATSITTY

Ach'íí'

I.

In my pocket: intestines
wrap fat, and it's so stiff
when cold. It looks like—

we shouldn't speak
so young. Instead, knead salt,
flour, and water.

Our toys, I've tasted them:
sheepherders or soldiers.
Should they harden

and be painted, or should
a hole be blown from the insides.
All that salt.

II.

Dad's baby brother, his intestines
broke, and he couldn't pee.
He died because he was so full.
Just like his grandmother,
the day she walked out of the hogan,
dropped to her knees, holding her
stomach—so mixed up inside
when it exploded.

III.

After all those explosions in Vietnam, it must've messed my uncle up
pretty good. He could never eat ach'íí' again. He had to have three Enemy
Ways done. We had to haul so many sheep. It's a long ride in the back
of a jeep all the way to Farmington to be baptized. I stood next to that
wall of bricks at the Apache Building, wearing my squash blossom: a line
of females v-ing down to the male, and there rested his tongue, almost
between my breasts.

IV.
I remember She Who Wasn't Spoken Of—
each Red Vine costed a nickel, that easy twine

across the street from our little red-bricked
house—They say she drove so fast

she whorled into a puff of smoke
behind Table Mesa the day she died.

Dad says he remembers the first time he died,
that long bus ride when they took him

to Utah for school. He had been memorizing
land formations: an angel the size of his hand

disappeared and after that, he was so empty
from crying and so full of remembering

rocks, he just fell asleep. He remembers
stealing pennies from his foster sister

to buy red licorice. He was always in trouble
for that or for sling-shotting chickens.

Only three survived the morning massacre.
Only one sheep was taken from the flock.

They stole it, all those Navajo boys,
led it to the mountain edge, where
they built a fire and slit its throat:

laughing into the dry
night, fat dripping
from their mouths.

Sunbeam

Around noontime on Highway 666, we are driving to town. It is Pepper's fifth birthday. My dad is working. He is probably running laps with students. *Cloudless.* Our two vehicles leave the Chuskas. I want a sucker. Cheii takes me south. There are six of them in the other car; they turn north. It is too bright today. Two weeks ago my mom dreamt of night birds chanting amidst juniper berries. Today, the land formations look like owls. I leave Little Water Trading Post with Minnie Mouse's heart in my mouth. Pepper is singing, "Jesus Wants Me for a Sunbeam" with our cousin sister when—Mom was holding Baby in the front passenger seat and shot a look over to her sister—My little brother sips root beer while Baby sleeps. It was May. I sit alone in the back of my Cheii's truck, wiping rouge across my eyelids. I don't understand the dream or the land—Grandma clenches my hand as we stand on the road, watching the sun take them:

pepper-grass gathered in a pink cup, here Daddy.

Nightsong: To the gorge dwellers

With no fire, you offer
nothing. Say,

a body found, fall creek
gorge. Eventual

it is, meaning to happen.
Meaning to say,

Dear fellow _____,
It is with deep

Name—Name—
Name, strung like

hair. Water strands
made old, made

white. Too close
to dark. Second tragedy

fall creek throat.
Repeated repeated loss.

Thirst-in almanac
of the gorges. Litany

of wrists. Look
down at your wrists,

down here where
the thick laps

the lips. Where you
haven't been taught:

pull yourself out of
the plunge pool

and look for fire, look
for rings shifted

to your thumb and
forefinger. There, like

vapor wrapping you
in strips. In this falling

moment, cities
sink into the depths,

drown. The earth
face carried up and

away in the current of
a whirlwind, where water

and mountains hide
in deep blue. What faces

bring: a reservoir filled,
following the night

when day fell into day,
soon followed by night

into night to night,
thrice with no moon,

thrice with no flame—
kept in the thick thick.

Evensong

I.
At the throat of this tree he sees me kneel,
steep into leaves and pockets of shale.
My voice hollows out veins in roots,

I look to you to see you: fallen mouth from the sky.
Up where lips round off over descant—
steep into leaves and pockets of shale.

Open: rain-beaded blossom. Uvular angles.
Where rocks fall out of themselves, utter
up where lips round off over descant.

I want to go back to ruth, mouth ever so filled
to the lips before the fall. Word spill,
where rocks fall out of themselves: utter

a prayer. Both limb and leaf bent skyward,
the calm before collapse. Creek-cut
at the lips before the fall. *A word-spill*

from leaf tongue, Father. From cracks,
the calm before collapse. Creek-cut
in the throat of this tree. He sees me kneel,
my voice hollows out veins in roots.

II.
Scoop to hollow the bend, calm
to bend calm. See my right palm—
I'm going to bend calm again. Rock wrens
of eventide begin to warble the easy ends:
cut. Into the air sweet water sprays; psalm

to the ever pouring gaze. A trickle bomb
as *my sore ran in the night.* When to embalm
this bubble stone walk and finally ascend,
scoop the hollowed.

Where the arrow current quells the qualm:
pierced, we say nothing. I glance at my palm—
it's where we began and didn't go, didn't lend
our eyes toward the current: whittled to bend,
a sand-swollen end, a silent opening.

III.
O Holy People, show me how I am human,
how I am soon to sliver. Stay please, for woman
or man's sake. Succor me from a telestial state,
where I long to be self-luminous in a slate
of granite. How easily I fall to shards, a hand

left to wane ungathered. How easily we
gather rocks for pockets. What drowns
is not the boulder but swivel water bait,
O Diyin Dinéé!

Hook me by the ribs, bear me up to human,
so I know to come here only when it's a male-
rain. This is how I dry my hair, kept from weight
of water. If all you can tell me is—*wait,*
let it be enough to know how sparkling can—
O Holy People.

Sovereignty and the Corn Soup Social
A Personal Reflection

MICHALYN STEELE

Among my earliest memories is wandering the halls and playing among the pews of the darkened chapel of The Church of Jesus Christ of Latter-Day Saints on the Cattaraugus Seneca Nation Indian Reservation in Western New York as my parents and my grandmother worked all night making Iroquois corn soup and Iroquois corn bread.

Traditional Iroquois corn soup is made from dried "squaw corn" or white corn, which has been soaked in lye then rinsed and rinsed again to release the dark inner kernel or "eye." It takes a long time and the black "eyes" of the kernels stick to your arms like freckles as you rinse, massaging the corn with your arms up to your elbows deep in the rinsing liquid. The corn is cooked with kidney beans and salt pork, yielding a salty gray broth and the corn softens into a hominy-like texture.

To make corn bread, the dried corn would be rinsed, and redried overnight on long tables covered with newspaper, then ground into a kind of masa. Kidney beans are folded into the masa and it is shaped into thick wheels the size of a children's red wagon wheel, and boiled. The result is a bit like boiled Play-Doh studded with beans. It is the ultimate comfort food, sliced and slathered with butter and salt.

These traditional foods require a significant investment of time and considerable skill to make, along with the right kind of corn. So the opportunity to eat these foods is treasured—featured at significant celebrations, but somewhat hard to get. As a kid, my local LDS Church was the place to eat these foods on the first Saturday of each month, the Corn Soup Social. On the first Saturday of every month, the Church held the Corn Soup Social, a gathering where people from around the reservation brought their own jars to purchase traditional corn soup by the quart or to enjoy a bowl and maybe a sandwich and a slice of corn bread at the tables set up in the church. Members of the congregation brought sandwiches and potato or macaroni salad to serve as a lunch plate.

The Corn Soup Social was one way our small branch of the LDS Church was working to earn money to build a new chapel. To be sure, the history of the relationship between The Church of Jesus Christ of Latter-day Saints and the Indian Nations of North America is fraught and complicated. But for me, my tribe (the Seneca Nation of Indians) and my Church (The Church of Jesus Christ of Latter-day Saints) meet inextricably in me and were the institutions that most colored my childhood on the Cattaraugus Reservation.

My two great-grandmothers, Florence Huff Parker and Nina Tallchief Seneca, joined the church in the 1940s as adults, responding to the message of young missionaries from the West, dressed in suits and fedoras. Soon thereafter, my grandmother, Norma Parker Seneca, was baptized in the Cattaraugus River, as was my mother, Carolyn Seneca Steele, when she was nine years old. For me, the faith of my mother and grandmothers is the LDS faith. They were committed to the gospel it taught, to the Book of Mormon, and to helping the Church grow in their community. My great-grandmothers baked pies and sold them to raise money for the original chapel that was eventually built on reservation land in the 1950s. The Church reached an extraordinary agreement with the Seneca Nation for the Church to use the parcel of land where it sits as long as it was used for Church purposes. Anyone from the reservation may also be buried in the cemetery behind the chapel, and I suppose I myself will someday be buried there with several generations of my Seneca ancestors.

In the years that have followed, the congregation has planted potatoes, corn, and an apple orchard on the land attached to the chapel to contribute to the Church welfare system. In 2015, my parents served a mission on the Cattaraugus Reservation with a special focus on helping reservation residents set up beehives and gain beekeeping skills to support the pollinators at the request of the Seneca Nation. They also helped the congregation build a corn crib behind the church.

In addition to the Corn Soup Socials, the congregation was working to raise money for a new, expanded chapel in the 1970s. I suppose because it was the 1970s, the golden era of the variety show, the congregation took a page from the Osmond playbook and the BYU performing groups, and formed a band and mounted a variety music, comedy, and dancing show comprised of members of the small congregation. I wore a shirt adorned with green sequins as a preteen backup singer for several of the musical numbers. For a few shows I performed a comedy routine that my mother had lifted from short humorous blurbs in *Reader's Digest*. There was hoop dancing and other traditional dances, there were hymns and an uplifting message, there were pop cover songs from *Grease*, from Linda Ronstadt, from the Doobie Brothers, and others. We played small crowds around Western New York and eastern Ohio. I was asked for my autograph after one show in Akron, Ohio because my corny comedy routine had killed.

As a legal academic, I have been keenly interested in studying the legal relationship between the federal government and tribes. I have been guided and inspired by the Two Row Wampum, which symbolizes the two parallel canoes of two sovereigns, moving side by side, neither endeavoring to steer the other. Surely the United States has not often been faithful to this vision of peacefully coexisting sovereigns, with much of the history of federal Indian policy marked by the effort of the United States to stamp out Indian culture and identity.

At least for me, the two identities of being a member of the Seneca Nation and of the LDS Church have peacefully coexisted. My experience in the Cattaraugus congregation, more often than not, was of a uniquely symbiotic, cooperative relationship between the Seneca Nation and the Church. The Church contributes to the community and is a gathering place. The Corn Soup Social preserved and perpetuated important cultural touchstones within the reservation community.

The expanded church that was built as a result stands to me as a monument of the Church's embrace of Seneca culture and community and the Seneca community's embrace of the Church as part of the community as well.

From Buffalo to Bread

DARREN PARRY

I loved to sit at the feet of my loving Grandmother, Mae Timbimboo Parry. She would sit for hours and tell me Shoshone stories about how the Coyote stole fire, or how the Sun got its name. As I attended school I developed a great love for history, and then one day I suddenly realized something. None of the stories my grandmother told me were in our history books. From our history books one can conclude that historical events are an absolute and have only one conclusion. But over the years I have come to realize that history is about perspective. Whose perspective?

For our people, history was just another battleground. We are often portrayed as uneducated, primitive, and cruel. Good for nothing except to teach the white people how to grow corn. The Mormon people of the Cache Valley often described my people as thieves and beggars. The irony in this is that the Mormon people themselves suffered hatred and injustices. It is hard to believe that they could be found guilty of doing the same. Peter Maughan, a Church leader in Cache Valley, just prior to the massacre at Bear River said, "With extraordinary good luck, the volunteers will 'wipe them out.' We wish this community rid of all such parties, and if Colonel Conner can be successful in reaching that Bastard class of humans, who play with the lives of the peaceable and the law abiding citizens in this way, we shall be pleased to acknowledge our obligations."

The events that took place on that cold January morning in 1863 have long been forgotten by most. Maybe guilt or remorse has silenced all of those who one day may have wanted to know the truth. I hope this new generation of people will have a desire to listen and to learn. Not because we are looking to have things made right, but because those who sacrificed so much have a God-given right to be heard. Their voices cry from the ground. Their stories need to be told.

If you are here at the massacre site at just the right time in the evening you can sit and hear the cries of our little ones calling to their mothers. Your senses tell you that you are among the spirits of more than 400 children of Damma Appa, that Great Spirit who created us all. You don't have to see things as they were, to know that a terrible injustice had taken place. You can feel it!

For Sagwitch and Bear Hunter and their small bands of Shoshone people, the reality of the situation became very real. After Bear Hunter's torture and murder, Sagwitch was left alone to witness almost the entire destruction of his people. No one would have blamed him for having feelings of hatred or resentment toward the Mormon settlers. But he chose a different path. One that not only saved his life, but that of generations to come. Ten years removed from the largest massacre of Native Americans in the history of the United States, Chief Sagwitch and the remaining survivors were baptized into the Mormon Church.

This massacre at Bear River does not define us. We have forgiven but we will never forget. There is a saying that we instill in our youth at an early age that says, "Give a man a fish and you feed him for a day; teach a man to fish and you feed him for a lifetime." Our tribal members know how to fish. We have more than 540 members today. The vast majority of us live along the Wasatch Front. We are your neighbors. We are active members in your communities. We have health care, housing, and education programs for our members. We have many of our children attending major universities around the country each semester. We realize that education gives our youth many options and opportunities. We have set up a trust account for the purchase of this massacre site. We currently own 30 acres and would love to have more.

Every Saturday morning we have cultural activities for our youth so that our heritage is not forgotten. We pride ourselves on being members of a society that makes a contribution.

Long ago our people worked hard every day just to make a living and survive. Every tribal member played a significant role in the well-being of our society. For the past 150 years the federal government has created an expectation that being a Native American means having a dependency on an entitlement program. We have chosen a different path and we have chosen to make our own destiny.

The most successful Native Americans today are those who can best balance Culture and Change. We honor our culture and honor our elders. Those who have gone before are important to us. We honor them and their traditions, but we realize that we live in an ever-changing world and we are preparing ourselves to change and succeed with it.

Part One

Native Experience with the Early LDS Church, Interpretation of Mormon Scripture, and Literary Representations

1

The Book of Mormon as Mormon Settler Colonialism

ELISE BOXER

Who are these tribes? They are called Indians, but it was a mistake that these Americans should ever have been given that name. Long before they were called Indians, most of them called themselves Lamanites. Their numerous people occupied America from north to south, and from east to west. When they broke up into many tribes with tribal names, they forgot the one general name by which they had once been known. The history of this old Lamanite nation is the most important record which has been translated into English since the translation of the Bible. It bears strong testimony of the Bible, and it was foretold by Bible prophets who said that it would become one with the Bible in the hands of the Lord for the accomplishment of [H]is purposes. This record is the Book of Mormon. It is a voice of love and assurance from prophets among the ancient Lamanites to the wandering remnant of their posterity. Nothing to compare with it is offered to them from any other source. It is the history of their people in ancient America; and the words of their great men and mighty leaders telling them who they are.[1]

Albert Robison Lyman's *A Voice Calling* is a small history of American Indians on the American Indian continent and their connection to the peoples of the Book of Mormon. Lyman articulates that before tribes broke up into various tribal nations and bands, they were in fact, all one nation: the Lamanites. This quote effectively highlights the belief that American Indians are not only the descendants of Lamanites found in the Book of Mormon, but simultaneously erases the diverse creation stories and histories unique to each tribe. The Book of Mormon is their history, or Lamanite history. Indigenous identity, history, sovereignty, and belief systems have not only been dismissed but replaced with a limited, racialized identity grounded in Mormon religious discourse. Lyman's short history illustrates the pervasive belief by general members of the LDS faith who believe American Indians are Lamanites and the Book of Mormon the history of this continent.

The Book of Mormon is not just a reflection of Mormon settler colonialism, but has been used to create a discourse that silences Indigenous voices and perspectives regarding their own history as a people on this continent. According to P. Jane Hafen, this is a "disruptive and colonizing act."[2] The Book of Mormon is utilized to construct a Lamanite identity and history in which Indigenous Peoples exist only to legitimize the presence of Mormon settlers on this continent and the religious narrative found in the Book of Mormon as accurate and true. By depicting Indigenous Peoples as Lamanites, or the first immigrants to this continent, the Book of Mormon provides the necessary justification for Indigenous removal and dispossession by Mormon settlers along the Mormon Corridor (Idaho, Utah, Arizona) in what is now the United States. The Book of Mormon reflects the nuanced ways in which Mormon settler colonialism is utilized to physically remove Indigenous people from their homelands while also demarcating Indigenous worldviews, identities, and histories as the racialized "other." The Book of Mormon reflects the nuanced ways in which Mormon settler colonialism functions by creating very distinct notions of Indigeneity.

Indigeneity, as defined by the Book of Mormon, is exhibited through the construction and application of "Lamanites" to American Indian Peoples. Lamanite identity is fluid, changing over time, but always in relation to Mormon Euro-American notions of Indigeneity. The use of the Book of Mormon as a historical and religious text of Lamanite identity and history on this continent erases the way Indigenous Peoples view their own creation as a people, their connection to the land, and their identity as a people. Instead, Indigenous Peoples are made to fit into Mormon creation stories and religious belief system. The erasure of Indigenous Peoples and history by Mormon settlers is an extension of the larger American colonial project of removal and genocide of Indigenous Peoples.

As Hafen has articulated, "Listening to Natives tell their own stories about their origins is a decolonizing act."[3] The use of diverse Indigenous histories and perspectives must be included to diversify current Mormon-Indian historiography. Currently, those tribal nations who had been early converts to Mormonism or which have a long history with Mormon settlers have dominated the literature. The inclusion of more diverse histories and perspectives will not only challenge current Mormon-Indian history, but reflect the diversity of tribal nations and experiences. There is no generic "American Indian" experience, or Mormon-Indian experience, nor is there a Lamanite identity that can be uniformly applied to all Indigenous Peoples. The inclusion of varied perspectives that challenge the Lamanite history and identity will enrich the historical narrative and empower tribal nations and peoples to tell their own histories. This chapter will use Dakota histories and worldviews as a framework and lens to challenge the notion of the Book of Mormon as Dakota history or Dakotas as Lamanites. Dakota Peoples' history and perspectives will be connected to the larger historiography and narrative of Mormon-Indian history. Finally, this rereading of the Book of Mormon is not about its veracity, or challenging its ecclesiastical authority, but rather how text operates as a definitive history of Indigenous Peoples in the Americas.

Theory and Terminology

The terminology used to discuss these issues must be precise and carefully selected. *American Indian* reflects terminology used in the Introduction to the Book of Mormon and various publications by LDS authors whereas the term Indigenous and/or Indigenous Peoples in my own analysis is used to acknowledge the diversity and sovereignty of tribal nations and tribal citizens. According to James Riding In and Susan A. Miller in *Native Historians Write Back: Decolonizing American Indian History* the use of *Indigenous* is not just about acknowledging *"original* occupation of an area ... but a set of principles that ... Indigenous Peoples live [by] in [their] communities."[4] Using specific tribal names when possible is vital because it is referencing a particular community's perspective and values.

Waziyatawin, Dakota historian, and Michael Yellow Bird, Mandan/Hidatsa sociologist, in *For Indigenous Eyes Only: A Decolonization Handbook*, defines "decolonization [a]s the intelligent, calculated, and active resistance to the forces of colonialism that perpetuate the subjugation and/or exploitation of our minds, bodies, and lands, and it is engaged for the ultimate purpose of overturning the colonial structure and realizing Indigenous liberation."[5] Decolonization is useful in challenging the Book of Mormon as a literal or religious history of Indigenous Peoples on this continent. By centering and privileging Dakota worldviews regarding their origins and history as a people, it disrupts the Mormon religious narrative that Dakota Peoples were/are Lamanites. By reclaiming Dakota history, a history that is not found or reflected in the Book of Mormon, it challenges the Mormon creation story of Lamanites as the first immigrants on this continent.

Mormon colonization can be defined as "the formal and informal methods (behaviors, ideologies, institutions, policies, and economies) that maintain the subjugation or exploitation of Indigenous Peoples, lands, and resources."[6] By this definition, The Church of Jesus Christ of Latter-day Saints can be viewed as a colonizing enterprise. The Book of Mormon became a powerful tool to subjugate Indigenous Peoples.

The Book of Mormon is a powerful extension of Mormon colonization because religious doctrine is used to define and shape Indigeneity. The Book of Mormon becomes the primary source of Lamanite history to Mormons, including American Indian Peoples who have been encouraged to read this text to better understand the history of their Lamanite ancestors. The Book of Mormon is not just about a religious, historical narrative that documents the rise and fall of Lamanite people; it also shaped early Mormon Euro-American views of American Indians. Like many other Americans in the nineteenth century, Mormon Euro-Americans viewed American Indian Peoples as a vanishing people, a people in need of saving via civilization. Lamanites could be saved vis-à-vis conversion to Mormonism. Civilization could be achieved only through their conversion to Mormonism, particularly their reclamation of the Book of Mormon as part of their Lamanite history and as an integral component of Lamanite identity. In addition to using colonization as a framework of analysis, settler colonialism is a useful tool when examining how the Book of Mormon codifies and justifies the erasure and removal of Indigenous Peoples. Mormon settler colonialism provides the necessary language and framework that names Indigenous removal, or what Patrick Wolfe terms "the logic of elimination" from the Book of Mormon.[7] Wolfe argues that the "restrictive racial classification of

Indians straightforwardly furthered the logic of elimination ... [race] is made in the targeting."[8] Indigenous Peoples are made into Lamanites, a process that begins in 1830 with the first printing of the Book of Mormon by Joseph Smith. The process of racializing Indigenous Peoples as Lamanites was to gain "access to territory."[9] The notion of American Indians as Lamanites changed over time, especially as Mormon settlers moved west and claimed Indigenous lands as their own. Wolfe further articulates, "settler colonialism destroys to replace."[10] The use of the Book of Mormon as the origins of Lamanite peoples is an act of settler colonialism, it replaces Indigenous histories and worldviews with a religious narrative that racializes and demarcates them as the racial and spiritual "other."

In addition to the work of Patrick Wolfe, Adria L. Imada's work on settler colonialist nostalgia in Hawaii is useful when examining how settler colonialism "relies on and produces an investment in uncomplicated, ahistorical fantasies."[11] The Book of Mormon replicates these "uncomplicated, ahistorical fantasies" by asserting that Indigenous Peoples on this continent were the first immigrants, whose title to land was contingent upon their righteousness and obedience. The book became a "genesis" of Indigenous Peoples on this continent. The ancestors of American Indians kept a written record, now known as the Book of Mormon. American Indians could lay claim to this rich heritage through their conversion to Mormonism. Their acceptance of this Lamanite identity legitimized the written record on this continent. Furthermore, Lamanites, and by extension, American Indian Peoples, lost their inheritance or rights to traditional homelands due to their own wickedness. Lamanites would lose their inheritance, or title to their land because of their status as a fallen people. Second, the settlement and colonization of this continent was inevitable. Mormon colonization was prophesized by Book of Mormon prophets or Lamanite ancestors. Read another way, Lamanite prophets prophesized the arrival of Mormon settlers and subsequently, their own dispossession because of their spiritual wickedness. American Indian removal and displacement was justified.

Michael Omi and Howard Winant in *Racial Formations in the United States: From the 1960s to the 1980s* explore and define racial formations as the "process by which social, economic, and political forces determine the content and importance of racial categories, and by which they are in turn shaped by racial meanings."[12] The creation of a Lamanite identity as a category of race in the Book of Mormon can be read as one such "racial formation." The Book of Mormon replicated larger processes of not just Mormon settler colonialism, but American

colonialism by assigning "racial meaning to a previously racially unclassified relationship, social practice, or group."[13] Mormon Euro-Americans interacted and
engaged Indigenous Peoples on the premise that they were Lamanites.

Book of Mormon-Conflicting Origins

The Introduction to the Book of Mormon was not part of the original text,
but was included for the first time in 1981 and later amended in 2006. The 1981
Introduction describes the text as "a volume of holy scripture . . . it is a record
of God's dealings with the ancient inhabitants of the Americas" and written
by ancient prophets.[14] This written record was not just a religious, historical
narrative, but became the foundation for Mormon religious beliefs beginning
in the nineteenth century, continuing through the twenty-first century. The 1981
introduction to the Book of Mormon connects American Indian Peoples to
their ancestors, Lamanites, "after thousands of years, all were destroyed except
the Lamanites," and "they are the principal ancestors of the American Indians."[15]
Mormon, a Book of Mormon prophet, becomes the last survivor to record his
people's history in the Book of Mormon and preserves this record for his descendants. Mormon delivers the Book of Mormon to his son, Moroni, who abridges
this historical and religious narrative onto gold plates. American Indian Peoples,
until 2006, remain the principal ancestors to the Book of Mormon Lamanites.

In 2006, the Introduction to the Book of Mormon was quietly changed.
The phrase "they are the principal ancestors of the American Indians" changed
to "they are among the ancestors of the American Indians."[16] While the change
may appear minor, it was an important change that stirred interest and debate
about American Indians as descendants of "Lamanites." The change from "the
principal" to "among the" set off a firestorm of public opinion the following year
in 2017. The *Salt Lake Tribune* and *Deseret News,* the two most widely circulated
newspapers in Salt Lake City, Utah, reported on this terminology change to
the Book of Mormon introduction. Carrie A. Moore, journalist for the *Deseret
News*, wrote that this change "reignited discussion among some Latter-day Saints
about the book's historicity, geography, and the descendants of those chronicled
within its pages."[17] Many members of The Church of Jesus Christ of Latter-day
Saints believe the Book of Mormon to be a literal and religious history of an
ancient civilization and American Indian Peoples to be direct descendants of

Lamanite peoples. Even with the changes in 2006, the Introduction to the Book of Mormon still links "Lamanites" primarily to American Indians in the United States, not all Indigenous Peoples in the North and South American continent. There is no specific or even exclusive mention of American Indians in the Book of Mormon. Rather, there are various examples that contradict this exclusive application to American Indian Peoples. For example, in 2 Nephi 1:5, it reads:

> we have obtained a land of promise, a land which is choice above all other lands; a land which the Lord God hath covenanted with me should be a land for the inheritance of my seed. Yea, the Lord hath covenanted this land unto me and to my children forever, and also those who should be led out of other countries by the hand of the Lord.

The mention of people seeking religious refuge fits into the larger narrative that this continent was populated by newly arrived immigrants. It is important to note that the Book of Mormon itself directly contradicts the notion that American Indian Peoples were the only descendants of Lamanites. Despite changes made to the introduction, American Indians in general are still considered to be "among" the descendants of the fallen "Lamanites."

The Introduction to the Book of Mormon and the history therein not only ignores the diversity of Indigenous Peoples completely, but ignores their unique history that intimately connects them to the land. For many tribal nations, they are not the first immigrants. In fact, Indigenous creation stories reveal how each Indigenous nation came into being as a people through the "emergence stories in which human beings come from lower worlds. In many Plains tribes, human beings fall through a hole in the sky. In some woodland tribes, a turtle or some other diver goes to the bottom of the ocean and brings back a patch of earth."[18] These creation stories connect a people to land, particularly sacred spaces that are central to existence of a people. According to these stories, Indigenous Peoples have existed as a people since time immemorial. Their creation stories are a reflection of how they came into being as a people and also provide a connection to the world around them. For example, Gwen Westerman and Bruce White's *Mni Sota Makoce: The Land of the Dakota*, examines how Dakota people "named it and left their marks in the landscape and in its history … Dakota connection to this region goes back beyond human memory and written history." Minnesotans rarely learn and know about Dakota history and how their presence is part of a larger narrative of removal of Dakota people from their homelands so that settlers could claim and tame Dakota homelands.[19]

Failing to understand a people's connection to land makes it impossible to understand their history and culture. When Indigenous Peoples have been depicted as immigrants to this continent, like the Book of Mormon's depiction of Lamanites or American Indians as immigrants seeking religious refuge, the goal is to extinguish tribal title to land. Vine Deloria Jr., Standing Rock Sioux, further interrogated this notion of American Indian Peoples as recent arrivals to this continent propagated by the Bering Strait theory. Deloria begins his discussion recounting Wounded Knee II in 1973 to introduce how the Bering Strait theory has been continually applied to American Indian Peoples to dismiss their claims to land. During these courthouse hearings, Deloria recalls how defendants cited the 1868 Fort Laramie Treaty and Lakota creation story where they emerged as a people from an "underground world near Wind Cave, South Dakota" to demonstrate their right to exist as a people and force the US government to fulfill treaty obligations.[20] Testimony by the academic community refuted these defendant's claims. Instead, they put forth the Bering Strait theory to make American Indians the first "immigrants to North America, [by which] they are able to deny the fact that we were the full, complete, and total owners of this continent."[21] Despite their tenuous assertions, these interpretations are taken as fact and American Indian creation stories that explain their being as a people are completely silenced and ignored. While the arrival of American Indians via a land or ice bridge differs from the arrival of American Indians by boats as depicted in the Book of Mormon, both these narratives perpetuate the notion that American Indians were the first, or were among the first, immigrants to this continent. Deloria's work further demonstrates that the depiction of American Indian Peoples as immigrants is not new or exclusive to Mormons or the Book of Mormon, but is part of a larger narrative that denies Indigenous creation stories and worldviews. In doing so, Indigenous claims to land and place can be completely extinguished.

Indigenous worldviews must be acknowledged and restored as an integral component to our understanding of the historical past. Reclaiming Indigenous history, specifically Dakota history, is the first step toward decolonization and challenging the way in which non-Indigenous Peoples have ignored and silenced Dakota (Indigenous) perspectives and voices when writing the history of this continent. By placing Dakota people and voices at the center of not just Dakota history, but the history of this continent, history changes. Indigenous Peoples, including Dakotas, can no longer be considered the first immigrants or possible ancestors to "Lamanites." The centering of Dakota voices at the center of history also challenges the Book of Mormon as a literal history of their people or even part of Dakota identity and culture. For example, Gwen Westerman and Bruce White's *Mni Sota Makoce: The Land of the Dakota* offers up an example of how history dramatically changes when Dakota/Indigenous voices are not just included, but are the driving force behind the writing of a people's history. *Mni Sota Makoce* coincided with the 150th anniversary of the U.S.-Dakota War of 1862, a history that has largely ignored Dakota oral histories and perspectives. Westerman and White articulate how history comes in various forms (stories, legends, traditions, folklores) and can take the oral or written form. These histories become "'master stories,' stories that express the important values of a people" and "master stories" could become part of the dominant narrative if the teller's status was highly respected.[22] Westerman and White assert that "the Dakota connection to this region goes back beyond human memory and written history, but Europeans did not know of the Dakota people until the mid-1600s."[23] Since contact, Dakota history has been written from a non-Dakota perspective. Dakota Peoples and their connection to traditional homelands has been erased by a historical narrative that fails to include the rich oral history of the Dakota. The exclusion of Dakota Peoples from the historical narrative is not accidental, it is yet another method utilized by settlers to erase Dakota Peoples' creation stories and their intimate connection to place.

Wanbdi Wakiya states, "The power of the Dakotas had always dwelt in the land, from the great forest to the open prairies. Long before the white man ever dreamed of our existence, the Dakota roamed this land."[24] Dakota Peoples' connection to land can be seen in their Otókahe, or beginning.[25] From *Mni Sota Makoce*, it is "land where the waters are so clear they reflect the clouds" and is the original homeland for Dakota Peoples.[26] Erin Griffin (Dakota) recalls, "this region was the home of Dakota people generations before us, and for generations after us it will remain our homeland. We are told that we were brought here to this land from the stars to the place where the Minnesota and Mississippi meet. This place known as Bdote is our place of genesis."[27] Dakota people believe they "came from the stars to be on the earth ... the Earth opened herself in that way, and from the mud the Creator made the first Dakota man and woman. Because Dakota were made from the Earth, she is called Ina, mother."[28] The nineteenth-century non-Dakota written record recognized the importance of this site: "The Mdewakanton think that the mouth of the Minnesota River is precisely over the center of the earth, and that they occupy the gate that opens into the western world."[29] Dakota people are connected to the world around them and they thrived at Bdote, or center, of their universe. These stories, including the non-Dakota written record, highlight how the historical narrative can be grounded in Dakota worldviews. It also reflects the importance of Dakota language to reveal the interconnectedness between land and people. Land was treated with respect because as their Ina—mother—she was always treated with respect. Ina gave life to the Dakota Peoples, both literally and metaphorically. In return, Dakotas have a deep respect for Ina, land.

Dakota worldviews directly contradict and challenge the Book of Mormon as a literal history of not just Dakota Peoples, but all Indigenous Peoples on this continent. The Book of Mormon has been touted as a record written by Lamanites that begins in 600 BC and ends in 400 AD. However, according to the Dakota creation story, Dakotas have lived on this continent long before 600 BC. Their genesis as a people originated directly from the land, at the very beginning. They did not arrive seeking religious refuge, instead, they were born from the land. Dakota connection to the land was also disrupted and severed when the Book of Mormon, including the introduction, asserts that Dakotas, or American Indians, are descendants of "Lamanites." When the Book of Mormon is read and used as a literal history of Indigenous Peoples in the Americas, tribal creation stories and histories become mythological stories that are seen as quaint or mythical and dismissed as fictional. Indigenous creation stories are an integral part of Indigenous history and worldview and when the Book of Mormon is branded as American Indian history, these creation stories are not just silenced, but are erased and replaced with stories that support the theory of recent migration to this continent. Dakota Peoples' genesis as a people cannot be found in the Book of Mormon. Instead, a Lamanite history and identity are imposed upon them. Bdote, the site of Dakota genesis, ceases to exist when the Book of Mormon is privileged as the only legitimate history of all American Indians, including Dakota Peoples. Dakota people cannot exist without Bdote. Their sacred connection to Ina, land, history and identity as Dakota Peoples are erased by the existence of the Book of Mormon and myths that continue to perpetuate this text as Dakota/American Indian history on this continent.

Book of Mormon-Lamanite Origins

The exact location of Lehi and his family is not known. Many Mormon schol-ars claim that it was probably in Mesoamerica.[30] Lehi, patriarch and colonizer, escaped from Jerusalem with his wife; his sons and their wives; daughters, and other followers due to religious persecution in Jerusalem. The first chapter in the Book of Mormon begins with an account of Lehi, his wife, Sariah, and their four sons: Laman, Lemuel, Sam, and Nephi. Nephi, one of Lehi's youngest sons, is the first prophet in the Book of Mormon to document the religious and secu-lar narrative of his family and followers as they colonized this continent. Upon their arrival to the Americas, Nephi began to be favored by his father, Lehi, and God, angering his elder brothers, Laman and Lemuel. Eventually, dissension arose within Lehi's family and among his followers, splitting the family into two groups. This division gave rise to one of the two major civilizations documented in the Book of Mormon: "Nephites" and "Lamanites."

According to the Book of Mormon, this family division primarily had to do with the willingness of Lehi's family and children to follow God's command-ments. Nephi was the son who had wanted to follow his father's counsel and by extension, God's counsel. Laman and Lemuel, the two eldest, did not want to follow their father and youngest brother, instead, they rebelled. Nephi decided to leave his brothers and to take his "family, and . . . all those who would go with me were those who believed in the warnings and the revelations of God" and create a separate, righteous civilization.[31] Nephites continued to remain righ-teous and followed God's teachings as revealed through Nephi's written account. Mormon religious discourse regarding Lamanites led to their racialization and marginalization as found in the Book of Mormon. For example, after the Neph-ites and Lamanites split into two civilizations, the factor distinguishing the two groups was based on not just their own personal righteousness but also their peoples' righteousness. Individuals who had rebelled were:

> cut off from his [God's] presence. And He caused the cursing to come upon them ... [and] had hardened their hearts against him [God] ... as they were white, and exceedingly fair and delightsome, that they might not be enticing unto my people [Nephites] the Lord God did cause a skin of blackness to come upon them. And thus saith the Lord God: I will cause that they shall be loathsome unto thy people, save they shall repent

of their iniquities. And cursed shall be the seed of him that mixeth with
their seed; for they shall be cursed even with the same cursing.[32]

Lamanites were cursed with a "skin of blackness." This curse could be reversed
if they repented of their wickedness. In contrast, Nephites were "white, and
exceedingly fair and delightsome," and rewarded for their righteousness, their
skin was not cursed. Despite moments of righteousness, the majority of Lamanites never fully rid themselves of their cursed, "blackened" skin thus reinforcing
a racialized hierarchy as found in the Book of Mormon.[33] They were moments
when Lamanites became white. For example, in Alma 28: 17–18, it reads:

> And it came to pass that they called their names Anti-Nephi-Lehies; and
> they were called by this name and were no more Lamanites. And they
> began to be a very industrious people; yea, and they were friendly with
> the Nephites; therefore, they did open a correspondence with them, and
> the curse of God did not follow them.

This "curse" was lifted. However, this curse was never permanently lifted or
uniformly applied to all American Indians. Their "blackened" skin continued
to demarcate them and their descendants as unrighteous. Nephites occupied a
more privileged status as found in the Book of Mormon. Due to their unrighteousness, Lamanites lose their inheritance and all claims to this land. Instead,
Lamanites can only secure their inheritance if they become righteous. Despite
claims in the Book of Mormon that state "neither were there Lamanites, nor any
manner of 'ites;' but they were one."[34] In this passage, all distinctions, including
Lamanites, ceased to exist. However, the Introduction to the Book of Mormon explicitly connects American Indians to their Lamanite ancestors, thereby,
directly challenging the textual passage that asserts "they were one." If Nephites
cease to exist as a people, so too should Lamanites. However, this racial identity
and marginalization of Indigenous Peoples persisted. Mormons used the Book
of Mormon to determine at various points in time and place, who was and was
not a Lamanite. American Indian Peoples had no control over their own identity and history as a people in official LDS discourse. This belief that American
Indians were a remnant of the tribes of Israel shaped how Mormons interacted
with and felt a unique responsibility to the redemption of American Indian
people as Lamanites in the nineteenth and twentieth centuries.

Joseph Smith and Lamanites

The recent release of the Joseph Smith Papers by the Church History Department of The Church of Jesus Christ of Latter-day Saints provides a glimpse into early LDS Church policies, attitudes, and relationships with American Indian Peoples. Smith and the Council of Fifty "reflected the Latter-day Saints' interest in American Indians."[35] The founder and first prophet of the LDS Church, Joseph Smith Jr., believed that the Book of Mormon was a record of "the forefathers of our western tribes of Indians ... we learn that our western tribes of Indians are descendants from that Joseph which was sold into Egypt, and that the land of America is a promised land unto them."[36] Joseph Smith's spiritual revelations coupled with the Book of Mormon's discussion of Lamanites resulted in missionaries being sent amongst various tribal nations. Joseph Smith "sent four missionaries to the American Indians in September 1830, only a few months after the Church was organized, and other missionaries followed throughout the Church's early history."[37] This "Lamanite mission" sought to convert the "the Senecas of the Iroquois Confederacy (Cattaraugus) near Buffalo, New York; the Wyandots in Ohio; and the Delaware's west of the Missouri River."[38] On March 12, 1835, the Council of Fifty charged Brigham Young to "open a door to the remnants of Joseph who dwelt among the Gentiles which was carri[e]d."[39] Young's mission to tribes in the West had largely differed from previous missionary attempts "as the call seemed to distinguish the indigenous populations in the eastern United States from the Indian nations in the West."[40] Mormons made efforts to convert American Indians because they believed them to be descendants of Lamanites.

Smith's leadership was pivotal in the early applications of the term "Lamanite" to American Indians in the nineteenth century. The LDS Church, originally called the Church of Christ, continued to grow, the use of "Lamanite" expanded to include other American Indian nations in the western part of the American continent.[41] The expansion of Lamanite identity coincided with Mormon explorations into the "Rocky Mountains, ... Texas, California or Oregon."[42] Smith's connection between "western tribes" and "Lamanites" reinforced the perspective of American Indians as foreigners to this continent. Early religious missions designed to convert American Indians into Mormons were tied to Mormon settler explorations of western lands and ushered in the first phases of Mormon settler colonialism. Mormon settler colonialism was about access to land, especially land in the West that fell outside the physical and political boundaries of the United States. Smith played a pivotal role in the application and dissemination of a Lamanite identity to not just members of the religion, but as a central tenet to Mormonism. When taken together, Mormon settler colonialism "destroy[ed] to replace" American Indians into "Lamanites."

In addition to the Book of Mormon, another religious text also greatly influenced Smith's understanding of American Indians as Lamanites. As the first prophet or religious leader of the LDS Church, Smith received "modern day revelation" from God in what would become the Doctrine and Covenants. The Doctrine and Covenants is "a collection of divine revelations and inspired declarations given for the establishment and regulation of the kingdom of God on the earth in the last days."[43] Unlike the Book of Mormon, the Doctrine and Covenants provides "modern revelation" to guide members of the LDS faith and documents early LDS Church history. The Doctrine and Covenants, like the Book of Mormon, continues to further the notion of American Indians as Lamanites. American Indians had been a promised people that would one day "blossom as a rose" through the acceptance and conversion to the LDS faith.[44]

This simile, "blossom as a rose," referenced the current state of Indigenous Peoples in the United States. Smith and subsequently other Mormon Euro-Americans believed American Indians to be living in a fallen state. They viewed the current status of American Indians who had been and were being dispossessed of their lands, resources, and traditional ways of living and being, as evidence of their fallen state. Their blossoming as a people could begin to take place only as they accepted and converted to Mormonism. Mormon Euro-Americans felt a great responsibility in aiding and uplifting "Lamanites" because it was mandated by religious doctrine. Similar to widely held ideas regarding racial uplift, Mormon Euro-Americans felt a moral obligation for the religious uplift of Lamanite peoples. The acceptance of the LDS faith would be the solution to perennial problems facing Indian country. Poverty, alcoholism, unemployment, and various other social ills facing tribal nations could all be treated if American Indians understood their rich heritage as "Lamanites." These widely held paternalistic ideas regarding Indigenous Peoples were also reflected by United States federal Indian policy.[45] The LDS Church, like the US federal government, treated Indigenous Peoples as wards of the state, individuals who must let go of their traditional beliefs and embrace Christianity, or in this context, Mormonism. Religious conversion became a sign of civilization or letting go of one's Indigenous identity. White Mormons, like Smith, viewed Mormonism as the solution to the "Indian problem."

Paul E. Felt, former president of the LDS Southwest Indian Mission from 1971–1974, cited the 1845 Proclamation of the Twelve Apostles regarding Lamanites and the Book of Mormon, in his talk titled "Remnants of Israel: Who? When Gathered?"[46] Felt's remarks demonstrate how American Indian Peoples were still considered Lamanites well into the twentieth century. It further demonstrates the longevity of Smith's influence in asserting American Indian Peoples as Lamanites and authority of nineteenth-century religious leaders on Mormon-Indian religious and racial policies. The 1845 Proclamation of the Twelve Apostles states:

> We also bear testimony that the Indians (Lamanites of North and South America) are a remnant of the tribes of Israel, as is now made manifest by the discovery and revelation of their ancient oracles and records. And that they are about to be gathered, civilized, and made one nation in this glorious land. They will also come to a knowledge of their forefathers, and of the fulness of the Gospel; and they will embrace it and become a righteous branch of the House of Israel.[47]

This proclamation highlights the centrality of American Indians to Mormon religious beliefs. American Indians were the physical manifestation of the truthfulness of the Book of Mormon. If Mormon missionaries could convert American Indian Peoples, they could redeem this fallen "branch of the House of Israel." Mormon settler colonialism was manifested in the power wielded by members of the Twelve Apostles in proclaiming the Book of Mormon as not just Lamanite history, but the "ancient oracles and records" of American Indian Peoples. The 1845 Proclamation of the Twelve Apostles further "destroys to replace" individual tribal sovereignty by asserting that American Indians were going to be "gathered, civilized and made one nation in this glorious land." This proclamation denies and ignores tribal diversity and sovereignty. This civilization rhetoric also reflected larger US colonial policies that pushed to assimilate American Indians into mainstream American society. Furthermore, Indigenous Peoples' historical, cultural, and spiritual ways of knowing were completely ignored and instead replaced with the notion that their belief system could actually be found in the "fullness of the Gospel [Mormonism]." This 1845 Proclamation and Felt's talk

over 100 years later in 1981 highlights how the history and identity of Indigenous Peoples are continually erased and replaced with an identity grounded in
Mormon religious beliefs. Indigenous Peoples' agency and control over their own
history and identity has been denied. Their histories have not been included in
the Mormon historical record, instead, they have been supplanted by a racialized
rhetoric in which Indigenous Peoples are erased from the Mormon historical
and religious narrative. Instead, Mormon religious discourse was used to preserve and maintain the notion of American Indian Peoples as Lamanites from
the nineteenth century into the twenty-first century.

Mormon religious discourse and text thus played pivotal roles in not just the
development of this Lamanite identity but its maintenance into the twenty-first
century. Mormon settler colonialism gave white settlers the power to name, identify, and shape Lamanite history and identity. Mormon Euro-Americans became
invested in the term and concept of "Lamanite" because it reinforced their belief
in their own racial superiority over American Indian Peoples. As Patrick Wolfe
has effectively argued, settler colonialism "erects a new colonial society on the
expropriated land base."[48] This new colonial society not only racialized American
Indians, but created a society in which Mormon religious beliefs dominated and
shaped all aspects of the political, religious, social, and physical landscape. This
is especially evident at the center of the LDS Church today: Temple Square in
Salt Lake City, Utah. There is very little evidence or mention of modern tribal
nations and traditional homelands in and around Salt Lake City, Utah, on which
LDS headquarters was built.

In addition to key religious texts, the Book of Mormon, and Doctrine and
Covenants, publications and public speeches made by Mormon leaders and
members demonstrated how they were able to define and widely disseminate
Lamanite identity to the Church's followers. Many of these publications occurred
during important, biannual, globally broadcast meetings: general conference.
These talks are also published in the LDS Church magazine, *Ensign*. These Mormon publications further embed and disseminate notions of Indigeneity. Largely
given and written by lay members of the LDS Church, including ranking Church
leaders, these publications demonstrate the ways in which Indigenous worldviews were erased from the mainstream Mormon historical narrative. Instead,
these speeches and publications reflect how LDS Church leaders understood the
connection between religious discourse and its applicability toward American
Indian Peoples. Because these speeches were published in official magazines of

the LDS Church, non-Lamanite members of the Church fail to interrogate or critique the material found therein. This becomes problematic because it reveals the power of religious discourse and the role that LDS Church leadership has in shaping Mormon conceptions of race, particularly in regard to American Indians. American Indian worldviews have largely been ignored unless they fit into the widely accepted definition of "Lamanite." The power exercised by LDS leaders has also played a pivotal role in the shaping of a Lamanite identity.

LDS publications allowed for the wide dissemination of a Lamanite identity. A 1975 article in the official Church magazine, *Ensign*, "Who and Where are the Lamanites?" by Lane Johnson, an instructor for the Church Education System, demonstrates the fluidity of the term "Lamanite." Lane outlines the numerous definitions of "Lamanite" and its applicability toward Indigenous people. Johnson carefully articulates that Lamanite peoples can be categorized as a "particular racial lineage, a political/religious group, a covenant people."[49] Johnson demonstrated the multiple and shifting definitions of "Lamanite." Initially, "Lamanite" referenced a religious identity, someone who had rejected the "gospel" or who had become "wicked." Johnson further asserts that after God cursed the "Lamanites" with a "skin of blackness," the term "Lamanite" then referred to a religious/political faction whose "distinguishing feature was its opposition to the Church." Reflecting the fluidity of identity in the Book of Mormon, "lineage became an increasingly minor factor, and later there are many examples of Lamanites becoming Nephites and Nephites becoming Lamanites," reflecting the fluidity of identity in the Book of Mormon.[50] Johnson's article demonstrated the evolution of "Lamanite" from a religious identity into a racialized identity when they became accursed with a "skin of blackness." Johnson also highlights how "Lamanite" is not a category of lineage, however, it continues to be applied to American Indian Peoples based on lineage: American Indians as descendants of "Lamanites." Johnson contradicts his own argument. Lineage does in fact play a factor and oftentimes, the only factor, in determining Lamanite identity. Despite claims made by Johnson that lineage did not matter, it did matter because LDS Church leaders largely relied on lineage to determine one's "Lamanite-ness." For example, the Introduction to the Book of Mormon relies on lineage, American Indians can be counted as "among" the descendants of "Lamanites."

Another Mormon writer, Gordon C. Thomasson, moves beyond the obvious categories of racial and religious identity and assumes that all Indigenous people are "Lamanites." Thomasson supports his claim by stating that "Lamanites either came to be called Lamanite or labeled themselves as Lamanites" or that "being a Lamanite was, in some sense, a matter of choice."[51] Theoretically, Indigenous people could decide whether or not they were "Lamanite." However, in practice, many Mormon Euro-Americans, including LDS Church leaders, determined who was or was not "Lamanite." Mormon settler colonialism was about power, the power to define and subjugate the "other," American Indians. The usage of "Lamanite" in the Book of Mormon and by LDS leaders demonstrates that American Indian Peoples do not have the power to define their own identity as a people or nation. American Indian Peoples are replaced with a Mormon religious narrative that normalized Mormon settler colonization, especially the dispossession of Indigenous land that has been guised as Lamanites losing their inheritance, land, due to their own unrighteousness.

In the twentieth century, Spencer W. Kimball, apostle and prophet, continued Smith's tradition of shaping LDS Church policies toward American Indians. Kimball was perhaps the most prolific and authoritative commentator regarding the physical "whitening" of Indigenous Peoples. Kimball fused religious ideologies found in the Book of Mormon with his personal understanding of Lamanites to further shape how non-Indigenous Mormon members viewed American Indian Peoples. He stated, "they [Indigenous Peoples] shall rejoice; for they shall know that it is a blessing unto them from the hand of God; and their scales of darkness shall begin to fall from their eyes; and many generations shall not pass among them [Lamanites] save they shall be a white and delightsome people."[52] Kimball interpreted this passage as, "their scales of darkness shall begin to fall from their eyes; and many generations shall not pass among them [Lamanites] save they shall be a white and delightsome people" to mean the physical and literal whitening of Indigenous Peoples.[53] In his talk "The Day of the Lamanites," Kimball states, "I saw a striking contrast in the progress of the Indian people today … they are fast becoming a white and delightsome people … The Day of the Lamanites is nigh. For years they have been growing delightsome, and they are now becoming white and delightsome, as they were promised."[54] Kimball's twentieth-century perspective perpetuates the notion that one's level of righteousness was tied to one's skin color and the lighter the complexion, the more righteous and by extension, civilized, an individual. Kimball was specifically mentioning the Indian Student Placement Program. He argued that Mormon American Indian students who participated in this LDS Church program would eventually become "white and delightsome," as promised by the Book of Mormon.

Kimball's comments not only provide a more contemporary view of Indige-nous Peoples, but also perpetuates racist notions of Indigenous Peoples. In his talk "Of Royal Blood," Kimball defined an all-encompassing Lamanite iden-tity that included "all Indians and Indian mixtures, such as the Polynesians, the Guatemalans, the Peruvians, as well as the Sioux, the Apache, the Mohawk, the Navajo, and others."[55] As the LDS Church president and prophet, Kim-ball was instrumental in popularizing the use of "Lamanite" in reference to not just American Indian Peoples, but Indigenous Peoples globally in the twentieth century. Various LDS Church programs, like the Indian Student Placement Program, targeted Indigenous Peoples in the United States for conversion into the faith, and to serve as a civilizing program for school-age children.[56]

Kimball's speeches coincided with the increasing numbers of American Indian conversions to Mormonism and participation of Mormon American Indian children in the Indian Student Placement Program. Lamanite conver-sion placed them on the pathway to becoming physically and culturally "white," or Mormon. Lamanite children who participated in the Indian Student Place-ment Program were praised and held up as an example of the truthfulness of this prophecy. Kimball's position as a prophet in the LDS Church gave him the power to define what it meant to be a Lamanite in the twentieth century with very little criticism from its membership, including Indigenous Peoples.

Finally, Indigenous Peoples were admonished to ignore any negative conno-tations of being Lamanite and instead, proudly claim a Lamanite identity. For example, Kimball encouraged Lamanites to not feel "a little bit ashamed that they are Lamanites. How can it be? ... You who are Lamanites remember this: Your Lamanite ancestors were no more rebellious than any of the other branches of the House of Israel."[57] Kimball wanted Indigenous Peoples to claim an iden-tity that did not reflect their lived experiences or value their cultural identity. Instead, this statement by Kimball reflects the problematic ways in which being a Lamanite was constantly forced upon Indigenous Peoples.

Conclusion

Dakota historian, Waziyatawin, argues that when writing about Indigenous Peoples and history, Indigenous sources must be utilized. If Indigenous voices are continually excluded from the historical narrative, the history being written continues to be a colonial interpretation of Indigenous Peoples and their history. The Book of Mormon is not Indigenous history. Instead, historians must challenge Indigenous histories that are being written without using and centering Indigenous voices and perspectives. Centering Dakota worldviews and reading the Book of Mormon through the lens of settler colonialism challenges the assumption that it is the history of American Indian Peoples or that American Indian Peoples are "Lamanites." In the United States today, there are 573 federally recognized tribes. It is nearly impossible to write a history that is reflective of these diverse people because their worldviews and lived experiences are dramatically different from one another. When using the Book of Mormon as a literal history of Indigenous Peoples on this continent, it silences the creation stories of tribal nations that explain how they came into being as a people. While many tribal creation stories may be similar to one another, they are just as diverse as the people themselves. These stories highlight the intimate connection Indigenous Peoples have to the world around them, especially their deep connections to their land. When the Book of Mormon is promoted as the history of the "ancient inhabitants" of the Americas, it effectively obliterates any Indigenous histories and claims to land because Mormon settler history is privileged as the most important, accurate history of Indigenous Peoples.

The Book of Mormon became the foundation of Lamanite identity in The Church of Jesus Christ of Latter-day Saints. Indigenous Peoples were expected to claim Lamanite identity as their own because it was their ancestors who wrote the Book of Mormon. The Book of Mormon reflects the insidious ways in which Mormon settler colonialism functioned because it created and gave meaning to Indigeneity through the lens of a Lamanite identity. Indigeneity of American Indian Peoples was revealed through the construction and application of Lamanite identity. The use of the Book of Mormon was a tool and manifestation of Mormon settler colonialism. It effectively erased the physical presence of Indigenous Peoples from their lands and their own history. Instead, the Book of Mormon became the "master story" of American Indian history and identity on this continent. Indigenous Peoples must reclaim their histories and identity as their own. History written about Indigenous Peoples must privilege Indigenous sources and worldviews. Mormon settler colonialism must be dismantled and space must be made for additional Indigenous voices and histories even if they challenge the "master narrative."

2

Other Scriptures

Restoring Voices of Gantowisas to an Open Canon

THOMAS W. MURPHY

Behold, other scriptures I would that ye should write, that ye have not.[1]

In an intriguing intertextual moment in the Book of Mormon the resurrected Jesus Christ chastised a group of Nephites for selective recording of prophecies of Samuel the Lamanite. Jesus spoke of other scriptures, as yet unwritten, and directed the recording of a prophecy of ministrations from the dead coinciding with his biblical resurrection. Elsewhere, the narrator acknowledges Jesus and Samuel had much more to say than was recorded.[2] Joseph Smith pointed to limitations of scripture by acknowledging, on the title page of the 1830 Book of Mormon, that the account may contain "the mistakes of men."[3] As an extrabiblical scriptural narrative the Book of Mormon proposed divine communication comes to humanity "according to their own language, unto their understanding."[4] Taken collectively these passages suggest that the Latter-day scriptural canon is self-consciously culturally bound and incomplete.

This essay employs autoethnographic reflection and decolonizing methodologies to amplify the radical message that the Creator speaks to all people in our own languages and cultures. The voices of ancestors emerge from Indigenous sacred narratives in ways that offer a counterbalance and corrective to records of colonial empires. I draw from Haudenosaunee (Iroquois), especially Mohawk

and Seneca, oral tradition to offer a decolonizing perspective on the Book of
Mormon that might serve Latter-day Saints seeking more effective ways to live
harmoniously in a multicultural world.

Emphasis on Mohawk and Seneca traditions highlights some resemblance
between Iroquois and Mormon thought.[5] Historian C. Stanley Banks con-
tended in a 1945 publication that "Tradition has it that the prophet Joseph
Smith, in his authorship of the Book [of Mormon], was greatly influenced by
his study of the beliefs of the Iroquois Indians of New York."[6] Essayist Edmund
Wilson recorded the conversion story of a Mohawk man from St. Regis a few
years later: "Philip Cook thought at first that Joseph Smith must have been
influenced by the Handsome Lake doctrine, through the Senecas of Western
New York, but then he concluded that no white man at that time could ever
have had access to their ceremonies or understood what was said if they had."[7]
Communications scholar Bruce Johansen, noted for his work on the influence of
Iroquois ideas on American democracy, asked in the early 1980s if the origins of
Mormonism might also "owe anything to the Iroquois?"[8] More recently, historian
Lori Taylor notes that the Seneca prophet Handsome Lake, Joseph Smith, and
Book of Mormon character Lehi each had guides in their visions and that the
Iroquois League and Book of Mormon cultures buried weapons as a renuncia-
tion of war.[9] Historians Philip J. Deloria (Dakota) and Clyde R. Forsberg have
likened Joseph Smith to nineteenth-century proto-ethnographer Lewis Henry
Morgan who created fraternal orders modeled after the Iroquois.[10] Former BYU
librarian Rick Grunder notes similarities between Mormon and Iroquois place
names (Oneida and Onondaga) and resemblances between Samson Occum,
a Mohegan preacher among the Oneida, and Samuel the Lamanite.[11]

Religion scholar Peter Manseau has amplified Lori Taylor's work on
Iroquois-Mormon connections in his new multicultural history of religion in
the United States, *One Nation, Under Gods*. Manseau identifies similarities
in visions and angelic visitors and an emphasis on sobriety but adds parallels
between an American Jesus and the Iroquois traditions of the Peacemaker and
visitations of Handsome Lake's three messengers and the "Three Nephites" to
suggest that the Book of Mormon became the visual representation of the Seneca prophet Handsome Lake's hidden scripture. Manseau suggests, "while the
birth of Mormonism is often considered in relation to ... other Second Great
Awakening movements of the Burned-Over District, in fact the similarities pale
in comparison to all that Smith's religious visions had in common with those of

Handsome Lake."[12] While some readers may desire to see validation of the Book of Mormon's historicity or, to the contrary, evidence of its nineteenth-century origin in these proposed parallels between the Iroquois and Mormons, neither approach is my intent here. Instead, I examine differences alongside similarities to ask a more fundamental question. How can Haudenosaunee perspectives on colonization, dreams and visions, seers and prophets, and siblings and peace help us decolonize the Book of Mormon?

Decolonization

Decolonizing methodologies challenge narratives that privilege the perspectives and authority of settler colonists and offer alternatives that bring Indigenous perspectives to the center of analysis.[13] Authors of decolonizing literature often situate themselves and their works within particular personal and cultural contexts, enabling readers to better contextualize the author's perspective.[14] Thus, I write as a seventh-generation descendant of Susannah Ferguson, born around 1786 in the Mohawk village of Tiononderoge, not far, in time and place, from the founding events of the Book of Mormon. Susannah's granddaughter, Lura Elmina Cole, would relocate to Kansas, convert to Mormonism, and eventually move to Albion, Idaho. I grew up in southern Idaho in the 1970s hearing stories of Susannah and her daughter Rachel as our "Lamanite" ancestors. As I heard the stories filtered through Book of Mormon prophecies, Lura's conversion to Mormonism, facilitated by intermarriage, helped lead to the presumed "white and delightsome" appearance of my family in recent generations.[15] Troubled and intrigued by these stories I pursued a career studying Native America and Mormonism.

The Mohawk are one of the Six Nations of the League of the Haudenosaunee (Seneca, Mohawk, Oneida, Cayuga, Onondaga, and Tuscarora) whose traditional territory includes today's Upstate New York and portions of Ohio and Pennsylvania. Joseph Smith would claim to find the gold plates in traditional lands of the Seneca. Reading Mormon scripture in light of Mohawk and Seneca oral tradition provides a way to decolonize this new American scripture. In other words, a reader might reject messages privileging power and authority of white colonizers as "mistakes of men" and find inspiration in elements that Mormonism shares with Indigenous Peoples from whose land this faith emerged. We can

then probe similarities and, more importantly, differences to see if there is any-
thing that colonizers might learn from Haudenosaunee narratives. In this effort
to rethink the Mormon canon I draw upon the teachings of Sakokweniónkwas
(Tom Porter), a Mohawk Bear clan elder, as compiled in *And Grandma Said . . .
Iroquois Teachings as passed down through oral tradition*.[16] I also draw significantly from scholarship of Seneca descendant Barbara Alice Mann, *Iroquoian
Women: The Gantowisas* and *Native Americans, Archaeologists, & the Mounds*.[17]
I personally find the teachings in these Haudenosaunee accounts inspiring and
of comparable value to scripture.

Indigenous Mormons have often found inspiration in oral tradition and in
written sacred narratives such as the *Code of Handsome Lake, Black Elk Speaks*,
and the *Popol Vuh*.[18] Too often, Mormon interest in Indigenous spirituality
is limited to its usefulness in authenticating or repudiating the Book of Mormon.[19] The reference to the existence of other scriptures could be read in a
more liberating manner.[20] Following decolonizing work of Native Christians
such as Richard Twiss, Taoyate Ob Najin (Lakota/Oglala), one might recognize
"that Creator's Spirit was already here long before Europeans came."[21] Mormons
might employ an open canon as validation of divinity in traditions of their own
ancestors, wherever they come from.[22] Or, Mormons might consider the even
more liberating prospect that Indigenous traditions are sufficient on their own
terms.[23]

Dreams and Visions

Dreams and visions are vitally important in both Haudenosaunee and Mormon
cultural traditions. For Haudenosaunee dreams expose latent desires that may
need to be acted upon, either literally or symbolically, to be satisfied. Sakokweniónkwas, for example, recorded the teachings of his grandmother Konwanataha (1889–1978), a well-respected Kanienkehaka (Mohawk) seer, after she
appeared to him in a dream instructing him to record her teachings.[24] Dream
work is traditionally a communal endeavor, as Barbara Alice Mann explains.

> The communal nature of dreamtime is part of the Iroquois consensus
> philosophy. Dreams are communication from the spirit realm containing
> messages, instructions, and/or warnings. Dream workers, traditionally

female for the most part, explain meanings (if they are not obvious) and prescribe ways to respond to a message, comply with instructions, and/or deal with warnings. These acknowledgements must involve the community, or at least a portion of it, or they will not be effective.[25]

Both cultural traditions consider dreams and visions to be fundamentally alike.[26] Yet the communal input appears to receive less value in the Book of Mormon. When Lehi shares a dream with his family, skeptical responses from his wife, Sariah, and sons Laman and Lemuel are downplayed in favor of that of the patriarch.[27] Haudenosaunee share with Mormons an intense interest in work of dreams and visions, but also recognize influence by personal desires and thus employ a system of community-based vetting.

Haudenosaunee and Mormons believe lost knowledge can be recovered through dreams, but Sakokweniónkwas perceptively warns, "it's *much*, much easier to not have to refind that knowledge from dreams or from trying to make yourself sensitive to those things. It's much easier just to listen to a grandma or a grandpa who knows." It's not just that it's easier to gain knowledge from the living than it is from the dead, but when your knowledge comes from dreams "you never know if it's real or not real."[28] Haudenosaunee dreams and visions are not expected to convey pure messages free from influence by culture, gender, personality, or limited understanding. The humility of Iroquois approaches to knowledge received in dreams can be an example for Mormons to emulate, especially when the Book of Mormon narrator's own self-conscious recognition of cultural bias is brought to the forefront.

We can look to the approach by Sakokweniónkwas to his own gap in knowledge—about spirit songs his grandmother and uncles passed on to him—to further develop a decolonizing approach. He warns his audience, "I'm not sure if this is correct what I'm going to tell you. But, it's the closest that I can deduce from my studies, and from my years of trying to understand." The sources of his knowledge prompted this uncertainty as he "had to depend on a dream, through prayer, to get the understanding and definition of this." "All I know," he explains, "is that's what spirits told me at that time. And I don't know if they were trying to trick me! Or if it's really true. But it sounds like it's logical."[29] When Sakokweniónkwas obtains knowledge from his dreams, he qualifies it. He first seeks it from his elders, but when his grandma is no longer available then he turns to prayer and dreams for answers.

When the Book of Mormon is read within the context of Haudenosaunee oral traditions, social and political functions of its account become apparent. Nephi's preference for his father's visionary experiences over his mother's skepticism is characteristic of a patriarchal culture.[30] In contrast, matrilineal Haudenosaunee traditions exhibit greater gender balance. Dream interpretation empowers women who mediate individual aspirations. When Nephi dismisses objections of Sariah, Laman, and Lemuel, he elevates his own social position vis-à-vis his mother and older brothers. This approach empowers Nephi while undermining the validity of his mother's and brother's perspectives. It thus helps to create inequity, perhaps contributing to perpetual warfare among his descendants.

Seers

In conjunction with shared respect for dreams and visions, Haudenosaunee and Mormon cultures maintain socially important roles for seers. Sakokweniónkwas describes his grandmother as a seer. He asks,

> Do you know what I mean when I say a 'seer'? We call it in my language teiaia'taréhtha. It means that she makes judgments or she finds out something. If somebody is sick, and you don't know why you're sick, or you have a problem—emotional or spiritual or physical—and you don't know why, you would go to my grandma or other people like her.[31]

He describes seers as "people who have the ability to see" and as "healer like."[32] Seers may have special insight, but that does not mean that all listeners trust them uncritically. "There are a lot of seers that are only there to make money," Sakokweniónkwas warns.[33] In fact, Mormon seer Joseph Smith reported temptations to use the gold plates for monetary gain.[34] Seers in both traditions occupy important social positions but their peculiar abilities do not make them immune from frailties of human motivations and temptations.

Joseph Smith and his contemporaries frequently employed Indigenous artifacts as media for seeing. The seer stone used in the translation of the Book of Mormon resembles the "exotic stones" traditionally prized by Haudenosaunee who "carried such items with them during life as amulets and articles of personal adornment and often took them to their graves."[35] The *Ulûñsû'tĭ* stones of the Iroquoian-speaking Cherokee have summoning and communicative powers, functionally similar to stones used by early Mormons.[36] Seers from the Smith and Whitmer families include gorgets, common artifacts found in Haudenosaunee burials.[37] Yet, another stone, found at Nauvoo, resembles a spindle whorl.[38] These various artifacts became the means through which Joseph Smith sought access to "the words of those who have slumbered in the dust."[39] While use of exotic stones for seeing and protective powers indicates some similarities between practices of the different cultures, use of items taken from burials would be highly problematic and deeply offensive in Haudenosaunee tradition.[40] These varying practices of seeing elucidate assumed privileges of a settler colonial culture.

Prophets

Lori Taylor and Peter Manseau have encouraged greater attention toward Seneca prophet Handsome Lake as a prelude to Joseph Smith.[41] Indigenous narrative portrays Mormonism as "an equivalent of Handsome Lake's Gaiwí:yo [Gaiwiio or Gai'wiio'], but for white people, maybe with a little more Christian emphasis, just like the Gaiwí:yo had a little more Iroquois emphasis mixed with Christianity."[42] Sganyadaí:yoh (Handsome Lake) was born in 1735 in the Seneca village of Conawagas on the Genesee River. He lived through a troubling time that saw loss of most Seneca land base through colonial violence, coercion, and fraud. Followers of Sganyadaí:yoh were well aware of "his personal weaknesses and failures" and included them in the telling of his story.[43] By the time his visions began in 1799, he had become "a hopeless drunk who finally gulped himself into a coma."[44] He emerged from his coma with stories of a vision, soon to be followed by others that changed his life and led him to establish a new religious movement advocating traditional ceremonies and clan structures blended with elements of Christianity. This Longhouse tradition condemned the use of alcohol, coercive spirit power, bad medicine, and abortion.[45] Each prophet founded new religious movements blending Haudenosaunee and Christian traditions, one serving primarily the settler colonists and the other the colonized.

Many shared ideas appear to resemble Christianized aspects of Handsome Lake's Gaiwí:yo or Code. As Mann explains, Sganyadaí:yoh refashioned traditional Haudenosaunee culture "to accommodate European concepts of male dominance and Christian concepts of a single creator in a world locked in the Manichean struggle of good *versus* evil."[46] Both traditions offered reassurance to the original peoples that they would not be entirely exterminated, a fate that white colonial violence had made seem all too possible.[47] The common themes of sibling rivalry, universal opposition, and of a resurrected Jesus in America are those emanating from the Gaiwí:yo with its apparent Quaker influence.

Siblings

Sibling relationships play foundational roles in Haudenosaunee traditions. In teachings recorded by Sakokweniónkwas, the daughter of Sky Woman gave birth to twins. The first twin was birthed normally but the second came out kicking and screaming, rupturing his mother's side and killing her. Sky Woman mounded dirt on the body of her daughter, Mother Earth, and from her grew three sisters: corn, beans, and squash. Sapling, the first twin, made medicines that could heal. Flint, the second twin, made medicines that sicken. Sapling made berries, Flint added thorns. Sapling created mountains and rivers while Flint scrambled them. Sapling associated with light, Flint with darkness. Sakokweniónkwas explains, "We don't like to refer to them as good and evil." We just credit one with making "nice things that help us" and the other "always made the mischievous things." The second twin is not "the evil one," rather he is "like a prankster." The first twin became the sun and the second, "the one who controls the night." "So there has to be death and there has to be birth. There has to be happiness, joy, and laughter. And there has to be tears and crying. And so it is that everything is balanced like that."[48] Maintaining balance is the twins' responsibility.

While balance and cooperation characterize Haudenosaunee sibling relationships, a more polarized sibling rivalry distinguishes Book of Mormon stories. Nephi and Laman, two sons of Lehi, emerge as antagonists. Nephi, a "record keeper," presents himself as "righteous" and portrays Laman as choosing "to do evil instead of good."[49] Rather than cooperation and balance (words that do not appear in the Book of Mormon), "opposition in all things" receives emphasis.[50] Nephi and Laman become primary progenitors of two groups, Nephites and Lamanites, whose violent struggles fill most of the narrative. These nations

appear divided by belief and disbelief, righteousness and wickedness, industry and idleness, and light and dark skin. There is nuance introduced into this
dichotomy, however, when Lamanites adopt Christianity and become more righteous than Nephites shortly before Christ's birth. These binary opposites in a
battle between good and evil were initially foreign concepts to Haudenosaunee.

The earliest Christian missionaries noted the absence of ideas such as good
and evil, God and Satan, and heaven and hell.[51] Mann explains, "The record is
quite clear: Oppositional thinking, sin, and sacrament, the Manichean dichotomy, and all the accoutrements of Christian oppositional thought were quite
foreign to the Iroquois at first contact. Prior to Christian meddling, there were
no such Manichean dichotomies as Heaven and Hell, God and the Devil."[52]
Elsewhere, Mann describes the term "Great Spirit" as one of several "old missionary perversions" that were products of colonial evangelization.[53] Mann elaborates, "It was in their determination to convey the glories of Christian theology
to the 'ignorant' Iroquois that the missionaries swiped the tale of the Twins and
recast it in the mold of their own god and devil, the quicker to proselytize the
Natives."[54] In fact, the Quaker missionary Henry Simmons recorded his own
melding of Genesis with Iroquois creation in a discussion at the home of Handsome Lake's brother Cornplanter a few months before Sganyadaí:yoh's visions.[55]
Christianized versions of Sapling and Flint downplayed or removed the female
characters Sky Woman and Mother Earth and dichotomized the Twins as good
and evil.

Parallels between Sapling and Flint and Nephi and Laman most closely
resemble Christianized versions that emerged out of dialogue with missionaries. There are no parallels to Sky Woman or Mother Earth. Nephi and Laman
appear as opposites while Sapling and Flint are complementary co-creators. The
Book of Mormon's starker dichotomy is illustrated in a passage which curiously
likens Laman to "flint." The Lord "had caused the cursing to come upon" Laman
and his followers, "yea, even a sore cursing, because of their iniquity. For behold,
they had hardened their hearts against him, that they had become like unto a
flint; wherefore, as they were white, and exceedingly fair and delightsome, that
they might not be enticing unto my people the Lord God did cause a skin of
blackness to come upon them." Nephi claims that because of the cursing, Lamanites "did become an idle people, full of mischief and subtlety, and did seek in
the wilderness for beasts of prey." Nephi also asserts a chosen status as "ruler"
and "teacher," claiming his people were "industrious," labored "with their hands,"

built buildings, sowed seeds, raised "flocks, and herds," worked "all manner of wood, and of iron, and of copper, and of brass, and of steel, and of gold, and of silver, and of precious ores."[56] This Manichean dichotomy of good and evil is racialized and extended ethnocentrically across cultures of their descendants.

Portrayals of Lamanites bear a striking resemblance to stereotypes of American Indians that emerged after the American Revolution. As settler colonists poured into lands they had seized they encountered impressive evidence of industry in the farms and mounds dotting the landscape. Mann explains:

> Settlers had an enormous stake in denying any cultural credit to Native Americans, inspiring Euroamericans to dream up a doomed, and by the time the myth was done, *white* race of Mound Builders in ancient America. The myth was the only way, psychologically, to reconcile their ongoing genocide and land seizure—openly justified by the 'savage' state of Native America—with the undeniable evidence of 'civilization' presented by the math, astronomy, and artistry of the mounds.[57]

Historian Alan Taylor describes the emerging dichotomy, "By telling themselves stories of their renewed creation of a wasteland, the victorious Americans erased from memory the accomplishments of the Indians." Stark contrasts "defined the Indians as solitary, idle, selfish, unchanging, unimproving and unimprovable, heathen savages who lived by hunting and fishing alone" and white Americans "as industrious Christians dedicated to agriculture, innovation, and civil institutions."[58] While helpful in alleviating settler colonial guilt for an atrocity, this polarization between civilized and savage peoples is neither an accurate description of ancient or colonial America.

The idea that an ancient white race was responsible for the mounds dotting American landscapes has long since been discredited by archaeologists.[59] Mann has summarized extensive documentary and oral traditions demonstrating "the Shawnee, the Iroquois, the Lenâpé, and the Cherokee," rather than an ancient white nation, were responsible for mound-building cultural traditions. "Europeans watched the Iroquois build mounds long before Mound Mania seized the country—indeed, long before the U.S. *was* a country."[60] Congregationalist minister Ethan Smith combined the mound builder myth with the popular idea that American Indians were the lost tribes of Israel in his book, *View of the Hebrews*, published in 1823 and 1825 in Poultney, Vermont.[61] Today, DNA evidence has added to the archaeological data and oral traditions to undermine such ideas.[62] The LDS Church has responded by changing the Introduction to the Book of Mormon, adjusting chapter headings to downplay racism, and with an essay on its website acknowledging the failure of genetic evidence to support an Israelite origin of American Indians. The new DNA essay reminds readers that "the primary purpose of the Book of Mormon is more spiritual than historical."[63] The recent efforts by the LDS Church leadership to reprioritize the scriptural status of the Book of Mormon over its historical claims complement long-standing Indigenous approaches to sacred narratives in which historicity is irrelevant.[64]

Androcentric missionary interpretations of Iroquois Sky narratives, like stories of Nephi and Laman, excised Haudenosaunee cultural values of complementarity and cooperation. Mann elaborates, "Recasting the Twins as the Christian God and Devil was undoubtedly the most destructive manipulation of the Sky tradition, after the expulsion of women from Creation. Separating the Twins from one another to present them as enemies cruelly betrayed the true meaning of bonded relationship, for Flint was not a 'destroyer,' nor Sapling a lone 'Creator.' Instead, *both* Twins were creators of life abundant—*as were their female elders before them*."[65] While the Book of Mormon's version does not cast Nephi and Laman as God and Devil, it does polarize them and casts ethnocentric aspersions on Laman's descendants while neglecting women.

"Iroquoian culture values cooperation above all else." The Twins were not competitors but "collaborators who, between them, brought forth the exhilarating and fruitful mixtures of the benign and the dangerous, the funny and the grave, the frightening and the comforting, that constitute the human world." Instead of battling each other, the Twins were "appropriately adjusting for each other's tendency to go too far in his own direction."[66] The Book of Mormon lacks the "reciprocity, mutuality, interdependence, and the complementary parallels." These "parallel agents of equal power function synchronously so as to maintain a balanced cosmos." In this respect, "Flint *completes* Sapling, just as Sapling *reciprocates* Flint." There is not a battle between the two, "only a ceremonial dance as each circles the council fire, perpetually re/treading the other's path which is also his own path." Likewise, gender is also an expression of the twinship principle, "the genders are seen as simultaneously independent, yet interdependent, each one half of a paired, human whole." Excising female Creators neglects "that each half must be meaningfully intertwined with the other, if cosmic balance is to be maintained."[67] When contrasted with Haudenosaunee culture, the Book of Mormon is an imbalanced narrative overlooking creative powers of women.

Great Peace

Although Nephi preached "all are alike unto God," even "male and female," his descendants would struggle to live up to these teachings.[68] The climax of Mormon scripture comes with an appearance of Jesus followed by two centuries of peace and equality. This narrative apogee is the most compelling of all proposed parallels between Haudenosaunee and Mormon traditions. The Great Peace may be the only event in the Book of Mormon supported by external sources.[69] Yet, the corroboration of the Great Peace in Haudenosaunee oral traditions complicates the Mormon narrative. The Peacemaker's appearance likely came later than suggested and peace was less utopian than indicated, lasted longer than claimed, and, most importantly, included a Mother of all Nations left out of the Nephite record. These lacunae amplify the statement attributed to Jesus, "Behold, other scriptures I would that ye should write, that ye have not."[70]

The most compelling parallels come from Christianized accounts of the Great Peace. In the version Sakokweniónkwas learned from his grandmother (as well as that of Roy Buck and Jake Thomas), one of the four sacred beings of the Sky World, came to Turtle Island (North America). He was born to an unmarried woman simultaneously with eleven other babies born to married women. These eleven other children were drawn by a magnetic pull to the fatherless child who became a Teacher and a seer. The Teacher shared the Thanksgiving Address, the clan system, and Four Sacred Rituals consisting of dances, a song, and a game.[71] After sharing these foundations of Iroquois culture, the Teacher took leave of Turtle Island. Addressing his eleven birth mates he informed them, "Across this big water, there's another people; they're different than us. And those people are worse than us, meaner than the people here, more violent; the killing and things going on over there.... They're in more need than here."[72] Leaving that message, the Teacher walked across the sea.

In old age the eleven birth mates were drawn again magnetically to shores of Turtle Island where they found their Teacher returning from across the water. Upon arrival he showed them his wounds and reported, "They don't want peace." The people across the sea had murdered him and rejected his message.

He opened his garment to show his wounds and scratches, including the holes in his chest, hands, and feet. The Teacher expressed appreciation for Onkwehón:we (original people of North America), "You didn't hurt me when I was here. Thank you, you opened yourselves, and you embraced the Creator's teachings. And you gave me great honor." The Teacher taught them his favorite game and left behind a big wooden bowl in which to play it.[73] Sakokweniónkwas learned from his grandmother, Konwanataha, narratives that validated matrilineal cultural traditions.

With a direct revelation from the Peacemaker, the Haudenosaunee need not convert to Christianity. In sharing these and other stories, Sakokweniónkwas, who describes himself as "pagan," expressed his embarrassment over the similarities with Christianity: "Some people say this story is very much like the story of Jesus Christ. And they have cause to think that." He noted that he thought the missionaries must have taught us and that we had "mixed our knowledge with theirs and got it all confused like muddy water." As he got older, he realized that all humans share the same sun and the same earth, so "there *have* to be commonalities." "It doesn't mean," he clarifies, "that because I'm an Indian, I can't have original truths" or that "until a missionary came and taught me something, I knew nothing." Colonized Indians often start to believe these assumptions that truth can only come from white cultural traditions. Yet, "we have to reclaim our independence and our freedom as well. That's the hardest thing for Indians to do, or anybody that's colonized to do, is to get back their freedom, the real freedom to think, be thinkers again." So, Sakokweniónkwas concludes, "I'm just gonna tell you just the way they told me, and then you can draw your own conclusions."[74]

The Gaiwí:yo, or Code of Handsome Lake, has a similar but shorter message and account. In one of his visions Handsome Lake saw an approaching man who greeted and turned to face him as they drew closer. "Then said the man, 'Sedwágo'waně, I must ask you a question. Did you never hear your grandfathers say that once there was a certain man upon the earth across the great waters who was slain by his own people?'" Sedwágo'waně answered in the affirmative. "Then answered the man, 'I am he.' (Sega^{n}hedŭs, *He who resurrects*). And he turned his palms upward and they were scarred and his feet likewise and his breast was pierced by a spear wound." Sega^{n}hedŭs explained, "They slew me because of their independence and unbelief. So I have gone home to shut the doors of heaven that they may not see me again until the earth passes away." He went on to ask

Sedwãgo'wanĕ if anyone believed his teachings. Segaⁿhedŭs told him, "You are more successful than I for some believe in you but none in me." He offered one last warning before departing, "Now tell your people that they will become lost when they follow the ways of the white man."[75] In these accounts missing from the Nephite record, the messenger's validations of Haudenosaunee culture are clear and unequivocal.

Mann attributes associations between Handsome Lake and Jesus to the influence of Christian missionaries. Christian ideas in the Gaiwí:yo include "monotheism, good and evil as inimical opposites, and heaven and hell as moralistic reward and punishment for behavior in life." "The similarities between Jesus and Sganyadaí:yoh were pressed, so that the Gaiwí:yo actually includes a testimonial from the lips of Jesus." Other ideas include "the confession of sins … the suggestion of a salvation, and haunting visions of the destruction of the world." Importantly, as the message of Handsome Lake spread, "women were put on the defensive, stripped of as much power as public sentiment would allow, with female spirit workers and Clan Mothers who opposed the Gaiwí:yo redefined as 'witches.'" She concludes, "*None* of these traits reflected traditional Iroquoian thought. *All* of them were borrowed from European Christianity." Despite the similarities, Longhouse adherents see them as complementary traditions, noting "the wishes of God were transmitted through Handsome Lake, to the Christians through Christ."[76] Appearing at the turn of the nineteenth century, Sganyadaí:yoh's new religion helped preserve the traditional clan and ceremonial systems even as it incorporated Christian interpretations.

Associations of Peacemaker and Handsome Lake with Jesus helped defend Haudenosaunee traditions against missionaries. It is from this intercultural milieu that one finds overlap between Book of Mormon and Iroquois traditions. The Peacemaker served a central role in ending a civil war and establishing a democratic League of Nations that brought peace and prosperity in its wake. Mann notes, "The Second Epoch civil war was an absolutely historical event, traceable today through archeology, astronomy, European primary-source written records (composed well after the event), and, most importantly, oral tradition."[77] This evidence might have generated more interest from scholars of the Book of Mormon if not for its timing.

Significant scholarly debate accompanies the dating of the founding of the League. Western scholars typically propose founding dates between 1450 and 1550 CE, but oral tradition suggests earlier dates ranging from as early as

1000 BCE and as late as 1390 CE.[78] The reasoning that the Cayuga Keeper Jake Thomas gives for the earliest proposed date was because "elders feel that the Peacemaker made the Laws and united the nations before he went across the great salt water to the land of the white race. We feel that it was the same prophet that the white race call Jesus as he was reborn again from a virgin mother and gave the white race the good tidings of peace on earth."[79] While this earlier date is more compatible with the Book of Mormon, it is not the one substantiated by archaeological, historical, astronomical, and oral data.[80] Mann and her co-author Jerry Fields, an astronomer and mathematician, have evaluated a broad swath of existing sources to identify an eclipse associated with the founding of the League. They conclude, "It is rare enough when archaeology and oral tradition agree. But when archaeology, oral tradition, historical records, and astronomical science *all* point to the same date, August 31, 1142, a significant mass of evidence is before us."[81] The founding of the League, possibly occurring in 1142 CE, made the Great Peace possible.

The Peacemaker brought a new political, social, and economic alliance that fostered peace but he did not work alone. He had assistance from interpreters and allies, Hiawatha and Mother of Nations. Prior to new teachings, people had begun to lose "spiritual knowledge" and "ceremonial life." "This period of time was perhaps the darkest, most violent, and hopeless of our entire history.... Things became so bad, at that time, that cannibalism evolved, and society became very sadistic."[82] As Sakokweniónkwas recounts, a mother and daughter from a Huron village came down near present-day Kingston, Ontario. There the daughter mysteriously became pregnant and gave birth to a baby that would become the Peacemaker. As an adult, the Peacemaker crossed the river and lake and began a journey among the Haudenosaunee. "There was a woman living over there, and her name was Tsikónhsase."[83] Called Jigonsaseh in Seneca traditions, the Peacemaker sought her out "in the very first act of his peace mission" and "recognized the Jigonsaseh not only as his cosmic mother, but as The Mother of Nations."[84] Along with Aionwahta (Hiawatha), the Mother of Nations served as an interpreter and political ally bringing together the five nations.

Jigonsaseh "guided the final negotiations leading to the Great Peace" and her name was subsequently born by a Seneca clan mother in "the gendered counterpart of the Men's Grand Council."[85] The Clan Mothers operated much like "the local level of government" but not in an inferior sense to the "federal level of government operated by the men." "The Clan Mothers' Council at Gaustauyea mirrored the Men's Grand Council at Onandaga, and vice versa."[86] This new government had three guiding principles of popular sovereignty, health, and righteousness, later echoed in the US Constitution.[87] The principles, clan system, ceremonies, and economy were central to establishing peace. This peace was not an absolute absence of war. "Political reality was never so simple."[88] The reduction in conflict, especially internally, enabled the Iroquoian women to develop "a form of communal economics that guaranteed social security and preservation from want to all members of society." Through cooperation, communal ownership of land and resources, generous gift giving, and reciprocity with Mother Earth, gantowisas built an affluent and egalitarian economy that flourished for centuries, despite increasing warfare with arrival of European colonial powers. Decline in the League's economic affluence and displacement from most of its traditional territory would not come until after General John Sullivan's army destroyed the fields and villages of the Haudenosaunee in his burnt earth campaign of 1779.[89]

These "other scriptures" tell a complicated but much more balanced story than Nephite narrators. Iroquois accounts testify to a period of extensive conflict followed by a Great Peace during which people unified under a democratic confederacy lived in relative affluence with minimal warfare. The gantowisas, under the able guidance of Jigonsaseh, built a gift-giving economic system that ensured equality and affluence up until they lost their land in the aftermath of the American Revolution. This holocaust, as the Seneca anthropologist Arthur Parker has called it, came not at the hands of Lamanites but from the invading revolutionary armies of Continental Congress in 1779.[90] While many Iroquois lost their lives and gantowisas lost most of the land, descendants have survived to continue to tell sacred stories, ones that have yet to garner sufficient attention from Latter-day Saints.[91]

Our Own Understanding

There is an inspiring message that appears in the Book of Mormon as words of Nephi, yet also echoes teachings of gantowisas. "For the Lord God giveth light unto the understanding; for he speaketh unto men according to their language, unto their understanding."[92] At first glance Nephi's statement might not appear to have much in common with wisdom of Iroquoian women but an explanation might elucidate that possibility.

Handsome Lake's visions came at a time of significant social turmoil as the United States, aided by the Quakers, sought to transform a female-controlled economy into a Jeffersonian community of yeoman farmers. Handsome Lake's new religion urged men to become the farmers, displacing the gantowisas, reframed traditional narratives in terms of good versus evil, and demonized the gantowisas by calling them witches and hunting them down.[93]

The gantowisas did not submit without a fight. Their struggle would help ameliorate androcentric ideology and suspend murder of "witches" by Handsome Lake's followers. In their gendered struggles against Sganyandaí:yoh and Christian missionaries the spokesperson for the gantowisas was a man named Sagoyewatha (Red Jacket). Sagoyewatha was one of the best-known Native orators in the new United States, and his famous 1805 speech to missionary Jacob Cram may be the "most often reprinted composition by a Native American author."[94] He challenged Reverend Cram, "We understand that your religion is written in a book. If it was intended for us as well as you, why has not the Great Spirit given to us, and not only to us, but why did he not give to our forefathers the knowledge of that book, with the means to understand it rightly?" As the spokesperson for women, Sagoyewatha continued, "Why may we not conclude that He has given us a different religion *according to our understanding?*" (Emphasis mine).[95] While outsiders saw Red Jacket as author of this speech, his socially ascribed responsibility was to speak the words of the gantowisas.[96]

In addition to this famous and widely reprinted speech, Sagoyewatha addressed a crowd in Palmyra, New York, in July of 1822 during which he expressed similar frustrations with Christian missionaries.[97] While we do not have a transcript of the latter speech, he likely repeated familiar refrains that echo Haudenosaunee oral traditions testifying to the existence of an alternative religion *according to our own understanding*. The Book of Mormon echoes the same inspired message, one that has yet to receive the attention it deserves.

Conclusion

Twenty-first century revelations from biological anthropology, coupled with evidence from archaeology and history, have unsettled Mormon beliefs about ancestral origins of Native Americans. It has become untenable to present the Book of Mormon as *the history* of Native America. The LDS Church has recently reminded its followers to approach scripture on spiritual rather than historical terms. In this sense, DNA evidence has helped liberate Mormons to look anew at scriptures and consider alternative ways to give them meaning. Decolonizing approaches to scripture provide Mormons with an opportunity to recognize and validate Indigenous voices.

The resurrected Christ, who initiated the Great Peace of the Book of Mormon, chastised Nephites for incomplete record keeping. The more culturally inclusive approach Christ encouraged can be pursued by turning to other sacred narratives like oral traditions of the Haundenosaunee that also testify of a Great Peace. In these accounts the Peacemaker acted in concert with the Mother of Nations. Reciprocity and tolerance of other scriptures may serve as a corrective for patriarchy and ethnocentrism that can now be bracketed as mistakes of men in the latter-day canon.[98]

More careful attention to insights of Haudenosaunee prophets and seers who also dream and have visions can help inform twenty-first-century approaches to scripture. Prophets and seers are human beings like the rest of us who function within cultured and gendered perspectives that limit understanding. When those dreams and visions are discussed, shared, and vetted within a community we can better collaborate in finding appropriate ways to act upon our inspirations. If we are to follow the example of the Haudenosaunee, women should be in leading roles in such dream work.

Joseph Smith, a seer from a colonizing society on land recently wrestled violently and fraudulently from Haudenosaunee, struggled to understand his own dreams and visions haunted as they were by holocaust. As Mormonism moves through another century, it needs to forthrightly confront the racism, sexism, and colonial legacies of its scriptural canon. Some Indigenous Mormons have found space for validation of their own traditions in the Book of Mormon's proclamation, echoing that of the gantowisas: that the Creator speaks to all according to our own understanding. A decolonized Mormonism might recognize *Code of Handsome Lake*, *Black Elk Speaks*, *Popol Vuh*, Haudenosaunee oral traditions, and similar narratives from cultures of its varied membership as other scriptures. In doing so, Mormons will better understand not just others but also ourselves.

3

Joseph Smith in Iroquois Country

A Mormon Creation Story

LORI ELAINE TAYLOR

The man whose experience most influenced how early Mormons thought and acted toward Indians was Joseph Smith, but histories of Joseph Smith say nothing of his interactions with American Indians before the establishment of the Church of Christ in 1830, which seems unusual considering his abiding interest and the focus of the book that changed his life, the Book of Mormon.[1]

The Mormon Creation Story

We may not find Joseph Smith and Indians in conventional histories or in the limited written records of his early life, but we can reach into a story of his contact with the Senecas, a story claiming a connection between Joseph Smith and Handsome Lake. This story came up in a conversation as I was talking to Nicholas Vrooman, the teller of the story. He suddenly looked at me. "You're a Mormon? Oh boy, do I have a good story to tell you."[2]

This specific story has been told since at least the 1960s.[3] Each teller makes the story their own, coaxing listeners toward their own understanding. When I tell the story, I talk about how it fits into my research, framing the story with an explanation of who Nicholas is and how he came to tell me the story (layered over his explanation of who his teller is and how he came to tell the story). In the story that follows, the teller asks Nicholas and others, "Hey! Hey you guys ever hear the story of how the Mormons came to be, the real story?"[4]

Handsome Lake, Joseph Smith, and the Word, told by Nicholas Vrooman

It was June … Summer Solstice … 1987. This is a story I heard.

We were on the Turtle Mountain Reservation in north-central North Dakota.… Sundance encampment was there.… Everybody's camps were pitched, and we had been out gathering pole materials to put up the lodge. And so now everybody was sort of just being quiet and hanging around camp.…

It was a potent time.… And, there's this one guy, his name is Wabanimki. He's an Ottawa, but he was adopted into the Seneca, to a family at Tonawanda.…

Those of us who were sitting around were dancers … we're whittling stakes and stuff, and our little skewers that we're going to use to pull rope with … somehow we got talking about—I think maybe it had something to do with my being raised in New York, too, and coming up with Iroquois, the Haudenosaunee.…

He says, Hey! Hey, you guys ever hear the story of how the Mormons came to be, the real story. Well, sure we want to hear the real story. Well he says, really it all came from the Iroquois, from the Seneca, there, because … Joseph Smith … he lived there in Seneca territory of New York.… he is the guy that is credited with bringing this Mormon religion to the people … he was a farmer there in New York in Seneca territory, and he had these Seneca guys that were working for him.

This is in the early 1800s.… after they suffered the final defeat after the War of 1812.… They were a real pitiful people. But you know what, the story is that everybody was pitiful then.… Everybody was struggling for a toehold in making this new country work.…

This Joseph Smith, he was a farmer and he was an optimistic man. He was a moral man. He was a spiritual man. And, he had these guys working for him. But they weren't like the rest of the Indians who he saw around them because these guys were real good guys. And he wanted to know how come when all the people around, so many of these Seneca people were just pitiful and into alcohol and debauchery and stuff, and how come these guys were so solid, so stable, so strong. And they say, well, they were followers of Handsome Lake. And, well, who is this Handsome Lake?

Well, Handsome Lake, he, too, suffered all the trauma that came along with the defeat of the Iroquois people.... he was into the alcohol and everything, too. But finally there was this one point where this guy, this Handsome Lake had ... two or three visions.... he was told these things and given these signs on how to help his people survive ... he became the prophet of the Haudenosaunee.... He was a holy man. And he found a way of taking the best of the old traditional ways of the Iroquois, the Seneca people, and mixed them with the best ways of the Christian white types coming from Europe, those Euro-American types. And he found a way of blending this together because his vision told him that the only way his people were going to survive is if they held on to the root, the main root of who they were throughout time that gave them a sense of identity and strength and consistency of heritage....

So these guys, there, that worked for this Joseph Smith, you know, they're telling this Joseph Smith this is who they are, that they are followers of this Handsome Lake and they are followers of the Word, the Gai-wiio, the Word.... And, so, this Joseph Smith said, By golly, this is just what the white people need because, because they're just as pitiful as the Indians are. And because it's a new world for everybody, what the white people need to do is to take the best of their Christian heritage and tra-ditions and stuff that come out of their European ways and mix it with the Indigenous ways of the people who have lived on this land for a long time, you know, like the Iroquois people....

And so, what about all these books, we say, this gold and stuff?.... And he said, Well, that's real easy. And, you know, because during the War of 1812 the Iroquois there, they sided with the British. And even though they lost, the British still had to pay up because basically they hired the Iroquois to fight with them.... and they paid them off in gold.

Anyhow, what they did was, they took this gold, and they say, Okay. Joseph Smith, you got it right. That's what you guys got to do. We'll be better, us Indians will be better off if you white people do just like we did to get along here in this new world. We'll be better off if you folks can understand us a little bit more by taking in some of our world view, too. So, we will help you ... bring the Word to your own people. This is what we're going to do ...

And, so, what Joseph Smith needed, what he knew he had to do was stage some kind of a media event to really get the attention of these people.... They said, What we'll do, Joseph Smith, is this.... We'll take this gold we got from the British.... we'll melt this gold down.... and we'll put it into these tablets like. And what we'll do is we'll take our writing on it and ... we'll write the Gaiwiio in our picture writing on these tablets. But we'll work with you on this. And you will emphasize it for your Christian ways, you know, so that your people will tune into it. And then we'll mix in with it our Indian ways in it so it will be a nice blending so we'll all get along through these words. And it will be the white equivalent of Handsome Lake's, Gaiwiio. And we'll put it on these gold tablets, and then we'll bury it there.... And then you will have these dreams and you will go and you will get these tablets and you will bring them up from the ground and you go, Look what I found! And everybody will stand up and they'll look and they'll listen....

It will make sense to these people, just like with us, it makes sense to us, you know, this blending now. This is a new world. We have to accept this.... they will listen to this new Word that you bring to them. And that way we will all get along much better.... we will all live under the new word, the Word, the Gaiwiio. And you will be the Handsome Lake for your people. You will be that.

And so ... we sit there at the Sundance camp. And we say, Oh, hmm. You know it makes a kind of a sense.... Where does this story come from now, we asked Wabanimki. And he said, back at Tonawanda, those tablets are still alive. Those tablets are still alive. There's people there that know this story. . . .

And now this Mormon religion becomes a big thing. Although it got watered down and changed here and there over time from what the real true Word was, from the way Gaiwiio spoke it. There was too much emphasis on the Christian thing, more than there used to be, more than the way that we passed it on, the Iroquois passed it on, the Seneca there to Joseph Smith. . . . And that's the way that happened, he told us. . . .

And, the sundance went on. It was a good sundance, and, Wabanimki . . . he was a good firekeeper. And, it was a good dance, a good thirsting dance.

So I always remembered that story. . . . I've only told it to a few people. . . . I think there's a story there. I think there's truth to it, you know, whatever, whether it's real or not, there's a truth there somehow. And, so, I just pass this on to you, just to say that this is what I heard. Like I say, this didn't come from me. This is just what I heard. And I told you who I heard it from. And he said he heard it from somebody else. And, that's how that goes.

Sacred Counter-history

The history of Joseph Smith is sacred history, not just in the sense that the majority of Mormons hold it close but in that it has been canonized in LDS scripture as *Joseph Smith–History*. Joseph Smith is the protagonist of Mormons' creation story—as Mormons emerged from chaos, distinguishing Us from Them and Now from Then. The Restoration is inevitably such a story of emergence.[5] A counter-creation story could, if it were believed among Mormons, crack the foundation of the sacred history by altering the accepted genesis of Mormon scripture. Who can tell a sacred counter-history? I have not heard Mormons tell the story of Joseph Smith and Handsome Lake.[6]

My friend Nicholas and I thought and talked together about this story for years. He later wrote me about it.

Why was it I "heard" this tale, and it sunk [sic] into me? It could have rolled off me like a tall tale coming from a crackerjack, or even a wiseass red tongue putting down a white boy. But no, I knew it was something else, and I held on to it, and told it around, because it seemed so much a sense-maker of a different America than the standard myth of who we are and where we come from. I know it touched me because it's about the America I choose to live in, a between the cracks America, an underlying America that lives just below the level of historic scrutiny and national- istic mythologizing, but is all pervasive and ever operative in the natural currents and earth memory of a deeper, more full truthtelling [sic] to our existence. And why was it you were the only one who heard me? What links in a chain of some larger continuity do we both serve as tellers of this story? If any ...

I think that may be why we, you and I, feel so much for what this story has to tell—whether it's true in the sense of actually occurring is not the point of the telling for us. It's that it *is truthful* about a greater humanity we so ache for in light of the suffering, misunderstanding, and exploita- tion we yet see all around us.

No little story we have here. For however it came into existence, the fact is, it is, and has all this to say, at least for me ... [7]

There is something valuable, even sacred, about this story of a syncretic Ameri- can religion, and I approach with care for the sacred. Spiritual histories of white Christians and American Indians cannot be written together unless they are understood in similar terms, but they cannot be understood in similar terms without collapsing one into the worldview of the other—at least not in conven- tional histories. In their process of assimilation, unified histories do violence to the sacred as sacred. The place for this story is not in consensus histories with unified visions of truth.

Neither the tone of this story's telling nor the implications of its claims fit tidily into Mormon history as it is so far, but it might fit messily. What can be done with conventional historiographic methods to see into the gaps in Joseph Smith's history where the followers of Handsome Lake might fit in?

Joseph Smith and the Iroquois

This Mormon creation story proposes not only that Joseph Smith interacted with Indigenous Peoples before the Book of Mormon but claims a role for nineteenth-century Indigenous Peoples in the coming forth of the Book of Mormon. However, no conventional records directly mention Joseph Smith meeting Iroquois people in New York.

Indians were not invisible during the time that people lived in shared spaces, but as long as they were seldom or not at all recorded, Indians become invisible to those writing later histories.[8] Most of those sources available for reconstructing Indian-white contacts that are made part of the public record are originally recorded and later told from a white view, but one can create a fair picture of contact as represented by the new Americans in the various phases of colonization. Many Native Peoples also kept records, though Native records of contact are seldom explored in written history because they may follow cultural forms determined within Native cultures—often (but not exclusively) oral narratives—that do not lend themselves immediately to print scholarship. With the records we have, we can still challenge both invisibility and stereotypical portrayals of unidirectional relationships between the peoples.

When one sees the implication of cultural transference or blending, the impulse might be to try to discover the original circumstances of contact and the extent of influence. For example, the traditional religion of the Haudenosaunee or Iroquois, was given by the Seneca prophet Handsome Lake from 1799 to 1815 in the form of recitations of visions and other teachings. There has been much speculation and a few studies of the origins of Handsome Lake's thought, which might include Quaker and Moravian influence along with the renewal of commitment to traditional Native culture. Studies of the new religion use as sources the stories of elders and the words of Handsome Lake preachers, as well as the documents of Quakers and other white observers in order to explore the specific elements that were brought together into the Longhouse religion as taught by Handsome Lake and, after continued evolution, as practiced today.[9]

Among Mormons there is another contemporary subculture with numerous indications of European- and Native American cross-cultural influence—but influence that has not been studied. There is silence in Mormon histories regarding possible firsthand contact between Joseph Smith and local Indians in his youth. Mormon history is well trod and minutely argued; any silence calls attention to itself.

Had previous scholars looked, they would find some intriguing cases of Mormon and Iroquois similarities: both Handsome Lake and Joseph Smith had guides in their visions—Handsome Lake had four messengers teach him, and one messenger, Moroni, returned to Joseph Smith four times. Handsome Lake had a guided vision of a journey on a Sky Road, during which he saw scenes symbolic of an afterlife, including crowds of people standing at the fork of a wide and rough road which led to a great lodge, the house of the Punisher where people cried for help, and a narrow road, lined with fruits and flowers, which led to the pleasant lands; and Lehi, an early character in the Book of Mormon, had a similar guided vision symbolic of earth life, including crowds of people attempting to walk along a narrow path, some holding on to an iron rod to avoid falling, all moving toward a tree whose fruit they wished to take, while people in a great and spacious building mocked their efforts.[10] At the time of a much earlier prophet to the Iroquois, when the Five Nations formed a confederacy, they buried their weapons of war beneath a white pine as a renunciation of war; a violent people in the Book of Mormon, the Anti-Nephi-Lehies, also buried their weapons as a renunciation of war.[11] There are also similarities in the size and authority of delegations to the civil governments of the Iroquois Confederacy and the Mormon Council of Fifty, in health restrictions in the Handsome Lake code and the teachings of Joseph Smith, and in ceremonies and in origin stories, which are not so easily compared. Any of these similarities could be investigated as possible cultural transferences.[12]

Joseph Smith in New York

The New York period of Mormon history begins in 1816, when Joseph Smith Sr. and Lucy Mack Smith moved with their children from Vermont to Palmyra, New York, and goes through 1831, by which time most of the early members of Joseph Smith's new religion had moved to Kirtland, in northeastern Ohio.[13] Joseph Smith Jr. first wrote about his own life in 1832; he mentioned the spiritual quest of his youth but nothing of the Iroquois.[14] Lucy Mack Smith wrote a biography of her son in 1853 in which she recalled that he told tales of Indians "as if he had spent his whole life among them," but she mentions no firsthand contact, either.[15]

Dozens of studies have been published attempting to understand the origins of Mormonism by looking to Joseph Smith's youth in Western New York. Scholars have convincingly broadened the analysis of Joseph Smith's life to include folk magic and the Primitivist Seekers, even seventeenth-century hermeticism.[16] But contemporary Iroquois appear so seldom as to be considered negligible in the histories written of early Mormonism.

If it is intellectually plausible to reach across oceans and centuries to find his influences, why has no one reached across the Genesee River to Joseph Smith's Seneca contemporaries?[17] I would suggest a simple answer: scholars in the Western tradition have not been trained to consider Native influences on political thought, lifeways, and religion.[18]

When white writers construct Indians as a unified whole relating to a white norm, such a construction does not tell us all there is to know of a Native experience of empire any more than it tells us all there is to know of a white experience of settlement.[19] The Genesee country in the early nineteenth century was an area of new white settlement, not only an area of transition between lifeways but an area where people who are theorized as binary opposites were in fact in frequent contact and exerting subtle influences upon one another.[20] To investigate whether Joseph Smith was likely to meet Iroquois people face-to-face and perhaps sit down with them and listen to the teachings of their prophet Handsome Lake, I look to the interactions of individual Iroquois and settlers.

Iroquois and Settlers in the Early Nineteenth Century

Settlers knew Iroquois people as individuals. Firsthand stories tell of specific, situated contacts. In reports from settlers in the upper Finger Lakes area of the Genesee country, I concentrate on the period after the War of 1812 (a time of upheaval for the Western New York Indians and of nationalism and social stabilization for white pioneers) and before 1838 (when, with the signing of the Treaty at Buffalo Creek, removal of the Iroquois seemed sure). This period includes the whole of early Mormon history in New York (1816–1832).

The land west and south from Sodus Bay was known as Nundawahgageh, the territory of the Seneca.[21] After General Sullivan and 5,000 men destroyed 40 villages in 1779 in retaliation for the Iroquois alliance with the British in the Revolutionary War, most Senecas stayed in villages west of the Genesee River.[22]

Ten Seneca Reservations were established in 1797 and by 1817 the Senecas were starving.[23] Tensions between Senecas and settlers persisted on the reservations and in nearby settlements.[24] As a solution to an uncomfortable situation, Governor De Witt Clinton suggested in 1818 that "it is presumed there can be no reasonable objection to their removal." Twelve Seneca chiefs signed a formal reply telling him, "We desire to let you know that wrong information has reached your ears."[25] Many people of the Iroquois Nations left the Finger Lakes in the generations between the 1780s and the 1830s.[26] In 1816, 4,492 Iroquois lived in New York.[27] Despite removals, 5,100 Iroquois lived in New York in 1829.[28]

Some of the soldiers who saw the fertile Genesee country during Sullivan's raid to destroy the Iroquois returned to settle the area. Sale of township lots opened in 1789.[29] By 1800 there were over 15,000 residents.[30] The War of 1812 interrupted new settlement, but the area (particularly Rochester) boomed after all hostilities in Western New York ceased.[31] By 1830, there were over 120,000 non-Iroquois people in Genesee country.[32]

Not all Iroquois lived on the reservations west of the Genesee. As late as 1813 "there were numerous families of Indians scattered around" the area that would become Rochester.[33] Even when Iroquois were no longer living in an area, they traveled through, visited, and stayed periodically in the lands most of them left in 1779.

Iroquois and settlers alike used the Indian trails that laced the Finger Lakes area. The Iroquois Trail connecting Geneva, Canandaigua, and Avon was the first main highway.[34] Iroquois walked the trails between the Seneca and Tuscarora lands in the west and Onondaga farther east. Handsome Lake, for example, walked every year between Allegany, Cattaraugus, Buffalo, Tonawanda, and Onondaga until he died in 1815.[35] After the codification of Handsome Lake's teachings in 1826, the Handsome Lake preacher walked the circuit annually.[36]

In the time of earliest settlement (1788), one could travel by water from the Mohawk Valley to what is now Palmyra, where Joseph Smith spent his youth. Palmyra was the former site of the Seneca village of Ganagweh, a town site chosen for its easy access by water.[37] Writers of histories of Wayne and Ontario Counties make many references to Iroquois visits to Ganargua or Mud Creek. Pioneers called the waterway Mud Creek because it was stagnant, a source of illness.[38] In the 1840s, by which time the creek had been cleared, "The dwellers in its valley were enabled, with the help of Lewis Morgan, Esq., of Rochester, to come at its ancient Seneca name, which they adopted."[39] The creek is still Mud

Creek south of Victor but is Ganargua Creek from Victor through Farmington, Macedon, Palmyra, Newark, and Lyons—where it now meets the Erie Canal near the Canandaigua Outlet.

In 1796, a local historian of Macedon, the township just west of Palmyra, remembered that there were a few Indian residents when the first white settlers arrived. "The favorite haunts of the red men of this section seem to have been along the valley of the Ganargua, as the flats are rich in Indian curiosities," meaning, the graves of their ancestors.[40] Up to 1803, Indian families built bark houses in Palmyra in the forest between Main Street and the Ganargua Creek; they hunted bear and deer and fished for "salmon and other now extinct varieties of fish in Mud Creek." The writer remembered them as "generally sober, honest and peaceful."[41]

Stephen Durfee, the son of Quaker pioneers who moved to Palmyra in 1792 when he was 16 years old, remembered the Iroquois presence at Ganargua Creek during his youth: "The Indians, were hunting and trapping, camping in our neighborhood, in all the earliest years. The flats of the Ganargua, and the adjoining up lands were favorite hunting grounds. Many of the sons of the early settlers were trappers."[42] Did the Iroquois trappers and the sons of settlers work cooperatively? In Manchester, the township just south of Palmyra, Iroquois hunters who camped along the Canandaigua Outlet did work cooperatively with whites who "would carry loads of venison to Canandaigua for them, where it would be bought up and the hams dried and sent to an eastern market. Trapping upon the outlet was profitable for both Indians and whites."[43]

On the western end of Ganargua Creek, Joseph Smith (not the Mormon), the first settler of Canandaigua and a man who had been a captive as a child and later acted as interpreter for the Seneca at treaty negotiations, built in 1793 a small framed grist mill in the Farmington area.[44] Because he was a Seneca speaker and a frequent interpreter, it is likely that he entertained Seneca and other Iroquois guests at his homes and businesses in Geneva, Canandaigua, and Farmington, then Leicester. Seneca speakers and Indian agents also lived in the vicinity of Palmyra and Canandaigua. Jasper Parrish, who had also been a captive and was adopted as a Mohawk, was appointed official government interpreter in 1792 at age 25;[45] he was made Indian Sub-agent at Canandaigua in 1803.[46] Captain Israel Chapin, at the request of Red Jacket, replaced his father General Israel Chapin as Indian Agent from 1795 to 1802. The family had lived at "'Chapin's Mills,' a few miles north of Canandaigua, on the Palmyra road,"[47] on land included in one of the two township lots bought by Israel Chapin.[48] In the early decades of white settlement, Iroquois would have traveled through the Finger Lakes area to visit Smith, Parrish, Chapin, and other government agents and traders.

Centers of trade would have been common places for Iroquois and settlers both to gather. Before the Phelps and Gorham Purchase was opened, Geneva, built near the former Seneca village of Kanedesaga, had become "the principal seat of the Indian trade for a wide region." Horatio Jones, another who had been a captive as a child and later served as an interpreter for the Iroquois, "was living in a log house covered with bark, on the bank of the Lake, and had a small stock of goods for the Indian trade."[49] After the establishment of Canandaigua, former site of the Seneca village of Ganundagwa, "the Cayuga, Oneida, Onondaga and Seneca Indians received their annuities at Canandaigua, which made it a place of annual gatherings of those nations, and the centre of Indian trade."[50] In Lyons, east of Palmyra, Judge Daniel Dorsey started merchandizing soon after 1800. "A large proportion of his early trade was with the Indians, who were encamped along the banks of the [Canandaigua] outlet and at Sodus. There used to be as many as thirty Indian huts along where William Street, of Lyons village, crosses the canal."[51] White merchants were not the only traders in the area. Nicholas Stansell, son of pioneers of Lyons, east of Palmyra at the junction of the Canandaigua Outlet and Ganargua Creek, recalled his family buying corn from Onondagas when the family's own provisions were exhausted.[52]

Some of the most interesting recollections of the Iroquois by white settlers reveal that spaces within people's houses were also open to Iroquois guests, sometimes uninvited. Rhoda Sawyer Swift was married to General John Swift, an Indian fighter who bought and settled the Palmyra township in 1789. The story is told in local histories of the evening she was making hasty pudding,

> when three Indians entered, and, without ceremony, took seats around the fire, and gravely watched her proceedings. Finally, their conduct gave umbrage to Dame Swift, who caught the poker, and assailed them so lustily that they were glad to make a hasty retreat. Her act is notable, from the fact that to later arrivals, from a sense of dread of offending, she gave of food needed for the family to satisfy their importunate demands.[53]

While this is certainly not a tale of fast friends, the story ends by referring to "later arrivals," implying that Indian visitors continued to visit her. Had they been visiting Ganargua Creek? Did they visit other settlers as well?

Other recollections tell us that the visits to Rhoda Swift were not isolated incidents. Charles Herendeen, who in 1896 collected just such stories for an article later published in a pioneer history of Macedon, the township just west of Palmyra, is unusual among local historians. He did not generalize about interactions with the Iroquois. He asked the old people of his town what they remembered and strung these memories together with a few comments. He creates a picture of firsthand contact without fear or resentment, not of two peoples inhabiting wholly different geographical and social spaces.

> Some of the old settlers, among whom were my grandparents, would find in the morning perhaps a half dozen Indians asleep on the floor before the fireplace, and receive from them a "grunt" of thanks and satisfaction. Doors were not locked and Indians availed themselves of a night's lodging without asking permission from their host, who had no fear of being harmed.

Whole families of Iroquois would stop for meals.[54] "Children," he wrote, "seemed to have no fear of them."

> It is known to be a fact the "Old Blue Sky" and "John Sky" and other chiefs came suddenly into a room where there were children, swung their tomahawks around their heads and then dropped their weapons and picked up the children and kissed and fondled them. They would "count Injun," which was like the following, "Scat sky, ski-e-ski, tickine sky, tuta and a-was-ski," speaking the last with a quick, loud voice and startling emphasis, thus playing "scare" with the children.[55]

Only two reports I found named the people they spoke of, making the Iroquois context of most of the individuals and incidents untraceable. Blue Sky and John Sky, however, we find in records of the Seneca. Both Tonawanda chiefs signed several documents in the 1800s.[56] Blue Sky traveled to Washington, DC, in 1802 to visit President Jefferson with Handsome Lake and a delegation of others of the Six Nations;[57] Blue Sky was also closely allied with Red Jacket during the War of 1812.[58] In July 1818, at the first Six Nations meeting to recall the teachings of Handsome Lake, John Sky spoke to the gathered council of the prophet's moral teachings for three hours. The game of "scare" which Herendeen cites would have been before January 1819, when John Sky died.[59]

Herendeen tells of one child who made an effort to learn the Seneca language just to facilitate friendly meetings. A 90-year-old woman remembered
greeting Seneca travelers in their own language in 1812, when she would have
been almost six years old. "She used to go out and meet the Indians when she
saw them coming toward her father's home and that she learned a few words of
their language, such as 'Sago' (good morning), and 'De-qua-chee' (how do you
do?), and that this seemed to please them greatly."[60]

The strength of individual acquaintances and friendships promoted the long
alliance of Senecas and Quakers. Griffith Cooper, for example, had long been
sought as an advocate for the Iroquois. Red Jacket visited Cooper in Pultneyville,
north of Palmyra on Lake Ontario, in 1827 to ask his assistance. Red Jacket, not
known for his willing alliance with white people, trusted the Quakers, whose
practices were in great contrast to missionary efforts that demanded open confession of allegiance to a Christian God.[61]

An associate of Cooper's was Mary Durfee of Williamson township, north
of Palmyra.[62] In her diary, she wrote her thoughts as a Quaker woman concerned
with "the natives of this country."[63] At Cooper's house, Mary Durfee wrote of
meeting three Seneca delegates from Buffalo who were seeking Quaker media-
tion.[64] She also met Seneca delegates at a meeting in Farmington, just south of
Palmyra.[65]

Local histories throughout the Genesee country often began with a chapter
on "the Indians," "the Iroquois," or "the Seneca," but few of those local histories
told of contemporary Senecas outside of treaty negotiations and laments over
their sorry state. Without the stories collected by local historians Orasmus
Turner and Charles Herendeen, and a few firsthand recollections, there would
be little to say beyond generalizations about the interactions of Iroquois and
settlers in this area.[66]

Joseph Smith and Red Jacket in Palmyra

Beyond reports of firsthand contacts, we can begin to connect individuals in
possibilities of contact by piecing together other facts. It is possible, for example,
that Joseph Smith heard a public speech of Red Jacket (who was Handsome
Lake's nephew but opposed his teachings).[67]

In July 1822, Red Jacket and four others (Blue Sky, William Sky, Peter Smoke and Twenty Canoes[68]) walked through Palmyra on their way to ask their trusted advocates, the Quakers, to intercede in their struggle to prevent missionaries from violating the 1821 New York law barring non-Indians from living on the reservations in Western New York. Perhaps Red Jacket was traveling north to visit Cooper as he did five years later. The delegation arrived in Palmyra about sunset and the people of the town pressed Red Jacket to speak to them. Red Jacket, the most widely-known Seneca of this period and one who spoke frequently and fervently against white encroachment on Seneca lands, delivered a speech that evening at the Palmyra Academy.

> His speech, if it had been properly interpreted, no doubt would have been both eloquent and interesting. But as it was, merely enough could be understood to *know* his object, while his native eloquence and rhetorical powers could only be *guessed* at, from his manner and appearance.[69] He commenced by representing the whole human race as the creatures of God, or the Great Spirit, and that both white men and red men were brethren of the same great family. He then mentioned the emigration of our forefathers from towards the rising of the sun, and their landing among their red brethren in this new discovered world. He next hinted at the success of our armies under the great Washington; our prosperity as a nation since the declaration of our independence; mentioned Gen. Washington's advice to red men to plough, and plant, and cultivate their lands. This, he said, they wished to do, but the white men took away their lands, and drove them further and further towards the setting sun;—and what was worse than all, had sent Missionaries to preach and hold meetings, stole their horses, drove off their cattle, and taxed their land.—These things he considered their greatest calamity—too grievous to be borne.

The writer went on to ask why "these our red brethren" opposed missionaries. "We know not; but the cause of pure religion and christian philanthropy requires their speedy investigation and public explanation."[70] Perhaps Red Jacket spoke as reported; perhaps not. Red Jacket did not speak or write English, so all of his reported words and ideas are translations.[71]

The visit of Red Jacket to Palmyra is perhaps the closest I have come to finding Joseph Smith Jr., then 16 years old, in the same place at the same time as any Iroquois person. Orasmus Turner, who was then an apprentice printer in Palmyra at the office of E.P. Grandin (who later printed the Book of Mormon), recalled that Joseph Smith "used to help us solve some portentous questions of moral or political ethics, in our juvenile debating club."[72] The debating club was established January 1822,[73] and Orasmus Turner finished his apprenticeship later that year, so Joseph Smith would have attended the club sometime during 1822. Red Jacket's visit and speech in Palmyra that summer brought excited notice throughout Wayne County, notice unlikely to be missed by the juvenile debating club. Did they discuss his opposition to missionaries? Did they debate the question whether "both white men and red men were brethren of the same great family"? We can only speculate whether Joseph Smith was in attendance at meetings after Red Jacket's speech or whether the club discussed his visit, but given Red Jacket's notoriety, the size of the town (3,724 in 1820),[74] and Joseph Smith's interest in local affairs, it is likely that Joseph Smith took notice of Red Jacket in 1822.

Like most of his contemporaries, Joseph Smith probably had extensive secondhand knowledge of American Indians. Palmyra newspapers carried frequent notices of Indian wars and removals in the southeast US, of discoveries of Indian mounds and antiquities in the upper Midwest, as well as occasional notices of the "civilization" and possible removal of New York Indians. But Joseph Smith, an inquisitive person with a particular interest in Indian antiquities, is likely to have gone out of his way to meet the Iroquois people who continued to visit Ganargua Creek and the towns near Palmyra during his youth and long after he left New York.

Stephen Harding came into close contact with Mormons several times in his life: he was present in the printing office in Palmyra when the proof was pulled of the title page of the Book of Mormon in 1829, and much later he was one of the federally appointed governors of Utah Territory. But he also remembered Joseph Smith, who was several years older than he, as a "long-legged, tow-headed boy ... who was generally fishing in the mill pond at Durfee's grist-mill, on Mud Creek, when my elder brother and I went to the mill." When Joseph Smith met him at the printing office, he did not think Smith remembered having seen him at Durfee's a decade earlier.[75]

Durfee's mill on Mud Creek, or Ganargua Creek, was at the north edge of the wood between Main Street and the creek. It was in this area where settlers reported that Indians "continued the custom of taking temporary possession of the forests at their pleasure."[76] Stephen Durfee remembered the Iroquois staying at Ganargua Creek during his youth.[77] If Joseph Smith was fishing at the pond, he would certainly have taken the opportunity to find out about the Iroquois who occasionally camped and hunted there.

The Finger Lakes area was still home to Senecas and other Iroquois even after they had been forced farther west. "An old gentleman told me," wrote Charles Herendeen, "that between 1845 and 1850 he well remembered that bands of Senecas, Cayugas, etc., would come to Macedon and remain there for some days, looking around the country. It was supposed that they were in search of 'landmarks,' graves, etc."[78] I include this report not despite but because of its late date. This recollection shows not just a continuing memory but a continuing Iroquois presence in the Finger Lakes into at least the third generation of settlement—a presence which could be extended through oral histories well into the twentieth century.

Iroquois certainly still traveled, and stayed periodically, in the upper Finger Lakes between 1816 and 1830, and they were people with whom Joseph Smith might have had firsthand contact. Firsthand contacts between Iroquois and settlers in the upper Finger Lakes in the first generations of white settlement complicate the idea of a binary opposition of Indian and white. I have attempted here to reach past Indian as "other than white" to show the variety of people in the area engaging in complex relationships.

Joseph Smith brought with him an astonishing variety of influences. I suggest that we must further open up the possibilities for understanding the web of his influences by acknowledging and exploring the potentially rich area of Iroquois contact.

Once the hard division between Indian and white or Iroquois and settler is abandoned, it does not seem unlikely that, as the story goes, followers of Handsome Lake met Joseph Smith while they were all working as field hands and, because Joseph was a boy curious about spiritual matters, they told him of the spiritual teachings of the Seneca prophet, who was less than ten years passed.[79]

Considering the Claims

Neither Joseph Smith Sr., nor Joseph Smith Jr., was in a position to employ field hands as the story claims, but Joseph Smith Jr. did occasionally get seasonal work in the fields as well as digging for treasure, which is much better documented. Did he meet Indian workers in the fields? Luman Walters, who is often claimed to have been Joseph Smith's "magician" mentor, had "an Indian herbalist" in his family. If Joseph Smith did have contact with him, could he have been a source of Indian knowledge or connections?[80] A Western New York newspaper reported that workers digging the Erie Canal found "several brass plates" with skeletons and pottery.[81] Could we find and make connections between metal plates and Iroquois people during the contact period?[82] What of similarities in Iroquois and Mormon stories, and ceremonies, and political structures?

What other comparisons have been made by those who are familiar with both the Iroquois Longhouse and Mormonism? Edmund Wilson, on a tour of the Six Nations for the *New Yorker* in the 1950s, visited Philip Cook, a Mohawk of Akwesasne. Wilson tells the story of Cook's rejection of various Christian churches, his difficulty in the Longhouse, and his eventual conversion to the LDS Church. Cook, through Wilson, makes an interesting observation: "Philip Cook thought at first that Smith must have been influenced by the Handsome Lake doctrine, through the Senecas of Western New York, but then he concluded that no white man at the time could ever have had access to their ceremonies or understood what was said if he had."[83]

Tracing the lines of acquaintances of all of the people I know who know the story, I find that one man knew them all or knew who told them. In another of Edmund Wilson's articles for the *New Yorker*, he wrote of Wallace "Mad Bear" Anderson, in 1958 a dynamic man of 31 years old. Mad Bear later became one of those elders who for young people in the 1960s and 1970s imparted Indian wisdom and stories. He also, in his travels, made connections with Indigenous Peoples around the world and worked to bring them together.[84] He spread Iroquois stories and his contemporary interpretations far and wide. Leslie Fiedler remembered Mad Bear telling of the Indian past on Atlantis and the future after the Chinese invasion to destroy white Americans. Fourteen sixty-foot giants were already roaming the land, and, as he told the story (before 1968) it was time to go to the woods for council before the riots began. The upheaval would leave only Indians on the continent.[85] Mad Bear told Edmund Wilson about the white serpent, the red serpent, and the black serpent who, as foretold a thousand years earlier, were then (1958) locked in battle, awaiting a great war in 1960. The villain in this story is Russia. He talked of a messenger who would come to them, "an Indian boy, possibly in his teens, who would be a choice seer."[86] Mad Bear

Anderson is the trickster figure in the story of Handsome Lake followers and Joseph Smith—possibly a source, possibly just a very strong teller of the tale.

Even if the story is not fact, and I do not know that it is or is not, is it truth? It is superficially violent to Mormon sacred traditions, though it may not be deeply so. It is disquieting for Mormons to consider. If the idea of Iroquois collaboration with Joseph Smith seems farfetched, then it is time to disprove it and ask a different set of questions: what meaning is made of this story, by whom, and to what end? The door is open to prove, disprove, analyze, reevaluate, or speculate. The only thing that has ended is silence about early Mormons and Indians.

Conclusion: Sounds True

I am surprised that my research, available as an unpublished dissertation since 2000, has been used to give the connection between Handsome Lake and Joseph Smith more solidity than can be supported by evidence.

In *One Nation Under Gods*, Peter Manseau compressed events and facts of Joseph Smith's life to serve his story of religious influence between the two prophets (putting golden plates in Joseph Smith's hands in 1822 rather than 1827, for example).[87] Compression, skimming, pulling highlights—that is how we slip stories from one context into another. Manseau added no additional evidence, however, of a potential connection between Handsome Lake and Joseph Smith. He traced the lines of my original scholarship to make them bolder.

When interviewed about Joseph Smith and Handsome Lake, Manseau implied that there is momentum in research into the topic. He told the interviewer that scholars are beginning "to investigate how Joseph Smith was influenced by Native American culture, and specifically by a movement such as Handsome Lake's."[88] The scholars investigating are: me, then him going through my work, and now Thomas Murphy citing both. We have original research into history, amplification of original research, an interview about amplification, then research into narrative. There is not an "increasing frequency with which scholars are identifying resemblances between Iroquois and Mormon thought."[89] What we have here is a game of telephone, and the connection between Handsome Lake and Joseph Smith grows tighter with each telling of the story.

And that is what I find most interesting about the story of Handsome Lake and Joseph Smith at this point: the story left the context of painful detail and footnotes in a doctoral dissertation to flow through a story of many American gods and a story of open scriptural canon. Those are interesting stories, and as stories they function not as history but as most stories do. They fulfill the wishes and needs of the tellers and of the listeners and readers. They sound true. They fit. You know, these stories ought to be true.

Following the path of stories in that way was exactly the broad point of my doctoral dissertation, "Telling Stories about Mormons and Indians." We tell stories that we want to be true. We tidy up the edges and reshape our memories, knowingly or not, until our stories become true.

Nevertheless, to say that Joseph Smith drew from Handsome Lake is wishful thinking. Claims lead back to a central trickster storyteller in the mid-twentieth century. If you read the original scholarship closely, there is no proof. I know because I spent years looking for that proof. I turned Western New York, Iroquoia, and Mormondom upside down and shook them to find every little clue. I dug into the story because I wanted it to be true. Maybe it will turn out to be so. Not all events of the past are recorded in ways we can access, so maybe it already is historically true even if not verifiable. When I act as a historian, however, I cannot go there. Perhaps someone will find a way to nudge the story closer to historical fact with new research. Until then, just repeating the story does not make it historically true, even when it feels truer with every telling.

No, we do not know that Joseph Smith knew of Handsome Lake. As history this is a story of plausibility or potentiality rather than a story of probability or actuality.

4

When Wakara Wrote Back

The Creation and Contestation of the "Paper Indian" in Early Mormon Utah

MAX PERRY MUELLER

Introduction

In 1851, Wakara wrote a letter to Brigham Young. Or at least Wakara tried to. To be sure, the powerful Timpanogos Ute leader and Indian slave trader who, a few years after he was baptized into The Church of Jesus Christ of Latter-day Saints and yet waged the so-called "Walker War" against his would-be brethren, was multilingual. According to the Mormons' great "gentile" champion Thomas Kane, Wakara learned English, Spanish, and other Indian dialects through his travels on the Old Spanish Trail, along which he traded his Indian slave wares. Kane recalled that Wakara was a "particularly eloquent master of the graceful alphabet of pantomime, which stranger tribes employ to communicate with one another." According to Kane, Wakara's linguistic faculties came in handy when he demanded "black mail salary" from weaker tribes—often in the form of Indian slaves—enforced by his troop of equestrian warriors.[1]

The written transcripts of his face-to-face meetings with Brigham Young also demonstrate that Wakara was a speaker who could, though a mixture of translation, hand gestures, and a few English phrases, hold his own with the most formidable of white interlocutors. The Mormons would quickly succeed in colonizing Wakara's ancestral lands—replacing the fish-eating Timpanogos'

61

sacred and fecund streams, rivers, and forests in the Utah Valley with dams, tilled fields, and rock and wood fences to fit their own white American model of agrarian civilization.[2] Yet in the early 1850s Wakara refused "Big Chief" Young's many offers to buy Ute land outright. Instead, Wakara stalled Mormon encroachment by negotiating land leases in exchange for grain, cattle, and firearms.[3]

Yet despite his linguistic efficacy, Wakara was not literate. Or more accurately, he wasn't lettered. As such, Wakara's letter (see below) is illegible. It is a set of looping lines, composed on a sheet of the yellow-tinted paper that the early Mormons in Utah preferred because of its durability and thickness. Some of the lines appear to be Ws written in nineteenth-century cursive, as if a young child attempted to imitate the writing of his parents or teachers. Yet the writing is not of a child, but of the 40-something-year-old warrior. On the flip side of the paper, in the distinct, compact hand of Thomas Bullock appear the words "Walker's writing."

Bullock knew Wakara well, even intimately. In May 1850, the English convert, onetime personal secretary of Joseph Smith Jr. and Brigham Young, and the clerk of the Church historian's office, recorded the minutes of the meeting between Young, other leading Mormons, and Wakara and his fellow Indian leaders during which the two sides first pledged to establish relations of trade, land sharing, and friendship. In May 1852, Bullock again met Wakara and other Ute leaders, this time to measure and record their physical characteristics. As the legend of Wakara's ferocity grew in the collective imagination of American Westerners who wrote about his exploits as a horse thief in California, as an Indian slave trader in New Mexico, and as a warlord in Utah, so would reports of his physical stature. Wakara's mid-twentieth-century Mormon-raised biographer, Paul Dayton Bailey, put his height at over six feet. However in 1852, Bullock measured Wakara at five feet seven inches and 164 pounds, a bit shorter and stouter than the rest of the Ute leaders of whom Bullock took stock that day.[4]

Bullock labeled the 1851 Wakara document "writing." Yet the Ute warrior clearly intended it to be a letter. Like other letter writers in early Mormon Utah, Wakara used one half of one side of the 15- by 12-inch sheet of paper. He strung together what appear to be distinct words in a series of rows from left to right and from top to bottom. The paper was then folded, so that this one sheet could serve as both the letter and its own envelope. On the front panel, which was

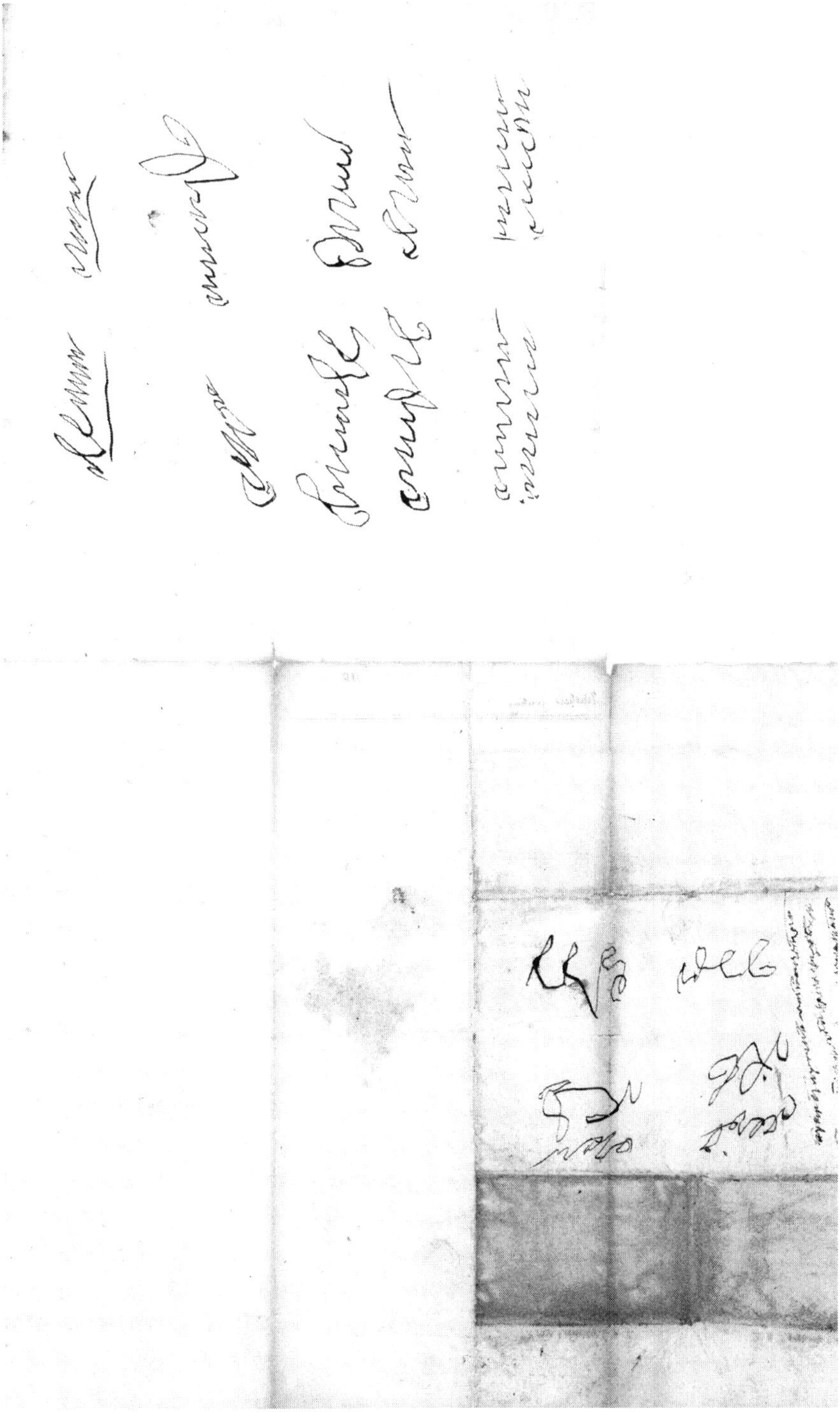

Figure 4.1. Thomas Bullock, "Walker's writing 1851," Box 74, Folder 44, Brigham Young Papers. Scanned from original by Michael Landon (LDS Church History Library).

Figure 4.2. Thomas Bullock's Notation, "Walker's writing 1851," Box 74, Folder 44, Brigham Young Papers. Scanned from original by Michael Landon (LDS Church History Library).

formed after the sheet was folded into tenths, Wakara wrote the address of the intended recipient. One can perhaps make out a series of cursive *B*s.

Wakara demonstrated that he could put pen to paper. But this act of writing (would-be) words on a page did not explicitly capture Wakara's meaning. While it cannot be read in a literal sense, this letter in fact has much to say.[5] Narrowly imagined, for Wakara this letter likely communicated the same message that much of his spoken words directed *to* or *about* his (at various times) Mormon trading partners, land tenants, brethren in the gospel, and enemies at war. More broadly considered, this letter also likely spoke to Wakara's understanding of the relative power and efficacy of the written word over the spoken word. Words on a page, because of their materiality, mattered more than words in the air. In both senses, when Wakara wrote his letter, he created a writerly self—a self that, in this new Mormon Utah constructed out of farms and fences as well as pen and paper, the writer and his intended reader had to contend with.[6]

Historians cannot read the lines of Wakara's letter. This chapter proposes to read between them. Perhaps there, based on other more legible archival material associated with Mormon-Ute relations from the 1840s and early 1850s, historians can find in Wakara's writing a rebuttal to the Mormons'"paper Indian." This paper Indian was a literary figure of unrepentant savagery that the Mormons created on the pages of their growing "Mormon archive" of sacred scriptures, Church records, epistles, court documents, speeches, and Utah territorial laws.[7] In the rhetoric and actions of the Mormons, these paper Indians took on literal flesh and bone bodies upon which the Mormons could act: to convert those "Indians" whom the Mormons described in their archive as most corrigible and build them into the "Lamanites"; to displace or kill those Indians like Wakara whose unrepentant savagery the Mormons described as a threat to the expanding kingdom of Zion.

Building Zion, Building Lamanites

It was only once they reached Utah in the late 1840s that the Latter-day Saints were able to sustain continual efforts to fulfill what they believed was their divine mandate to convert large numbers of Native Americans. But this was not for a lack of trying. Even before the early Latter-day Saints left Mormonism's birthplace in Western New York, Joseph Smith Jr. revealed the future role of

Native Americans in the restored Church. For Mormons, America's Indigenous Peoples were much more than "Indians"—often seen as both a burden to
the white American republic and a hindrance to the nation's westward expansion.[8] In the Book of Mormon, the Indians are the present-day descendants of
the "Lamanites," the last remaining remnant of a family of Israelites who, like
the "gentile" founders of white America, fled to the New World to escape religious persecution some six centuries before the birth of Christ. Because their
conversion was so vital to the unfolding of the prophesied events of the latter
days, in a September 1830 revelation Smith sent Oliver Cowdery, the Church's
second-ranking official and Smith's chief Book of Mormon scribe, on the first
official mission in Mormon history. "Go unto the Lamanites and preach [the]
gospel unto them," Smith commanded, specifically to the Lamanites gathering in
"Indian Country" west of the state of Missouri as a result of the Indian removal
policy.[9] Smith and Cowdery expected that this gospel would naturally appeal
to the Indians. After all, the Book of Mormon was the Indians' own long-lost
family history, "a record of the people of Nephi and also of the Lamanites," as the
book's title page states.

Unlike many Americans who saw no place for Natives in their visions of a
Columbia stretching from sea to sea—President Andrew Jackson signed into
law the Indian Removal Act the same year that the Book of Mormon was first
published—the Mormons understood their own exodus from the United States
in the late 1840s as a providential move toward the Indians. They believed that
the ultimate success of their own covenantal community was incumbent upon
turning Indians into Lamanites, who would eventually become (literally and
figuratively) white Mormons. After all, the Indians were "the house of Israel,"
as prolific pioneer diarist and Vanguard Company member Levi Jackman called
them in late July 1847, "the children of the covenant seed unto whom belongs the
priesthood and the oricals [sic] of God." The realization of the mandate to covenant with the Indians was finally at hand. And though Jackman acknowledged
that they were currently little more than "filthey [sic], degraded and miserable
beings," it was in the Great Basin where the Mormons would find "a people
to commence" this work with. The stakes were high. Jackman recognized that
nothing less than the creation of "Zion [to] be built up no more to be throne
[sic] down" was contingent on building up the "Lamanites."[10] In the interest of
both their particular Christian duty and economic practicality—"cheaper to
feed them, than to fight them" was Young's axiom—the Mormons reached out

to the Indians as the Book of Mormon taught them they should: to nurse them up to the standards of their would-be white brethren (1 Nephi 22:6–12).

Young wanted to clearly communicate this divine mandate of paternalistic redemption. When he did not meet with them himself, Young sent emissaries to the Utah leaders. For example, as the Mormons moved south in the late 1840s, Young sent interpreter Dimick Huntington to Fort Utah. The settlement was built near the fishing villages of Wakara's Timpanogos Utes in the Utah Valley, which served as the gateway through the mountains to the fertile plains of southern Utah. In the spring of 1849, Huntington reported to Young that while there were many "very friendly" Indians in the area, the mood was precarious. Through Huntington, they told Young that they needed both carrot and stick—guns to forge Indian friendship and a stronger show of force to frighten the fence-sitting Indians into compliance. "We fired the [fort's] cannon once and it had good effect," Huntington wrote to Young.[11] In response to Indian attacks in the Utah Valley, in January 1850 Young ordered the creation of a company of "minutemen" drawn from the best fighters in the Nauvoo Legion. After the first skirmish with the Timpanogos, General Daniel H. Wells authorized the legionnaires to "act as the circumstances may require exterminating [Indian fighters] such as do not separate themselves from their hostile clans."[12]

Of course, the Mormons had personal experiences with orders of extermination. When he announced his 1838 "extermination order," Missouri Governor Lilburn Boggs deemed the Mormons enemies of the state. In contrast, Wells cautioned his minutemen that when possible, "sue for peace," and "exercise every principle of humanity compatible with the laws of war."[13] Yet as the makers of the laws of the land, the Mormons believed they had the authority to deploy violence as a tool of state formation. In February 1850, the militia swept through the Utah Valley, tracking down and killing several dozen Timpanogos. According to John Gunnison, a military officer and explorer who surveyed Utah for thruways for the transcontinental railroad, Mormon fighters coaxed a group of Indians into surrendering. The Mormons then executed them en masse. One of Gunnison's expeditionary colleagues, the surgeon James Blake, helped the Mormons decapitate the Indians. Blake wanted to box up the 40 to 50 Indian heads and send them back to Washington for study. The headless bodies were left to freeze and then to rot in the warming Utah spring air.[14]

For his part, Gunnison approved of this use of violence as an act of state-sponsored "chastisement" of "insolent" Indians who refused to recognize the

Mormons' authority over the land.[15] However, the Mormons' claim that they had the authority to deploy violence because they were representatives of the state was based on a fallacious tautology. The Mormons could use violence to suppress threats to their settlements not because they enjoyed legal authority, but because they enjoyed superior tools of war. Such tools included bullets, cannons, forts, and well-trained militias. Such tools also included a seemingly unending stream of migrants who brought with them communicable diseases against which the Indians had no immune defense. The migrants also brought with them oxen, plows, seeds, and irrigation systems, which remade the Utah landscape in the name of an American Zion and in the image of the Mormons' ancestral homes of New and Old England. These changes to the land eventually led to famine among the game- and fish-eating Utah Natives and to the desertification of much of the once-verdant Utah landscape.[16]

In the midst of their first Indian war, the Mormon military leadership understood the seeming incongruity between their mandate to bring the gospel to the remnant of Israel and the massacre of these very same people.[17] Yet the message from the Mormon leadership was that the Mormons need not cry over a few dead Indians. During a February 1850 meeting of Church and legion officials, Young cited a previously unrecorded (and likely apocryphal) prophecy from the Mormons' first prophet. In the process of restoring the Lamanites, Joseph Smith himself foresaw that "many of the Lamanites will have to be slain by us." These unredeemable Indians would be "better off on the other side of the vail [sic]" than continue to live in open opposition to Zion.[18] During this meeting, Parley P. Pratt, who was part of the first mission to the Lamanites in 1831, agreed that it was "best to kill the Indians." By *Indian*, Pratt meant male Indians. Unlike an Indian "brave," Pratt believed that women and children were malleable to the civilizing will of the Latter-day Saints. Young agreed to limit this extermination to Indian men. While "we have no peace until the men are killed off," Young proposed to "let the women and children live if they behave themselves."[19]

The Nauvoo Legion executed this plan. After turning them into widows and orphans, the militiamen brought several "squaws & children" north to Salt Lake. There, John Gunnison observed, they were "placed [in Mormon homes] as servants to make white people of them."[20] Gunnison was only half right. The Mormons had greater aspirations for the captives: to make them into Lamanites who could be eventually folded into the white, Mormon people. Yet the Mormon leadership soon recognized that it overestimated these Indian women and children's ability and desire to be made into Lamanites. After feeding them and caring for them through the rest of the winter, many "ran back to their Indian camps," while others died, recalled Daniel Wells.[21]

Constructing Paper Indians

The Mormon settlers also deployed another tool of war and colonization, arguably as insidious as smallpox, as devastating as canon fire, and as pernicious as fencerows and irrigation ditches: the written word. To be sure, long before the arrival of the Mormons, Wakara's Utes had been exposed to reading and writing.[22] In 1776, the Franciscan friars Selvestra Velez de Escalante and Francisco Atanasio Domínguez led an expedition north from Santa Fe into the lands of Wakara's ancestors. The friars sought a more northerly route to the Spanish missions at Monterey, California, and preached Christianity and civilization to the Natives whom they encountered along their way through present-day Utah and Colorado. In the expedition's journal, the friars employed words to mark off "friendly" Indian from foe and to lay claim to the fertile lands around the "Lake of the Timpanogos" (Utah Lake), to which they hoped to soon return.[23]

While a permanent Spanish settlement was never established, the friars' *entrada* into central Utah helped integrate Wakara's Ute ancestors more fully into the Spanish trade system, especially the trade in flesh—horses, animal pelts, and Indian slaves.[24] The *entrada* also marked the entrance of the Roman script in which Wakara's ancestors—and later Wakara himself—were constructed on paper as archetypal marauding, savage Indians. According to contemporaneous and later historical accounts, Wakara began to dominate the Old Spanish Trail in the 1830s and 1840s with his cavalry made up of Utes, Shoshone, and Paiute fighters as well as famed mountain men James Beckwourth and Thomas "Pegleg" Smith. He stole thousands of horses from the California *rancheros*—daring feats that earned him the moniker the "greatest horse thief in history."[25] In southern Utah, he enslaved nonequestrian Paiutes—mostly women and children—and sold his booty in auctions in New Mexico. The sales of slaves were recorded in words and numbers on ledgers, with "boys fetching on an average $100, girls from $150 to $200," recalled Daniel Jones who led the first Mormon mission into Mexico. Girls made better "house servants," though the potential for concubinage also added to their value. Jones, who described "Walker" as horrific and as "systematic in this [Indian slave] trade as ever were the slavers [of Africans] on the seas," was not alone archiving his disgust for Indian slaving. Since the mid-1700s, Catholic priests preserved in writing the ill treatment of Natives, including ritualized public beatings and rapes of captives by "barbarians" like Wakara. Torture, the padres wrote in letters to the colonial authorities, was a bargaining technique used to exact a higher price from the soft-hearted Mexicans, especially Catholic priests. The priests justified their purchase of these slaves—almost always women—as a means to save their bodies and souls. In preparation for the baptismal font, the priests stripped them of the "Indian" name and replaced it with a Catholic one before they were added to the Church membership rolls.[26]

At either ends of the Old Spanish Trail—the California missions in the West and the New Mexico trading outposts in the southeast—Wakara already occupied a world of the written word when the Mormons marched into the Great Basin in July 1847. Yet the Mormons were the first to use the technology of the pen (and soon the printing press) to sustain a textual imposition over the land and over the people of Utah, which Wakara had for the previous decade dominated with the technology of his horse and musket. The Mormons initially recognized Wakara's control over the Great Basin. The renowned Western explorer Jim Bridger told Young that the Salt Lake Valley was caught between the often-warring Utes to the south and Shoshone to the north.[27] Young was careful not to cross paths too soon with the Ute warrior known to most white Americans as "Walker." The Mormon leader understood that Wakara could either ease or obstruct the building up of Zion.[28]

Brigham Young and his counselors thought it both impractical and unchristian to kill off all male Natives. During the first few years in Utah, the Mormons hoped to turn Wakara and other members of his family, which constituted the elite of the Northern Utes, into exemplars to which lesser Indians would aspire. To be sure, the Mormons abhorred Wakara's slave trading, which they considered fratricide of fellow Lamanite kin. Yet Mormons and non-Mormons alike wrote that Wakara's travels on the Old Spanish Trail had refined him to some degree. Conversant in several Indian dialects as well as Spanish and English, Wakara was viewed as something of a cosmopolitan Indian. He occupied a state between savage and civilized; a liminality exemplified in his dress. In March 1850, Thomas Kane told the Historical Society of Pennsylvania that Wakara wore "a full suit of the richest broadcloth, generally brown and cut in European fashion, with a shining beaver hat and fine cambric shirt." To this ensemble, the warrior added "his own gaudy Indian trimmings."[29]

In the late 1840s and early 1850s, Young frequently met in person with or sent letters to Wakara. Young hoped to win the Ute leader's support for Mormon plans to expand into the fertile land of southern Utah as well as to missionize southern Utah's Natives. In a November 1849 letter, which Dimick Huntington read to Wakara, Young explained what Wakara might gain from an alliance with the Mormons. If Wakara allowed them to settle the Utah Valley, then the Mormons would instruct Wakara's people on how to cultivate the land.[30] "Deer are few, and you must make corn this year, and learn to work like white men," Young told Wakara in a May 1850 letter.[31]

Young's didactic written messages point to a central goal of the Mormons' relations with Utah's Native Peoples: the Mormons wished to become teachers to their Indian pupils, bringing what the Mormons viewed as knowledge of modern civilization and the ancient truth of the Indians' Israelite identity. In another November 1849 letter that he had Huntington read to Wakara, Young explained, "We are sent here by the Great Spirit to teach you, and do all of you good."[32] Young expected that Wakara would accept this lesson as would a child. After all, in May 1849, Huntington reported to Young that after spending a peaceful night with the Utes in the Utah Valley, during which they displayed their happiness by singing "around the Fort" and warming themselves by a fire, "Walker lay in my arms . . . I told [the Utes] of the Book of Mormon [and that] they must be our friends, & we yours."[33]

According to the Mormons, most of the Timpanogos Utes had proven that they were unable to receive such instruction. And Young predicted this would hold true for most Indians who were too set in their heathen, horse-stealing ways to respect Mormon property, let alone to "enter into the new and everlasting covenanting" with the Latter-day Saints.[34] Young thus responded to Huntington's campfire dispatch with a letter admonishing the Utah Valley settlers to finish the fort and cease fraternizing with the Indians.[35] To Young's mind, the subsequent Indian attacks at Fort Utah demonstrated that he was right not to confuse Indian kindness with weakness. However, soon after the Fort Utah battles, followed by a measles outbreak that killed a large number of his tribe, on March 13, 1850, Wakara asked Isaac Morley, the head of the new Manti settlement in the Sanpete Valley of southern Utah, to baptize him in Manti's City Creek. Following this, Wakara began what the Mormons likely viewed as missionary work, encouraging others to enter the waters and "wash away [their] sins." With Wakara's blessing, Manti was established ostensibly as a mission to cultivate the Indians: to convert them from nomadic hunters, gatherers, and horsemen into landed farmers. The hope was that a peaceful Lamanite neighborhood would be in place when white Mormons moved in.[36]

The plan seemed to work. According to written correspondence between Young and Morley, by summer, more than 100 Indians followed Wakara into the baptismal waters and were confirmed members of the Church branch in Manti. Their names were then added to the Church's rolls.[37] Fellow Ute leaders Arapine (Arapeen or Arapene) and Sowiette were also baptized. In May, the three leaders were ordained Church elders. Young was elated. He saw these baptisms and ordinations as fulfillment of ancient prophecy. "The spirit of the Lord is beginning to operate upon the hearts of the Lamanites," Young wrote to Morley. The prophet hoped that the spirit's work would be so complete that these Lamanites would leave their Indian ways behind and only "do good."[38]

The Book of Mormon taught that Wakara's ancient ancestors had periodically been good too. But Wakara's ancestors did not record the gospel's truths in a manner that could be passed down from generation to generation. This illiteracy meant forgetting the ways of the Lord. For the incipient goodness to endure in the hearts of Wakara and other modern-day Lamanites, the Mormons believed that these new Church members had to be further converted: from an oral people to a people of the book. Young explained to Morley that Wakara must learn to read. "The Book of Mormon might be a great blessing to [him] . . . & through him to ma[n]y of his kindred." Young told Morley that he should translate the Book of Mormon into the Indian language. And as any attentive tutor would, Morley should see to it that Wakara "apply himself diligently by study & also by faith."[39]

The Mormons hoped that they could convert Wakara not only into a Mormon economic ally and Mormon brother in the gospel, but also into a partner-in-arms in the fight to abolish the Indian slave trade. To do so, as did the padres in New Mexico, the Mormon response to the trafficking and often the brutal killing of Indian children was to purchase them. "Buy up the Lamanite children," Young told the settlers at Parowan in southern Utah in 1851, "and educate them and teach them the Gospel." On its face this business of slave trading was pure evil, Young explained. Yet below the surface, Young detected God's providential hand at work. "The Lord could not have devised a better plan, than to have put the Saints where they were, in order to accomplish the redemption of the

Lamanites." Before they were lost either to slavery or savagery, the Mormons would purchase the innocent and place them in Mormon homes where they would learn the truths of civilization and Christianity. This work would be done "so that many generations would not pass," Young pointed to the Book of Mormon's most famous passage regarding racial restoration, 2 Nephi 30:6, "ere they should become a white and delightsome people."[40]

For a time, following his baptism and ordination, even Wakara was enlisted to assist in what the Mormons believed was this salvific work. In March 1851, the founder of the Parowan settlement, George A. Smith, sent a "talking paper" north with Wakara, certifying that "Captain Walker" and his band of Utes had "showed themselves Friends and gentlemen." Those Mormons to whom Wakara presented Smith's written certificate should accord the Indians goodwill and trade with him for his "horses, Buckskins and Piede children."[41] Having helped the Mormons settle southern Utah, having dedicated himself to the gospel, and having led other Indians into the baptismal waters, Smith reasoned that Wakara had been transformed from an Indian purveyor of human flesh to a protector of his Lamanite brethren. Yet less than a year later, as Brigham Young testified in the January 1852 trial of the Mexican slave trader Don Pedro León Luján, "Indian Walker" had not made such a transformation, but instead continued to "traffic" in Indian slaves. "He offers them for sale," Young testified during the trial, which served as a test case against the Indian slave trade in the Utah territory. "When [Walker] cannot get what he thinks they are worth, he says he will take them to the Navahoe [sic] Indians, or Spaniards, and sell them, or kill them which he frequently does."[42]

Luján lost. An all-Mormon jury found him guilty of trading with Indians without a license. He was fined $500. And his slaves were also confiscated and placed in Mormon homes.[43] Within the year, Wakara lost, too. The Mormons succeeded in ending the 300-year history of the Indian slave trade between New Mexico and southern Utah. In early 1852, with the support of Governor Young, the all-Mormon Utah Territorial Legislature passed a law that made it legal for Mormons to purchase Indians from slavers like Wakara. The law also empowered the Mormon settlers to recoup the purchase cost through indentured servitude of up to twenty years.[44] No longer able to send their human wares south, the Utes relied even more on the only market left open to them—the Mormons. And when that market proved disappointing, the Mormons described how the Indian slavers learned to deploy violence as a sales tactic. The archive of Young's tenure leading US Indian Affairs in Utah as well as the memoirs of Daniel Jones included one particularly gruesome incident. In early summer of 1853, just before the breakout of hostilities between the Wakara-led Utes and the Mormons, "Arapine, Walker's brother," enraged that the Mormons had prevented the sale of Indian children to the Mexicans, came to Provo to tell the Mormons "that they had no right to do so, unless they bought them themselves." When the Mormons refused to give Arapine the price he sought, Jones recalls, Arapine "took one of these children by the heels and dashed its brains out on the hard ground, telling us we had no hearts, or we would have bought it and saved its life." It was a strange argument, "the argument of an enraged savage." But it was also often an effective one. Jones reported that after the summer of 1853, "I never heard of any successful attempts to buy children by the Mexicans."[45]

The paternalistic Mormon ideology of buying slaves in order to free them was designed to distinguish the Mormon home in Utah, in which Indian women and children would be legally and lovingly placed for a time-limited indenture, from what the Mormons imagined were the brutal slave auction blocs of Santa Fe, where Natives were mere property, to be bought, sold, and abused. However, in reality, the economic and social mechanics of the Mormons' slavery enterprise were similar to those of the Spanish colonial system. As was the case in New Mexico, once purchased, these slaves were baptized, given a Mormon name, and integrated into Mormon home economics as adopted children, servants—even polygamous wives—and they performed essential work for the labor-intensive settler-colonial communities.[46] Not only was the Mormons' system not that different from the Spanish's, it wasn't necessarily that different from the Indians'. As James F. Brooks has argued, among the tribes of the American southwestern borderlands, "slave" captivity held many meanings—meanings that were not based on the same "racial dichotomization" that defined the "African" chattel slavery of the American South. A "slave" frequently moved "between statutes"— from servant, to adopted kin, to spouse.[47] The Mormons drew no such parallels between how they treated the slaves and the brutality that Wakara and his fellow slaving warriors performed on the bodies of their slaves especially at the point of sale. To the contrary, the Mormons wrote about this performed violence to distinguish Wakara's slaving from their own and to justify their own participation in a system that they viewed as fundamentally evil.

In the summer of 1853, tensions with the Wakara-led Utes over the Mormons' disruption of Wakara's slave-trading operations, as well as the Mormons' further encroachment into Ute land, led to open conflict after a Mormon man killed one of Wakara's relatives during a trade deal gone bad. Over a 10-month period, Utes sporadically attacked Mormon communities in southern Utah—communities that Wakara had helped establish only a few years before. Though not always under Wakara's direct orders, Ute warriors engaged in what the Mormons described as "Indian depredations." They pilfered Mormon cattle, stole crops and horses, and destroyed settlers' infrastructure. Along with an untold number of Indians, perhaps a half dozen Mormons were killed. Mormons living in outlying areas abandoned homes and crops still in the ground to find shelter in fortified towns.[48] At the same time, the Nauvoo Legion went on the offensive. They attacked Ute villages with indiscriminate violence. A mile from Wakara's camp in the Utah Valley, a group of Ute noncombatants sought shelter in the Mormon fort at Nephi. Yet there they were "shot down like so many dogs," remembered Adelia Wilcox, one of Heber C. Kimball's plural wives who witnessed the massacre. Their bodies were "picked up with pitch forks, put on a sleigh and hauled away" to be dumped in a mass grave. "The squaw they took prisoner" and sent north to Salt Lake.[49]

In the short term, the "Walker War" was a draw, or perhaps even a victory for the Utes. The Mormons were forced for a time to seek shelter in their more established settlements. But as Jill Lepore has argued in her study of the "war" (1675–1678) between the settler colonialists of the Massachusetts Bay Colony and the Native American leader "King Philip," whom the New England settlers had at one time also called a friend, white Americans might have lost the war of wounds; Philip's (Metacomet) pan-tribal alliance initially pushed the settlers off Wampanoag land and back to their coastal communities. But the English prevailed in the war of words. In the history books of white American and Native encounters, those who controlled the means of production of history—paper, ink, and printing presses—also controlled who was portrayed as civilized and savage. In his *A Narrative of the Troubles with the Indians* (1677), William Hubbard described a scene in which colonial soldiers came upon burned-out English houses. There they also found "a Bible newly torn, and the Leaves scattered about by the Enemy in Hatred."[50] Such accounts of Indian assaults against the written gospel parallel the Book of Mormon's descriptions of the Lamanites' desire to destroy the gospel that Joseph Smith would restore in the latter days (at the end of the Book of Mormon saga, Mormon buries the Plates of Nephi on the Hill Cumorah to spare them the fate that would befall the Puritans' Bible (Mormon 6:6)). Two centuries later, compiled in Peter Gottfredson's

The History of Indian Depredations in Utah (1919) the Mormon witnesses to "Walker's" attacks described them as unprovoked acts of aggression against the benevolent settlers who only wished to raise up the benighted, savage Indians to the Latter-day Saints' level of piety and civilization.[51]

And yet, seventeenth-century white American colonists and nineteenth-century Mormon pioneers enjoyed what Lepore has called a "literal advantage" over the Native Americans whom they tried to convert, displace, and kill. And this literal advantage was insidiously circular: illiterate non-whites could not respond in writing to writers who labeled them as less than human—ahistorical beasts.[52] Even the names of these two wars obliterate the Wampanoag "Metacomet" and Timpanogos "Wakara" from the historical memory while the Indians "Philip" and "Walker" become the belligerents. The English become the victims of unwarranted aggression as well as the courageous victors who used words to set up ramparts between themselves and the natives, between civility and barbarity.[53]

Wakara Writes Back

The early Mormon archive presents a clear view of how the Mormons understood their role in building a certain portion of Utah's Indians into Lamanites. The Mormons would be the mothers and fathers, teachers and masters to their would-be Lamanite sons and daughters. The few Indians who proved themselves redeemable would be the Latter-day Saints' obedient children, students, and servants. However, most Indians would prove themselves to be like Wakara, unrepentant savages who left their mark in the archive through their acts of violence. In response, the Mormons wrote how force was justified to clear these Indians from the Great Basin, land that God had given to the Mormons as their Zion. This dual project of Lamanite building and Indian removal was literal—taking place on flesh-and-bone bodies—and literary—taking place on the pages of the growing archive of Mormon-Native encounters. Yet Wakara also understood the power of the written word as a tool of politics and war. From his earliest encounters with the Mormons in the late 1840s to his death in 1855, Wakara and other Indian leaders witnessed Mormon emissaries and interpreters read letters that contained messages for them sent from Brigham Young. These leaders then witnessed Mormon scribes transform their own spoken responses into written words, which were carried back to the Mormon prophet. Thus when he put pen to paper in 1851, Wakara wanted to write back against the construction of the Mormons' paper Indian, of which "Walker" himself became the prime example.

Wakara was perhaps at the height of his power and wealth when he penned his letter in 1851. The previous decade had been a profitable one for him. From California, Wakara and his men had stolen horses by the thousands and brought them along the Old Spanish Trail for sale in Santa Fe. And from Utah between 1840–1849, records indicate that he and other slavers brought at least 225 captive Indians, mostly Paiutes, to market in New Mexico.[54] And yet by 1851, Wakara was also surely aware that the fortune of his own wealth and the well-being of his people's way of life was under threat. Mormon growth along the Wasatch Front had likely already begun to disrupt the fish and game resources upon which Wakara's Timpanogos band relied for bodily and spiritual sustenance. By the time Wakara died four years later, disruption had been replaced by destruction. At the July 1855 Mormon-Ute gathering at Provo, the Timpanogos leader High-forehead described the lush forests that used to grow next to the fish-eating Utes' streams. But now "the ground is hard and we cannot eat it."[55]

By 1851, disease had also begun to decimate Wakara's Utes as well as the Pai-utes. Measles and other Old World pathogens ravaged both the Natives and the Mormons during the first year of settlement in the Sanpete Valley. These micro-scopic pests, combined with the New World's own diseases, colonialism, warfare, slavery, and forced migration, created an almost apocalyptic cocktail for Utah's native inhabitants. At the end of July 1853 during the first outbreak of conflict with Wakara, Brigham Young took note of the precipitous decline in Native popula-tion. "The Indians in these mountains are continually on the decrease. Bands that numbered 150 warriors when we first came here number not more than 35 now."[56]

The recently arrived Mormons had also already disrupted Wakara's slave trade, and they promised to end it altogether. For Wakara, Indian slavery was not the unmitigated horror that the Mormons made it out to be. The Utes did not share the Mormons' view that all Indians were one people descended from one common Israelite ancestor. The century before, while the southern Paiutes remained pedestrian and relied on local food sources, the Utes became feared horsemen, traveling throughout the Rockies and the Great Plains to hunt buf-falo and to capture and sell other Indians, especially their poorer, Paiute neigh-bors.[57] Of course, Brigham Young too believed in a hierarchy of peoples. In a set of speeches in early 1852 to the Utah legislature, which legalized a form of "Afri-can" chattel slavery in the territory, he explained why he felt morally justified to support the enslavement of people of African descent, whom he believed were spiritually and intellectually inferior to whites due to their descent from cursed biblical anti-heroes.[58] As such, Wakara might have viewed efforts to abolish Indian slavery as Brigham viewed efforts to abolish African slavery—an affront to the culturally and theologically prescribed order of humanity.

And yet the Mormons did not dismantle the Indian slave trade. Through their claims to legal and doctrinal exigencies, as well as through displays of force, the Mormons usurped control over it from the Utes. They continued to purchase Paiute children and place them in Mormon homes long after they ended the Ute slave trade.[59] Thus, instead of trading partners and friendly neighbors, the Mormons became existential threats to the Utes' traditional way of life. As the federal Indian agent Jacob Holeman explained in a series of reports that he wrote in the early 1850s to his bosses in Washington, the Mormons and other white settlers had destroyed the Utes' hunting and foraging grounds. As such, the Utes were forced to rely even more on trading humans for the guns and horses they needed to hunt ever-vanishing game, to defend their lands, and to steal Mormon cattle and grain.[60] The same year that Wakara penned his own letter, in January 1851 another Indian agent, H. R. Day reported that the Utes considered Mormon thievery of land and resources, including Indian slaves, as the cause of the escalating Mormon-Indian tensions. Day reported a conversation he had with Sowiette, a Ute leader who, along with Wakara and Arapine, had been ordained Mormon elders just a few months before. "The old chief ... said to me, American—good! Morman—no good! American—friend, Morman-Kill-Steal," wrote Day.[61]

For these Indians, what the Mormons called the depredations of unrepentant savages—grain stealing, horse, and cattle thievery—could have been seen as attempts to restore unjust imbalances in Mormon-Ute relations. In May 1850, Brigham Young and other leading Mormons met Wakara, Sowiette, and Arapine in the Utah Valley. The Mormons and the Utes formed covenants of trade, land use, and friendship.[62] Such agreements established relationships of reciprocity. The Indians believed that they were entitled to the fruits produced on these lands—fat cows, golden grains—which they shared with the Mormons. What the Mormons called their Indian policy of largesse—feeding the Indians, instead of fighting them—was to the Indians just deserts. If the Mormons broke the covenants by not providing the Indians their fair share, then the Indians were justified in taking what they needed, and with force if necessary. Even at the height of the Mormon-Ute 1853–1854 conflict, Wakara told the Mormons as much. As he explained in a letter to Nauvoo Legion Colonel George A. Smith, Wakara did not intend the Mormons any bodily harm. What he wanted was to take the share of cattle he believed was his due for allowing the Mormons to live on his land.[63] From this perspective, the Indians saw the Mormons, not themselves, as the dishonest, violent aggressors against whom the Indians had no choice but to fight back to protect their lands and their lives once it was clear that the Mormons could not be held to their word.

On July 6, 1853, just days before the outbreak of Mormon-Ute conflict, a veteran Mexican fur trader M. S. Martenas interviewed Wakara. In the transcript of the interview, Martenas noted that he had known Wakara and his kin for more than three decades. "They talk freely with me," Martenas wrote, "and express their feelings and wishes without reserve." In Spanish, the polyglot Ute leader provided a counter-narrative to what had already become the dominant Mormon view of Mormon-Indian relations in Utah. Though not employing the same ontological Lamanite lens through which the Mormons read Wakara and other Indians of Utah, Wakara explained to Martenas that his claim to the lands of Utah was, in fact, inherited. These were the lands "on which his band resides and on which they have resided since his childhood, and his parents before him." Wakara did acknowledge that, "when [the Mormons] first commenced the settlement of Salt Lake Valley ... [they were] friendly, and promised many comforts, and lasting friendship." The Mormons' neighborly behavior continued for a short time "until they became strong in numbers, then their conduct and treatment toward the Indians changed—they were not only treated unkindly, but many were much abused." The Mormon settlements also expanded farther into the Utes' "hunting grounds in the valleys" without consideration of the disruption that such sprawl caused their native neighbors, trading partners, and would-be religious brethren. "And the graves of their fathers have been torn up by the whites."[64]

According to Wakara, this was the state of Mormon-Indian relations in July 1853. Ironically, instead of helping the Indians create permanent settlements as they had pledged to do, the Mormons' ever-expanding kingdom had forced the Utes to become refugees on their own lands, "driven by this population," as Wakara explained to Martenas, "from place to place." Martenas added his own observations about the "present excitement" between the Utes and Mormons and fears about the coming conflagration. Not only had the invaders trampled across their lands, killing fish and game in the process, and disturbing the final resting place of the Indians' fathers, the Mormons had also interfered "with the long established Spanish trade," the main source of the equestrian Utes wealth, power, and prestige. "I greatly fear that much difficulty will grow out of this present excited condition of the Indians," Martenas concluded, "should the Mormons continue their unkind treatment."[65]

Over the next ten months, "excitement" begot violence as Wakara and his forces attempted to push back Mormon encroachment. But by May 1854, Wakara made peace with the whites, smoking a peace pipe with Young and other Mormon leaders near the Mormon settlement at Nephi. Though Mormons saw it this way, the Indian leader most likely did not interpret his decision to sue for peace as submission to white supremacy. (In fact, Wakara insisted that Young travel south from Salt Lake to his camp at Chicken Creek for the peace parley, and to come bearing gifts of cattle, blankets, ammunition, and whiskey.[66]) Instead, Wakara likely understood it as a recognition of a new future in which the Indians would have to live with the whites. Peace became a strategy of negotiation, though one that rarely worked, by which Wakara hoped to create a future with some dignity for his people.

Wakara is no innocent. Like his "big chief" counterpart Brigham Young, Wakara has blood on his hands; that of the Mormons whom he and his braves killed; and that of the Paiute and Shoshone women and children whom he enslaved, abused, and murdered. But Wakara's attempt at letter writing suggests that he also did not want to be reduced to a character in the Mormons' faith-promoting history, in which the faith of the Latter-day Saints in their own delightsome worthiness is contrasted with the dark-skinned and dark-hearted Indian. Consciously or unconsciously, Wakara recognized that writing was the means by which he could become a historical subject in the new, lettered world that the Latter-day Saints were building up around him. As much as the forts, farms, and roads that the Mormons constructed on the land of his forefathers— and according to Wakara, sometimes literally digging up his forefathers' graves to do so—the written word was a keystone to the infrastructure of Zion.

Conclusion

After Wakara wrote it in 1851, his letter most likely joined other correspondence from the southern Mormon colonies traveling north in saddlebags, perhaps even Thomas Bullock's. It made the trip along the dusty wagon road between Salt

Lake City and the settlements in Sanpete. We will never know if Brigham Young himself ever saw it. And even if he did, of course, he would not have been able to read it, at least not in the traditional sense. Instead either in the field or at home in the Church historian's office, in his own distinct hand Bullock added a critical notation on the "writing's" provenance and then filed it with the growing corpus of Brigham Young's office files.

It is possible that Bullock understood Wakara's attempt at letter writing as more of an artifact than an archive. Perhaps he viewed "Walker's writing" as material proof that Wakara's failure to communicate anything in writing signified the unbridgeable gap between Mormons and Natives as historical subjects as well as history's recorders. Though Wakara's intention was just the opposite, for Bullock "Walker's writing" demonstrated how Wakara himself participated in the creation of the paper Indian. The juxtaposition of legible descriptions produced by white Mormon witnesses to and participants in the "Walker War" archived with Wakara's unlettered scribbles on the page only served to further embody the distinction between the innately savage, ahistorical Indians and the civilized and historical Mormons.[67]

And yet, at the May 1854 peace meeting, in which Young and Wakara promised to reestablish brotherly affection and trade, Wakara once again demonstrated that he recognized the authority that the written word carried in the expanding Kingdom of Zion. "Walker wished President Young to write a Letter," Wilford Woodruff recorded in his journal, "so [Wakara] could show it to the people & let them know that we were at peace." Young obliged.[68] Wakara understood that a letter from Young would allow even a much-despised Indian to travel through the territory unmolested. Wakara however would have only ten months to take advantage of these traveling papers. Early the next year, he became an indirect casualty of the war that would bear his name. On January 29, 1855 the once-feared and famed warrior, slaver, and horse thief—probably no older than fifty years old—succumbed to some communicable disease he likely caught after attending the trial of a group of Paiutes who had been accused of the murder of John Gunnison. The early chronicler of early Mormon-Indian encounters had been killed in the fall of 1853 at the height of the "Walker War" when his party was attacked by Pahvant Utes near Sevier Lake in central Utah.[69]

George A. Smith reported that on his deathbed, Wakara "expressed great anxiety for peace with the whites." But his burial ceremony shocked his would-be white friends, making manifest how Wakara's unrepentant savagery would extend past his own mortal life. According to Smith, along with a letter from Brigham Young (perhaps the letter issued at the May 1854 peace treaty), Wakara was buried with fourteen of his best horses, which had been slaughtered for the occasion, along with "two or three Piede Squaws, and some prisoners."[70] Wakara, however, would not stay buried for long. Like the graves of his own forefathers, Wakara's would also be torn up by whites. Under the auspices of the Bureau of American Ethnology, in the 1870s the naturalist and surgeon Henry C. Yarrow led the excavation of Wakara's remains. Yarrow sent the skull of "Wah-ker, a celebrated Ute warrior, long the terror of the People of Utah, New Mexico, and California," as he explained in his published study of Wakara's burial site, as well as the "cranial bones of a Piede or Piute Indian said to have been buried with him" to the Army Medical Museum in Washington, DC. Like Thomas Bullock before them, Yarrow explained that he and his colleagues were interested in measuring the warrior's body—in particular his cranial volume—in order to compare them with dimensions of other "races."[71]

The only known body of Wakara's written work stayed buried longer. To be sure, for at least a century, Wakara has appeared at the center of studies of Mormon-Ute relations—with Wakara fulfilling the role of the Indian marauder in Mormon pioneer historical narratives and folklore.[72] Yet until now, Wakara's own words on the matter have gone unexamined. This is probably the case because his writing cannot be read, and thus remained for much of its history a curious artifact. Today, however, "Walker's writing" is accessible digitally on the LDS Church History's online catalog. It is filed in the subcategory "Indians, 1850–1865" in Brigham Young's office files. Among other documents related to early Mormon-Native encounters, this digital folder includes Bullock's 1852 recording of the weights and heights of Utah Indian leaders, other transcripts of meetings with Wakara and leading Mormons, baptisms of Indians (including Wakara), as well as lists of Indians killed as part of the Walker War.[73]

Much is lost in digitization. The yellow color of the paper. The brown dirt creased into the folds and plastered on the backside of one of the panels, which perhaps was most exposed to the elements, or to the inside of a saddlebag. The watermark from the Walter & Winthrop Laflin Company. The different color pen, which was used to write the smaller, more compact set of "words"—words that seem to be written by a more skilled hand. (This potential third hand produced what appear to be diacritic lines over certain "letters" in some unidentified language.)[74]

Digitization reduces this artifact. It literally flattens it into two dimensions. But digitization also elevates "Walker's writing" in two important ways. First, it compels the historian to treat it as an archive and attempt to read it as such. Second, it allows this archive to be replicated infinitely. "Walker's writing" is always just a few keystrokes away from appearing on any computer screen of anyone wishing to read it. Wakara thus is present today—perhaps more present than he has ever been before—even though he is long gone. To be sure, since neither Wakara nor any of his Native descendants are behind this literary replication, the meaning of Wakara's writing exists in a different category than, say the proliferation of Native-led printing of Indian political and cultural writings in the nineteenth century, which emerged as a direct and public response to the existential threat that Indian removal represented to flesh and blood Indian existence.[75] Ironically Wakara's (digital) presence today is facilitated by the very same institution most responsible for his and his people's (bodily and cultural) demise. In terms of this specific document and this specific historical figure, the act of "re-presenting" marginalized non-whites in the Mormon past to which they've long been excluded, is likely not a conscious one by the LDS Church.[76] Yet more broadly, this act of not just opening up the archive to the world, but making it accessible digitally to "every nation, kindred, tongue and people" (2 Nephi 26:13) is part of the Church's effort to expand the idea of what it has meant historically to be a Mormon and who can study Mormon history.[77]

The act of digitizing Wakara's letter makes it (potentially) omnipresent. Yet it nevertheless remains wedded to a specific archival space, a specific geographical location, and a specific historical moment. As such, it implicates Wakara as a historical actor—one could even argue a historian—of early Mormon-Native encounters. When one digs into the archive and begins to use these newly uncovered (or newly digitized) sources to deconstruct a singular, normative "history" (what Foucault called the "archeological method"), a set of competing *histories* emerges. These histories alter the meaning of the archival material itself.[78] The Mormon-constructed "paper Indian" and "pious pioneer"—built upon a particular reading of "Walker's writing" and the Mormons' records of "Walker's War"—is confronted by "Wakara," the chronicler of his Native American people's last stand (think Mormon at Cumorah (Mormon 6)). This Wakara wrote back. He used words in an attempt to repel a violent army of colonizers (think the Lamanites) bent on seizing his Native American land and destroying his Native American way of life.

Figure 4.3. Hi-Res Scan from original.

Figure 4.4. Lo-Res Scan available at the LDS Church History Library online catalog.

5

In the Literature of the Lamanites

(Un)settling Mormonism in the Literary Record of Native North America, 1830–1930

MICHAEL P. TAYLOR

O Stop and tell me, Red Man,
Who are ye? Why you roam?
And how you get your living?
Have you no God;—no home?
—William W. Phelps

William W. Phelps's "Oh stop and tell me, Red Man," which was included in the LDS Church's official hymnal from 1835–1927, captures the theological and cultural underpinnings of early LDS representations and understandings of Native North America: a continent peopled by a branch of ancient Israel who have since fallen from grace into their current state of idleness and idolatry. The hymn concludes with a call for Latter-day Saints to proselytize American Indians from their "savage customs" into "pure religion" in order to "fill [their] bosoms" with eternal joy.[1] Although this hymn has since been removed from the Church's official songbook, Phelps's depiction of American Indians as a fallen branch of Israel—direct descendants of the Lamanites from the Book of Mormon—to whom God is now offering the restored gospel of Jesus Christ through white American settler-evangelists, has remained central to contemporary LDS theological understandings and cultural practices.

In his 2012 general conference address, Elder Larry Echo Hawk (Pawnee) reiterated the themes of Phelps's lyrics, describing the near extermination of his people as the fulfillment of Book of Mormon prophecy.[2] Echo Hawk then coupled his own LDS conversion narrative with an entreaty to all American Indians to reconsider their relationship with Jesus Christ through the Book of Mormon: "I exhort all people to read the Book of Mormon. I especially ask the remnant of the house of Israel, the descendants of the people of the Book of Mormon, wherever you may be, to read and reread the Book of Mormon."[3] At the time of Echo Hawk's general conference address, I was working through the first year of my doctoral studies in Indigenous North American and Pacific literatures at the University of British Columbia. As a Mormon-settler scholar working within the intellectually and emotionally challenging field of Indigenous studies, his words caused me to step back and reconsider my own positionality and methodological practices. Then in a resulting period of intense self-doubt, I approached my dissertation supervisor, renowned Cherokee author and critic Daniel Heath Justice, and asked, "What can I as a settler scholar really do to contribute to the field of Indigenous Studies?" His response was immediate, simple, and direct: "Be humble. And listen." Such humble reconsidering though is an ongoing, daily process of learning, making mistakes, seeking forgiveness, relearning, and forging relationships across both inherent and constructed racial, religious, and experiential differences.

Fundamental to this reconsidering has been researching my own ancestry and the normalized narratives that have circulated within and around my family for generations. I descend from a particular pedigree of LDS evangelists among the Indigenous Peoples of what are now recognized as the states and territories of the United States. In October 1830, the Prophet Joseph Smith sent my paternal ancestor Elder Parley Parker Pratt "into the wilderness, among the Lamanites."[4] Pratt's first LDS mission into Indian Country included the Seneca near Buffalo, New York, as well as the Shawnee and Delaware living west of Missouri.[5] Two generations later, my great-great-grandfather, Joseph Henry Dean, served two missions to the Hawaiian Islands and subsequently opened the first LDS mission in Samoa. Another two generations later, my paternal grandfather moved his family to Holbrook, Arizona, to preside for three years over what was then the Church's Southwest Indian Mission. Now two final generations later, I recognize that as a result of being raised within this long line of LDS leaders and missionaries among the Indigenous Peoples of North America and the Pacific, my personal history of American Indians and Mormons has been shaped by the zealous lens of restored Christ-centered salvation.

This proselyting perspective has also included the often selective narratives published by LDS scholars, historians, anthropologists, and enthusiasts, who have read American Indian stories, languages, archeological sites, and even human genomes in ways that seek to corroborate, or at least draw parallels to, the prophetic claims of the Book of Mormon and Latter-day prophets. As renowned American historian Daniel Walker Howe describes, such writers have turned to what could be described as the literature of the Lamanites and focus, for example, on the early nineteenth-century sermons of William Apess (Pequot) because they seem to similarly embrace the Lost Tribe of Israel ancestral model.[6] Other writers emphasize the ostensible similarities between the recorded visions of Black Elk (Oglala Sioux) and the revelations of Joseph Smith and ancient Book of Mormon prophets.[7] Still others interpret the Christ-like virginal birth of Deganawidah, the great peacemaker of the Haudenosaunee Confederacy, as the climactic Book of Mormon visitation of Christ to the Americas.[8] As intriguing as such parallels can be for LDS readers, such connections remain purely speculative. And while such speculative scholarship is, of course, not limited to Latter-day Saints, there is within the Church a cultural and even curricular tendency, as anthropologist Stuart Kirsch observes within American Christianity at large, to "remake the histories of Indigenous Peoples" through an exclusively LDS cosmology.[9] By reinterpreting Mormon-like moments in American Indian literatures, such subjective narratives simultaneously erase distinct American Indian histories and contexts, and disregard how Apess, Black Elk, and other nineteenth- and early twentieth-century Indigenous writers and thinkers actually viewed, wrote, and spoke about the early LDS Church and its members.[10]

In fact, despite many attempts to interpret Apess, Black Elk, and others as validations of LDS claims about doctrine, deity, and American Indian ancestry, neither Apess nor Black Elk seem to have ever mentioned Mormonism in any of their published writings. Even such well-known American Indian literary figures as Zitkala-Ša (Yankton Sioux), who lived and worked from 1902–1916 on the Uintah and Ouray Reservation in Utah, attended women's conventions in Salt Lake City, collaborated with BYU music professor William F. Hanson to compose the first Native American opera, worked closely with LDS attorney and later Brigham Young University president Ernest L. Wilkinson, and whose 1938 funeral service was held in an LDS chapel, never directly discusses Mormonism in her opera, poetry, two collections of stories, and more than twenty-five published essays.[11] The fact that even Zitkala-Ša, considering her extensive social, political, literary, and legal interactions with early Latter-day Saints, seems to have never addressed Mormonism in her published writings places the early Church far on the periphery of American Indian intellectual, political, and popular discourse throughout the nineteenth and early twentieth centuries despite the centrality of American Indians within contemporaneous LDS discourse.

There were, however, a number of influential nineteenth- and early twentieth-century American Indian writers who did occasionally address Mormonism in ways that continue to challenge the Church's cultural, spiritual, political, and physical settlements throughout Native North America.[12] Because recovering and reclaiming American Indian writers from the archived centuries of systematic silencing and colonial neglect is an ongoing process, the authors discussed in this essay should be read as the first step toward (un)settling Mormonism in the literary record of Native North America rather than as any attempt at a comprehensive survey. And rather than delving into the often divisive debates of deity and discovery that subjective parallelisms and the rightfully reactionary work of Indigenous and allied scholars and writers invoke, my hope is to analyze published American Indian perspectives on the early Church in a way that neither unilaterally celebrates Indigenous conversion nor belabors the fraught historical and contemporary moments of American Indian–Mormon relationships. Instead, as Indigenous and allied scholars continue to reframe the Book of Mormon and its resulting theological and cultural histories and practices through Indigenous cultural, spiritual, and intellectual histories, contexts, perspectives, and epistemologies, my goal is to invite readers to reconsider past and present American Indian–Mormon relationships by returning to the published writings of nineteenth- and early twentieth-century Native North America.[13]

In other words, the goal of this essay is to encourage readers to humbly listen and seek to respectfully respond to past and present American Indian observers, experiencers, and writers of Mormonism in order to more reciprocally repair, remake, and retain these crucial relationships. And to that end, although such popular American Indian authors as John Rollin Ridge (Cherokee), Alexander Posey (Muscogee Creek), and Will Rogers (Cherokee) occasionally address Mormon politics, rumored retaliation against apostates, and the breadth of

Brother Brigham's bed, similar to such popular non–American Indian writers as Mark Twain, Zane Grey, and Arthur Conan Doyle, this paper focuses specifically on those few American Indian writers who discuss American Indian–Mormon relationships from a more overtly American Indian perspective.[14]

Imagining Collaborative Resistance

But before we listen to the literary record of 1830–1930 Native America, let us consider two contemporary American Indian authors, Martin Cruz Smith (Isleta Pueblo) and Leslie Marmon Silko (Laguna Pueblo), in order to establish an imaginative framework through which we can more productively reconsider the first century of American Indian–Mormon relationships. Rather than emphasizing moments of American Indian–Mormon conflict and violence, both authors choose to reimagine early American Indian–Mormon relationships as collaborative, not in any attempt to reify religious truth claims maintained by one group over the other, but rather as friends and allies in mutual resistance against US federal restrictions on territorial and spiritual sovereignty. To reimagine such collaborative resistance, both Cruz Smith and Silko build their narratives around the explicit parallels between Book of Mormon prophecy, the prophet Wovoka (Northern Paiute), and the late nineteenth-century Ghost Dance Movement.

In her 1999 novel, *Gardens in the Dunes*, Silko depicts what the novel's front flap describes as "the fatal collision between two cultures" as her young protagonist, Indigo, navigates her way through the US government school, England's elite, the Brazilian jungles, Gilded Age America, and the American Southwest. Yet, as Silko depicts such often violent cultural collisions, her narration of American Indian–Mormon relationships remains more congenial and collaborative than combative. Silko begins her novel as Indigo's older sister, Sister Salt, looks back at her childhood and tells of when the police first arrived to quell the growing Ghost Dance Movement that she and her people participated in. Among those arrested, Sister Salt explains, were "the white people, mostly Mormons, who came to dance for the Messiah."[15]

Small groups of Mormons came because the Mormons had been waiting for the Messiah's return; they became very excited after they heard

Wovoka preach. Mormons began to dance *hand in hand* with the other dancers; these Mormons who believed in Wovoka were generous and donated meat for the dancers. The white canvas for the dancers shawls was donated by the Mormons.[16]

In this opening recollection, Sister Salt singles out Mormons as those who physically and spiritually supported, participated in, and suffered punishment because of the Ghost Dance. Silko's Mormons did not attend as curious onlookers or spiritual skeptics. Instead, Sister Salt remembers dancing "hand in hand" with Mormons in their shared hope for the fulfillment of Pueblo prophecy. But why the Mormons?

As Sister Salt's recollection continues, the Messiah soon arrives to bless both the Indian and Mormon dancers:

When the Mormons approached the Messiah, Sister Salt stayed nearby to listen for herself; she was amazed. As the Messiah gave his blessing to the Mormons, Sister Salt distinctly heard the words he spoke as Sand Lizard, not English, yet the Mormons understood the words and murmured their thanks to him.[17]

Silko's Messianic-Mormon communion highlights two fundamental realities at the outset of the novel. First, Mormons and Ghost Dance Indians share the prophetic belief that a messianic savior will return to rid the continent of settler-colonial violence and sacrilege. Second, American Indians and Mormons share a common creator with whom they can communicate with equal efficacy.

As settler resistance to the Ghost Dance increases, federal police and Indian agents enforce the near starvation of Sister Salt's Sand Lizard people, forcing many to begin to migrate to town where Silko again highlights the possibilities of American Indian–Mormon solidarity:

Grandma Fleet did not like the idea of town, but with a baby and a little girl to feed, they hadn't much choice: to stay at the old gardens meant starvation.... Their first years there were very difficult, but the Walapai women and the Paiute women shared the little food they had; a kind Mormon woman brought them old clothing. As long as there was no trouble, the authorities left them alone.[18]

In town, Silko describes how her characters' American Indian–Mormon relationships exceeded participation in parallel prophecies. Here, Mormon women
become charitable collaborators, alongside other American Indian women,
in the succor of arriving Ghost Dance refugees.

Through this intersecting network of shared prophecy, persecution, and
providing/receiving relief, Silko goes on to outline how American Indian and
Mormon women began to develop meaningful, reciprocal friendships:

> Grandma Fleet and one old Mormon woman were released from gov-
> ernment custody. Grandma and the Mormon woman became friends
> on their walk down the river. They did not talk so much as they pointed
> out things to each other, then smiled and nodded to each other while
> they walked along.[19]

Notice how Silko describes the forming of American Indian–Mormon solidarity. Neither woman seems to say much. Instead, they walk together and express
their own observations. Better yet, while each outlines her own interests, the
other woman smiles and nods in reciprocity, respect, and sincere acknowledgment. By doing so, each voice is heard, each observation is validated, and each
woman embodies a commitment to further friendship.

As Silko's novel continues, the friendship between American Indians and
Mormons begins to fade, perhaps because, as Grandma Fleet suggests, Mormons
simply "got tired of resisting the U.S. government."[20] In a conversation between
Grandma Fleet and her Mormon friend, Silko explains, "The old Mormons
believed they were related to the Indians, and the U.S. government feared the
old Mormons and Indians might band together against the government. The old
Mormons who answered the call of Wovoka were hated most of all. How dare
these Mormons take an Indian to be the Messiah?"[21] Silko's novel concludes with
a final dance for the Messiah, but this time, "no old-time Mormons showed up like
they had last time; but who could blame them after their punishment?"[22] Silko's
Gardens in the Dunes imagines American Indian–Mormon solidarity in fulfilling
shared prophecies, in suffering persecution, and in caring for the persecuted in
a way that challenges the dominant narrative of American Indian–Mormonism.
She simultaneously hints at federal and public fear of such collaborative resistance.

It turns out that Silko's gesturing toward the possibilities and fear of American Indian–Mormon solidarity is more historical fact than contemporary

fiction. Indeed, the Book of Mormon prophesies that if the Euro-American "gentiles" remain unrepentant the Lamanites will "go forth among them . . . as a young lion among the flocks of sheep, who, if he goeth through both treadeth down and teareth in pieces, and none can deliver.[23] And as the recently published *Council of Fifty Minutes* volume of the ongoing *Joseph Smith Papers* project clearly describes, after the martyrdoms of Joseph and Hyrum Smith, early LDS leaders, including subsequent prophet and president Brigham Young, turned in their anger to such Book of Mormon passages and concluded that "at some future point violence might be divinely condoned or required."[24] Brigham Young and other council members argued that Latter-day Saints should form an alliance with American Indians in preparation to be called upon to carry out a continental cataclysm in the name of Christ.[25] And such arguments did not only arise as a result of anger-driven, post-martyrdom debate. They also came in the form of visions received in early LDS temples. During an 1845 evening of song, dance, and speaking in tongues led by Young in the Nauvoo temple, for example, Young interpreted Elizabeth Ann Whitney as she spoke in tongues and prophesied, "The 'Lamanites' . . . would soon convert and 'join in the dance before the Lord of Hosts, when our Enemies shall be crumble[d] to dust & fall to rise no more.'"[26] Indeed, one of the Council's founding commissions was to "cultivate relations with American Indians."[27] And in response, some American Indian Nations also sent reciprocal delegations back to Nauvoo.

On April 4, 1844, for example, eleven Potawatomi Indians arrived in Nauvoo, reportedly seeking both alliance and advice "to avoid losing their land."[28] At a church conference held two days later, Joseph Smith invited the delegates to attend and sit on the stand.[29] After the conference, the council continued to reach out to encourage American Indians to become a more unified force, and to form potential American Indian–Mormon alliances.[30] Whether in anger, in fear, or in accordance with modern revelation, the Council of Fifty remained committed to achieving both spiritual and sociopolitical solidarity with American Indians across the continent. As council member Orson Spencer reported, Joseph Smith prophesied prior to his death that such an alliance would be essential to the ultimate survival of both American Indians and Mormons: "'If the Lamanites won't hearken to our council, they shall be oppressed & killed until they will do it.' The gospel to them is, they have been killed and scattered in consequence of their rejecting the everlasting Priesthood, and if they will return

Figure 5.1. "Joseph the Prophet Addressing the Lamanites." Lithograph by H. R. Robinson, 1844. Image from the LDS Church History Library, Salt Lake City.

to the Priesthood and hearken to council, they shall have council enough, that shall save both them and us."[31]

While Silko explores the possibilities of American Indian–Mormon collaboration based on shared struggles for spiritual sovereignty, a reimagined resistance that is interestingly rooted in the doctrine and dialogue of early Latter-day Saints, Cruz Smith's debut novel, *The Indians Won* (1970), imagines an American Indian–Mormon solidarity that is capable of revolutionary resistance in protection of American Indian lives and lands. *The Indians Won* presents an anti-colonialist alternate history in which American Indians from across the continent combine to take back America from the diminished forces of the post–Civil War United States. In Cruz Smith's narrative, the Mormon-Wovoka connection that Silko highlights becomes central to the success of Cruz Smith's Indian insurgence. As the story goes, Wovoka and a paler-skinned Mandan Indian, known among the whites as John Setter, travel from nation to nation preaching Wovoka's prophecy of an Indian Messiah and precolonial continental renewal, as well as the need to join together and fight to aid in the fulfillment of the prophecy. After meeting with a delegation of American Indian leaders and messengers from various nations across the continent, Setter heads west with a contingent of American Indian–Mormon converts to the "Great Salt Lake to see men who call themselves ... Saints."[32]

In Salt Lake City, Setter meets with leading Mormon officials, including President John Taylor. Setter relays Wovoka's prophecy and the resulting organizing movement of American Indians in order to persuade Taylor and his adherent Saints to join in the prophetic revolution:

> "What does this mean?" President John Taylor asked from his throne overlooking the Empire of Deseret.... "It means," Setter said, drawing his hand in a wide sweep over the map, "that the United States has ceased to be the authority over this land. They are only a party to the struggle, the losing party."

Hearing Setter's proposal, one of Taylor's fellow apostles, Orson Pratt, exclaims, "It is God's hand write [*sic*] large.... The Gentiles have been thrown back by the Lamanites. It is the Judgment of God, the test that brings the Indians, the Sons of Laman son of Lehi, back to grace. Why do we hesitate?"[33]

While Taylor remains less inclined to immediately see the hand of God in anticolonial Indian resistance, he does begin to wonder: "Could there actually be common cause between savages and the Latter Day Saints who walked the wide streets of the Salt Lake City?"[34] Mulling over such questions, Taylor turns again to interrogate Setter:

> "Tell me what a white man like yourself, Mr. Setter, is doing in this war? What's in it for you?" Setter folded his arms. "It's very simple, President Taylor. I am not white, I am Indian. Mandan. It is a trait among the Mandan for many to be born with paler skin and lighter hair. Albinism, some say.

Again, Pratt cannot contain his excitement at the possibility of participating in the direct fulfilment of prophecy: "That explains it.... A Mandan, one of the last Sons of Nephi."[35] Still unconvinced, Taylor asks Setter and his company to leave so that Taylor can commune on the issue with God. Pratt accompanies them and ensures eventual Mormon support:

> Don't worry ... President Taylor will see the light. It's just that he did not have the experience of accompanying Brigham to the Rio Grande Valley and finding the ruins of the Ho-ho-kim, your ancestors. Oh, there was no doubt in Brigham's mind that the children of the bad brother Laman would be brought back to the path of Mormon. I don't think [Taylor] could help being impressed by the fact that you are a son of Nephi and Moroni."[36]

Setter leaves Salt Lake City with no firm commitment of Mormon support, but leaves Taylor with a desire to explore the plausibility of Wovoka's prophecy: "'I can't help but believe that there is some responsibility on us to fulfill the prophecy of the return of the Lamanites. If we don't, who will?' he said sincerely."[37] As Cruz Smith's alternate history continues, Pratt's assurance soon becomes a reality and ten thousand Mormon soldiers join the growing force of the Indian Nation.[38]

As the novel's title so subtly describes, with the help of Mormon reinforcements, Cruz Smith's Indians win back the North American continent. And as they do, they return to Salt Lake City to persuade Taylor and others to accept

Wovoka as an additional prophet and accept the Indian Nation into full Mormon membership. "President Taylor's announcement of March 2, 1881, marked the beginning of Indian Mormonism."[39] Cruz Smith then concludes with some overt levity:

> The following year, Chief Taylor of Salt Lake City died in a fit. Wovoka was left as the leader of the Mormon Church and innovations came quickly.... Tavibo [Wovoka's father] was raised to the level of Moroni in the Mormon hierarchy. Joseph Smith was declared to have Indian ancestry.[40]

Then with a seriousness that speaks to the present push within and beyond this collection to recenter Indigenous perspectives and presence within contemporary Mormon discourse, Cruz Smith writes, "As might be expected, a great number of the original Mormons packed up and left the Indian Nation. A surprising number, however, almost half, were impressed by Wovoka's monumental sincerity and remained true to their beliefs."[41] After all Wovoka's revelatory beliefs of a Messiah coming to usher in an era of peace and renewal of the American continent are not so different from certain fundamental LDS beliefs:

> We believe in the literal gathering of Israel and in the restoration of the Ten Tribes; that Zion (the New Jerusalem) will be built upon the American continent; that Christ will reign personally upon the earth; and, that the earth will be renewed and receive its paradisiacal glory.[42]

As many contemporary Latter-day Saints fear what they see as an increasing attack on religious freedom, and as contemporary Indigenous Peoples within and beyond the United States continue to resist ongoing encroachments on their lands and livelihoods, Silko's and Cruz Smith's reimaginings of mid-nineteenth-century American Indian–Mormon collaborative resistance provide both the significance and underlying framework of this essay. Both novels explicitly emphasize the shared desire for spiritual and territorial sovereignty, the shared struggle to resist federal mandates, and as a result the shared potential in supporting one another toward maintaining/regaining our shared and starkly distinct realizations of sovereignty. So, in this spirit of American Indian–Mormon solidarity that Silko and Cruz Smith imagine, and Brigham Young and Joseph

Smith sought, let us more accountably listen to the first 100 years of published American Indian perspectives on the prophesies, politics, and practices of the early Latter-day Saints in order to (un)settle Mormonism away from the widely internalized settler-colonial ideologies that have and continue to normalize cultural, sociopolitical, and literal violence within the expanding circles of LDS discourse and influence.

"This is the Place": American Indians and the "Mormon City"

Throughout the earliest years of the Church, Cherokee author John Rollin Ridge (Yellow Bird) became Mormonism's first widely published American Indian critic. Ridge was a prolific newspaper editor, poet, and author, remembered most for publishing the first American Indian novel, *The Life and Adventures of Joaquín Murieta: The Celebrated California Bandit* (1854).[43] He first encountered Latter-day Saints in 1850 while traveling from the Cherokee Nation to seek fortune in the California Gold Rush. And his resulting bitterness from what he experienced echoed through his newspaper editorials for the subsequent seventeen years. Yet Ridge's coverage of Mormonism had little to do with the direct relationships between American Indians and Mormons. Instead, Ridge's writings focus largely on the Church's politico-economic control of Salt Lake City and the Utah territory, what Ridge refers to as the "Mormon City." Yet while the bulk of Ridge's writings on Mormonism have little to do with American Indian issues, this first moment of Mormonism in the literary record of Native North America establishes a perspective that carries throughout the writings of the other overtly American Indian writers remembered throughout this essay.

In a letter written to his mother and published in 1853 in the *Fort Smith Herald*, Ridge describes the many challenges of westward emigration and locates them specifically in Salt Lake City:

> We got to the Salt Lake ... burned up with "mountain fever" and suffering excruciating torture ... from pain in our backs that seemed to enter the very spinal marrow! ... When we reached the Mormon City ... all our animals were failing. We concluded to recruit at the Salt Lake, both ourselves and our beasts.... After much trouble questioning the Mormons we found a range for our mules.

Ridge goes on to describe his frustration from having to negotiate with Latter-day Saints who "even charged toll on the 44 miles of the road to the city."[44] Although his letter does not specifically criticize the Church or individual Latter-day Saints, Ridge's initial encounter with the Mormon City left him embittered against what he saw as exploitative LDS economics.

Unlike Ridge, who had left the Cherokee Nation in search of fame and fortune as a mainstream American author, Paiute writer, speaker, and activist Sarah Winnemucca wrote from her traditional territory in what is now Nevada. Yet despite her proximity, she mentions Salt Lake City only once in her 1882 tribal story, *Life Among the Piutes: Their Wrongs and Claims*. And when she does, Winnemucca addresses Salt Lake City's direct relationship with corrupt federal Indian agents in the colonial economics of the American West. Describing an Agent Batemann, whom she accompanied as interpreter to deliver federally issued supplies to a group of Shoshone Indians, Winnemucca writes:

> A family numbering eight persons got two blankets, three shirts, no dress-goods. Some got a fishhook and line; some got one and a half yards of flannel, blue and red; the largest issue was to families that camped together, numbering twenty-three persons: four blankets, three pieces of red flannel, and some of blue, three shirts, three hooks and lines, two kettles. It was the saddest affair I ever saw.

She continues, "There were ready-made clothes of all kinds, hats, shoes, and shawls, and farming utensils of all kinds. Bales upon bales of clothing were sent away to Salt Lake City."[45] Similar to Ridge's earlier account of passing through the Mormon City, Winnemucca's singular mentioning of Salt Lake City does not discuss Mormonism or accuse individual Latter-day Saints of any direct wrongdoing.[46] Instead, she places the Mormon City as both the financier and beneficiary of profiteering federal Indian agents and their ongoing exploitation of their impoverished Indian wards. She leaves her readers to draw their own conclusions regarding the Church's participation in the ongoing economic exploitation of reservation Indians.

Rather than delve into the doctrines and dogmas of LDS theology and cultural practice, Winnemucca and Ridge both describe the Mormon City as an intricate economic epicenter, one Winnemucca identifies as participating in and profiting from the direct exploitation of Indigenous Peoples and lands. Each writer describes Salt Lake City as a leader in the political and economic ventures of the American frontier, and Winnemucca specifically emphasizes how such ventures continue to seek to remove Indigenous Peoples from their lands and resources. As Winnemucca goes on to address, transforming the Great Basin into a profitable LDS settlement was not only accomplished through bargaining with fraudulent federal Indian Agents. Such financial stability was also maintained, at times, through direct acts of settler-colonial violence.

"Like a Roaring Lion": Reporting Mormon-Settler Violence

Beyond Ridge's initial experience traveling through Salt Lake City, Ridge seems to base much of his subsequent Mormon-focused editorials on hearsay, lacing his writings with the rumored practices of assassinating Mormon apostates, stoning unfaithful polygamous wives, and other such acts of religious fanaticism.[47] Winnemucca, Simon Pokagon (Potawatomi), and Charles Alexander Eastman (Santee Dakota), on the other hand, provide straightforward accounts of Mormon-settler violence that place Mormon settlers as participants within the US settler-colonial regime.

Winnemucca, for example, provides a Paiute-specific narrative of LDS settlement that emphasizes the problematic relationship between religious prophecy and practice. Yet, rather than indict Latter-day Saints directly, Winnemucca chooses not to distinguish between Mormon settlers and other white settlers. To Winnemucca, all settlers, Mormons and/or otherwise, were quite the same: "[The white people] came like a lion, yes, like a roaring lion, and have continued ever since." Her grandfather, on the other hand, upon hearing of the whites' arrival, "jumped up and clasped his hands together, and cried aloud, "My white brothers—my long–looked for white brothers have come at last!"[48] In this introductory passage, Winnemucca juxtaposes her own perspective of white leonine violence and her grandfather's perspective of the fulfillment of traditional Paiute prophecy. While LDS readers may latch onto the prophecy because of its surface similarity with the Book of Mormon's Nephite-Lamanite narrative, Winnemucca describes the arrival of the whites as the introduction of widespread violence among her people.

Indeed, it would not be long until Winnemucca's people would begin to suffer the devastating results of Promised Land prophecies and manifest destinies that have motivated the colonial masses to take up the White Man's burden at the expense of those deemed inferior.[49] Among these envisioned white settlers arriving in Paiute territory were the more than 250 Latter-day Saints sent between 1849–1855 by Brigham Young, remembered by many as the "Lion of the Lord," "to establish political control of the area and to proselytize and 'civilize' the Indians of that region."[50] Winnemucca remembers, "The Mormons came in a great many wagons and settled down in Carson Valley."[51] Surprisingly, this is the first and only time Winnemucca uses the term "Mormon" throughout her tribal story to distinguish between LDS and other white settlers.

Although Young called many of these initial Latter-day Saints back to Salt Lake City in preparation to defend the Church against the approaching US military, LDS missionary efforts continued in Paiute territory. As taught by the Church Education System, "The Las Vegas Mission was founded in 1855 to proselytize local Indians and teach them agriculture and peaceful ways. Latter-day Saints there labored among the Paiutes, converting many of them and establishing a farm for them."[52] In contrast to the Church's curricular narrative, Western Shoshone historian Ned Blackhawk describes this same period as "the Crisis of Mormon Settlement,"[53] and Winnemucca entitles the chapter in which this increased number of Mormon settlers arrived as "Wars and Their Causes."

According to Winnemucca, soon after Mormons arrived to assert political control of the territory, two wealthy settlers were found dead and the murderers had placed arrows into the bullet holes in order to frame men from the neighboring Washoe Tribe. Although the Washoe chief denied the charges, he sacrificed three of his young men as prisoners. Winnemucca writes, "Next morning all the white people came to see them. Some said, 'Hang the red devils right off,' and the white boys threw stones at them, and used most shameful language to them."[54] But before a final verdict was spoken, the three Washoe men tried to escape. The settlers immediately shot all three, killing one instantly and fatally wounding the other two.[55] Although Winnemucca does not directly censure Latter-day Saints in this tragic scene, the numbers suggest that LDS men and boys were among the settlers calling to hang the "red devils," throwing stones, shouting insults, and shooting three innocent Washoe men to death. At the very least, LDS settlers were within earshot, knew what was going on, and gave Winnemucca no reason to record that they had either condemned the violent actions or counteracted the cultural norms that had emboldened such violence. While the Church's narrative of LDS settlement revolves around proselytization, Winnemucca's Paiute history of Mormon arrival is one of increased conflict and violence. Not once does she mention missionaries or pioneers. Instead, she identifies Mormons as unexceptional white settlers both in purpose and practice. By introducing the arrival of the whites in Paiute territory through her grandfather's prophecy, one that some might interpret to support similar Book of Mormon prophecies, Winnemucca calls on her Christian audience, and in the context of this collection, her contemporary LDS audience, to remember that whether the coming of Euro-American settlers and the inexplicable suffering they have brought with them for the Indigenous Peoples of North America has been divinely decreed or not, participating in such violence involves individual agency.

In contrast to Winnemucca, Pokagon was decidedly more direct in his accusation against Mormon-settler violence and the role it played in the larger, ongoing oppression of American Indians. Pokagon was one of the most formidable American Indian literary figures in nineteenth-century North America. And while he wrote and spoke from his own Potawatomi context, he and his writings circulated throughout literary and activist circles of Chicago and the Northeast to the extent that he was invited as a featured speaker at Chicago's 1893 World's Columbia Exposition as a renowned representative of all American Indians. As American Studies scholar Kiara Vigil suggests, "Pokagon urges white readers to consider revising their views on American history in relation to the usurpation of Indigenous lands and culture."[56] Likewise, Pokagon's discussion of Mormon-settler violence, specifically the Mountain Meadows Massacre, should cause contemporary LDS readers to work to revise dominant cultural views on American Indian–Mormon relationships, as well as the Church's participation within the ongoing appropriation and exploitation of Indigenous Peoples, lands, and cultures.

In 1888, Pokagon published an essay entitled "The Future of the Red Man," in which he begins, "Often in the stillness of the night, when all nature seems asleep about me, there comes a gentle rapping at the door of my heart. I open it; and a voice inquires, 'Pokagon, what of your people? What will their future be?'"[57] Judging "the future by the present and the past," Pokagon concedes to the mainstream colonial narrative and predicts that within the coming generation "all Indian reservation and tribal relations will have passed away."[58] But what were the events, past and present, that caused Pokagon to ostensibly surrender to the colonial narrative of "the vanishing Indian" so prevalent throughout the nineteenth and early twentieth centuries? Pokagon begins with the 1492 coming of Columbus and the ensuing enslavement and slaughter of Indigenous Caribbean Peoples. Pokagon then jumps from the 1513 landing of Juan Ponce de León in what is now Florida to the French and Indian War (1754–1763) and the deliberate introduction of smallpox. Next comes the Revolutionary War (1775–1783) and the introduction of "Awsh-kon-tay Ne-besh (fire water)." The War of 1812 and the 1813 Battle of the Thames in Canada soon follow. Pokagon writes, "I always think of my people in those days as the dog kept by the school-master to be whipped whenever a child disobeyed.... At one time I felt that our race was doomed to extermination."[59] And right in the center of Pokagon's nearly 400-year history of genocidal colonial violence against Indigenous North Americans, he writes, "These outrages were generally planned, and frequently executed, by white men, as was, in after years, the Mountain Meadow [sic] Massacre, of Mormon notoriety, for which also we were persecuted and suffered untold disgrace."[60]

The Church Education System currently introduces adolescent seminary students to the Mountain Meadows Massacre within the context of the Utah War of 1857–1858 and the increasing tensions between Latter-day Saints in Salt Lake City and the US federal government.[61] The lesson manual reads, "Motivated by anger and fear, some Latter-day Saints in southern Utah planned and carried out the massacre of about 120 emigrants traveling to California." Before describing the details of the massacre, the manual encourages teachers to pose the following question: "If you had been a Latter-day Saint in 1857 and had heard that a large army was approaching your city, what concerns might you have had?" The suggested lesson plan then provides the details of the Mormon militiamen's deceit, disguise, and the resulting massacre in order to encourage students to more honestly and immediately resolve personal conflicts, and face the consequences of individual sin.[62] The lesson then concludes with an official expression of regret issued by Elder Henry B. Eyring, now a member of the Church's First Presidency, to commemorate the massacre's 150th anniversary in which he apologizes "to the Paiute people who have unjustly borne for too long the principal blame for what occurred."[63] For many young Latter-day Saints, such a lesson is their first encounter with the Mountain Meadows Massacre, one of the touchstone topics of Mormon controversy, and represents the Church's ongoing attempt to offer greater transparency into the more challenging moments in Church history that Church education manuals had until recently only glossed over. Yet, such a lesson and such a statement of regret, as honorable as both are, divorce the massacre from the colonial history within which Pokagon and Winnemucca place early Mormon-settler violence within.

In 1918, Santee Dakota physician, activist, and writer Charles Alexander Eastman published a series of short biographies entitled *Indian Heroes and Great Chieftains* in which he catalogues, among other conflicts and episodes of exemplary American Indian leadership, moments of American Indian–Mormon altercations. Widely read for his ethnographic stories and legends published in mainstream American magazines, as well as for his two autobiographies, *Indian Boyhood* (1902) and *From the Deep Woods to Civilization* (1916), *Indian Heroes and Great Chieftains* (1918) seems to be the last time Eastman published anything about Mormonism. And he does so in connection to three of the fifteen American Indian leaders he features: Red Cloud (Oglala Lakota), Spotted Tail (Lakota Sioux), and Roman Nose (Cheyenne).

It was in 1854 when Red Cloud first encountered Mormon emigrants, "who left a footsore cow behind," on their way to the Salt Lake Valley:

> The young men killed her for food. The next day, to their astonishment, an officer with thirty men appeared at the Indian camp and demanded of old Conquering Bear that they be given up.... It would seem that either the officer was under the influence of liquor, or else had a mind to bully the Indians, for he would accept neither explanation nor payment, but demanded point-blank that the young men who had killed the cow be delivered up to summary punishment. The old chief refused to be intimidated and was shot dead on the spot.[64]

As Eastman explains, Red Cloud and his band of Oglala warriors retaliated and "not one soldier ever reached the gate of Fort Laramie" in what settler histories have remembered as the Grattan Massacre.[65] Like Winnemucca, here Eastman does not directly blame Mormon emigrants, who had passed through the Oglala territory in peace, for the resulting violence. However, he also does not plead their innocence. It was, after all, someone among that train of Mormon emigrants who reported the killing of an abandoned cow and sent the officer, intoxicated either with alcohol or a normalized feeling of white supremacy, to "punish" the Indians.

In his brief biography of Spotted Tail, Eastman again places Latter-day Saints as participants in the settler-colonial violence against American Indians.

Eastman writes, "At this time, the presence of many Mormon emigrants on their way to the settlements in Utah and Wyoming added to the perils of the situation, as they constantly maneuvered for purposes of their own to bring about a clash between the soldiers and the Indians."[66] Similar to Winnemucca, who juxtaposes the mass arrival of Mormon settlers in Paiute territory with the causes of war, Eastman suggests that Mormon settlers, "for purposes their own," intentionally initiated conflict between military officials and American Indian tribes that they encountered on their way west. Eastman reports that Mormon settlers were not only similar to other white settlers, but were settlers who purposely "added to the perils" of the already fraught sociopolitical situation of Native North America.

Eastman's accusations prepare his readers to almost celebrate with the Cheyenne war chief, Roman Nose, after his attack on a large group of emigrant Latter-day Saints:

> In this instance the Mormons had time to form a corral with their wagons and shelter their women, children, and horses. The men stood outside and met the Indians with well-aimed volleys, but they circled the wagons with whirlwind speed, and whenever a white man fell, it was the signal for Roman Nose to charge and count the "coup." The hat of one of the dead men was off, and although he had heavy hair and beard, the top of his head was bald from the forehead up. As custom required such a deed to be announced on the spot, the chief yelled at the top of his voice: "Your Roman Nose has counted the first coup on the longest-faced white man who was ever killed!"[67]

Why is it that out of the eight years, in which Roman Nose ostensibly "attacked more emigrants going west on the Oregon Trail" than any other Indian chief, Eastman chose to highlight a particular attack on Mormon emigrants? On the one hand, perhaps Eastman's largely non-LDS readers would be less likely to condemn American Indian violence against Mormons than they might with such aggression against non-Mormon white settlers. On the other hand, by choosing to feature Roman Nose's attack on Mormons from the array of Roman Nose's other successful campaigns in defense of his Cheyenne people and lands, Eastman reinforces the prominent role he saw LDS settlers playing in the increasing violence against American Indians in the American West. In their discussions of

Mormon-settler violence, Eastman, Pokagon, Winnemucca, and Ridge remind readers that no matter how divinely destined Latter-day Saints believe westward migration and settlement to be, and while anger of past injustices and fear of future persecution surely motivated some acts of Mormon-settler violence, many emigrating Latter-day Saints carried with them notions of white-Christian superiority that normalized Mormon-settler violence against American Indians.

Mormon Women, Mormon Wives

Beyond Mormons' reported complacency and/or committing of settler-colonial violence along the American frontier, American Indian authors also considered the widely criticized practice of polygamy and its perceived violence against women. And while such authors as Ridge and Rogers take a more mainstream approach of both condemning and caricaturing Mormon polygamy, another contemporaneous Cherokee intellectual and author, John Milton Oskison, shifts away from Mormon-national politics to challenge, instead, the dominating dogma of US Christian monogamy and its simultaneous effects on tradition-ally nonmonogamous American Indian familial traditions. Although Oskison published prolifically and quite popularly throughout the early twentieth cen-tury, his only mention of Mormonism comes in his now-canonized short story, "The Problem of Old Harjo" (1907).[68]

In this story, a young missionary, Miss Evans, learns to appreciate the affec-tionate relationship between Harjo and his two wives while Harjo also begins to accept Christianity. However, Harjo's baptism is stalled by Miss Evans's superior, Mrs. Rowell, because he refuses to stop practicing polygamy. Oskison describes Mrs. Rowell as a strict patriot whose "cousin was an earnest crusader against Mormonism.""Possessed of but one enthusiasm—that for saving souls," Oskison writes, Miss Evans set out to "rehabilitate Old Harjo morally," by per-suading him to put away one of his wives. Harjo understands the missionary's command as jest and replies, "You tell me, my friend, which one I give up." His wives then humorously suggest that the two run a race to decide. As Miss Evans makes the seriousness of her request apparent, Harjo asks her to leave and she expresses her disgust from being treated so disrespectfully "by an ignorant old bigamist!" Oskison continues: "Then the humor of it burst upon her, and its human aspect. In her anxiety concerning the spiritual welfare of the sinner

Harjo, she had insulted the man Harjo." She returns to beg forgiveness and asks Harjo to explain why he had married multiple wives:

> Well, five years 'Liz and me, we live here and work hard. But there was no child. Then the old mother of Jennie she died, and Jennie got no family left in this part of the country. So 'Liz say to me, "Why don't you take Jennie in here?" I say, "You don't care?" and she say, "No, maybe we have children here then." But we have no children—never have children. We do not like that, but God He would not let it be. So, we have lived here thirty years very happy. Only just now you make me sad.

Miss Evans leaves in regret, determined to find a way for Harjo to be saved without disrupting the harmoniousness of the Harjos' nonconforming familial relationships. It is here that Oskison returns to Mormonism through Miss Evans's internal conflict: "If she was sometimes tempted to say to the old man, 'Stop worrying about your soul; you'll get to Heaven as surely as any of us,' there was always Mrs. Rowell to remind her that she was not a Mormon missionary." Oskison leaves Mormonism in the words of Mrs. Rowell. And he leaves the happy Old Harjo as the "impossible convert" who would haunt Miss Evans until death.[69]

Yet Oskison never discusses Mormonism head-on. In fact, in an intriguing sense of irony, Oskison seems to strike a balance between Mrs. Rowell's criticism, which directly reflects popular antipolygamy criticisms, and the honest Old Harjo. Rather than condemning Mormonism, Oskison mentions Mormon polygamy in order to criticize the antipolygamous attempts to disrupt traditional kinship relationships among American Indians. Oskison's story celebrates the complex humanity of American Indian, and perhaps unintentionally LDS, familial structures that extend kinship opportunities and responsibilities beyond the limitations of US Christian monogamy. Clearly, Oskison remains more interested in how anti-Mormon politics affect American Indian Nations than how polygamous politics allegedly affect the US nation-state.

Mormon Communalism and American Indian Self-Sufficiency

The only other American Indian literary figure I have found to publish about the early Church was Haudenosaunee activist, orator, and author Laura Cornelius

Kellogg. As a widely recognized representative of the Haudenosaunee Confederacy and cofounder, alongside Eastman, of the Society of American Indians, Kellogg was, as American cultural studies scholar Cristina Stanciu appropriately suggests, "an Indian Woman of Many Hats."[70] One of Kellogg's most fundamental commitments was to find ways for American Indian communities to become self-sufficient again rather than having to rely on faulty federal promises and philanthropic friends. Her solution was to create Indian industrial villages based on a combination of "the foreign Garden City with the Mormon idea of communistic cooperation."[71]

In 1911, Kellogg asked, "How did [the Mormon] go into the desert with his destitute colony and establish economic freedom to every individual man the way it has never been done in the history of the white man in Western civilization?" She answers:

> He had men and he had the soil.... Labor must do it, and it did. The Mormon practiced irrigation twenty years before the rest of the country did. He did it without money because he capitalized on labor. Men were worth just exactly what they will always be worth when the estimate is right: men were worth just what they could do for the community.[72]

Kellogg continued to outline how early LDS settlers established a watering system, seeded the ground, and cultivated the land through communally committed individual labor without the help of the federal government. Surprisingly, she seems to laud what her contemporary American Indian writers condemn, observing how "traveling [Mormon] missionaries were men more bent upon learning the local conditions, the proper methods, the secret of successes, the market requirements, the development and advancement of every locality, than upon converts." Kellogg then concludes:

> The foreign American and European idea of the division of dividends to the shareholder is a communistic idea of capital and not of men. The Mormon idea is a communistic idea of men.... Mormons today are the richest people per capita in the world. There is one precaution they took among other things. And that is they fortified themselves against the lazy man.... I believe that were the [Indian] Industrial Village organized with the Mormon ideas of capitalization, combined with the European

and American idea of the market, that we would secure the maximum advantage.... To reach a state of economic equity we must follow the Mormon idea of making men the capital of the community.[73]

In 1913, Kellogg voiced similar praise of what she described as Mormon communism in her testimony before the US Senate. This time she qualified her views, declaring: "I am not versed in the ethical questions of the Mormon institution. I do not advocate Mormonism, but I certainly do the industrial system of the Mormons."[74] Finally, in her 1920 book, *Our Democracy and the American Indian*, Kellogg addresses Mormon communalism again as part of what she describes as the only plan to "atone for crushed spirits, broken hopes, plundered fortunes, wasted lives" and "obtain, secure, and maintain real independence."[75] Kellogg's discussion of what she explains as a Mormon communistic industrial system says nothing of the controversial realities expressed by her contemporaries, that the economic success of the Mormon City, for example, often came at the expense of American Indians. She says nothing about Mormon-settler violence, polygamy, or any other controversial characteristic of the first century of Mormonism. Instead, she celebrates what she observed as the successful instillation of individual accountability within LDS communities and encourages American Indian readers to similarly recommit themselves and their resources toward regaining communal independence.

Conclusion

As I began to seriously reconsider my position as a Mormon-settler scholar within the field of Indigenous Studies near the beginning of my doctoral studies, I received the transformative formula for working toward more meaningful dialogue, more reciprocal relationships, and more collaborative scholarship and activism: "Be humble. And listen." The purpose of this essay has been to invite readers to join me in more humbly and more openly listening to the literary record of Native North America in order to reconsider and rearticulate the simultaneously brutal and beautiful past and present relationships of American Indians and Mormons in order to forge more mutually thoughtful, considerate, and critical relationships into the future. Listening to Ridge's criticism of the early Church leaves readers to wonder how his perception may have differed had he been treated with compassion, fairness, and respect while he traveled through the Mormon City. Listening to Winnemucca and Eastman causes readers to question whether they might have chosen to distinguish between Mormon settlers and other settlers differently if Latter-day Saints would have transcended the normalized racist ideologies of colonial America in order to maintain a more mutual balance between individual religious realities and communal responsibilities and relationships. Pokagon challenges readers to see beyond the bias of divine decrees in order to reconsider LDS history within the broader context of US settler colonialism. Oskison entreats readers to prioritize human relationships over individual religious convictions and popular political rhetoric. Finally, listening to Kellogg reminds readers of our individual ability and accountability to learn from one another and to collaborate in order to build up our respective communities. Finally, Rogers reminds readers to slow down amidst all the controversy of the past and present and have a good laugh. Together, from their distinct cultural, political, spiritual, and experiential backgrounds, these writers encourage the cultural, academic, and ecclesiastical discourse of American Indians and Mormons to remain committed to "the attentive care we give to the ongoing processes of balanced rights and responsibilities."[76] Rather than speculating on perceived parallels between Mormons and American Indians, these American Indian writers publishing throughout the first 100 years of Mormon–American Indian history encourage all of us to hold ourselves and each other more accountable, individually and institutionally, for past and present lapses in our imperfect attention and care as we strive together toward more bilaterally respectful and beneficial future relationships.

Part Two

Native Mormon Experiences
in the Twentieth Century

6

Mormonism and the Catawba Indian Nation

STANLEY J. THAYNE

In 1929 anthropologist Frank Speck declared in a publication on Catawba religious beliefs and customs that "the case of the Catawba" is "unique, so far as available information goes, in the history of evangelical mission labors among Indians of North America." "The event of a mass conversion of the tribe to the Mormon church is," Speck felt assured, "one unequaled in the history of Indian missions."[1] By the 1920s, by most counts, over 90 percent of the Catawba people in the Catawba Nation were listed on the rolls of The Church of Jesus Christ of Latter-day Saints (Mormons). And while the same is not exactly true today, nearly all Catawba people are still connected in one way or another to Mormonism. Speck, as an anthropologist, found this situation of Catawba-Mormon conversion lamentable. He was there to investigate, discern, and above all collect "native concepts." The interposition of Mormonism, as he saw it, only made his task all the more difficult. How could he sift the "pure" nuggets of Native culture from the "garbled notions of Christian theology" and the additional layers of Mormonism he found in the Catawba Nation? Speck investigated each of the items he collected with a careful "suspicion of Mormon teachings." He seemed to long for that time when they had "remained untouched as a group" by Mormonism or "any of the numerous denominational proselyting agencies." Speck based his nostalgic quest for "pure" Catawba teachings on an assumption that he paints as prelude to this article: "Until about 1850 we may picture the Catawba as retaining some of the form and content of their original beliefs and rituals." Clearly, Speck imagined a static state of anthropological purity in place prior to the intervention of European colonialism, after which everything became altered.[2]

However, if Speck saw Mormonism as continuing this process, he does not identify Mormonism as the primary culprit for this "loss." In Speck's view, by the time the Mormons arrived, the damage had already been done. He blames this state of affairs on what he calls a "period of dispossession" or an "era of vagrancy." Following the loss of and expulsion from their 25-square-mile tract of territorial homeland—recognized in the British Treaty of Augusta—"the Catawba went into social and economic exile, dispersed throughout the counties adjoining the great river which gave them name and character." The inevitable consequence of this dispersion, Speck avers, "was to prevent the ancient spiritualistic legacy from being handed down through teaching, practice or imitation." What the younger generation carried with them from this time were "the poignant memories of poverty and plague," not the "narratives and rituals of the past."[3]

There is some truth to this. This period of dispossession and wandering surely did disrupt ceremonial practice, as had the plagues, diseases, and other challenges that preceded it—including the very stark fact of massive population loss. European and American colonialism had dealt a severe blow to the Catawba people. But, this qualified truth notwithstanding, Speck's basic assumptions represent an anthropological fantasy: the "pure native." By its very nature, such a way of looking at Catawba culture and peoplehood cannot view change and adaptation as anything but corruption, dissolution, or "contamination." It does not allow the Catawba people to be people. People adapt and change, and to change is not to cease to exist. Colonialism and Mormonism both brought profound changes for Catawba people, to be sure, but that did not mean they stopped being Catawba.[4]

Speck's way of thinking was, of course, very common among anthropologists and many other Europeans and Americans during the nineteenth and twentieth centuries, and similar conceptions continue to shape and inform ideas about Native identity today. But some scholars have proposed other models for thinking about culture and Indigeneity that are premised on the idea that culture is dynamic, that people adapt to their circumstances—including religious conversion—and that change is a part of being Native.[5] One example, focusing on Mormonism in an Indigenous setting, is Hokulani Aikau's work *A Chosen People, A Promised Land: Mormonism and Race in Hawai'i*. While not uncritical of the influence of Mormonism in Hawai'i, Aikau demonstrates that, for better or worse, Mormonism has become a profound part of many Hawaiians' lives and family histories. In a very real sense, then, one cannot write about what it means to be Hawaiian, for many Hawaiians, without addressing and taking into account Mormonism and its influence on Hawaiian Indigeneity. And Aikau argues this point from the position of an explicitly *Hawaiian* epistemology:

> Within a Hawaiian worldview we cannot move forward if we do not know where we came from. Thus the path ahead in many ways is dictated by how well we know the paths already traveled. For [many Hawaiians], a critical aspect of the path already traveled includes the LDS Church and its history in Hawai'i.[6]

Similarly for people from Catawba: whether actively involved in the Church today or not, for nearly every Catawba individual, their grandparents or cousins or tribal leaders are or were affiliated or connected to Mormon institutions in some way. It is part of the path they, as a people, have traveled, and for many, it is the path they are on. For many, it profoundly influences what it means to be Catawba.

But if Catawba people tend to view the advent of Mormonism among them in rather different terms than Speck, some Catawba people also view Mormonism as something that came to replace something that was lost. As one Catawba woman explained: "We were kind of lookin', because we had lost our tribal religion—it had been lost early on ... And then the Mormon missionaries came to the area and they were accepted by the Catawbas."[7] Some view the arrival of the Mormons as providential, even foretold. Prominent Catawba leader Samuel Taylor Blue is remembered as saying that the missionaries brought a book that was "a direct history of our forefather, which we had no other history of before this book came along."[8] In other words, Mormon missionaries restored to them something that was already theirs—their own history, in the Book of Mormon. Some Catawba people believe that, had it not been for the cohesive force of Mormon community and leadership, the Catawba people may not have survived the challenges of the late nineteenth and early twentieth centuries. As a group of Catawbas told a group of other Christians who proposed to build them a church on the reservation, after the Mormons had come: "We have found what we have been looking for!"[9]

What follows is an ethnographic and historical portrait of Mormonism among Catawba people, based on historical research and ethnographic field-work conducted in the Catawba Indian Nation and among Western Catawba descendants between 2012–2015. It is a partial portrait, since I did not talk to and cannot represent everyone, and some Catawba families are more repre-sented than others. This is the nature of ethnography; "partial truths," as James Clifford put it.[10] While many Catawba people may not see themselves or their conception of what it means to be Catawba represented here, I have done my best to represent those I did have the opportunity to interact with. This chapter is based off a chapter in my dissertation, "The Blood of Father Lehi: The Book of Mormon and Indigenous Peoples."[11]

Mormon Missionaries and the Catawba Nation Branch

The latter half of the nineteenth century, prior to the encounter of the Catawba people with Mormon missionaries, had been a time of great uncertainty and many hardships for the Catawba people. In the 1840 Treaty of Nation Ford the state of South Carolina dissolved the Catawba homeland with a guarantee of an equivalent plot of land in the mountains of North Carolina, away from the encroachment of white settlers. When the state of North Carolina refused to negotiate these terms, the Catawba people were left without any title to ter-ritory. Some took up residence with the Eastern Cherokees in western North Carolina; others scattered elsewhere.[12] A few returned to South Carolina and were able to secure a small, one-square-mile plot of land, held in trust by the state as a reservation, on which, by most accounts, they were barely able to eke out a subsistence. By the 1870s and 1880s many returned from their sojourn in North Carolina and coalesced around this small area near Rock Hill, South Carolina—the site of the current reservation and Nation headquarters.[13]

The first Mormon missionaries known to enter the Catawba Nation did so shortly after this, in May of 1883. One of these missionaries noted, "We have been to see a remnant of a tribe of Indians called the Catawba Indians." The term "remnant" was used frequently in Mormon writings to refer to Indige-nous Peoples as a remnant of ancient Israel—a belief based in the Book of

Mormon, which describes Indigenous Peoples as Israelites, or "Lamanites," who sailed to the Americas—but here it seems to refer to the depleted condition of this once populous and powerful nation. Robison, one of the missionaries, wrote that "they are almost run out and badly mixed with the whites," but also noted that "they seem very taken with us." In October of that year two Mormon elders preached to a crowd of 50 Catawba people who invited them to return. Two weeks later James Patterson was the first Catawba individual to apply for baptism and about a month later four more applied and all were baptized in the Catawba River.[14] Shortly after that more were baptized, including several prominent tribal members, whose example led others to follow suit.[15] Just over a year after the missionaries' initial arrival, missionary Joseph Willey noted in his journal: "We organized a Branch of The Church of Jesus Christ of Later Day Saints [sic] and set Bro. James Patterson apart to Preside over the Branch ... The Saints numbered 31 in all, 25 of the number was Lamanites." ("Lamanite" is a Book of Mormon term that many Latter-day Saints use to refer to Indigenous Peoples of the Western Hemisphere.) Willey also noted that "The Indians called us there [sic] preachers and the white people called us the Indian preachers."[16]

Mormon missionaries faced violent opposition throughout much of the South during this period—including in York County, South Carolina—due largely to the Mormon practice of polygamy and the perceived threat it posed to Southern womanhood—as conceived of and protected by Southern chivalry—as well as general nativist distrust of outsiders.[17] Many in the Catawba Nation today recount stories about their grandparents who hid missionaries in their homes or helped them hide in the woods and swamps to protect them from mob violence.

The opposition to Mormon missionaries became so violent in the region that in November of 1884 the Rock Hill Branch was temporarily disbanded and the missionaries along with 22 Catawba Church members relocated to the farm of Mormon Church member James Russell in Spartansburg, South Carolina, about 63 miles west of Rock Hill. Several Catawba converts also migrated to Utah beginning in 1884.[18] But a few months later most of the Catawba people had returned to their homes, though threats of mob violence against the missionaries did not cease. At its height one missionary was shot and wounded while his companion was captured, stripped, and whipped. Nevertheless, the missionaries persisted and on August 2, 1885, missionaries organized the Catawba Nation Branch—a Mormon congregation—and set apart Alonzo Canty as branch president. Historian Jerry Lee claims this "was the first Indian Branch of the Church to be staffed entirely by Indians."[19] Several current Catawba Ward members tout the Catawba Ward as the longest continually meeting Lamanite unit in the Church.[20] By 1887 three quarters of the Catawba people identified with the Mormon Church.[21] In 1885 two Catawba men, Pinkney Head and Alonzo Canty, were sent as missionaries to preach "among the Cherokee Lamintes [sic] in North Carolina."[22] It apparently did not take long for Catawba converts to accept and to implement Mormon terms, such as *Lamanite*, in reference to themselves and other Indigenous Peoples.

The Western Catawba

All of this occurred while Southern States Mission president John Morgan was leading a mass exodus of Mormon converts out of the South to settle in the San Luis Valley of Colorado. By 1885 Morgan had become aware of the Catawba people and their conversion to Mormonism and began making plans to migrate the entire group as part of the Mormon gathering and settlement in the West.[23] He noted in a letter to Church president John Taylor:

> Among those that the Elders have come in contact with are the remanents of the once numerous and powerful Catawha [sic] tribe of Indians now numbering only 93 souls, they live on a reservation, consisting of 660 acres of land, and receive an annuity of $800.00 per annum from the state of South Carolina.

He indicated that "about two thirds of the tribe have embraced the Gospel, with very fair prospects of all or nearly all being baptized" and informed him of his plans to relocate the entire tribe to the West: "At the coming session of the Legislature we shall endeavor to secure an act, empowering them to sell their land, with a view of gathering them out to the appointed gathering place."[24]

Morgan's plan to arrange the sale of Catawba land never came to fruition, and neither did his plan to relocate the entire group en masse. But several Catawba families and individuals did make their way west. Lewis Scaife indicates that "a few" Catawba families relocated to Utah as early as 1884, and a Church publication in 1905 indicated that of the 26 Catawba people living on the Catawba

Reservation, 38 had migrated west.[25] Prior to the arrival of the anticipated Catawba migrants to the San Luis Valley in Southern Colorado, mission president John Morgan expressed some concern about settling the Catawba Saints in the San Luis Valley, due to its harsh climate. "We feel at some loss where to counsel them to gather," Morgan wrote to Church president John Taylor seeking advice. "They come from a comparatively warm climate, and this high, cold, valley may not be the most appropriate place for them to come to."[26] Taylor apparently recommended trying to settle them in Arizona Territory; Morgan replied that "acting on your counsel we have written Pres. H. C. Rogers of Maricopa Stake for information as to the feasibility of locating our Catawba brethren in that section."[27] Morgan received a positive reply from the president of the Maricopa Stake, regarding the settlement of Catawba people there, but the Catawba Saints wanted to go to Colorado.[28] As Morgan indicated in a follow-up letter to Taylor,

> We have consulted with our Catawba brethren, relative to their location, and find them very much in favor of going to Colo. in preference to any other location, and find that it will require positive counsel, to cause them to go elsewhere: under the circumstances we deem it prudent to allow those that go with this company to go there, and try it. Should they not be pleased, we can then transfer them to some other locality.[29]

The core group of Catawba emigrants whose descendants have come to be known as the Western Catawba began with the five families that emigrated with John Morgan's Southern States Mission migration to the San Luis Valley in Colorado between 1886 and 1890. They have come to be known among many of their descendants as *the* Five Families. These included the families of James and Elizabeth M. White Patterson, Pinkney and Martha J. (Patterson) Chappel Head, John Alonzo and Georgia H. Patterson Canty, Hillery and Rachel Tims Harris, and Alexander and Sarah Head Tims. Western Catawba genealogist Judy Canty Martin has determined that this group consisted of approximately twenty-six individuals.[30] In addition to these five, at least two other families who subsequently migrated have joined to some extent the network of people who identify or are identified as Western Catawba. Most Western Catawba people can trace their ancestry to one of these individuals, and the names Canty, Head, and Harris continue to be prominent among them. Though these Catawba families had set out to build a new life with the Saints in the West, some of them continued to maintain ties with the Catawba Nation and the state of South Carolina and they continued to identify as Catawba and as Indigenous. However, as historian Mikaela Adams explains, "their geographical distance from the core Catawba community in South Carolina eventually called into question their rights as tribal citizens" and eventually led to a loss of citizenship in the Catawba Nation.[31] This was a complicated process, and a detailed account of it is beyond the scope of this paper, but this distinction between enrollment and nonenrollment is a major issue that divides citizens of the Catawba Indian Nation from Western Catawba descendants.[32]

Catawba settlers in the San Luis Valley initially settled in a town they called Manasa, presumably after the biblical Jacob's son Manasseh (one of the other early Mormon settlements in the valley was Ephraim), a name that holds scriptural significance in Mormon ideology and is often associated with Indigenous Peoples (more on this below)—but most of them shortly after moved a few miles north to Sanford, Colorado. While they seem to have successfully established themselves in the community, one Western Catawba individual recalled that this "was a pretty contentious place. They had the Danish and the English [Southerners] that didn't get along, and … my Indians, you know … they're really in trouble [laughs], cause they're not white."[33] Perhaps at least in part due to these circumstances, many of them did not stay long but ranged out into other parts of the valley to establish homes, and gradually some began to leave the San Luis Valley. In 1903 the family of Pinkney Head and Martha Patterson Head loaded a "prairie schooner" and moved south to New Mexico Territory, where they established a small farm in the recently incorporated town of Farmington, near the Mormon settlement of Kirtland and right on the eastern edge of the Navajo Nation.[34]

Today only a few Western Catawba families remain in the San Luis Valley. Many live in New Mexico, Utah, Idaho, Montana, and other parts of Colorado, among other places. Many are still actively involved in the Mormon Church, while others have joined other Christian denominations or left organized religion altogether. They intermarried with white and Chicanx populations, the latter of whom often faced discrimination, not only as Indian but as Mexican or Chicanx. Some members of the Garcia family, descendants of James and Martha Head Patterson, changed their name to Garce, hoping that would protect them from discrimination, and one individual took his mother's Catawba maiden name to try to avoid discrimination. Those who intermarried with white settlers have often found themselves in an ambiguous ethnic position. Judy Canty Martin described this feeling of racial and ethnic ambiguity: "I'm not white enough to be white and I'm not Indian enough to be Indian."

But if the San Luis Valley lacked a racial category for people like Judy Canty Martin to fit into, and if her ancestors' migration from the nation called her Catawba identity into question, Mormonism provided Indigenous categories she could identify with. When asked what it means "to be Catawba or not Catawba," she replied, "My patriarchal blessing says I am of the lineage of Manasseh, so I just took it at that ... and I've always considered myself Indian." In the Book of Mormon, the prophet Lehi—whom many Mormons believe to be the common ancestor of Indigenous Peoples of the Americas—is described as being from the lineage of Manasseh, and as a result Manasseh has become strongly associated with Indigenous Americans.[35] Hence, because she was revealed to be of the lineage of Manasseh, she felt confirmed in her identity as American Indian.

The patriarch who gave Judy Canty Martin this blessing was William "Buck" Canty, a descendant of John Alonzo Canty, one of the original Five Families migrants who settled in the San Luis Valley. As Canty Martin explained, the nickname "Buck" began as a racial slur, but he adopted it and it became how he was generally known. He became a respected member of San Luis Valley communities and well-known in the LDS Church as the "first Lamanite patriarch." Patriarch is a priesthood office in the LDS Church, assigned typically to an elderly man in each local area who fulfills the special function of giving "patriarchal blessings," which, in addition to providing counsel and a basic blueprint for one's spiritual life, also declares one's Israelite identity. Patriarchs are typically highly esteemed members of local LDS communities, considered to be spiritually mature individuals who can receive revelation on the behalf of others. In addition to giving over a thousand patriarchal blessings in the San Luis Valley and perhaps beyond, Canty was often invited to speak at Lamanite youth conferences and other gatherings of Native American Latter-day Saints, "urging the young Indians to be proud of their Lamanite heritage."[36] In this way, Canty became a strong and visible symbol of Lamanite presence and leadership in the San Luis Valley and in wider Latter-day Saint Native communities.

In 1978 Canty and his wife toured Europe as "spiritual leaders" with a Native performance group from Brigham Young University known as Lamanite Generation. At some point in connection with this tour, Canty was presented with a Plains Indian–style headdress by John Maestas (Taos Pueblo), director of the BYU Indian Education Department, on behalf of another BYU Indian organization known as the Tribe of Many Feathers. At the conclusion of the tour and after returning home, Canty wore this headdress and "other articles of tribal regalia" during the annual 24th of July pageant (Mormon Pioneer Day) held in his hometown of Sanford, Colorado.[37] In doing so, he was continuing a long-standing tradition; pictures of Canty as a young man depict him riding in town parades bedecked in a full-length headdress and Navajo blanket.[38] While Western Catawba people of younger generations, often children of interracial marriages, such as Judy Canty Martin, have sometimes faced an uphill battle gaining recognition as Native American, members of their parents' and grand-parents' generations were much more visibly recognized and celebrated as American Indian people. In the case of William "Buck" Canty, celebration of his status as the first Lamanite patriarch and material symbols of Indianness, such as a Plains-style headdress, mixed and reinforced one another.

Kyle Canty, a direct descendant of William Canty, explained that he attributes much of his own awareness of his Catawba identity and heritage, and his San Luis Valley neighbors' awareness of it, to the high esteem his father and grandfather held in the valley.[39] "I am living on the benefits of my dad and my grandpa, and uncle Pete," individuals who were well-known and generally liked in the valley communities, Canty explained. "We ride the wave on that." He and other Western Catawba people I have met seem less certain, however, as I interpreted it, about the degree to which riding that wave will be possible for succeeding generations who become increasingly less recognizably Native and generationally more removed from such visual symbols of Lamanite and American Indian identity, such as Buck Canty and Elbert Garce.

The Catawba Nation

Among those who remained in the Catawba Nation in the Southeast, affiliation with Mormonism continued to grow.[40] By 1900 there were approximately 125 members of the Catawba Nation LDS Branch and by 1912 there were 166 baptized members, the majority of whom were citizens of the Catawba Nation (the branch has probably always included some non-Catawba people). This constituted about three-fourths of the tribe at the time.[41] Missionary instruction also included education; missionaries began teaching reading and spelling to Catawba children as early as 1888, and in 1890 the Church assigned full-time teaching missionaries as teachers. Though they did face some competition from others—including a Presbyterian school from 1896–1905—Mormons for the most part conducted the formal schooling of many Catawba children until 1943 when the Bureau of Indian Affairs established a school for Catawba children.[42] Today most Catawba children attend public school, including a Head Start elementary school located within the Catawba Nation.

The Five Families who migrated to Colorado in the 1890s and others who migrated before that were not the only ones to migrate west. Several nation members relocated to the West as well. If they left after their family names were recorded on the 1943 roll, they were able to retain citizenship in the nation. For example, in 1956, just after being released as branch president of the Catwaba LDS Ward, William Watts moved his family to Salt Lake City, and his children and grandchildren continue to reside in Utah and the West as enrolled members of the nation. John Beck, also an enrolled Catawba citizen, lives in Salt Lake Valley as well and is a director of LDS Institute courses in Salt Lake City.[43] In 1961, as indicated by the final termination roll, there were fourteen enrolled Catawba citizens living in Utah and five in Colorado. That number has fluctuated and generally increased since then, as Catawba citizens have moved to Utah to attend Brigham Young University, the LDS Business College, or for other opportunities. While for many this is a temporary move, several Catawba families have opted to stay there. And while motivations for leaving are varied, the LDS Church has been a major factor motivating travel and relocation of many Catawba people to Utah and other parts of the West. Even among those who stay in the South, many have family, business, or personal connections to Utah. But a core has always remained in close proximity to the nation's territorial land base. Today there are Catawba Nation citizens throughout the United States. Still, the vast majority are located in York County, South Carolina, and surrounding counties, within what is referred to as the nation's "service area," for whom the benefits of full tribal services are available.

The nation expanded its tribal land base in 1943 when the state of South Carolina allocated $75,000 for the purchase of additional tax-exempt lands. The expansion, which included a 3,482.8-acre tract of land, became known as the "New Reservation," which was placed in federal trust and administered by the BIA. This section was broken up into allotments and either assigned to tribal members in severalty or sold when the tribe was terminated in 1962—at the instigation of Utah senator and prominent Mormon Arthur Watkins ("God rest his soul," one Catawba man said of him). A 135-acre parcel was placed in trust of the Mormon Church for the Catawba Ward and a ward farm, placing the Church in the peculiar quasi-governmental position as something like a "ward" to the Catawba people, in terms of holding a portion of tribal property in trust for them. The 630-acre "Old Reservation," however, continued to be held in trust by the state of South Carolina and administered as a state reservation.[44]

Explaining Catawba Conversion

Several explanations have been put forward to explain why the Catawba people embraced Mormonism, both by Catawbas themselves and by observers. Anthropologist Charles Hudson, who conducted fieldwork in the Catawba Nation in the early 1960s, suggested that, at least in part, Catawbas converted to "bolster ... their distinctiveness" after "their culture was almost defunct." Hudson believes that Mormonism provided them with "a source of alternative values" and racial distinction. "At a time when they were becoming physically and culturally like whites," Hudson explains, Mormonism "set them apart from whites, mestizos, and Negroes and made them feel they were in some sense a chosen people." Based on his fieldwork, Hudson constructed four "dominant themes in the Catawba view of their own history": "(1) the belief that they are descended from 'Lamanites'; (2) the belief that they were too friendly toward the white colonists; (3) the belief that Mormon missionaries were the first Christians who helped them; and (4) the belief that they have progressed" (as opposed to the dominant outside local belief that they have declined). Hudson suggested that conversion to Mormonism repositioned their more diffuse relationship of conflict with neighboring whites in terms of religious conflict, which, he points out, is socially acceptable as "part of the ideological fabric of American society." He points out that Mormon affiliation and Lamanite identity served to bolster claims of distinctiveness from African Americans. Hudson noted a strong denial, during his fieldwork in the late 1950s and early '60s, of any intermarriage or sexual "admixture" with African Americans. In the context of the early and mid-twentieth-century South, where being categorized as "colored" or "Negro" brought significant political and social disadvantages, the strategic reasons for articulating such a distinction are obvious. While these motivations are not limited to Mormonism, Church teachings served to bolster this distinction and antipathy toward the idea of intermarriage with African American people, as has been noted by others and is reflected in early twentieth-century Church publications.[45] Related to each of these formative influences, Hudson states that in Catawba "folk history," the coming of the Mormon missionaries "is perhaps the most crucial single event in their past."[46]

In Church meetings and other gatherings, Catawba Latter-day Saints frequently recount the coming of the first Mormon missionaries, the persecution they faced, and Catawba efforts to protect them from their violent neighbors by hiding them and helping then sneak in and out of the nation. In a sense, this inaugural moment in modern Catawba history and collective memory seems to serve as something of an ethnogenesis narrative: *this is how we, as Mormon Catawbas, came to be.* There are other narratives. The river, for example, is a strong symbol of ethnogenesis. The Catawba people are, in their own tongue, the *Iswa*, the "people of the river." Catawba pottery, shaped from clay dug from the banks of the river, shaped by the people of the river, and burned in Catawba soil, is also a strong symbol of Catawba identity. But when asked about Mormonism in the Catawba Nation, the story typically begins with passed-down memories of Catawba ancestors hiding Mormon missionaries in their homes to protect them from their angry and violent neighbors. Many people recount stories of their grandparents who hid the missionaries or gave them their bed to sleep in. (For example, Travis Blue remembers learning that his grandfather gave the missionaries his bed as he went out into the woods to sleep.) As far as Mormonism in Catawba is concerned, that is where the story typically begins.

In this sense, Mormonism in Catawba is again similar to how Mormonism has been incorporated into other Indigenous communities. Hokulani Aikau explains how prominent early Mormon missionaries such as George Q. Cannon and Joseph F. Smith have been remembered in Hawaiian-LDS oral tradition and even counted among the *kupuna*, the ancestors, of some Hawaiian Latter-day Saint communities.[47] While I have not heard Catawba individuals refer to the early missionaries as ancestors or as kin, they are remembered and invoked, sometimes by name but more often as "the missionaries" or "the elders," as crucial figures in Catawba community history.

But if the coming-of-the-missionaries might be read, in a limited sense, as a moment of Catawba Latter-day Saint ethnogenesis, it is also narrated as a compensation for or restoration of something lost through the Catawba encounter and experience of colonialism. As one Catawba woman told me, "We were kind of lookin', because we had lost our tribal religion—it had been lost early on … And then the Mormon missionaries came to the area and they were accepted by the Catawbas." She pointed out similarities between Catwaba traditional beliefs and practices and Mormonism, practices such as prayer and blessing by the laying on of hands. "We believe in giving blessings. That was one thing, I think, that the people were looking for—something that was similar to what they believed in. And so they found it in the Latter-day Saints." Similarly, respected Catawba elder Sarah Ayers is quoted as saying that "the early Catawbas were 'just waiting for the true Church before they were baptized,'" and that "the Church is just a way of life for us."[48]

The Book of Mormon is often pointed to as a major reason for Catawba acceptance of the missionaries' message. According to a local reporter in 1985, "Bishop [Carson] Blue said the Indians' gravitation toward the Mormon faith is natural. 'It's the only church that tells the Indians where they come from and who they are,' he said. 'For the Indians, it just tells the truth about themselves.'"[49] Former Chief Donald Rodgers explained that the Book of Mormon told the Catawba people where they came from, which was different from anthropological theories that told them they came across a land bridge. He explained that they began to see how the Book of Mormon was similar to and worked with their own traditions. In a Sunday school class a Catawba woman mentioned at the end of her lesson on pioneers that Chief Sam Blue was a "pioneer in our own area." She explained how Chief Blue told the Catawba people to embrace the Book of Mormon as a record of their ancestors. An audience member raised her hand and commented that at this time everyone disrespected Indians and called them savages, but Heavenly Father was aware of them and knew who they were. The implication seemed to be that the Book of Mormon gave the Catawba people a venerable identity, one that their neighbors were ignorant of and disrespected, but God knew who they were and revealed it to them through the Book of Mormon.

Church and Tribe

Charles Hudson, who conducted his fieldwork immediately following termination[50] in the early 1960s, stated, "At the time of my field work the two things that still served to hold the Catawbas together—albeit tenuously—were the Old Reservation and the Mormon church." The Old Reservation, which refers to the 630-acre state reservation, provided several tribal members with a place to live and provided others with a place of security. (It also provided them with state trust land and the maintenance of state recognition.) The Church, he explained, provided an "important social bond," though even then it was not as strong as it once had been, since the ward had been split.[51] As one Catawba citizen told me, he doesn't believe the nation could have survived the challenges of the late-nineteenth and the twentieth centuries without the cohesive strength of the Mormon Church holding the people together.

The close correlation between Church and tribe in the Catawba Nation is demonstrated by corrected slips of the tongue in interviews. One Catawba citizen, for example, stated that her father "served as bishop for the tribe, or—*for the tribe!*—for the *church*", and another described how his grandfather's role as chief gave him a "sense of pride that I'm a member of the church—or member of the *tribe*, and the church." Since the same person can and often does serve in both roles, as a religious leader and tribal leader, over the course of their life or even simultaneously, it can be hard to keep the two cognitively separate. Through linguistic slip, the two are often articulated together.

Another element that demonstrates the entanglement of Church and tribe are the prayers that open tribal meetings and other official functions. During a tribal council meeting demonstration held for a group of Catawba children at the Catawba Cultural Center, one of the executive committee members, whom I recognized from the Catawba LDS Ward, was called upon to open the meeting by offering an opening prayer. The prayer sounded very much like one you would hear at Church, addressed to Heavenly Father and closed "in the name of Jesus Christ," though also with reference to paths laid down by others and paths for little ones to follow. While sometimes these prayers vary, depending on who gives them, the prevalence of Latter-day Saints in the tribe means that the prayers often sound like prayers one would hear in LDS worship services.[52]

Tribal leaders are often prominent Church members and leaders as well. As Jerry Lee points out, every Catawba chief from William George, who was chief at the time the missionaries first came, until Albert Sanders, who was chief at termination (1877–1886), were members of the LDS Church. When the tribe was restored after the settlement, Chief Gilbert Blue, the grandson of Samuel Taylor Blue, was a prominent Church member. He was followed by Donald

Rodgers, also an active Mormon. The current chief when I conducted field work, Chief William Harris was reportedly raised Mormon, but his involvement in the LDS Church was not apparent to me or most I talked to on the matter. As for many in the Catawba Nation, lack of attendance does not automatically cancel out a sense of belonging, or at least connection, in some way or another, to Mormonism. One Catawba man who has left the church—or has been trying to leave it—told me, quite adamantly: I am *not* a Lamanite and I am *not* from the tribe of Manasseh. But the fact that he had to emphatically declare this in an effort to break that link demonstrates just how strong the association has become connecting Catawba people to Mormonism and the Book of Mormon.

Chief Samuel Taylor Blue

For many Catawba people, Chief Samuel Taylor Blue (c.1872–1959)—often referred to as Chief Sam Blue or simply as Chief Blue—looms large as a symbol of the relationship between the Catawba Nation and the Mormon Church. So large, in fact, that some people remember him as being chief at the time the first Mormon missionaries came—an impressive feat since he would have been about 10 years old at the time. But he was old enough to remember when the first missionaries came and he reportedly told stories about helping missionaries sneak in and out of the nation when he was a child and young man. One Church publication recalled that "during the days of persecution, he had carried the missionaries across the river on his back to protect them from the mobs."[53]

Blue became chief of the Catawba Nation in the early 1930s and served during most of that decade and intermittently in that capacity several times over the course of his life.[54] He also served as president of the Catawba Branch and as a respected elder and leader both in the Church and the Catawba Nation, which were not easily distinguishable to many. While he has not always been regarded in quite the same light by all Nation members, he is probably the most prominent single figure in the history of the modern Catawba Nation and is highly esteemed by his descendants and many other Nation members to this day. He was also quite well known outside of the Catawba Nation among the local community and in the Church, and continues to be to a significant extent. This is particularly true in the LDS Church. In 1950 he and his wife, Louisa, traveled to Salt Lake City to attend general conference and to be sealed in the temple.

While there, Blue was spontaneously called upon to speak in the conference before the general body of the Church—an event that is not only remembered but still held in digital copy by some of his descendants (I watched a recording of Chief Blue's talk at the home of Travis Blue, a great-grandson).

A good example of Chief Blue's legacy among his descendants and in the LDS Church is the way his great-great-grandson, Matt Burris, describes him. "When it comes to the tribe and the church," Burris explained, "I always think of him ... because he was a very good example, as a member of the church and a member of the tribe." In Burris's memory of the Catawba past, from the stories he's been told, the years that his great-great-grandfather served as chief were something like a golden era of Catawba history. "During his time, he was chief, ninety-nine or even a hundred percent of the tribe were members of the church.... and at the time," Burris shared his opinion, "there was kind of a big happiness in the tribe, there weren't any problems or things like that." Burris tied this period of perfect Church attendance to a scriptural promise he recalls from the Book of Enos in the Book of Mormon about the Lamanite people: "there was a promise that if they obeyed the commandments they would blossom like a rose into a beautiful—beautiful people. And ... at the time when my great-great-grandpa was chief, the people were following the commandments and doing what they were supposed to, and they were a beautiful people." Burris contrasted this with the present. "Now, very sadly, it's the opposite. The majority of the tribe aren't members, and if they are members they don't come to church. There's a very big problem with inactive members in the tribe right now." Burris also seemed to imply that the tribe is also politically less united than he imagines it was then. He spoke of conflicts and divisions within the tribe and of his own extended family's withdrawal from politics after his grandfather and other relatives resigned from their positions in tribal leadership. While several members of the Blue family have withdrawn from formal politics, they remain active in the LDS Church and find family solidarity there.

Burris in fact carried his great-great-grandfather's legacy with him on his LDS mission to Chile. He also found that, much to his surprise, parts of that legacy were already there, and he also, quite literally, carried part of it back home with him. There is a story about Chief Blue that has achieved some level of prominence and familiarity among some Church members by being included in a number of Church publications.[55] Burris carried a copy of the story with him on his mission and used it in his teachings, only to discover that his mission president was already familiar with it. Burris described feeling shocked that this man who had spent his entire life in Argentina had heard of Catawbas and of Chief Blue. The mission president had the story translated into Spanish, distributed it to the mission, and referred to it in his talks. Thus, Chief Blue and Catawba Mormonism became part of the Mormon missionary curriculum in Chile. Further, Burris described connecting with Indigenous Peoples in Chile when they discovered that he was Native American; he said that many Chileans, particularly those of the Mapuche Tribe, identified as Lamanites, an Indigenous Mormon identity that also linked them, since Burris identifies the Catawba people as Lamanites. Before leaving the mission, he had a special leather case made for his scriptures with two images burned into it, based on prints he had brought with him. On one side is a depiction of the Book of Mormon character Enos, known for his long and soul-wrenching prayer for the descendants of the Lamanite people. On the other side is an image of his great-great-grandfather, Chief Blue. Thus, holding together his scriptures, like two bookends, is a Nephite prophet praying for the welfare of the future Lamanites, and the Latter-day Lamanite Catawba Chief Samuel Taylor Blue, quite literally now a part of the Book of Mormon, burned into the cover of his great-great-grandson's missionary scriptures.

Catawba "Pride Cycle": Reading Catawba History through the Book of Mormon

A cycle emerges from the Book of Mormon that has become popularly known as "the pride cycle." Though that phrase does not appear in the Book of Mormon, it was popularized through a Church video made in 1995 and shown as part of the standard curriculum in Church seminary and Sunday school classes, and probably predates that. It has become part of the standard Mormon parlance. A diagram illustrating this cycle, published as an appendix to the Church-produced *Book of Mormon Student Manual*, reveals five stages of that cycle: 1. blessings and prosperity are followed by 2. pride and wickedness which leads to 3. warning by prophecy which, when rejected, leads to 4. destruction and suffering, resulting in 5. humility and repentance, which leads back to number one. The manual describes this as "a recurring cycle that underlies the rise and fall of nations as well as individuals," revealed by the Book of Mormon.

Ultimately, as the Book of Mormon teaches, it was pride that led to the over-throw of the Nephites, a fact reiterated by Joseph Smith's later revelations and by more recent prophets who quote the warning: "beware of pride, lest ye become as the Nephites of old."[56]

Some Catawba Latter-day Saints feel they can see a "pride cycle" at play in the history of the Catawba people. For example, one person explained that her father felt that:

> When you see the pride cycle that's referred to in the Book of Mormon, of people getting closer to Heavenly Father when things are maybe not going so great, and then when things do start going well then they allow themselves to have other influences enter in because they feel like things are going well now—he really likened that to the tribe and how, through the ups and downs of the tribe, throughout its history, there were times when things weren't going well and the people really pulled together and came closer to Heavenly Father and closer to the church, had more attending church and a better feeling at church; and then when things were going well, then other things entered in like jealousy and money and greed, and it affected how people lived their lives and it affected the spirituality of the people as a whole, and some even fell away from church because of things they saw other church members doing within the tribe. The tribal government itself. So he always felt like the history of the church correlated. Or he could see a lot of that pride cycle in the people here.[57]

This individual was hesitant to say she saw that cycle clearly at play, explaining that it is harder to really pin down now because there are a lot of tribal members attending other churches, if they even attend church. She identifies this as a fairly new development, even within her own life. As she explained, "it used to be a lot more centralized where ... all the tribal members that were church members were all going to Catawba Ward, for the most part." However, as more Latter-day Saints have moved into the surrounding area, wards and meeting-houses have proliferated and the geographical boundaries have shrunk. As more and more people have moved out from the reservation and immediate vicinity, it now means they attend different wards on those communities. The Catawba Ward has also been split and is now attended by as many or more non-Catawbas as Catawbas. Some Catawba people recall those good old days when it was nearly the entire Catawba community gathered together as one each Sunday for Church meetings. Church meeting was a tribal gathering then. However, as the ward has split, nontribal members have moved in, and many Catawba people have begun attending other wards, the de facto Catawba-Mormon congregation became fragmented, and as a result many stopped attending. When the Church body no longer correlated with the tribal body, it seems to have lost its appeal for many Catawba people.

But if the individual mentioned above was hesitant to impose the pride cycle onto Catawba history as a model with perfect explanatory force, she did identify the events surrounding the 1993 settlement as a moment when the pride cycle seemed to become apparent, and used it as a template for understanding that political climate. She explained that in the late 1970s "the tribe had kind of come together ... especially the ones that felt they wanted to regain the federal recognition." That was the period of struggle and unity. However, when they were successful, and "once we received the settlement in 1993, there was a lot of money that came with that." And so, naturally, with prosperity there came divisions. "You have this group of people who kind of have control over this fifty million dollars, and how it's spent, and then you have these people that are on the outside who think they know how the money should be spent or not spent, and it just ... there became a lot of fighting between the two groups." She explained that "there were people in both of those groups who were church members, so, it affected a lot of things, not just for the tribe but at church." Some people stopped attending Church. "So it really affected a lot of people, and from what I understand, it's even caused some barriers for missionaries even until today, because ... they'll say, 'Well, I'm not going there because so-and-so spent all the tribe's money.' ... after all these years, it's still causing barriers to getting people to come back to church." While she felt it's still too early to tell if the settlement was a watershed moment for defining Church affiliations in the tribe, she did state that "I do feel like it was a little bit of a turning point, from what I can see at this point in our history."

Another person who used the Book of Mormon pride cycle to describe tribal politics stated that "Every time around elections the pride gets way up here [reaches above his head]. Everybody's better than everybody else. It's sad.... It's like you live among the Gadianton Robbers"[58] (conspiring characters in the Book of Mormon). Even this he explained as a possible fulfillment of the Book of Mormon, which states "that there's opposition in all things." "Maybe that's a part of the scriptures that some of these people held to." Though he also feels like the Book of Mormon provide an antidote: "But, I think that it's just, they need to partake of the blessings of the Book of Mormon. Because if they don't, then they see what happens. They see they are led away, led astray, and they don't live by the things that they need to do."

With the pride cycle reading by Catawba people, it becomes clear that the Book of Mormon is not just a narrative read onto Indigenous Peoples by white Mormons. Some Catawba people read their own history and community through the Book of Mormon and through Book of Mormon–inspired narrative models such as the pride cycle. The Book of Mormon is read onto Catawba history and Catawba history is read through the Book of Mormon. Not only, then, is the Book of Mormon taken to be a "history of the American Indians," but the history of the Catawba people is read to be an ongoing narrative extension of the Book of Mormon. Political factions become, in effect, the Nephites and the Lamanites. Periods of conflict are the natural result of straying from the God of the Book of Mormon. Catawbas are, in some readings at least, quite literally, a people of the book.

Conclusion: Linking East and West

So, I will tell you a little of the oral history that has been passed down.... I don't know about the truth of it, but it is what it is. It's as accurate as I remember it.... The story goes that Granddad Patterson ... was in the fields plowing ... This must have been in the 1870s ... He stopped his mule to rest and he went to sit under a tree. And as he was sitting there he saw two men approaching him, off in the distance. And he waited and waited ... and finally they got to him and they said, 'We want to show you that we have a history of your people.' And it was the Book of Mormon. And ... he threw open his arms and he said, 'Where have you been? We knew you were coming. We've been waiting for you.' And so, he received the missionaries, and received the lessons, and he wasn't the first Catawba to be baptized ... but Granddad Patterson was the first elder in the church. So, when the missionaries were there, there was a lot of persecution from other religious sects. And Granddad Patterson hid the missionaries in his cabin multiple times,

and fed them, and one time there was a mob that was coming for the mis-
sionaries, and he got the missionaries out and took them into the woods and
told them where to hide, and that kind of thing. But the first LDS services
were held in his cabin, there on the land. So, I don't know if it was . . . any
kind of a premonition for Granddad Patterson to join the church and then
to migrate . . . to be closer to the headquarters of the church—or not. But . . .
probably with religious freedom, and acceptance for being Lamanites, and
then being part of the church probably helped them direct their migration
movement to Colorado.[59]

I begin this concluding section with this passage from an interview with David
Garce, a Western Catawba descendent, because it encapsulates several themes
articulated by both Western Catawba descendants and citizens of the Catawba
Nation: passed-down memories of the persecuted first Mormon missionaries
to visit the Catawba and of Catawba ancestors hiding these missionaries from
their persecutors. In this version, their coming is not a surprise but something
anticipated by Catawba leaders. In this Western Catawba version it is Granddad
Patterson. In the Catawba Nation it is often Chief Blue who is remembered
in a similar position, as escort and protector of the missionaries. The above
passage also seeks to explain why the Western Catawba left, but it begins with
the coming of the missionaries. If, as I suggest above, we can think of this as a
pivotal moment in Catawba collective memory—as Lamanites, as Mormons,
as a Church-tribe entanglement that not every Catawba person totally agrees
with today, but every one of them feels the effect of—then this is something
shared by both citizens and descendants alike, east and west. Both have passed
down stories about the early missionaries who came and changed the way they
think about who they are—brought them a book to teach them (or remind
them, some would say) of who they are. It is a book many of them continue to
read, believe in, and use to articulate what it means to be Catawba and to be
Indigenous.

For some Western Catawba people, being a Catawba descendent and being
a descendant of Book of Mormon peoples becomes entangled and inseparable.
When I asked Thomas Croasman, a retired professor at Brigham Young University–Idaho and a Western Catawba descendant, what it means to be Catawba,
he replied, "Oh, it just means that that's our heritage, you know—the blood of
father Lehi flowing in my veins." That answer is twofold. On the one hand, it is

heritage. "Some people are glad that they're Italian, or glad that they're from England, or Ireland, or whatever, and that's fine. They should be. And we're just proud to be Catawba." For Croasman, as a nonenrolled descendent, Catawba descent is a national heritage, much like that of migrants from other nations overseas (you might say he's Catawba-American). It is also something he carries in his veins: "the blood of father Lehi."

David Garce, a Western Catawba descendant of James Patterson, also sees Book of Mormon identity as a more expansive category to which Catawba people, east and west, do or can belong. When asked how Mormonism fits into the story of the Western Catawba, he replied,

> It sure fits in with Book of Mormon promises. And certainly the Cataw-bas were Lamanites, or descendants of Lamanites, and, as we know, the Book of Mormon was written for the Lamanites, and ... it's a story of our people ... Catawbas back in the Nation have done wonderful things as members of the church. And they're doing Christian things. And it's great. And I think, there's not a conflict, but there's a parallel track between what we're doing out here and they're doing back there. I think the religious part of it has something to do with our heritage, in that we can, we can almost claim blessings from the Book of Mormon, and our faithfulness to the gospel principles that are taught in the Book of Mormon.... But they seem to be not, not so much parallel with being Catawba, but rather being Lamanite. I don't know if that makes any sense or not.... So you can be a Catawba, for sure, and have all kinds of squabbles and disagreements and everything, but you can also be a Latter-day Saint who is a Lamanite and claim those blessings, and the pride of knowing that you are a descendant of Father Lehi, and all of the prophets that have come down from him.

This idea of a parallel track—that is, the idea that Eastern and Western Catawba have had a similar experience in their respective locations (the American Southeast and the American West, the Nation and diaspora)—is one that some Catawba Nation citizens articulate as well. And while the Western Catawba descendants, in diaspora, may face a very difficult task in trying to gain enrollment or recognition as Catawba, Lamanite identity is something that, in the minds of many Catawbas, links all of them to a much larger Indigeneity.

A spiritualized Indigeneity that is still, nonetheless, often located in the blood: "the blood of Father Lehi." If geography, nationalism, and politics divide them, Indigeneity and the "blood of Father Lehi" is still something that many of them, on both sides, believe they share. And while this is not a narrative that all Catawba people agree upon, for many it is a powerful and expansive shared Indigenous identity. For Thomas Croasman, to be Catawba is to have the blood of Father Lehi in your veins. Similarly, Sarah Ayers, late Catawba elder and master potter remembered by many in the Catawba Nation today, also felt the presence of Father Lehi. Speaking of her pottery she said, "I know who I'm representing with my work. I was once blessed that Father Lehi would help me in all endeavors that stand for the tribe in honor of our heritage."[60] Clay from the Catawba River shaped by hands guided by Father Lehi. The people of the river are a people of the book. They shape and are shaped by both.

7

Reclamation, Redemption, and Political Maneuvering in Diné Bikéyah, 1947–1980

ERIKA BSUMEK

On September 22, 1966, Secretary of the Interior Stewart Udall, First Lady Lady Bird Johnson, and Chairman of the Navajo Tribal Council Raymond Nakai, along with a host of other national and local politicians, attended the dedication of Glen Canyon Dam. At the beginning of the day's events, Udall proclaimed that the local surroundings featured "the most dramatic and spectacular part of Arizona." As the dedication ceremony wore on, it began to rival the dramatic scenery in terms of rhetoric and spectacle. Udall himself raised the stakes when he commented on the superlative aspects of the region's man-made and natural wonders. "We have right in our view the highest steel arch bridge in the world. We're standing on one of the highest dams of the world. And not to be satisfied with only a man-made arch, there is upstream about 50 miles from here the largest stone arch in the world, Rainbow Bridge."[1]

Lady Bird Johnson, taking the podium to dedicate the dam, was a bit more poetic but no less effusive. She claimed that the geographic area surrounding the dam was more than visually stunning, it also chronicled "eons of time laid bare" inscribed "on stone pages and in the treasure troves of Indian myths and arti-facts." Shifting her gaze from the past to the present, she noted that the new dam brought to light the important relationship between technology, conservation, spirituality, and recreation. "To me, the appealing genius of conservation is that it combines the energetic feats of technology—like this dam—with the gentle humility that leaves some corners of the earth untouched—alone—free of technology—to be a spiritual touchstone and a recreation asset." Johnson thought that the combination of natural and man-made wonders would inevitably make the rapidly filling reservoir "a magnet for tourists" and thus economically beneficial to all of the region's inhabitants.[2]

Elder Theodore Burton, one of the less well-known figures at the ceremony, represented The Church of Jesus Christ of Latter-day Saints (LDS or Mormons) at the event. He also remarked upon the ties between technology, commerce, and spirituality in his dedicatory prayer:

> Oh God, the Eternal Father, ... we thank Thee for this work which has been created. ... May the power that comes from the generators turn the wheels of industry to create new products ... and may the light which goes on in the homes ... of men be reflected in the light which comes into their eyes.[3]

Burton's comments reflected more than his own faith; they mirrored an entire set of local and national aspirations. The dam and its water storage capacity justified and reinforced the faith that Americans placed in technology. Thus, the ceremony celebrated more than the hope certain segments of society placed in the awe-inspiring 710-foot-high dam, the anticipation of more than 2,000 miles of shoreline the reservoir would create, or even the dam's capacity to generate 1.35 million kilowatts of electricity. Elder Burton's presence at the dam dedication, seated alongside a delegation of Navajo and white politicians, underscores connections between US Indian policy, reclamation, and Mormonism.

On the surface, the reclamation of water and the policy which was designed to terminate the federal government's trust responsibilities toward Native Americans appear to be completely separate policy initiatives. A deeper analysis reveals they were linked by a deeply ingrained belief system held by the key legislators and politicians who advocated for both policies as a way to spur regional growth, "uplift" Navajos from poverty, and solve what they referred to as "the Indian problem." Although both can be seen as part of longer historical trends associated with Indian assimilation, dispossession, and the domination of nature, they were also connected by the legislative efforts of regional politicians who saw them as complementary goals.

Drawing the connection between the two policies shows how and why Navajo Nation leaders were drawn into—and willingly engaged with—the era's political contests as they sought to establish their political influence in the region and foster economic opportunity for their constituency. Attempts to bring large-scale economic development schemes to the region led Navajo leaders, such as Sam Ahkeah, Paul Jones, and Raymond Nakai to support the Bureau of Reclamation's proposed Upper Colorado River Storage Project (UCRSP) and the construction of Glen Canyon Dam. The Tribal Council's decision to support the dam's construction in the early 1950s, reveals how and why some politically powerful Navajos found themselves aligned, however reluctantly, with key supporters of the federal policy of termination at a key moment when other Native American leaders and the National Congress of American Indians (NCAI) were actively fighting the policy and those white politicians who proposed it.[4]

Examining the links between water reclamation and the federal government's efforts to terminate its trust responsibilities toward Native American fills an important gap. Most scholars who have written about the Bureau of Reclamation in the 1950s haven generally delineated how the national political debates surrounding UCRSP explain either the evolution of American technical innovation or the rise of modern environmentalism.[5] Almost no attention has been paid to how the US Indian policy of termination and the Western water policy of reclamation were connected by a host of factors, including Western politics and the same core religious philosophies found in Mormonism. Indeed, some of the key backers of termination were LDS politicians who were also some of the most vocal supporters of the UCRSP. More importantly, arguments over regional economic development eventually spurred public discussions (and legal rulings) regarding what constituted a religion. Especially prominent in such debates were the questions of what (or who) was sacred in the landscape surrounding the dam and how different cultural definitions of "the sacred" would be valued. Ties between reclamation, termination, and religious freedom have gone almost completely unexplored in previous histories of the dam. A deeper look into the story of Navajos and Glen Canyon Dam demonstrates that religious ideology influenced regional economic development, governed ideas regarding natural resource uses, and shaped US Indian policy in unexpected and sometimes dramatic ways. LDS ideas of "redeeming the Lamanites" and "reclaiming the desert" were connected, not coincidental propositions. This essay explores the complex and intertwined history surrounding access to land and water, the expression and protection of religious freedom, and the political maneuvering that encompassed both on the Colorado Plateau.

Raymond Nakai, the Dam, and Economic Optimism

Although some speakers at the dedication of the dam paid tribute to God and feats of engineering at least one honored guest was thinking more about the region's Indigenous inhabitants than the vast concrete walls that now regulated the flow of the Colorado River. As Navajo Tribal chairman Raymond Nakai sat up on the podium listening to the others talk he was no doubt thinking of the speech he wrote to mark the occasion. In his prepared remarks, which ultimately Nakai would not get to deliver because other speakers exceeded their allotted time and the program organizers cut him from the program, Nakai had focused his attention on a question often posed to him by his Navajo constituents. When asked, "What has made our country great?" Nakai found himself inclined to answer, "personal and individual opportunity."[6] Yet, for many Navajos, that promise remained unrealized. Nakai had wanted to remind those present of resources more elusive to Indians than water, coal, natural gas, or oil: financial independence and economic opportunity. In a cruel irony, he was not given the opportunity to do so.

Still, as a firm believer in the American dream, Nakai thought that increased access to economic opportunities would eventually lead Navajos, like other Americans, to produce and consume more goods. More production and consumption would ultimately improve the quality of life for everyone, thereby strengthening the nation as a whole. "We are in this country ... untapping [sic] one of the greatest resources this continent possesses and that is the opportunity for all segments of our population to become ever more productive and in this way, provide ever more of the necessities and comforts of life for the greatest number of people."[7] Although Nakai thought that technology could spark consumerism—and consumerism had the power to transform society—he knew that such changes could easily be rendered meaningless without genuine social reform. While he did not speak for the entire tribe, he did represent a specific faction of the tribal council who wished to foster economic development to the reservation.

If in 1966 Nakai was unconvinced that the dam would bring a flood of opportunity to the reservation, he had become more hopeful about the tribe's overall economic prospects by the time the reservoir filled up. In 1969, while speaking at the Lake Powell reservoir dedication, Nakai reflected on the ties between water, nature, and jobs. Nakai noted that as an amateur photographer, he had spent many a weekend capturing images of "some of the beauties of the remote areas of the reservation." As a result of these excursions, he had become convinced that Lake Powell would enhance the grandeur of the region more than detract from it. "No one deliberately took it upon himself to destroy the beauty of this area thoughtlessly, and no one can say that this 'Jewel of the Colorado,' is not equally as beautiful as the area now under water." The clear blue lake that sparkled before his eyes was "a prize worth having" for he believed that it would ultimately enhance more than the scenery. "We are excited with the prospect of building up our tourist trade through these prospective recreational areas. This too will bring employment for the Navajo people."[8] In 1969, Nakai called up the heated environmental controversy that surrounded construction of the dam by referencing the publication of *The Jewel of the Colorado*, which the Department of the Interior published in direct response to the Sierra Club's efforts to stop additional large-scale reclamation efforts. He also made clear he was buoyed by the economic optimism associated with the development surrounding Lake Powell.[9]

While Nakai's comments focused on natural beauty and jobs, Johnson, Udall, and Burton had all remarked on the value of nature, faith in progress, and the power of technology to assist in the reclamation of water for human consumption. All of these views foreshadowed the key issues raised in the future litigation surrounding Glen Canyon Dam and its flooding of Rainbow Bridge National Monument in the 1970s and 1980s. At that time, state and federal judges were ultimately given the task of weighing the economic value of the dam against the cultural significance of place, nature, and religion.

Within the ensuing debate, Navajo leaders who once celebrated the completion of the dam found themselves allied with those Navajos who had been less enthusiastically vocal about its construction.[10] While Navajo leaders had wanted the economic opportunity promised them in the UCRSP, of which Glen Canyon Dam was part, they, along with a number of residents of the region surrounding Navajo Mountain also wished to insure the preservation of one of their most sacred places: Rainbow Bridge.

Navajo leaders had wanted the jobs, energy, and water that they hoped the dam would bring to the reservation, but few had initially realized that the dam

and its promise of economic growth would endanger their own religious traditions. They were not simply being naïve in failing to see that Rainbow Bridge
might be damaged as Lake Powell's waters inundated the area under the bridge.
Congress had, after all, promised to protect Rainbow Bridge National Monument with a diversion dam when it approved the Upper Colorado River Storage
Project.[11] We will never know whether Navajo leaders would have approved of
the Glen Canyon dam without that assurance.

Since litigation (*Badoni v. Higginson*, 1977, 1981) followed congressional
refusal to appropriate funds to protect the monument, judges had to decide
how to balance the economic and recreational benefits the dam provided to
a majority of Westerners against the constitutional status of an individual's
(or group of individuals') right to worship on land deemed sacred. Before one
can fully understand the concerns addressed in that case, one must examine the
history of development and resource allocation within the region as well as the
evolution of *different religions* that eventually shaped the political contours of the
area. Although often ignored by white scholars, Navajos assumed an important
role in the regional and national political debate surrounding reclamation.

Navajos, Sanctity, and Rainbow Bridge

Navajos have long considered Rainbow Bridge (Tsé Nan'í áhígíí) to be sacred.
Long before Udall touted Rainbow Bridge's majesty or Lady Bird Johnson made
note of its glory, the 42-foot-high arch was a site of great cultural significance
to the area's Indigenous Peoples. It is but one of many of the region's geological
formations that are sacred to Navajos.[12] Many Diné (Navajo word meaning
"the people") consider Rainbow Bridge—and many other of the region's rock
formations—as "the actual incarnate forms of Navajo gods," and archaeological
evidence indicates that the region's Indigenous populations have performed ceremonies on and around Rainbow Bridge for centuries.[13] Rainbow Bridge plays
an integral part in Navajo origin stories, especially the story of the cosmological
figures of the Hero Twins, sons of White Shell Woman and the Sun. The Hero
Twins traveled great distances across the western oceans to visit their mother,
White Shell Woman. In order to travel such distances, they used a magic rainbow to bridge space. Other Holy People followed in their tracks in order to visit
White Shell Woman, in part to counter ever-increasing disharmony among

different beings. Eventually, those who sought out White Shell Woman returned to the Navajo Mountain area (another sacred geographic marker in the region) and placed the magic rainbow in the safest place they could imagine, Bridge Canyon, below Navajo Mountain. The rainbow then turned to stone, creating a stunning red rock arch.[14]

Navajo cosmology also relates that two other gods—Monster Slayer and Born for Water—were raised in the cradle of Bridge Canyon, and the stone rainbow formed the handle of their cradle board. When they reached maturity, the two traveled to meet their father, the Sun, and used the stone rainbow to facilitate their journey.[15] The bridge plays other roles in Navajo sacred traditions. All of the Navajo residents of the Navajo Mountain community interviewed for a National Park Service administrative history in the 1970s detailed the significance of the bridge to their origin story.[16]

In addition to being a valued religious site, Rainbow Bridge is a historical site of great consequence for Navajos. Many Navajos who escaped Kit Carson's efforts to intern them in 1864 fled to Navajo Mountain and hid in the shadow of Rainbow Bridge for the duration of the Long Walk, a disaster instigated by the federal government that ended in 1868. The fact that Rainbow Bridge provided the refugees a hiding place within the area marked by their four sacred mountains had religious overtones as well. It was, for many Navajos, a sign that Navajo gods were protecting them. Given such a history, it is not surprising that the Navajo Protectionway Ceremony is one of the most commonly held religious ceremonies at Rainbow Bridge. Others, including the Blessingway ceremony and rain-requesting rituals, are also associated with the site. Local Navajos continue to leave prayer offerings for their deities at the bridge and in surrounding areas and have done so since at least 1909 when whites first observed the remnants of such offerings.[17] Navajos contend that the practice dates back long before that moment, as of course they must—why would they have suddenly begun to perform ceremonies there only in 1909? Yet determining the age of such rituals became important to the courts in the 1970s and 1980s when questions about the validity and authenticity of Navajo religion surfaced as part of *Badoni v. Higginson*.

Beyond Navajos, other Indigenous and non-Indigenous groups who lived, and continue to live, in proximity to Rainbow Bridge consider many locations in the region to have sacred meaning. Hopis, Apaches, Utes, Paiutes, and Puebloan Peoples have claimed a deep spiritual connection to the bridge, if not the region as a whole. Native Americans are not alone in their reverence of place. Members of The Church of Jesus Christ of Latter-day Saints, or Mormons, also laid a special claim to the Intermountain West. As one can tell from names of towns and counties that were culled from the Book of Mormon found throughout Utah and beyond, Mormons consider the region their Zion. They also maintained that they had a special relationship to the Indigenous Peoples of the Americas, and considered the Indigenous Peoples throughout the region, like the Navajos, to be "Lamanites"—descendants of the peoples described in the Book of Mormon. Understanding how Mormon ideas about the landscape and the original inhabitants of the region influenced policies surrounding the reclamation of water and the termination of the federal government's trust responsibilities toward Native Americans necessitates a closer examination of the actions of Mormon settlers and politicians.

Navajos and Mormons

A brief history of Mormon-Navajo interaction reveals that LDS leadership did not make the conversion of the Diné a priority during the first century of contact. For the most part, Mormon settlers to Navajo country initially focused on irrigation and productive land use rather than Indian "redemption" but even during the early phase of colonization the two initiatives could not be easily separated. After building cities such as Salt Lake City and Provo, the Church's prophet and president, Brigham Young, wasted little time in sending out small groups to form satellite communities. By 1877, the church had established over 300 settlements throughout North America, most in the Intermountain West. Those sent to establish such communities were expressly told to settle in close proximity to American Indians. By the 1880s, Mormons had established a host of small communities in the Four Corners region.[18]

Because annual precipitation for the region was less than 400 mm per year, which made farming almost impossible without irrigation, the Mormons quickly established a pattern of dam construction to create a watering system for their crops. In St. Joseph, Arizona, for example, Mormon emigrants built five dams between 1876 and 1884. Such dams tended to be relatively small barrier dams and were periodically destroyed when the Little Colorado River surged. It was not until 1924 that the community constructed its first permanent dam.[19]

Subsequent dam building made the settlement of the towns of St. Joseph, Sunset, and Brigham City, Arizona, possible. Mormon dam builders also saw themselves as "agents of God's great plan for the earth" and they wove together the ideas of "redeeming the remnant" and "reclaiming the desert" so it could "blossom as a rose" in scripture and through their settlement practices.[20] Irrigation efforts were both practical and religiously inspired. So too was their contact with Navajos. The settlers' close proximity to the Navajo Reservation meant that while many Mormons farmed, others worked to establish stable trade relationships with Navajos in order to solidify their stronghold in the region.

Trade relationships between Mormons and Navajos were fraught with tension and ripe with cultural misunderstanding. While members of the first Mormon expedition to Navajo country in 1854 reported that raiding Navajos were "cannibals" they sought trade with them nonetheless. Historian William Lyon reports that Mormon hostility toward the Navajo continued until 1870. Correspondence shows that Erastus Snow anticipated there might be a need to use violence to keep the peace even after Navajos were released from Fort Sumner or Bosque Redondo in 1868.[21] Conflict between Mormons and Navajos eased somewhat in 1871 when Mormon trader and federal Indian agent, Jacob Hamblin, helped negotiate an end to periodic skirmishes. Hamblin's agreement, however, was short-lived. As Mormon settlements in the region expanded, and Indigenous Peoples lost access to the water, land, and animals upon which they had depended, ill will between the groups increased. Even so, trade remained the primary vehicle of interaction.[22] In general, the Mormon traders who sought out contact with Navajos believed that Navajos, as Lamanites, might eventually be made "white and delightsome." As historian Robert S. McPherson noted, "These men ... shared ... a belief about these Indians' origins and their destiny."[23]

Despite continual contact with Navajos and the Mormon belief that Indigenous Peoples were "redeemable," widespread efforts to convert Navajos did not begin in earnest until 1942 when George Albert Smith, designated by LDS leadership as an "apostle and special friend to Native Americans," organized the first Mormon mission to Navajos in Gallup, New Mexico.[24] Efforts to reach Navajos continued throughout the 1940s. Missionary efforts expanded in 1954 when the LDS Church started what it called the Indian Student Placement Program (ISPP) where young Navajos would be sent to live with Mormon families during the school year to be educated alongside Mormon children and assimilated into Mormon culture.[25] By the 1950s, Utah politicians celebrated both Mormon outreach and Mormon irrigation endeavors. George Dewey Clyde, a devout Mormon and governor of the state of Utah from 1957–1965, even issued the bold claim that Mormons invented "modern irrigation."[26]

Because of early settlement patterns Mormons established a stronghold in both northern Utah and the Four Corners region. As their population grew, Mormons came into more frequent contact with Navajos and, by the 1950s, sought in earnest to convert them through missionary work, educational efforts, and adoption practices. By that time, Mormons had also become a dominant force in regional politics. They not only celebrated agriculture by advocating for increased irrigation and dam construction they also fundamentally believed that Indians should be fully assimilated into American society. Regional politicians, at least those in Utah, cast irrigation and Indian assimilation as complementary legislative objectives.

National Politics and Regional Development: Reclamation and Termination

For Senator Arthur V. Watkins reclaiming water for agricultural use and Mormonism went hand in hand. By the 1950s, reclamation would become part of a larger regional political drive, led in part by Watkins and other Utah politicians who felt that it would not only help their state's economic growth, but that it was also part of their larger religious mission.[27] Similarly, as the so-called "Indian problem" moved to the foreground in Cold War political debates when politicians compared reservations to communist communities, Mormon politicians, like Watkins, entered the fray and offered a solution. Given their background and belief system, most Mormon residents of cities and small towns throughout the West eventually worked to pass two key pieces of legislation. One promised the construction of dams along the Colorado River and its significant tributaries, while the other sought to reconfigure the government's relationship with American Indian Nations.[28] These residents wanted to transform what they saw as "wasted lands" and make them useful via reclamation while simultaneously pushing American Indians across the region to assimilate.[29]

In 1950, in order to guarantee that the states of Colorado, Utah, New Mexico, Wyoming, and Arizona would have access to their share of the Colorado River, the Bureau of Reclamation devised the UCRSP. The original plan called for the construction of nine dams including one called Echo Park Dam within the Dinosaur National Monument—just outside of Watkins's former home in Vernal, Utah, as well as a host of other proposed reclamation projects throughout the arid West. Given the Mormon communities' proclivity for dam building, Mormon residents and government officials, including Senator Dawson (R, Utah) and Watkins (R, Utah), strongly supported (and helped to craft) the plan. Debates about the size and scope of the project raged in the early 1950s and culminated in 1956 with the passage of the Colorado River Storage Project Act.

The same politicians, however, were also involved in other legislation of significance to American Indians during the 1950s. In 1953, the year just prior to the inception of the Indian Student Placement Program, Watkins introduced legislation to terminate the government's trust responsibilities to Indians.[30] The government's new Indian policy agenda reflected, unbeknownst to many non-Mormons, Watkins's own religious views and ideas of Indian "uplift."[31] Watkins—along with a handful of others who were influenced by their own faith—worked to simultaneously engineer the passage of Indian policy, water policy, and land use policy that reflected his religious faith and economic philosophy. These policies would eventually have the cumulative effect of undermining Native American religious freedom.[32]

As a devout Latter-day Saint, Watkins cared deeply about local issues, especially those related to irrigation and Indians. Shortly after graduating from Columbia Law School in 1912, Watkins returned to his hometown of Vernal, Utah, and became involved in Church and city affairs. He also wrote editorials for the local paper, ran a farm, and became a community leader. He moved to northern Utah in the 1930s and continually worked to strengthen his influence in Utah politics and his position within the church by studying Mormon theology. His integration of religion and politics can be seen in his first political campaign. In 1946, Watkins ran a successful campaign for the United States Senate by avoiding "political debate and stressing religious themes." In 1947, less than a month after Watkins entered the Senate he was appointed to chair the Senate Subcommittee on Indian Affairs. For Watkins the diversity of Indian communities was, according to historian Warren Metcalf, "a *problem* to be solved through the process of conversion."[33] This view fit neatly with the senator's understanding of Lamanites, their role in Mormon doctrine, and the larger effort to convert Navajos and other Indians—which Watkins supported and spearheaded. Watkins was also an advocate of the UCRSP and saw it as a divinely inspired policy.

The senator made this clear to Sierra Club's executive director, David Brower, in 1954 when the outspoken anti-dam activist testified before the Senate Subcommittee on Reclamation and Irrigation. Watkins took the chance to lecture Brower on how even God supported the UCRSP:

> In the first chapter of Genesis it's written—the first commandment given is, 'multiply and replenish the earth, and subdue it.' And we believe that God intended us to subdue it. So we've heard from Him and we know what He wants us to do, and that's what we're out there to do, and that's what this project is all about ... We're following the commandments of God.[34]

Clearly, in Watkins's view, the Lamanites were not the only ones who had a key role to play in the region. According to his reading of both the Bible and the Book of Mormon, Americans should also work to make the region's "wasted" arid land submit to efforts to irrigate it. The lands of southern Utah and northern Arizona targeted by the UCRSP then were sacred for both Navajos and Mormons albeit in different ways. Yet the Mormon idea that the land was sacred as A Zion in need of man's assistance fit well within the larger dominant white culture's desire for water, energy, and the dominion over nature. The fact that the Diné considered Rainbow Bridge sacred and worthy of protection would not become a contentious issue of debate until the 1970s.

Local Support for the UCRSP and Indian Assimilation

Watkins was certainly not the only resident of the American West to support reclamation and termination. He knew he could also count on his Mormon and Republican constituencies to support both his Indian policy and his water conservation strategy. Advocates for both policies abounded but those who supported the UCRSP were especially well organized, well funded, and enthusiastic. In the early 1950s, an organization called The Upper Colorado Grass Roots, Inc. adopted the nickname of "Aqualante." The new name was shorter and catchier than the group's official title and played on the idea that the organization's members were "water vigilantes." As water vigilantes, their stated mission was to take matters into their own hands and fight *for* the UCRSP. The 100,000 members of the organization saw the UCRSP as a plan that guaranteed a rich agricultural future in the region. In short, they believed that building dams would "put the waters of the Colorado River in four states—Colorado, New Mexico, Utah, and Wyoming—to use." No longer would they lie in waste.[35] Putting the waters of the Colorado River to use had long been the desire of settlers, ranchers, politicians, businessmen, and farmers. Who better to lead the fight than Mormon politicians from Utah?

To rally the public around the construction of the dams, the organization led by water engineer and the future governor of Utah, George Dewey Clyde, hired the Dave Evans Public Relations Firm to launch a pro-dam campaign. As lobbyists, the firm took in the single largest payment in congressional history.[36] The public relations firm mailed out thousands of pages of promotional materials to citizens and organizations across the Four Corners region. Some of that material came in the form of an Aqualante "speaker's kit," but the firm also issued press releases, letter templates, and advertisements. Children could become honorary vigilantes by purchasing an Aqualante enforcers' badge. Information packets were primarily distributed to the region's LDS membership through distribution at local Mormon ward meetinghouses. The firm sent the public relation's kits to national politicians, local state officials, and other community organizations such as the Boy Scouts troops throughout Utah, Wyoming, New Mexico, Arizona, and Colorado. Citizens responded to the rallying cry by joining the organization, picking up their pens, and conducting a letter-writing campaign to spread word of their cause. The firm assisted would-be authors in such endeavors by providing them with prewritten "suggested editorial" texts that could be copied and mailed to local papers. Aqualante explicitly aimed to counter the Sierra Club's opposition to UCRSP and its many dams.[37]

Aqualante worked especially hard to inspire its membership in 1954–1955 to fight for Glen Canyon Dam after the Sierra Club's efforts to save Dinosaur National Monument from the Echo Park Dam succeeded. In a post–Echo Park climate, Aqualante members strove to combat the "false information [put out by organizations like the Sierra Club and all of its East Coast supporters] by writing letters to friends and associates in other states, giving them the facts and urging them to write their Congressmen."[38] Importantly, it was because of the Echo Park debate that Congress had been forced to agree to a provision that protected Rainbow Bridge National Monument from Glen Canyon Dam's waters when it approved the UCRSP legislation in 1956.[39] Although much has been written about the Echo Park debate and the birth of modern environmentalism, Aqualante also warrants attention for the way that it pulled Native Americans, and specifically Navajos, into this national—but intensively regional—debate.

Aqualante members based their support of the UCRSP primarily on national defense, industrial development, the need to irrigate crops, and what they described as a plan to "uplift" Indians. As stressed in their promotional literature, the area's natural resources (i.e. oil, natural gas, and recently discovered uranium) could not enhance the nation's defense without sufficient water and power. Beyond that, the organization argued that the project would aid not just the larger national economy but would also help residents of the Navajo reservation in particular. Aqualante literature claimed that the UCRSP would enable the "people of the Navajo Indian Tribe—the largest tribe in existence" to "help themselves." "This," the group noted, "will reduce the need for federal aid" a claim that made a hash of budgetary reality, but that meshed perfectly with the prevailing political sentiment that it was time to terminate the government's trust responsibilities toward American Indians.[40] By addressing both Indian and government concerns, Aqualante assumed a moral high ground. They sought to build dams that would aid the development of white communities but also so that water and power would propel Navajos into the "modern" world.

Aqualante made its case through its propaganda literature by profiling a Navajo farmer named Mr. Yellowman and by evoking the failure of another government run "conservation" program, Navajo stock reduction. In a prewritten speech, Aqualante claimed that "one of the most envied men on the Navajo Reservation in New Mexico is one Mr. Yellowman. Why? Well, Mr. Yellowman has about a 20-acre farm with water to irrigate it. He is able to rotate his crops . . . He is able to provide a good living for his family." Unfortunately, Aqualante noted, Mr. Yellowman was exceptional. Echoing rhetoric from the Bureau of Reclamation, the Soil Conservation Corp, and the Bureau of Indian Affairs almost 20 years earlier, Aqualante claimed, "Most of the Navajos have only overgrazed and eroded wasteland . . . land that is almost barren of vegetation . . . land that takes as much as 18 acres to support even one sheep."[41] The government had previously cited such information to justify a devasting program that dramatically reduced the number of sheep on the Navajo reservation and resulted in an increase of reservation-wide poverty. The plan, in operation from 1932 to 1945, had the effect of drastically undermining Navajo economic self-sufficiency.[42]

The outward rationale for stock reduction was that Navajo land was over-grazed. Federal officials rationalized that a reduction in sheep would help safe-guard the future of the Navajo livestock economy and preserve the Navajo's land base. Government ecologists and engineers had bigger worries though, worries that stemmed from a massive reclamation project. Namely, they feared that soil erosion on the reservation might lead to a silt-filled Lake Mead. As the Bureau of Indian Affairs saw it, Navajo sheep herds would have to be reduced (i.e. killed) for the sake of the operation of Hoover Dam. Among Navajos, stock reduction was a wholesale disaster. The policy caused starvation, further eroded the land, and destroyed Navajos trust of BIA officials.[43] Given that it was such a dismal failure, why would anyone—let alone a Navajo—believe a new government conservation program would be any different?

Aqualante provided the answer to such a question. "What the Navajos want," continued the same brochure that highlighted Mr. Yellowman's story, "is the same chance that Mr. Yellowman has ... Water will give them a chance to help themselves."[44] Not content to end their case with one man's story, Aqualante argued that water and power would help the tribe educate their children—and better-educated Navajos would make better Americans. It was not so much that they envisioned that all Navajos would have increased access to water, however, as it was that more Navajos would move to the "better-irrigated" areas. Once relocated, Aqualante members claimed it would be easier for Navajos to send their children to schools.[45]

This plan proposed by Aqualante is interesting given that it neatly mirrors one put forth by Watkins in a joint subcommittee meeting on the "Termination of Federal Supervision over Certain Indian Tribes" in February of 1954. With Watkins chairing the hearing, he pressed Bureau of Indian Affairs commissioner Glenn L. Emmons, a former banker from Gallup, New Mexico, on the issue of Navajo education as an avenue for "self-help" and assimilation. As Emmons stated: "we know that we have not only to educate the Navahos, but integrate them as quickly as we can with the American school system." Watkins replied to Emmons, by introducing the topic of water scarcity into the discussion: "I think that would be a very desirable objective for the simple reason that in the area of the Navaho Reservation there are very few places where you can build schools because of lack of water." Watkins and Emmons agreed that the Navajo education "problem" was the biggest challenge the Bureau faced. Both men believed that relocating Navajo children in particular to non-Indian homes off-reservation, offered one solution.[46] Not coincidentally, Mormons had already started the ISPP for a similar purpose in addition to their larger mission to convert Navajos. Both men viewed getting water to the reservation, and controlling how such waters were used, as strategies that would facilitate assimilation and provide a solution to the larger Navajo "problem" of governmental reliance. While Watkins apparently did not seek Navajo testimony, Aqualante sought to represent Navajo opinion on the matter.

Aqualante press releases claimed that Navajos supported UCRSP. They noted the Glen Canyon Dam had the support of an unnamed chairman of the Navajo Tribal Council who believed that the UCRSP "will enable us to help support ourselves with the dignity and human satisfaction to which every citizen is entitled." Another anonymous Navajo spokesperson asserted that more than 15,000 Navajo would benefit directly from the project saying "This will be a wonderful thing for us; it will enable us to take our rightful place in society. But, it will also be wonderful for the United States. It will mean, 15,600 more really useful citizens living as well as we all want US citizens to live."[47] As dams were being designed, Aqualante advanced a complementary program of Navajo education and uplift that paralleled the goals of termination. That both water conservation and Indian assimilation shared the same constituency of motivated Mormon politicians and local residents has been overlooked in the historical record. The fact that Indian assimilation became part of a promotional campaign to get the dams built begs for an assessment of how leaders of the Navajo Nation responded to the UCRSP project. Additionally, the fact that religion played such a large role in the formulation of both policies bears consideration.

A Navajo Leader's Perspective

The unnamed tribal chairman Aqualante quoted was, in all likelihood, Sam Ahkeah. In his testimony before the 83rd Congress in 1954, approximately two years *after* the Aqualante kits were mailed out to speakers, Ahkeah voiced his support for the UCRSP. With Utah's own Senator Watkins chairing the hearings, Akheah made his position crystal clear. "For about 100 years we have waited for such a project which could irrigate a very large area of the reservation ... When the land is irrigated, it will make about 1,500 farms of a size sufficient to support a Navaho family. This means 1,500 families supporting themselves directly from the project."[48] Akheah and his lawyer estimated that about 7,800 people would directly benefit from the UCRSP and that an additional 7,800 would receive indirect benefits.[49]

Akheah's testimony before Congress was almost an exact transcript of the earlier mentioned Aqualante press release. Yet, Aqualante and Akheah were not in complete agreement. In particular, they held divergent definitions of farming. For Akheah a farm was an area primarily planted with "pasture grasses and forage for raising livestock and a small area used to grow garden produce and row crops." "Navajos," he stated, "are successful in the livestock industry" and he saw the dam as one way to renew stock herds, not help Navajos grow crops.[50] A surge in stock raising would foster financial independence. It would mean Navajos would open "stores, filling stations, and all kinds of service businesses" to meet the demands of livestock industry personnel as well as an influx of tourists from Glen Canyon's reservoir, Lake Powell. In his view, the larger Navajo community would support the UCRSP because it would enable them to "become self-sufficient," "live with dignity," and "become taxpayers."[51] What motivated Akheah? While we don't know for certain, there are some strong indications that Akheah had his own reasons for sticking to the Aqualante script.

Importantly, the Navajo chairman then made a very strong case for the reinsertion of the recently removed Navajo Dam into the UCRSP bill. Accordingly, the smaller Navajo Dam did again become part of the project under Senator Watkins's watchful eye. Akheah's statements show that some Navajos clearly supported development efforts—but it also demonstrates they wanted them on their own terms. Concurrent with Akheah's testimony in front of Watkins, the senator was pursuing his plan to terminate the federal government's trust responsibilities to American Indians. Likewise, Watkins was soliciting testimony regarding the Navajo Nation during termination hearings held that very year.

Akheah's successor, Paul Jones, also spoke out in favor of the UCRSP, but he was a bit more circumspect in his assertions. Writing an article titled "Reclamation and the Indian," for publication in the *Utah Historical Quarterly* in 1959, Jones, like those before him, invoked the story of Mr. Yellowman. This time, however, he used the farmer's story as a cautionary tale. Although Mr. Yellowman had been chosen as "the best farmer in San Juan County," Jones noted that Mr. Yellowman "frankly admits he cannot make a living from his farm." Launching a critique of the government's—and the Aqualante-supported—plan

to cluster Navajos into irrigation districts, he opined that crowding the "maximum number of Indians on each Indian irrigation project," would surely meet
"with uniformly unsuccessful results." Thus, he used Utah's history journal to
appeal for changes to the pending Navajo Indian Irrigation Project in New
Mexico, a participating unit in the UCRSP. He clearly had a specific audience
of educated, policy-oriented leaders, who valued Utah's history, in mind when
he asked for an increase in the size of the basic "farm" from 90 to 120 acres. Jones
noted that the tribe did want to be financially independent, and had already
taken matters into their own hands by starting an unnamed "farm" school, and
hired a farm manager named Clifford Hansen, to lead the school. But, like
Ahkeah, Jones envisioned that "farms" would primarily support sheep, hence the
need for increased acreage. Jones backed the Navajo Irrigation Project because
it had the ability to transform land that had supported only 5,116 sheep into
land that could support "436,000 sheep." In a place where a common refrain is:
"sheep equal life," irrigation was, in the chairman's words, "a life or death matter."[52]
Neither Jones nor Akheah addressed the matter of Rainbow Bridge. Nor did
Watkins broach the matter. Once the legislation had passed, it seemed likely that
Navajos felt that the wording in the bill would provide the necessary protection.

Aqualante, Navajos, and a Politics of Progress

If Sam Akheah suspected his appeal for increased water for Navajo irrigation
projects to Watkins and other politicians would receive a warm reception,
he was right. After all, it was a request that hewed closely to the one featured
in Aqualante literature. Although it appears that Aqualante was a simple grassroots organization that developed to champion the needs of small-town farmers
and Navajo Indians, it was, as indicated earlier, actually the brainchild of two
prominent Utahans: George Dewey Clyde and David W. Evans; both Utahans
had political aspirations and both had been involved with Aqualante from the
organization's inception.

George D. Clyde placed water issues at the foundation of his political career
starting in 1934 when he was appointed as the State of Utah water conservator.
By the 1940s, he had been elected director of the Utah Water Users Association.
In 1945, Clyde was appointed chief of the Division of Irrigation Engineering
and Water Conservation and Research for the U.S. Soil Conservation Service.

He moved on to become the director of the Utah Water and Power Board in 1953. A devout Mormon, he was elected governor of Utah in 1956. Before that, however, when serving as the director of the Utah Water and Power Board, Clyde commissioned David W. Evans's public relations firm to help the water and power industry campaign for the UCRSP. Evans created Aqualante and, with the help of state and Church officials, turned it into a high-profile organization. Clyde's relationship to Aqualante can be seen in a letter he wrote to William A. Dawson, who served in Congress from 1953–1959. In 1957, when Clyde feared environmental groups such as the Sierra Club would again mobilize their members to fight against Glen Canyon Dam, he informed Dawson that he had already passed along the suggestion to the "four governors" in Wyoming, Arizona, New Mexico, and Colorado that "the [Aqualante] Grass Roots organization in each state be activated."[53] This may make the Aqualantes the first "astroturf," or faux grassroots, movement in the United States.[54]

Given that Senator Watkins was a close political ally of Clyde, an Aqualante supporter, and the chair of the Senate Interior Committee Subcommittee on Indian Affairs, it is apparent that Utah politicians were involved in crafting Indian policy and water policy alongside each other. That prominent Utah politicians assumed important roles in both Indian affairs and water conservation make it possible to interpret their maneuvering within a framework put forth by historians such as Donald Worster. Worster argued that the very nature of consolidating water into dams put vast amounts of water in the hands of a few businesses whose interests aligned with powerful politicians.[55] It's not surprising that Clyde was closely tied to the water and power industry and that in 1959 he had become a prominent partner in the construction company that received the government contract to build Page, Arizona—the town directly next to Glen Canyon Dam, on land that once belonged to the Navajo tribe.

If one examines the actions of politicians like Watkins and Clyde, one must look at Akheah's and Jones's roles as well. Were they also fulfilling the role Worster assigned to politicians? If not, what does one make of Ahkeah's involvement with Aqualante and the UCRSP, especially in light of termination? Akheah clearly knew that by supporting the UCRSP he would please Watkins. Watkins, in turn, reinserted the smaller Navajo Dam back into the bill. In light of stock reduction, could Ahkeah's testimony in support of the dam represent one strategy that Navajos used to get the water the government had promised in earlier treaties—water that could revive decimated herds? Ahkeah was willing to embrace development if it would provide *his* constituents with the water they needed to rebuild their sheep flocks, which were an essential part of the Navajo economy, their culture, and their cosmology.

Paul Jones also used his position as tribal chairman to advocate for the Navajo Indian Irrigation Project (NIIP). He sought to make his case at the moment NIIP was being debated before Congress before an audience of Utah politicians that included Clyde. Like Ahkeah, Jones was familiar with the organizations and politicians who had influence over reclamation projects. Not only did Jones also use the example of Mr. Yellowman in his *Utah Historical Quarterly* article, either he or the editors also used a photograph of the Navajo Tribal Council meeting, provided by David W. Evans's public relations firm, to illustrate the publication. While we cannot be certain that Jones selected this photograph, the fact that Aqualante's founder provided the illustration the *Quarterly* used to illustrate the tribal chairman's appeal seems more than coincidental. As a politician who had his own constituency to consider, Jones had met with Clyde and Evans at the American Association of State and Local History (AASLH) conference earlier that year.[56] Jones and Clyde had appeared on a panel at the AASLH together and their remarks provided the foundation for their articles that appeared in the *Quarterly*.

In his article, Jones took the opportunity to correct George Dewey Clyde's assertion that Mormons invented irrigation as well as to advocate for his tribe. After reminding his audience that Indigenous people had been irrigating the region long "before there was reclamation law and even many years before the Mormon settlers at Salt Lake City or the Spanish settlers in New Mexico started to build irrigation works" he went on to request a revision of the current NIIP bill that was before Congress. His primary concern was that whereas the bill called "for farm units of ninety acres the Advisory Committee of the Navajo Tribal Council has requested a figure be revised to 120 acres."[57] In all likelihood, Jones hoped that Clyde and Evans, along with their influential political network, could help the Navajo get the water they needed.

Navajo leaders sought irrigation projects and they worked with Utah's Mormon politicians in order to serve what they perceived to be the needs of their people. They financially supported Aqualante and borrowed prose from their literature. They took advice from Watkins and Clyde when it was strategic to do so. Sometimes it paid off—but not always to the degree Navajo leaders hoped. By the time the Glen Canyon Dam was completed, approximately 1,000 Navajos had been employed by firms building it. Five thousand additional jobs went to non-Indian workers. While Navajo leaders had hoped that more Navajos would be employed, their maneuvering clearly did some good. But completion of the dam brought more acute disappointments as well. Ahkeah's intial view of the dam, for instance, would change when, in 1974 when reservoir waters reached Rainbow Bridge, the Bureau of Reclamation, Mormon politicians, and the National Park Service did little, if anything, to protect this Navajo sacred site.[58]

Sacred Spaces and Litigation

By 1974, Jones's and Ahkeah's hope that irrigated lands would rebuild herds had proven an illusion. Moreover, instead of precluding the "impairment of the Rainbow Bridge National Monument" as Congress promised in section one of the UCRSP, the dam had turned it into one of Lake Powell's key tourist attractions.[59] As Nakai had hoped, boaters flocked to Glen Canyon. From there they inundated Rainbow Bridge National Monument. One touring company ran 56-foot luxury boats that accommodated up to 88 tourists from Wahweap to Rainbow Bridge daily. By the late 1970s, approximately 100,000 people visited Rainbow Bridge annually. While there, they engaged in behavior that seemed more profane than sacred to Navajos. Boaters played loud music, drank alcohol, and swam below the bridge. All of this offended Navajo spiritual leaders and politicians.[60]

Eight Navajos, including three Navajo spiritual leaders, or *haatahli*, sued the Bureau of Reclamation, the National Park Service, and the Department of the Interior "to take adequate measures preventing further desecration and destruction of the Rainbow Bridge area by tourists, and otherwise to take adequate measures to preclude impairment of the Rainbow Bridge National Monument."[61] In *Badoni v. Higginson* Navajos asked the court to stop people from "acting in such a manner as to destroy and desecrate the Navajo gods and sacred sites threatened by the rising waters of Lake Powell and by the influx of tourists."[62] Legal scholar Brian Edward Brown has shown that they cited the First Amendment, claiming that the submersion of "the land base at Rainbow Bridge constituted an unconstitutional infringement of the right to free exercise of the Indians' religion."[63] Although a previous generation of Navajo leadership had supported building the dam, now another group of Navajo religious leaders sought to limit the harmful effects the rising reservoir created.

Two court rulings struggled with the inherent tension between religious freedom and economic development. First, the Utah district court ruled that the plaintiffs (Navajos) had no property interest in Rainbow Bridge National Monument and thus no standing to sue. In other words, since Rainbow Bridge was not owned by the tribe, Navajos had no legal claim to the area regardless of their long-standing belief that it was sacred. Nonetheless the court addressed what it defined as a "hypothetical" issue of religion involving an imaginary "plaintiff who petitioned a federal court to restrict public access to the Lincoln Memorial because he had had a[n] intense religious experience there."[64] The court used this hypothetical to chastise Navajos, reminding them that they were allowed to worship at Rainbow Bridge only as a courtesy from the National Park Service who managed the monument.

Navajos appealed, hoping that the federal Tenth Circuit Court of Appeals would reach a different decision. Ultimately, the Court offered a telling rationale for rejecting Navajo claims in *Badoni*. The Tenth Circuit Court agreed "with the trial court that the government's interest in maintaining the capacity for Lake Powell at a level that intrudes into the Monument outweighs the plaintiffs' religious interest."[65] It, at least, had engaged with the "religious claims" of Native Americans rather than dismissing them as abstractions, but the Court's decision clearly implied that the Indians' desire to protect the sacred was less important than the material "good" provided by the dam. As Brother Burton's dedicatory prayer reminds us, though, such "good" had religiously specific overtones as well.

Interestingly, as early as 1964, Navajo chairman Raymond Nakai anticipated a clash between Navajo religious beliefs and Christian beliefs. In a speech titled "An Alien God" he told his largely Navajo audience that they would continue to face challenges to their religion. Nakai, however, believed they had an avenue of redress, if such issues arose: The Declaration of Independence. "It is up to us to tell our brethren whose religious beliefs may center around the 'changing woman' that our forefathers had reference to all gods when they set forth in our Declaration of Independence the fact that the most precious right inherent to man is the right to do homage to God in whatever form he chooses." The hopeful Nakai envisioned a world where Navajo deities would get the same respect, as would the Christian God. Instead, the court eventually offered him a world in which Navajo traditions received the same respect as New Age visions, and far less respect than that accorded to either Christianity or the gospel of efficiency and the conservation of natural resources for non-Indians.

Conclusion

There are clear links between the history of Mormonism, reclamation, termination, and the ways in which Navajo leaders faced pressure (directly or indirectly) from Mormons as they attempted to obtain more irrigated land to assist in the rehabilitation of their sheep herds. This essay specifically shows how the history surrounding the Rainbow Bridge controversy and the history of the UCRSP and Glen Canyon Dam were connected. It demonstrates the ways that important policy makers invoked the concepts of self-sufficiency and economic growth when they discussed both the reclamation of water and the termination of the federal government's trust responsibilities toward Native Americans. Yet it also attempts to uncover how policy makers invoked such concepts in ways that more closely reflected Mormon belief systems while wholly simultaneously ignoring Navajo culturally specific land use and religious practices. As Raymond Nakai's presence at the dedication ceremony and Sam Akheah's congressional testimony indicate, Navajos participated in regional development efforts, but neither Nakai nor Akheah intended to abandon their culture in support of the dam. Nor did they fully ascribe to the vision of self-sufficiency through farming put forth by Watkins, Clyde, and Aqualante. Moreover, Navajo spiritual thought was not absent from Navajo interaction with politicians—at least when the dam was concerned. There were, after all, moments when dam advocates at least paid symbolic tribute to Navajo religion, moments when Navajo and Christian religious traditions peaceably coexisted.

During the dedication ceremony, speakers invoked references to a Mormon God, but organizers also included a Navajo rug—an item deeply imbued with religious symbolism for Navajos. Lady Bird Johnson, for instance, lifted a Navajo rug to "unveil" the Glen Canyon Dam dedicatory plaque. This moment embodies an important element in the controversy: the tension between the material and the spiritual. Navajos wove rugs not just as a way to honor Spiderwoman, but also to trade them as Spiderwoman—who bequeathed the skill of weaving to Navajos—intended. Rugs had both spiritual and market value for the Diné who did not necessarily view religion and opportunity as contradictory categories. Navajo leaders pursued economic opportunity but did so in ways that maintained harmony with their understanding of the sacred—a link perfectly embodied in the rug that Johnson lifted.

Early Mormon pioneers had come to occupy sacred Indigenous land in the Southwest and imbued it with their own sense of value—spiritually and monetarily. By the mid-twentieth century, both groups had embraced faith in economic progress in which the land and the water were resources. For Mormons, however, "development" became part of a larger mission whereas for Navajos such practices reflected cultural persistence. Though both groups traveled along roughly parallel trails for a good part of the 1950s and 1960s, the *Badoni* case shows that the paths forged by Watkins and Clyde and walked by Ahkeah, Jones, and Nakai were never the same. The disputes surrounding Rainbow Bridge mark one of those moments when the formerly parallel paths began to diverge. As had happened so often when American Indians attempted to find a balance between the material and the spiritual, the compromise they sought to strike was transformed into loss when the flooding of their sacred monument produced a flood of "economic opportunity" for others.

8

Aloha in Diné Bikéyah

Mormon Hawaiians and Navajos, 1949 to 1990

FARINA NOELANI KING

My search to understand the presence of Mormon Pacific Islander missionaries in Diné Bikéyah (Navajo lands) begins with my name. I am Bilagáanaa dóó Diné (white Navajo) named after Indigenous Pacific Islanders. My given names are Farina Noelani. I am of white American descent on my mother's side, and born for the Kinyaa'áanii (Towering House clan) of the Diné on my father's side.[1] Both of my parents converted to The Church of Jesus Christ of Latter-day Saints in their youth. During the 1980s and early 1990s, my family lived on the Navajo Reservation, where we participated in local LDS congregations in Montezuma Creek, Utah; Tuba City, Arizona; and Saint Michaels, Arizona. I was born in Tuba City during the mid-1980s. The LDS community became family to us, which consisted primarily of Navajos, whites, and Polynesians on the reservation. Two influential Polynesian Mormon families lived in the area at the time: the Kalaulis and the Tahus. The patriarchs of these families, respectively Mitchell Davis Kapuni Kalauli (Kānaka Māoli or Native Hawaiian) and Hector Tahu (Māori) both served as missionaries for the LDS Southwest Indian Mission during the 1960s, which included Diné Bikéyah.

As educators, Kalauli and Tahu later returned to the Navajo Reservation with their families. They both recruited LDS Polynesians to join them as employees of Diné education, developing a cohort. This group not only shaped Diné education during the self-determination era but also helped to establish the first LDS stakes on the reservation, which symbolized a growing Mormon community and network.[2] Kalauli became one of the first vice principals of the Whitehorse High School in Montezuma Creek, Utah, during the late 1970s and early 1980s. He convinced my namesake, Farina McCarthy (Māori), to work there as a counselor. They knew each other at Brigham Young University–Hawaii. My other namesake, a Kānaka Māoli named Noelani Tahu née Kauhaune, lived in Montezuma Creek with her husband, Hector Tahu, while he was the assistant principal at the high school.[3] My family used to live next door to the Tahus. My mother and father named me after Farina and Noelani because they "both were very active women who gave much great service to the church and community. Both attended the temple and were worthy, and always ready to serve and help others."[4]

My mother told me how Farina and Noelani exemplified devout members of the LDS community. For example, Noelani "dug in and did the work necessary when she saw the need" by donating a car to LeRoy Mexican. After my mother praised Mexican in an LDS testimony meeting for hitchhiking from Red Lake to Tuba City, 26 miles each way, to come to Church every Sunday, "the Tahus donated a good running old car to [Mexican's family]. They didn't know him well and were tight on funds, but [Noelani] was one of great compassion and was able to make things happen."[5] In such cases, Noelani epitomized "The Aloha Spirit" in Diné Bikéyah, which both Navajos and LDS Polynesians perceived as acts of generosity, welcome, and kindness. But some Pacific Islanders sought the welcome of Navajos, as they proselytized for the LDS Church in Diné Bikéyah.

Aloha forms a foundational part of ancestral Kānaka Māoli culture similarly to how the Diné relate to the teachings of Si'ąh Naagháí Bik'eh Hózhǫ́ (SNBH). Scholars have translated SNBH as "Walk in Beauty."[6] This concept permeates every aspect of life as a central Navajo principle to seek after harmony in all our relationships and movements. As Navajos, we aspire to live a long life, maintaining and restoring hózhǫ́, the beauty of harmony. Hawaiian conceptualizations of aloha also emphasize reciprocity and balance with all beings and things. In her oral history, Mo'olelo o na Po Makole, a Native Hawaiian of Kamalo, Moloka'i, explained: "Aloha is being a part of all and all being a part of me.... I respect all that is as part of the Creator and part of me."[7] One of my Diné elders, Uncle Albert Smith, taught "what we are and who we are" as "examples of Mother Earth." As Navajos, he said that "we use all that we have. We use the plants, the animals, the minerals, and parts of our body."[8] Like the Kānaka Māoli, Diné philosophies and ancestral teachings focus on maintaining, fostering, and restoring beauty in the relationships with the world that we consider as part of us.

Although the Kānaka Māoli stress reciprocity by saying, *Aloha mai no, aloha aku* (when love is given, love should be returned)," aloha signifies much giving.[9] As Noelani Tahu demonstrated to my parents and LeRoy Mexican, the Kānaka Māoli did not hesitate to "offer *kokua* (aid)" with aloha even if their resources were limited.[10] My family and many other Navajos, especially in the LDS Church, noticed and respected these Mormon Pacific Islanders' service and spirit of aloha as hózhǫ́, which restored harmony and reciprocity. I later learned that my parents may have never known Farina and Noelani if LDS officials did not assign Mitchell Kalauli and Hector Tahu to the Southwest Indian Mission (SWIM). In the aftermath of Euro-American settler colonialism, Mormon missionaries initially entered Diné Bikéyah as intruders. In 1949, the LDS Church established the Southwest Indian Mission, which included regions of the Navajo Reservation although the Navajo Tribal Council withheld its permission until 1953.[11] Many Kānaka Māoli missionaries, young men and women mostly between the ages of 19 and 25 years old, came as outsiders to Diné Bikéyah in the couple decades that followed.

Navajos called Hawaiian missionaries *bilasáanaa diwozhí*, the "Pineapples," with a sense of humor.[12] Mormon officials showed an interest in Indigenous populations that they considered "Lamanites," including Polynesians, Latin Americans, and Native Americans. Under the leadership of Spencer W. Kimball, especially between 1950 and 1980, some Latter-day Saints upheld what Kimball called the "Lamanite Cause." This cause represented efforts to proselytize, convert, and strengthen the LDS Church among the descendants of Lamanites, who Mormons believed to be ancient peoples of the Americas depicted in the Book of Mormon.[13] Whether they related as "Lamanites" or not, Kānaka Māoli missionaries and Navajos identified with one another as Indigenous. Scholars have increasingly engaged with global Indigenous networks and relationships, while exploring shared meanings of identities, experiences, and efforts to decolonize.[14] In this case, I have reached out to former Native Hawaiian missionaries who left their homeland to offer Navajos not only teachings of the LDS faith but also of their Indigenous cultures, which initiated bonds of mutual acceptance and appreciation between them and many Diné. Navajos recognized how Kānaka Māoli missionaries carried their "Indigeneity" with them to Diné Bikéyah.[15]

The Kānaka Māoli played a major role in the growth of the LDS Church on the Navajo Nation. This article examines the relationships and influence between the Kānaka Māoli and Diné through the experiences and perspectives of former LDS missionaries and Indigenous Latter-day Saints. Why did the LDS Church assign Kānaka Māoli and other Pacific Islanders to Diné Bikéyah in the Southwest Indian Mission and the missions that followed it? Why did these missionaries accept their assignment, and how did they experience the mission? What kind of exchange did the Kānaka Māoli and Diné sustain in the mission? How did they view and affect one another? Kānaka Māoli scholar Hokulani Aikau presents a significant query to people who occupy colonized Indigenous spaces, which I consider regarding Native Hawaiian missionaries in Diné Bikéyah: "What should our responsibilities be to the peoples whose land we dwell upon?"[16] Such questions guide the interpretations of these personal experiences, oral histories, interviews, and documentary evidence.

Prior to the 1990s, many Mormon leaders defined Indigenous Peoples of the Pacific and those of the Americas under the generic term of "Lamanites."[17] As white missionaries taught and converted Indigenous Peoples, the LDS Church began to assign more Lamanite missionaries to proselytize among other Lamanites, especially during the latter half of the twentieth century. Lane John-son, the assistant editor of the LDS Church magazine *Ensign*, published a map of "Who and Where are the Lamanites? Worldwide Distribution of Lamanites" in 1975. The map depicts Indigenous Peoples of North America, Central Amer-ica, South America, and parts of the Pacific Islands as "Descendants of the Book of Mormon peoples."[18]

Because of these interpretations, many twentieth-century Latter-day Saints considered the Diné and Kānaka Māoli as "Lamanite cousins" who descended from Joseph, through Ephraim or Manasseh. They would be closely related to most Euro-American Mormons who belonged to the tribe of Ephraim.[19] Such ideas correlated with larger trends including scientific discourse in nineteenth-and twentieth-century American scholarship that simultaneously focused on biological ties between Indigenous Pacific Islanders and Caucasians to justify settler colonialism in the Pacific.[20] Recent genetic studies into the twenty-first century stress Asian origins of Indigenous Pacific Islanders and Native Amer-icans. Some Mormon scholars have rejected that Native Americans descend from Lamanites because of such genetic research. I concentrate on some Kānaka Māoli and Diné Mormons who believed they were Lamanites or who were considered Lamanites between 1949 and 1990. During that period, they did not emphasize debates about the genetic research and DNA connecting them to Asians.[21]

Some Mormons characterized Native Americans and certain Indigenous Pacific Islanders as "chosen people," while they also perpetuated paternalistic systems of settler colonialism and white supremacy.[22] Gina Colvin, a Māori scholar, asserts: "Mormonism at its heart is a white, American, patriarchal, colonizing tradition that sometimes carves crude and bumpy tracks where its wagons roll."[23] In the context of settler colonialism, Mormons used rhetoric concerning their common lineage of the House of Israel as a strategy to convert Native Hawaiians and other Indigenous communities.[24] Although this narrative focuses on Native Hawaiian and Navajo connections as "Lamanites," other peoples related to one another under the banner of "Lamanite" identity, including Amerindians of Central and South America.[25]

In "Arts of the Contact Zone," scholar Mary Louise Pratt addresses how "relations of power" reverberate in the contact zone of settler colonialism.[26] Cultural collisions of the contact zone could be constructive as well as destructive but involve some change and shattering. In the case of Native Hawaiian missionaries encountering Navajos, the Southwest Indian Mission became a contact zone, but the power dynamics were not clear-cut as portrayed in a typical framework of colonialism. LDS missionaries have been shaped by colonial dynamics, since most Christian missions opened following the colonization of Indigenous lands and people. Yet, for many Indigenous missionaries and converts, they found some personal liberation and self-realization through endorsing and supporting the LDS Church.[27] Native Hawaiian missionaries served alongside Navajo missionaries who joined the Church. They believed that Mormonism applied to them and provided their path to salvation as Indigenous People and human beings.

Pratt's idea of "autoethnographic text" relates to this form of my autoethnographic narrative, as I address "representations that others have made of" Navajos and my own communities.[28] Native Hawaiian missionaries' oral histories stand for autoethnography because they were trying to understand the ways that others, including whites and Navajos, represented and thought of them. Both Indigenous missionaries "[engaged] with representations" that white Mormons "[made] of them."[29] I concentrate on how they represented and engaged with each other in the context of an arbitrary mission boundary that encompassed

Diné Bikéyah. The power dynamics differed from those of other settler colonialism frameworks in that Native Hawaiian missionaries were not settlers. Native Hawaiians were visitors on Navajo land, occupying another Indigenous space, while they shared the experience of coming from marginalized and colonized but culturally rich communities.

Because LDS missionaries have proselytized among Native Hawaiians since the mid-nineteenth century, some Kānaka Māoli accepted Mormon teachings decades before the Southwest Indian Mission began. Some Mormons referred to Elder George Q. Cannon's vision in 1851 of Hawaiians as descendants of Israel through the lineage of Lehi, a prophet and forefather of the Nephites and Lamanites in the Book of Mormon. These theories posit that children of the House of Israel came through the mainland of the Americas to inhabit the Pacific Isles such as Hawai'i. Other Mormons have supported these claims with passages in the scriptures, especially the "story of Hagoth, an adventurer and shipbuilder, who sailed 'forth into the west sea'" with a group of Nephites.[30] Some Native Hawaiian Latter-day Saints have believed these teachings to this day, tracing their genealogy to Israel.

Despite the entanglements of Mormon settler colonial power dynamics, some Latter-day Saints, especially of the Diné and Kānaka Māoli, have embraced the Lamanite identity as a form of Indigenous pride and unity. When I attended the LDS Native American congregation in Provo, known then (between 2011 and 2012) as the Franklin Second Ward, a Kānaka Māoli woman bore her testimony during a sacrament meeting about her gratitude to worship with fellow "Lamanites" that share such a unique heritage. Unlike most LDS congregations, Mormons voluntarily chose to attend this ward because of a common sense of culture and Indigeneity. Several Native Hawaiians joined this predominantly Native American ward, including former SWIM missionaries. Known as "Bradah Ned," Ned Kaili Aikau, who passed away in 2010, was one of the Kānaka Māoli missionaries to serve in the Southwest Indian Mission.[31] Aikau and some fellow Mormon Kānaka Māoli revered the LDS gospel and applied it to reorient toward ancestral life pathways.[32] Some Navajos and Kānaka Māoli converted wholeheartedly to the Mormon faith, and they willingly served the LDS Church as Lamanite missionaries among Indigenous communities and throughout the world.

LDS General Authorities possibly envisioned that Lamanites could best convert one another because of their shared "blood of Israel." General Authorities assigned enough Pacific Islander missionaries that they developed a presence in Diné Bikéyah through the Southwest Indian Mission, although the LDS Church did not officially publicize the reasons and statistics of the callings. SWIM operated until the LDS Church integrated it into the New Mexico-Arizona Mission in 1972. Earlier Mormon missions existed in the southwest Indian territories, regardless of Diné approval, but the LDS Church did not establish the mission officially called the "Southwest Indian Mission" until 1949. By 1974, the mission covering the Navajo Reservation became the Arizona Holbrook Mission. The Pacific Islanders built networks and cultural exchanges in Diné Bikéyah, especially as missionaries between the 1960s and 1970s. Some Polynesians, like the Tahu and Kalauli families, returned and settled on the reservation and influenced the LDS Church there for decades.

The LDS Church does not divulge specific information about how it calls and assigns missionaries to areas, which obscures the intent of Church authorities to send Kānaka Māoli missionaries to the Navajo Reservation. Native Hawaiian missionaries also served in noticeable numbers on other American Indian reservations. This study does not include missions outside of the Navajo Reservation, but some interviewees referred to Hawaiian family and peers who went to other Indian missions such as the Northern Indian Mission. Harvard C. S. Kim, for example, recalled that most of his LDS Native Hawaiian peers "had already served either in the Southwest Indian Mission or the Northern Indian Mission." When he received his mission call to the Southwest Indian Mission, in 1972, he believed that "all Hawaiians go" to the Southwest Indian Mission.[33] Native Americans from the region of the Northern Indian Mission have also told me about the positive impressions of Polynesian missionaries. One of my friends, Mary Pine of the Standing Rock Sioux Reservation, received LDS lessons from some Polynesian missionaries because of their "strong spirit" and "beautiful culture and music" that they shared.[34]

Mormons believe that Church leaders determine the missionary assignments by divine revelation. Scholars have not calculated the exact numbers of Native Hawaiian or Pacific Islander missionaries who served on American Indian reservations in missions such as the Northern Indian Mission and Southwest Indian Mission. The SWIM manuscript history and other LDS Church documents present, however, several indicators of the LDS Pacific Islander presence in Diné Bikéyah. In February 1966, for example, a SWIM newsletter reported a total of thirty-eight "True Israel" or "Lamanite" missionaries. Native Hawaiians often constituted the largest group of Lamanite missionaries. Of the thirty-eight Lamanite missionaries, the mission leaders identified eighteen from Hawai'i, five from Samoa, two from New Zealand, one from Alaska, one from Tonga, and four non-Navajo Native Americans.[35]

Some cultural misunderstandings and racial discrimination between whites and Navajos impeded missionary work among American Indians during the years of the Southwest Indian Mission (1949–1972), possibly prompting the LDS Church to assign Pacific Islander missionaries who could relate to Native Americans through their cultures. Some Navajo Mormons expressed frustration with the treatment that American Indians had received from LDS missionaries. Julius Chavez, a Diné Mormon convert, pointed out that "the missionaries that go in there [the Navajo Reservation] are not prepared to deal with the depth of the traditional religion." They tried to reinforce "the white concept of families and the white concept of blessings" instead of respecting traditional Navajo values. The missionaries attempted to convert his uncle, a hataałii (commonly translated as "medicine man"), but "they ended up insulting him rather than helping him." Chavez criticized the missionaries' lack of preparation, stressing their need to "have the spirit" and "bear down pure testimony."[36] To Chavez, Indigenous Pacific Islanders shared a sense of spirituality with Navajos unlike white missionaries.

Millie Garrett, a Navajo LDS convert, claimed: "I think when missionaries go to the reservation that they should be screened." Her friend served with a married missionary couple who disrespected the First Nations in Canada. The sister missionary wore white gloves to avoid touching the Indigenous people. She racialized First Nations as "dirty" and "untouchable." Church officials eventually sent the couple elsewhere, since the sister missionary refused to work with Indigenous communities. This story affected Garrett's perception of LDS missionaries, upsetting her: "But what did that do for that group of Indians there? That left something they won't forget, 'This is how these Mormons treated us.'"[37] While missionaries represented the face of the LDS Church and Mormonism, their racial proclivities could disrupt relationships of trust and exchange between Mormons and Native American communities.

The LDS Church addressed part of these issues concerning cultural and racial differences by calling Native Americans and Pacific Islanders to serve in SWIM. To some degree, these "Lamanite" missionaries regained the Navajo People's trust of Mormons. Navajos often affiliated more closely with brown-skinned missionaries due to shared experiences of marginalization based on colorism.[38] They also listened to Navajo missionaries who shared their heritage and oftentimes understood their language and culture. Gabriel Cinniginnie, a Navajo Mormon convert, admitted that he accepted a couple of missionaries because they were Māoris instead of white Americans. He had previously rejected white missionaries that tried to visit him. "Since these two were Maoris, brown-colored, I decided I'd listen to them," Cinniginnie explained. "If they had been Anglos, maybe it'd be a different story. Since they were Māoris, I decided I'd go ahead and trust them because they were the same color as my skin."[39] Cinniginnie preferred learning the gospel from people that not only resembled him but also bore the same skin tone that marked them as minorities and "others" in dominant US society.

Some LDS Navajos have understood their connections to the Kānaka Māoli according to their own terms through oral tradition. Tiyarra Roanhorse, an LDS Navajo convert who went to Brigham Young University–Hawaii in 2016, learned by Diné oral traditions that Native Hawaiians were her distant relatives. "One of the old stories was that our Mother created us and helped Heavenly Father create the Earth," Roanhorse described. "Her name was White Shell Woman. When she was done creating the land and the people and making our Navajo Tribe, they believe she descended here to Hawai'i and settled on the Hawaiian island, and here she remained."[40] Roanhorse referred to "Heavenly Father" in these ancestral teachings, interpreting Diné oral traditions as a Latter-day Saint in the English language. In 1976, Ch'ahádiniini' Binálí, a Diné elder, discussed how the original Navajo clans came from White Shell Woman (also known as Changing Woman).[41] After teaching the Blessing Way ceremony to her children, he said, "Changing Woman then left toward the West where she was supposed to live with the Sun on an island in the middle of the ocean."[42] 'Asdzą́ą́ Nádleehé (Changing Woman) and Jóhonaa'éí (Sun) united in the western ocean. Roanhorse translated this oral tradition as "Heavenly Father" and "Mother," specifically Yoołgai 'Asdzą́ą́ (White Shell Woman), who created both Navajos and Native Hawaiians.

Julius Chavez, who embraced a Lamanite identity, also relied on Diné oral traditions to relate to Kānaka Māoli and other "brown" peoples. Chavez concentrated on the physical "link" of brown skin and black hair that diverse people shared with him. He remembered the teachings of his grandparents, which address these ties:

They said, 'That our creator went through many, many millions and millions of trouble to carve our bodies, to carve our hair out of black flint,
and to make every strand. It took them millions of years to do that.' ...
I look at that when I see other Lamanites or other Indians. I say to
myself, 'It is true. It was a hard work to create that person.' That's my
link to other Native Americans, to other brown people, even to the black
people, and to the Oriental people because they have stories too. Our
tribe has stories about them and how they were created.[43]

Chavez viewed other Native Americans and Indigenous Pacific Islanders as
Lamanites, but he continued to value his elders' stories. To Chavez, "other
Lamanites" and "brown people" were special, because the Creator "suffered" and
endured much to create them. He accepted the Book of Mormon and Lamanite identity but still adhered to Diné ancestral teachings to understand fellow
brown-skinned and black-haired people.

Zenobia Kapahulehua Iese expressed a bond that formed between Kānaka
Māoli missionaries and Navajos: "We loved them and they loved us. They
opened their doors to us."[44] Navajos accepted Iese and other missionaries immediately after they self-identified as Kānaka Māoli. Iese came from Kaua'i to
serve in SWIM between April 1971 and October 1972. The LDS Church also
assigned her sisters, Cynthia Kapahulehua and Charlyne Kaulukukui, and her
future husband from Samoa, Tavita Iese, to the Southwest Indian Mission. Iese
remembered that "it was easier for the Hawaiian and Polynesian missionaries
to get into the home to be able to relate to the [Navajo] families than it was for
the Anglo missionaries." Because of love and trust, according to Iese, Navajos
willingly listened to her and fellow Kānaka Māoli missionaries.

Some Navajos identified with her and other Pacific Islander missionaries in
temporal, historical, and spiritual ways. Iese recognized physical and cultural similarities as well as common Indigenous historical experiences of Navajos and Native
Hawaiians. Navajos were reserved toward her at first, but they welcomed her and
other Kānaka Māoli missionaries once they knew "we shared the same history."[45]
Iese considered how Navajos and Kānaka Māoli faced parallel settler-colonial
struggles with Euro-American imperialism as "the same history." The Diné and
Kānaka Māoli both suffered land dispossession and displacement at the hands
of the US government and white settlers. They have also shared a common cause
of decolonization and Indigenous sovereignty despite settler-colonial legacies.[46]

Iese expounded: "Navajos were there, the Yavapai, the Apaches, all the Native Americans were there before the foreigners (white men) came, before the *Mayflower* arrived. You cannot say that Captain Cook 'discovered' America, because there were people there already."[47] Iese compared Captain James Cook, the British explorer who reached the Hawaiian Islands, to the Pilgrims that established some of the earliest English settlements in North America. Native Americans and Kānaka Māoli both claim homelands and Indigeneity in the onslaught of the Euro-American Doctrine of Discovery and Manifest Destiny. Despite the violent histories of settler colonialism, the survival and ongoing presence of Indigenous Peoples fortified Iese's LDS faith. Speaking of Native Americans and Pacific Islanders, she noted, "They have a rich history and culture already that is embedded in wherever we live. You go through Canyon de Chelly, the homes that were built within these walls. Again, Book of Mormon times, there were people living here already." She related the Navajos' ancestral ties to the lands of Canyon de Chelly, where ancient dwellings remain, to "Book of Mormon times." Instead of referring to Native Americans as "Lamanites," she emphasized the Indigeneity and status of First Peoples that connect the Diné and Kānaka Māoli.

Iese and other Kānaka Māoli missionaries focused on interpretations of the Book of Mormon, other than a common Lamanite identity, to understand the Diné. She did not want to "categorize" anyone as a Lamanite, since the term carried negative connotations. Iese turned to scriptures such as 3 Nephi 16:1 that tell how Christ appeared to the Nephites in the Americas and taught them: "And verily, verily, I say unto you that I have other sheep, which are not of this land, neither of the land of Jerusalem, neither in any parts of that land round about whither I have been to minister." Iese believed that her mission among Native Americans fulfilled this scripture and "brought the Book of Mormon to life," as "the Lord, more and more, is being open to us finding each other and sharing our testimony with each other." To her, the "other sheep" included the Diné and Indigenous Peoples.[48]

Iese asserted that her and her husband's mission "has strengthened our testimony even more in the gospel, of the Book of Mormon, and of Jesus Christ coming to 'other sheep have I.' The Navajo people and all these other tribes, all these 'other sheep,' he talked about." Iese could not call herself or Navajos "Lamanites," but she sensed a kinship with them as "God's children," "lost tribes," "other sheep," and Indigenous people that survived settler colonialism.[49] Dennis Little, an LDS Navajo who served in SWIM between 1970 and 1972, confirmed that

Kānaka Māoli missionaries "understood us [the Diné]" because of shared experiences under white American colonization.[50] He remembered several Kānaka Māoli missionaries who could relate to the poverty on the Navajo Reservation, since they came from economically disadvantaged homes and communities. Kānaka Māoli missionaries tended to accept and embrace Diné people and their living conditions, even in cases of lacking amenities and conveniences due to socioeconomic disparities, because "they were used to it."[51]

Other Mormon Native Hawaiians viewed and respected Navajos as Lamanites and fellow minorities but personally rejected a Lamanite identity such as Deborah Pe'a Tsinnijinnie, who served in the Arizona Holbrook Mission in 1976. Tsinnijinnie did not elaborate on why she did not identify as a Lamanite, but she pointed out that "it was not a Lamanite thing [in Hawai'i] as much as it was" on the Navajo Reservation and US mainland. To her, Lamanite identity pertained more to the North American continent and Native American ties to Book of Mormon histories. She related to the Diné as a "minority" in both the United States and the LDS Church.[52] Some Indigenous Mormons viewed Lamanite identity as another label and category that separated them from other Latter-day Saints. Others regarded the term as offensive, since some Book of Mormon histories depict Lamanites as a fallen people that were cursed with "a skin of blackness" for their iniquities.[53] For some LDS Navajos and Kānaka Māoli, according to Dennis Little, the Book of Mormon and "being all Lamanite brought us together ... like cousins."[54] Mormons have understood and lived according to LDS teachings and doctrine in many ways, including diverse Diné and Kānaka Māoli.

Like Tsinnijinnie and Iese, William Keoniana Kelly underscored similarities between Indigenous Peoples as minorities in the LDS Church. Kelly wanted to serve a mission among the Diné after hearing a returned Kānaka Māoli missionary highlight his experiences. Kelly "was so excited to hear what he talked about working with the Navajo Indians and how they were similar to our people, the Hawaiian people." He received his assignment to SWIM in July 1967, and he worked in the mission office for twenty-one months as a secretary and assistant to the president. Kelly remembered, "My aloha went out more to the Polynesians, and I tried to help them as much as possible. I also felt a kinship to the Indian missionaries that were in the field at the time and also some other minority groups like the Hispanic missionaries."[55] He focused on assisting fellow Pacific Islanders and non-white minorities in the field as a mission leader, emphasizing their need to support one another. LDS missionaries also dedicated their efforts to humanitarian service. Navajos recognized missionaries like Kelly, for example, who reportedly "prepared gifts for thousands of Indian children in the Southwest" with his partner Elder Stuart Palmer according to the *Navajo Times* in 1969.[56]

Reflecting on what brings the Diné and different Indigenous Peoples together, Julius Chavez found that "no matter what kind of dancing it is, it's dancing for everyone in the world."[57] Navajos enjoyed and participated in LDS Polynesian dances and "luaus" on the reservation. Dennis Little stressed that Indigenous Pacific Islanders and Native Americans "shared each other's culture" in the mission.[58] He continued to note that "Anglo-Americans are still search-ing for their culture." Unlike the Polynesian and Native American missionar-ies, "[white American missionaries] didn't bring" culture to share on the same platforms.[59]

A Brigham Young University student dance and song troupe, known as Lamanite Generation, developed from the missionary cultural shows. In 1971, Janie Thompson and a returned SWIM missionary, Danny Stewart, formed Lamanite Generation at Brigham Young University. Lamanite Generation, a team of predominately Native American and later Polynesian and Latin Amer-ican dancers and singers, traveled and held shows, especially on the Navajo and other Native American reservations. Some scholars point out that presidents of the Southwest Indian Mission, Dale Tingey (1968–1971) and Paul Felt (1971–1972 who became president of the newly formed New Mexico-Arizona Mission, 1972–1974), encouraged the development of the group, basing the idea on the missionary performance tours.[60]

Harvard Kim recalled how Pacific Islanders included Diné communities in their traditions and celebrations to promote missionary work. By the 1970s, some Pacific Islander former missionaries returned to live on the Navajo Reser-vation with their spouses and families. They often received leadership positions in local congregations such as Vii Pita, a Samoan who was the branch president in Many Farms, Arizona. The branch president and his wife, Carmen Pita, orga-nized the largest luau during Kim's mission because "they were so excited that an Elder from Hawaii was there." Kim described the preparations:

We dug the *imu* (underground oven) with snow still on the ground and frozen. We used river rocks instead of volcanic rocks, and we used lots

of old lettuce leaves (discarded by the school and trading post) instead
of banana leaves and stomps to create the steam in the *imu*.[61]

Indigenous Pacific Islanders created a luau experience for a diverse Mormon
community in Diné Bikéyah, involving Navajos in the efforts. This experience
served as a gift of cultural exchange, as Pacific Islander missionaries occupied
Diné space. LDS Pacific Islanders gathered from different parts near and on the
Navajo Reservation, including former SWIM missionaries who then taught
in San Juan County, Utah, public schools. Polynesian missionaries assigned to
other areas received permission to attend the event. Many of them came to
perform songs and dances at the luau.

Kim's parents sent a couple cases of pineapples from Hawai'i just for the event,
which a member of his congregation retrieved from the Holbrook airport. Kim
reminisced: "The entire Many Farms Branch pitched in and we had a blast—good
food, good entertainment, and good company."[62] Some Navajo members of the
branch dedicated hours to painting a mural for the luau that depicted a Hawaiian
beach.[63] The Many Farms Branch luau represented the diverse but unified community that LDS Pacific Islanders and Navajos formed in Diné Bikéyah between
the 1960s and 1980s. LDS Pacific Islanders, such as the Pitas, prepared and held
gatherings that celebrated and disseminated their culture among Navajos and
people who associated with Mormons in Diné Bikéyah. Navajos reciprocated by
assisting, donating their resources, and learning and sharing different Indigenous
cultures. The influence of Pacific Islanders in Diné congregations came primarily
through cultural exchange and personal relationships.

As a sister missionary, Zenobia Iese taught dances and crafts to Navajos such
as making poi balls and cooking with SPAM. In turn, Navajos showed her how
to make Diné jewelry and fry bread. Iese remarked how Native Americans and
Pacific Islanders may live in "different places, yet we have some great similarities
when it came to family and traditions and the ceremonial dances." She compared
the Hawaiian oli (chants traditionally unaccompanied by dance), mele (general
songs and chants), and ahu (the feather cloak or cape worn by leaders) to Native
American songs, chants, dances, and ceremonial clothing respectively.[64] Missionaries reached out to Diné communities through cultural dance and music,
which relied on their Indigenous ancestral teachings and traditions.

Native Hawaiians and Navajos continued to play a major role in missionary
work on the Navajo Reservation after SWIM, especially under the leadership

of George P. Lee, a Navajo who had served as a young missionary in the Southwest Indian Mission. In 1975, Lee became the first Native American member of the LDS Quorum of Seventy (a high leadership role in the Church). The LDS Church later excommunicated him, in 1989, for "apostasy and other conduct unbecoming a member of the church."[65] Before Lee's excommunication, he served as the president of the Arizona Holbrook Mission. As a sister missionary, Deborah Tsinnijinnie respected Lee as her mission president and developed a strong affinity for the Diné. I do not elaborate on Lee's impact among LDS Navajos, since the interviewees did not discuss him in depth. Tsinnijinnie emphasized, however, that she honored him for his service and leadership in the Church during the mid-1970s.

Tsinnijinnie went on a two-month tour with a group of missionaries throughout the Navajo Reservation and bordering towns of the Holbrook Mission. The group performed Hawaiian and Samoan songs and dances to fundraise for youth missions. Tsinnijinnie found many opportunities for cultural exchange on the show tours, which "perpetuated [her] own culture" while she learned Diné ways of life such as making fry bread and mutton stew, beading, weaving, and sheepherding. Navajos often asked her about Hawai'i, providing her occasions to discuss Kānaka Māoli culture, language, and heritage. My father, who is a Navajo convert and former SWIM missionary, remembered how Polynesian dance, music, and culture fascinated the Diné as "spectacles," but Navajos also respected seeing other Indigenous people continuing their traditions.[66] Tsinnijinnie taught some Diné youth Hawaiian hula that she had danced since the age of four in her hālau (hula school group). Mormon Kānaka Māoli in her home congregation from Hilo, Hawai'i, had organized her hālau, exemplifying how the LDS Church encouraged Tsinnijinnie to connect with Kānaka Māoli culture and ancestral lifeways.

Navajos educated Tsinnijinnie more about their language, culture, and people throughout her mission. She adored and respected the Diné, especially the sáanii (elderly women). She recounted: "I blended right in. They accepted me. I never had a hard time. They let me in their home. We [missionaries] did door to door in the snow, in the rain, in the mud. They always let us in. They were kind. I never was rejected by the Navajo people on my mission." According to Tsinnijinnie, her skin tone, mannerisms, and spirituality enabled her to "blend in" with the Diné, as she developed a kinship with them on her mission like Kānaka Māoli missionaries did previously on the Southwest Indian Mission.

Their distinct culture and dances created a forum of exchange and engagement with Navajos.

Tsinnijinnie became a part of a Lamanite community and family after her mission in Provo, where she attended college and met her husband Thomas Tsinnijinnie, who is Diné from Navajo Mountain, Utah. She accepted the Lamanite Award to receive student funding at Brigham Young University. Several Kānaka Māoli missionaries followed similar life courses after serving in Diné Bikéyah: they attended a Church-owned school with Lamanite programs and opportunities where they courted and married fellow Lamanites.

Like Tsinnijinnie, some of them married Diné Mormons and relocated permanently to the Southwest and Diné Bikéyah. LDS Kānaka Māoli and Diné formed what many Mormons considered "Lamanite" families through intermarriage, and they often played crucial roles in the leadership of Native American congregations. Thomas Tsinnijinnie, for example, served as the bishop of the Papago Ward, a Native American congregational unit in the Salt River Pima-Maricopa Indian Community and Phoenix area. Deborah Tsinnijinnie fulfilled various assignments for the ward, particularly involving the Relief Society for female members and youth programs. Bishop Tsinnijinnie referred to his wife's missionary experiences as strengthening to his faith in the LDS Church.[67] Some Kānaka Māoli missionaries would influence Navajos and their relationship with the LDS Church beyond their time on the mission.

As some Pacific Islander missionaries returned to work on the Navajo Reservation after their missions, they became leaders in the LDS Church like Mitchell Kalauli. In 1962, Kalauli became one of the first Pacific Islanders to serve in the Southwest Indian Mission. Prior to that time, Kalauli knew about Native Americans only from Hollywood movies. Once called to be a mission leader, he developed a stronger connection with Native Americans. Kalauli dedicated himself to two personal goals: the first, to complete his missionary work, and the second, to be a forerunner for his Hawaiian people. He reached out to people on his mission by using his musical and cultural talents of singing and playing songs on his guitar. Kalauli later decided to live with his family on the Navajo Reservation, serving as the bishop of the Tuba City Ward in 1992 during the development of the first LDS stakes on the Navajo Reservation.[68]

On Valentine's Day of 2016, a Navajo Latter-day Saint, Fred Talker, spoke to the local Mormon congregation in Monument Valley, Utah. He dedicated his talk to the most significant role models in his life, especially Kalauli, who influenced his life as an LDS bishop. He demonstrated to Talker that "the soft heart has nothing to do with being a coward. The bravest are soft in heart." When Talker's mother was struggling as a single parent, Kalauli helped her find employment at the Whitehorse High School. Talker considered Kalauli as a father and recognized how he "shaped people."[69]

After Kalauli passed away, he appeared to Talker in a dream, telling him to "put his family in order." Talker decided to recommit to his faith in the LDS Church. LDS Kānaka Māoli such as Kalauli connected with Navajos initially through the Southwest Indian Mission, but they continued to support the growth of the LDS Church in Diné Bikéyah by sustaining relationships with the Diné throughout their lives. For Talker, his relationship with Kalauli persevered past death, since his former bishop bequeathed him a legacy of "priesthood" and "fatherhood."[70] Kalauli also represented the first generation of "Lamanite" leaders in the twentieth-century LDS Church among the Diné.

LDS Church officials called Edwin Tano, a Kānaka Māoli from Wahiawā, O'ahu, as the first Chinle Stake president on the Navajo Reservation. Church officials respected Tano since he spoke Navajo, lived on the reservation, and married a Diné woman.[71] Tano claimed that he "never left his mission" and has lived in Diné Bikéyah for decades as an educator.[72] He received his assignment to the Southwest Indian Mission in 1966. He was offered his "dream job" just after completing his mission application and realized that "the mission call was a choice between either making money or giving money." He would give to Navajos throughout his life based on Kānaka Māoli teachings of aloha. Tano found connections with the Diné, although he knew very little about them before his mission. He participated in mission performance tours and luaus by dancing and playing the ukulele. Tano noted that he and several Pacific Islander missionaries had worked at the Polynesian Cultural Center in Lai'e, Hawai'i, where they learned dances and songs that they later showcased on the mission.[73] According to Tano, they held luaus to show Navajos that "we had our culture but we were embedded with Christ."[74]

Reflecting on how the Navajos reacted to him as a missionary, he asserted, "Hawaiians were always accepted because of aloha, our naturalness and welcomeness." He concluded from his mission experience, "I have a mission. The Lord has a mission for everybody. The Lord provides a way to succeed in the place he wants us to build his kingdom." Tano viewed his calling as sharing the LDS gospel with fellow Lamanites and supporting Indigenous Peoples, especially the

Diné. He remained in Diné Bikéyah, where he married Sara Singer (a Navajo Mormon), raised their family, served in various Church callings, taught in high school, and coached football for over 30 years.[75] Before becoming a stake president, Tano worked in the Elders' Quorum and later became the first Lamanite (or non-white) bishop in the Tuba City area. He served as the first stake president of the Tuba City, Arizona, Stake in 1995 as well.[76]

When LDS Church authorities asked Tano if he would accept the position as the new Chinle Stake president in 1992, he "told them that the day of the Lamanite people to be hand-fed, patted on their heads and constantly reminded that they were a chosen people had to come to an end if they would even expect to rise to their true stature."[77] Tano identified as a Lamanite, as did some Navajos with whom he served. He believed that the organization of the Chinle Stake marked a transformative event for Lamanites, and that Navajos would fulfill their potential as Latter-day Saints. He envisioned a promising future of the Church unit, because he believed that the stake "is the chlorophyll of the plant that makes it grow, not the external water or fertilizer."[78] According to this opinion, LDS Navajos should embrace their self-determination, decreasing the "external" assistance of non-Navajos in the LDS Church.

Tano and some Church leaders scrutinized reliance on other Latter-day Saints, especially those considered as white and Anglo-American, in temporal and spiritual terms. Tano criticized the extent, for example, to which Native American converts "have gone through the motions" and imitated other Mormons' lives without fully understanding LDS practices and principles for themselves.[79] The formation and operations of the Chinle Stake through Lamanite leadership would enable Navajos to develop their own testimonies of the LDS Church by eliminating previous dependency upon white Mormons.

As a bishop, Tano valued Native American congregations and stakes, recognizing their potential to advance Indigenous faith-based self-determination. In 1979, a previous stake president organized two congregations in Kayenta, Arizona, a "Lamanite" ward for Native Americans and a non-Native American branch. When Tano became bishop, he maintained these separate congregations. He justified this decision in 1991: "From the natural man's eyes, we want to be racially equal. . . . But when you do that, you again deprive the Lamanites of taking of anything because they are going to back slide [sic] and sit in the back." Tano referred to the conceptualizations of racial integration and segregation.

He differentiated his ideas of LDS ethnic congregations, specifically Lamanite wards, from the national discourse of racial segregation and inequalities.

In his opinion, Native American congregations presented Navajos with more opportunities to serve as equal members of the LDS Church, because branches and wards needed and relied on them. "Without this Kayenta Ward or Lamanite ward, [the members] wouldn't have the opportunity to socialize into the Church and realize that the gospel is also socialization," Tano explained.[80] Diné Mormons related more closely to other Navajos and Lamanites, which fostered connections between the members and strengthened LDS Navajo networks. Tano and other Indigenous Mormons supported the Diné stake in the hope that Native American congregational units encouraged greater devotion and salvation through the LDS gospel. Some Native Americans have followed these efforts to promote LDS Diné participation in self-sustaining Native American congregations, including my father and the current Chinle Stake president Romero Brown (who are both Diné).[81]

As the bishop of the Tuba City Ward in 1992, Mitchell Kalauli compared the early Chinle Stake with his mission in SWIM to trace the growth of the LDS Church in Diné Bikéyah. After serving as a SWIM missionary during the 1960s, Kalauli worked for the LDS Indian seminary program on the Navajo Reservation. Kalauli noticed positive changes among LDS Navajo congregations since the creation of the Chinle Stake. According to him, Church leadership, membership, and presence increased. Not only were more Diné converts worthy of attending the LDS temple services, but they also found ways to travel to the nearest temples for worship, sometimes located hundreds of miles from their homes. By the mid-1990s, wards began to develop with fully staffed leaders and auxiliaries who were both Navajo and non-Navajo.

The rise and decline of the Indian Student Placement Program (ISPP), which placed Native American students with Mormon families during part of the year for schooling, correlated with SWIM and the expansion of the LDS Church on the Navajo Reservation.[82] Kalauli appreciated the impacts of the ISPP on several Navajo missionaries serving in Diné Bikéyah, which he credited for preparing them for missions. He regarded, however, the suspension of ISPP as necessary. He criticized the program for removing the youth leadership from Diné Bikéyah, which prevented the stake from becoming "local and [flourishing]."[83]

Despite the collaborations and empathy between Kānaka Māoli and Diné Mormons, some Navajos viewed Native Hawaiians as outsiders who detracted from Diné authority in the LDS Church. Dan K. Smith, a Navajo LDS convert and member of the Chinle Stake, expressed some concerns with the role of the LDS Pacific Islanders in leadership positions following the major changes in the LDS congregational organizations on the reservation. He initially regarded the stake boundaries to be too large, but he later realized that the expansion provided opportunities for the Native American members to become more devout and independent in the LDS Church.

Although he respected some of the help from non-Navajo stakes, as a former branch president, counselor, and district president, Smith stressed that the LDS Diné needed less assistance from nontribal members including Native Hawaiians. Although they often accepted and understood Church leader assignments as callings from divine revelation, LDS Pacific Islanders sometimes represented an extension of outside control in Navajo communities. Smith explained, for example, that some Navajos resented how a Kānaka Māoli served as stake president.[84] Navajos still depended on non-Navajo Church leaders and members, whites and Polynesians in particular, which he thought stalled the growth of a Diné stake such as Chinle. Victor Black, a Navajo from Tuba City, received priesthood authority in the LDS Church after most Pacific Islanders left his area. He recalled, "When I joined [the LDS Church], the Samoans or members from Hawaii held those leadership positions. Over the past twenty-four years, I have noticed that gradual change so that the native local brethren have stepped up to the plate." When most "Hawaiians, Samoans, and non-Native teachers" moved away, Victor Black and other Navajo men felt obligated to fulfill the duties of priesthood holders and leaders because no one else would assume them.[85]

When Edwin Tano accepted the calling as the Chinle Stake president, a Navajo approached him and "wanted [him] to take back his temple recommend," a document that allows Latter-day Saints to enter their temples. When he returned his recommend to Tano, this Diné Mormon told him, "I don't need this anymore." Tano did not understand what offended this member of the stake, but he wondered if the man was upset that a Kānaka Māoli became the stake president.[86] To Tano, he felt Kānaka Māoli Mormons came with resolve, experiences, and aloha to strengthen and assist Navajos in their growth as Latter-day Saints. He followed the encouragement of LDS church officials such as Harvey Gardner who assured him:

Now you will be able to tell them [Navajos] what we (bilagaanas) have been trying to tell them for years but were not successful. But now they will listen to you because you will know how to speak to them and they will trust you and accept what you say.[87]

The Diné terms of *bilagaanas* or *bilagáana* translate as *whites* or *Anglos*. Harvey asserted that Navajos would respond and adhere to Kānaka Māoli Mormons as missionaries and leaders. In 2013, Tano expressed satisfaction that "now there are much more natives in leadership positions [on the reservation] which was the intention in the first place. I always believed that church leadership should be vested in those 'whose bones will be buried in this land.'"[88]

Despite the possible differences and even tensions between Kānaka Māoli and Diné Latter-day Saints, diverse Mormons continued to unify and harmonize in LDS communities throughout Diné Bikéyah. Pacific Islanders served as missionaries and Church authorities, established the base of the LDS Church on the Navajo Reservation, and converted many Navajos alongside other Native American, white, and non-white Mormons. Some Native Hawaiian missionaries settled on the reservation to support the infrastructure of the LDS Church, spearheading the formation of the first stakes in Diné Bikéyah. Some Kānaka Māoli and Diné Mormons intermarried starting Navajo-Hawaiian families that hybridized two different heritages under the banner of Lamanites and Latter-day Saints. Native Hawaiians planted the spirit of aloha among Navajo Mormons through their service as missionaries, Church leaders, and cultural ambassadors.

The exchange between Kānaka Māoli aloha and Diné Bikéyah was reciprocal, as Native Hawaiian missionaries brought their memories of Navajo land back home with them to the islands. In 2013, Zenobia Iese described how former SWIM missionaries gathered in Lai'e, Hawai'i, since several of them had returned to Hawai'i and formed a social network based on their shared experiences on the Navajo Reservation. Iese looked forward to their next reunion, emphasizing their closeness and efforts to visit one another.[89] Diné ancestral teachings of Si'ah Naagháí Bik'eh Hózhǫ́ (SNBH) live in the people and their homelands, which resonated with Kānaka Māoli Mormons who also embraced their Indigeneity. By their encounters with Kānaka Māoli Mormons on the reservation, Navajos glimpsed how aloha intertwines with the land and people of Hawai'i.

Although Church officials and scholars have not reported specifically on the number and personal information of Kānaka Māoli that served the LDS

Church in Diné Bikéyah, Navajos recognized and felt the presence of these
Native Hawaiians. When I attended the Southwest Indian Mission Reunion
with my father on April 5, 2013, the representation of the aloha culture and spirit
did not surprise me. Several Native Hawaiians traveled from Hawai'i to attend
the reunion in Orem, Utah. In homage to past days of luaus on the Southwest
Indian Mission, they gathered on the stage of the Church gymnasium, introduced themselves in Navajo, and then performed Kānaka Māoli songs and hulas.
They adorned several former missionaries with leis, including the past SWIM
president Dale Tingey. Photos of former missionaries covered one of the walls,
and a third of them were Indigenous Pacific Islanders. The reunion reminded
everyone, although not exclusively, of LDS Native Hawaiians' influence and
contributions in the mission.

After a recent conversation with "Auntie" Farina, my namesake, she sent me
documents with a list and pictures of LDS Indigenous Pacific Islanders who
lived and taught in schools on the Navajo Reservation during the 1980s. Farina
and many of those names and faces have become a part of my extended family.
As Fred Talker and other Navajos have shown me, LDS Kānaka Māoli and
Indigenous Pacific Islanders did not teach my family alone of aloha—giving
and service—on the reservation. This article highlights only a few of the LDS
Kānaka Māoli and Pacific Islanders who came to Diné Bikéyah as missionaries,
and some who returned to work in Diné education as they continued to support
Mormon congregations and networks.

The bilasáanaa diwozhí ("Pineapples") formed an integral part of the LDS
Church in Diné Bikéyah, because the Diné and Kānaka Māoli related to one
another in myriad ways. Whether they viewed each other as fellow Lamanites,
as the "True Israel," or as Indigenous Peoples with respective concepts of SNBH
and aloha, diverse LDS Navajos and Native Hawaiians willingly embraced the
Mormon faith and became brothers and sisters in the Church. While LDS
Church officials identified them both as "Lamanites," they found alternative
connections between 1949 and 1990 through friendship, kinship, and aloha
lasting to this day. While LDS Native Hawaiians sought to "serve" Navajos,
they relied on the generosity and assistance of Navajos to live and connect with
Diné communities. When these missionaries embraced this dependency, seeking
with humility, Navajos often obliged and welcomed Native Hawaiians, and they
would engage in the discussions about the LDS Church, learn, and share the
teachings of faith and diverse cultures.

9

Grafting Indians and Mormons Together on Great Plains Reservations

A History of the LDS Northern Indian Mission, 1964–1973

JAY H. BUCKLEY, KATHRYN COCHRAN, TAYLOR BROOKS, AND KRISTEN HOLLIST[1]

"There is something different about you Mormons," a Lakota man told LDS Northern Indian Mission president Rex C. Reeve Jr., "something in your faces, you're just different."[2] Indians living on reservations encompassed within the Northern Indian Mission (NIM) boundaries really did notice peculiarities when Mormon missionaries—emissaries for The Church of Jesus Christ of Latter-day Saints (LDS)—arrived on the reservation during the 1960s. LDS missionaries spent nearly as much time chopping wood, coaching basketball, and serving in the community as they did teaching gospel lessons in Indian Country.[3] This service created bonds of friendship and trust between missionaries and Indian communities, helped establish LDS congregations on and near reservations, and provided educational, economical, and religious opportunities and experiences for those inclined to participate. Yet, some Indigenous Peoples viewed this Mormon intrusion into Indian Country as another well-intentioned colonialist, Christian, paternalistic organization endeavoring to "save the Indian" through conversion and acculturation into the dominant society.[4]

The elders, sisters, and couples called to the Northern Indian Mission shared their gospel message to Indigenous Peoples living on reservations in Montana, Wyoming, North and South Dakota, Nebraska, and Minnesota. Instead of the symbolic motif comparing saving souls to harvesting wheat by thrusting in the sickle, NIM missionaries altered their methods of reservation proselyting to resemble grafting—joining LDS teachings and cultural practices with existing Indian beliefs, identities, and cultures that enabled them to inosculate or grow together over time. Latter-day Saints take seriously the injunction to gather scattered Israel through inviting all to come unto Christ through sharing the gospel. Believers literally become the seed of Abraham and will receive the blessings of the Abrahamic Covenant, including: inheritance in a Promised Land; innumerable posterity; and access to priesthood and temple blessings. Latter-day Saints also believe Natives are descendants from the House of Israel, especially the tribe of Joseph, through his sons Ephraim and Manasseh, and repeatedly refer to the proselytization of Indigenous Peoples as "redeeming the remnant."[5]

Like the grafting of roses or fruit trees, which requires patience and practice to graft the natural branches into the mother vine, LDS leaders and members believed the lives of American Indians would grow stronger and improve when infused with Christ's teachings to fulfill the LDS scriptural promise that "Jacob shall flourish in the wilderness, and the Lamanites shall blossom as the rose."[6] They endeavored to accomplish this grafting by building relationships of trust and endeavoring to connect LDS teachings and scriptures to American Indian cultures and beliefs whenever possible. Natives decided whether they wanted to listen, accept, reject, or oppose those messengers and their teachings.

The Missionary Training Center (MTC) briefly introduced missionaries called to the Northern Indian Mission to a simplified and distorted white European view of American Indians.[7] Once in the field, some missionaries learned greetings and words in Lakota and other Native languages, as well as greater empathy and understanding when Indigenous Peoples shared their culture and history with them.[8] The Church and its missionaries established programs to encourage education, agricultural production, and economic self-sufficiency as well as to share the gospel. Northern Indian Mission missionaries' methods of reaching out to community leaders, building friendships and conducting community service before teaching missionary lessons, and focusing on specialized youth programs like seminary, youth sports, and community activities established goodwill in some Indian communities and aided in the establishment of several Latter-day Saints congregations in Indian Country.

This essay is the first published history of the LDS Northern Indian Mission, describing its origin, objectives, and expiration. We are the first to use the records kept by the presidents of that mission, and the first to distill their various visions and points of emphasis. As an LDS mission history, our essay often casts the proselytizing of Native Peoples in a favorable light because that is the story the mission records reveal.

We also point out the shortsightedness and shortcomings of the mission. The mission presidents and missionaries did not concern themselves nor question that they engaged in a form of colonialism, making undeniable efforts to transform Indigenous minds and bodies into alternative images largely shaped by Mormon Americans. Latter-day Saints both introduced—and perhaps occasionally imposed—beliefs and cultural contexts upon those who professed faith in the LDS Church, inscribing new Mormon identities upon Native hearts and minds.

In order to counterbalance these mission-produced sources, my co-authors and I have conducted and transcribed dozens of oral history interviews with Native individuals and Native missionaries, as well as utilized other oral history interviews, memoirs, and correspondence to provide Native voices and perspectives describing their own experiences and Native realities. Many of these Native voices are favorable to the Church. Others are not. We have included selections from both.

We have also utilized newspaper accounts and other sources to provide non-Native voices that opposed the expansion of LDS missionary work onto Great Plains reservations. We hope readers will come to understand that instead of viewing LDS ecclesiastical and educational efforts among Native nations from within a binary of right or wrong, they will realize that the history of the LDS Northern Indian Mission contains more nuances than they initially supposed. Finally, we ask readers to put aside their own preconceptions or judgments to allow Native members who embraced the Church to articulate their own LDS Indigenous identities and cosmologies they created through exercising their own agency throughout this grafting process.

Historical Context of LDS Indian Missions

Since its founding on April 6, 1830, The Church of Jesus Christ of Latter-day Saints has emphasized the importance of missionary work to proclaim unto all the world what they believe to be the restored gospel of Jesus Christ. The publication of the Book of Mormon in 1830 revealed an American religious text offering an interpretation that some American Indians were among a remnant of the House of Israel through the lineage of Joseph (through his sons Ephraim and Manasseh). Book of Mormon authors Nephi, Mormon, and Moroni each commented that the sacred scriptural record was written to the descendants of the children of Lehi—called Lamanites after Lehi's eldest son Laman. Latter-day Saints have felt a special calling to share the Book of Mormon with American Indians, believing that their acceptance of the ancient record would "bring them to a knowledge of their Fathers."[9]

Church president Joseph Smith initiated the first official LDS mission when he called Oliver Cowdery, Peter Whitmer Jr., Parley Pratt, and Ziba Peterson as missionaries to teach the gospel to the so-called "Lamanites."[10] The missionary foursome traveled to the borders of Indian Territory in 1830 sharing their message that the once powerful Indigenous Peoples should accept the gospel message and regain the promises God had made to their forefathers—that the Americas would be a promised land to those who worshipped the Lord. Elder Pratt promised them "if the red man would receive this Book [of Mormon] and learn the things written in it, and do according thereunto, they should be restored to all their rights and privileges ... and should be in favor with the Great Spirit."[11]

The missionaries' efforts did not yield any Indian converts. Later, after the Latter-day Saints emigrated west, they established additional Indian missions there too, with mixed results.[12] LDS interest in Indian missions diminished between the Civil War and World War II.[13] By the mid-twentieth century, however, the LDS Church expressed renewed interest in establishing Indian missions. They organized the Navajo-Zuni Mission in 1943, the first LDS Indian mission in the twentieth century, rechristened five years later as the Southwest Indian Mission (SWIM)(see Table 9.1).[14]

Genesis of the Northern Indian Mission:
President Grant Farmer, 1964–1967

In the summer of 1963, Elder Spencer W. Kimball asked Southwest Indian Mission president J. Edwin Baird if he would extend his mission another year "for the purpose of opening up the work for Indians in what became the Northern Indian Mission." Kimball prophesied that "the work among the Lamanites

Table 9.1 Indian Mission Timeline and Northern Indian Mission Presidents

1943	Navajo-Zuni Mission created
1948	Renamed Southwest Indian Mission
1961–1965	J. Edwin Baird, Southwest Indian Mission President, initiated and presided over Northern Division
1964	Northern Indian Mission created
1964–1967	Grant R. Farmer, Northern Indian Mission President
1967–1970	Harvey A. Dahl, Northern Indian Mission President
1970–1973	Rex C. Reeve, Jr., Northern Indian Mission President
1970	North Central States Mission renamed Manitoba-Minnesota Mission
1972	Southwest Indian Mission reorganized as New Mexico-Arizona Mission
1973	Northern Indian Mission reorganized as Dakota-Manitoba Mission
	Reservations in MT and WY transferred to Montana Billings Mission
	Reservations in MN transferred to Minnesota Minneapolis Mission
	Reservations in NE transferred to the Missouri Independence Mission
1974	Northern Indian Mission reorganized as South Dakota Rapid City Mission; President Clarence Bishop (1973–1976)
1974	New Mexico-Arizona reorganized as Arizona Holbrook Mission; President George P. Lee (first American Indian Mission President)
1975	New Mexico-Arizona reorganized as New Mexico Albuquerque Mission; President Stanley D. Roberts (1974–1977)
1975–1989	George P. Lee serves as first American Indian General Authority

would move forward in the future 'at a greatly accelerated level, as never before.'" Baird and his wife led a caravan of "thirty experienced missionaries from the SWIM and went north, placing then in isolated locations on various reservations" in what became known as the "Northern Division of the Southwest Indian Mission." (See Figure 9.1)[15] There they set up permanent full-time missionary work on eleven reservations in Wyoming, Montana, and the Dakotas (see Figure 9.2).[16] The missionaries, along with five full-time seminary leaders, found places to rent and commenced teaching. For twenty-one months, Baird directed the work in the Southern and Northern Divisions, traveling thousands of miles making visits and conducting affairs.[17]

LDS leaders separated the Southwest and Northern Divisions by creating an independent Northern Indian Mission (NIM) with headquarters in Rapid City, South Dakota, on 1 April 1964.[18] They called Grant Farmer—a building contractor from Boise, Idaho, who had served as a missionary in the Northern States Mission twice (1946–1947 and 1952–1954) and as a stake missionary [a stake is a unit comprised of several wards and branches] to Indian tribes south of Boise—as president. When Farmer arrived in Rapid City in the summer of

Figure 9.1. Southwest and Northwest Indian Mission President J. Edwin Baird and Indigenous Elders and Sisters Missionaries. Courtesy of Rex C. Reeve, Jr., Northern Indian Mission Collection, MSS 8816, L. Tom Perry Special Collections, Harold B. Lee Library, Provo, Utah.

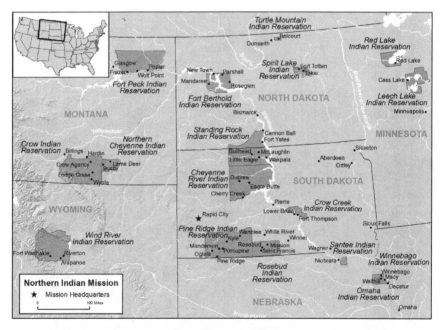

Figure 9.2. Map of Northern Indian Mission boundaries. Map courtesy of BYU Think Spatial Lab.

1964, he had 65 missionaries.[19] Farmer built the mission—the largest geographical mission in the US—from scratch from his motel room. He rented a mission office at 615½ 7th Street, and trained the missionaries called to this new mission. Over the next few months the number of missionaries increased from 65 to 100. Missionaries who had been serving for a few weeks or months suddenly became senior companions to the newcomers, and pairs of elders were sent hundreds of miles away from mission headquarters into unfamiliar areas with the parting words, "May the Lord be with you Elders!"[20] About 30 Pacific Islanders, from Hawaii to New Zealand, served in the NIM as well as a number of Indigenous missionaries, mostly from the American Southwest. By 1966, the NIM and SWIM each had around 175 English-speaking full-time missionaries.[21]

Farmer believed the teachings and practices of the LDS Church held answers to many problems he saw confronting Indians. He held a paternalistic perspective that exposure to Latter-day Saints and their programs would help Indians progress spiritually and temporally. In many ways, LDS Church programs resembled other social welfare and federal and institutional efforts aimed at the acculturation of Indians into Western modes of thought and belief.[22] Farmer assigned between four and twenty missionaries to each reservation (depending upon the size).[23] Many Natives belonged to the Native American Church or to Catholic or Protestant denominations, and this represented their initial exposure to the Latter-day Saint tradition. Most knew little about the LDS Church and were not even sure whether Mormons were Christians.[24]

Farmer stressed the importance of contacting tribal leaders and council members and he facilitated relationships with them to gain their trust. "All over the mission many Indian leaders know President Farmer and count him as their close personal friend," Reeve wrote. "This has required many hours of waiting in offices, and hundreds of missed appointments."[25] Cato Volandra (Brulé Lakota), tribal chairman of the Brulé Sioux on the Rosebud Reservation commented, "I have never met a more persistent man than President Farmer."[26]

Working with leaders occasionally produced favorable results. Farmer organized trips for tribal leaders to visit Utah to learn about the Church firsthand. In July 1967, Robert Philbrick (Lakota), chairman of the Crow Creek and Sioux Indian Tribal Council from Chamberlain, South Dakota, and three other council members traveled with Farmer and Reeve to visit Salt Lake City. Accompanying them were Malvina Shields (Crow Creek Sioux) and her friends Brenda and Janet Pease and Mary Not Help Him, all recent LDS converts. Moreover, the tribal chairman's son, Douglas, had joined the Church the previous year. Philbrick's entourage visited Church offices, met LDS leaders, and toured Temple Square, Welfare Square, Deseret Industries, and Primary Children's Hospital. After visiting a stake farm near Utah Lake, they toured the campus of LDS Church–owned Brigham Young University.[27]

Farmer articulated his enthusiasm for missionary work and his professed love for Indigenous Peoples in the messages he sent out in the monthly NIM publication *The Lamanite* (see Figures 9.3 and 9.4). For him and other Latter-day Saint contemporaries, the term "Lamanites" referred to all the Indigenous Peoples of the Americas and Polynesia.[28] Farmer believed in an Indian heritage he referred to as "Indian Israel" and emphasized the importance of helping to gather this scattered branch of Israel to the truth.[29] He always reminded the missionaries that it was a great privilege to serve among Indigenous Peoples: "How glorious to labor in the midst of our Savior's vineyard, in the very heart of his field—for the Lamanites *are* his sheep! How marvelous to see in their eyes the light of wonder, recognition of their Shepherd's voice and acceptance of his Church!"[30]

Farmer organized mission tours (by Polynesian missionaries, a mission band, Indigenous elders and sisters, a mission softball team, and a mission basketball team) as community outreach endeavors.[31] Indian communities accepted Polynesian and Native elders and sisters more easily and the missionaries related how their Native cultures enabled them to understand, appreciate, and teach LDS concepts more effectively from a Native point of view. Alvin Watchman (Navajo) remarked he "joyfully entered the temple for the first time" and felt "somewhat at home because of the spiritual preparation he had received and also because his knowledge of traditional Navajo ceremonies and teachings enhanced, increased and magnified his temple experience. Also, some of the symbolism seemed familiar to him." While in the MTC, preparing to serve in the South Dakota Rapid City Mission, he met his future wife Edna Crane (Sarcee/Canadian Sioux) who worked in the cafeteria and had recently returned from the Northern Indian Mission. After his mission, they became reacquainted at a birthday party and married. Watchman recounted that "one benefit of serving a Church mission was how much my reading ability improved because we had to do so much reading. Improved reading and the good study habits from my mission really helped me with my schooling." Watchman later served as bishop of the Native American Ward in Provo, Utah.[32]

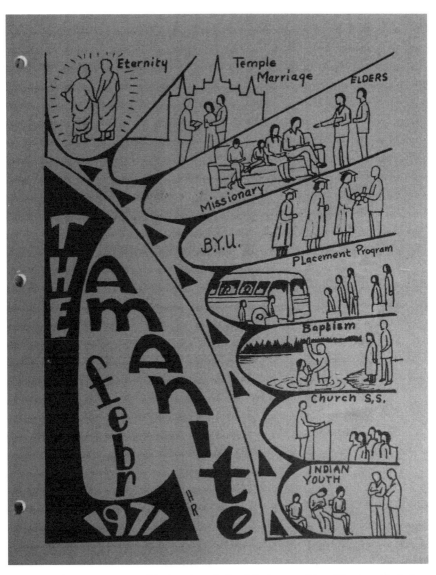

Figure 9.3. February 1971 cover of the Northern Indian Mission monthly publication, *The Lamanite*. Artwork by Herman Red Elk and E.B. Hatch. Courtesy of Rex C. Reeve, Jr., Northern Indian Mission Collection, MSS 8816, L. Tom Perry Special Collections, Harold B. Lee Library, Provo, Utah.

GO MY SON, GET AN EDUCATION, LEARN THE WAYS OF GOD.

Figure 9.4. May 1973 cover of the Northern Indian Mission monthly publication, *The Lamanite*, featuring the song *Go My Son*, which emphasized the importance of getting an education. Artwork by Herman Red Elk. Courtesy of Rex C. Reeve Jr., Northern Indian Mission Collection, MSS 8816, L. Tom Perry Special Collections, Harold B. Lee Library, Provo, Utah.

Donald Pine (Lakota) from Fort Yates, Standing Rock Sioux Reservation, noted that after he received his mission call to the Portugal Porto Mission "my heritage proved to be a great asset during my mission: being a Sioux Indian created an unusual interest in the Spanish people, which allowed me to teach when others were unable to. People were curious to know where I was from, and then after hearing I was Sioux, which was the Indian Tribe about which they had the greatest curiosity, they asked me questions about my people. I was able to share my Lamanite Book of Mormon heritage and teach the gospel."[33]

Traveling Church dignitaries also relished listening to the testimonies of Native converts. In July 1967, President N. Eldon Tanner of the First Presidency and Elder Delbert L. Stapley of the Quorum of the Twelve Apostles visited the NIM. Nearly 200 people attended a conference in Pierre, South Dakota, where Indian members "expressed appreciation for learning about their ancestors from the Book of Mormon and the promising opportunities to serve in the different branches (small congregations) of the Church on the reservations." The next day Tanner and Stapley met with Brulé Sioux Tribal Council Chairman Cato Valandra, who reported a favorable response to Church efforts among his tribe.[34] After only two and a half years, the Northern Indian Mission had grown from nothing to "2,000 Lamanite members in 16 branches scattered among 17 tribes on 22 reservations."[35] Farmer oversaw the construction of Church buildings on the 11 reservation headquarters at Poplar, Lodge Grass, Dunmore, Lame Deer, Fort Yates, Cass Lake, Macy, Winnebago, Rosebud, Cherry Creek, and Eagle Butte.[36]

Emphasis on Agricultural and Educational Pursuits: President Harvey A. Dahl, 1967–1970

In July 1967, Church leaders called Harvey Dahl to serve as NIM president. Dahl, a cattle rancher from Deeth, Nevada, had served in the Farm Home Administration as a special assistant to US secretary of agriculture Ezra Taft Benson. Not understanding nor acknowledging Indigenous land use nor Indigenous religious identities, Dahl paternalistically believed that "the Indians need economic help as much as spiritual help." He said that the aim of the mission was "to build men to be good ranchers and farmers, heads of their homes and good priesthood holders."[37]

One of those was Gerald Red Elk (Assiniboine/Dakota) from Poplar, Montana. His wife was an active member but Gerald struggled with alcohol. With the help of missionaries and local leaders, he gave up the bottle and returned to Church activity, eventually serving as branch president. His brother Herman Red Elk (Assiniboine/Dakota) served as the artist who drew many of the covers for *The Lamanite*.

Hoera Tetuhi Marei Kura Kingi (Māori), who served as a NIM missionary, returned to Pine Ridge after his mission. He met Elizabeth Mousseaux (Oglala Lakota), and introduced her to the Church. They married and had five children. After living in New Zealand from 1981–1990, they returned to Pine Ridge where he provided education and vocational training in Pine Ridge and served as Pine Ridge branch president.[38]

Dahl, a six-foot-four-inch cowboy, traveled the Indian rodeo circuit and was a pickup rider for the bronc riding events. He met hundreds of Indian men at these rodeos and struck up conversations and formed friendships. He believed farming and ranching could economically empower people living on poverty-stricken reservations. Dahl organized agricultural projects in every state within the NIM boundaries. He believed that assisting Indian farming and ranching programs served perfectly in helping them become self-reliant, and members and nonmembers all had access to these programs. "We hope that it will be possible for as many Indians as have the desire to farm and graze their own lands on the reservation" Dahl opined. "We want to help all Lamanite people—both Church members and non-members."[39]

Reservation conditions created obstacles to overcome. The Church owned no land, had no Church buildings, very few members, and no priesthood leadership to organize and run the branches. The missionaries and senior couples had to carry the load of establishing each branch.[40] Linda Uranga (Rosebud Sioux) remembers that she liked the missionary lessons, especially their teachings about the Heavenly Father and Jesus Christ, which made more sense to her than the Catholic teaching of the Trinity. After her baptism at Pine Ridge, they held Sunday meetings at the American Legion hall. Her family and the Arrow family were the only ones. The missionaries said the opening prayer, they sang a song, blessed the sacrament, passed it, gave a talk, and closed with prayer. Later, when they established a formal branch, she thought "Gee, Church service is a lot longer than it used to be!"[41]

Many missionaries did not have running water or indoor plumbing, and cooked with woodburning stoves. Driving distances created logistical problems. Bitter cold winds, deep snow, and ice made winter driving hazardous. Renting trailers and getting missionary housing proved a never-ending challenge, as well as keeping the cars and pickups in the fleet functioning. Missionaries sought to build relationships of trust in the community through service with the slogan "first a friend, then a contact."[42] Service projects included: hauling and stacking hay, herding cattle, harvesting corn, creating fun games to care for youth during powwows, chopping wood, repairing fences, planting community gardens, and other forms of chores and community service. When a flood hit Rapid City, the missionaries distributed truckloads of supplies to the entire community.[43]

Reservation life involved uphill battles against unemployment, educational attainment, alcoholism, and poverty. Roy Watchman (Sioux: Cheyenne River/ Standing Rock/Turtle Mountain) grew up in Mobridge, South Dakota, along the Missouri River. "When you are in the middle of a lot of poverty, you don't realize how poor you are," he recounted. Watchman lived in a "one-room log cabin of about 600 square feet with a dirt floor and a stove in the middle. We slept around the stove. We didn't live in a home with indoor plumbing until I was about 15 years old."[44] Sister missionary Flora Dude (San Carlos Apache) was assigned to Hardin, Montana, near the Crow Reservation. "Some of the families we visited had old houses and used cardboard to cover their walls." They visited an elderly grandmother who invited them in. "We talked to them about the Church and they listened and they were quiet even though they probably did not understand all of what we said because they spoke Crow. Their granddaughter translated for us. The grandmother came over and gave me a hug and offered us food." Indigenous generosity was not dependent upon material bounty.[45]

Dahl knew Indians had good land so he assigned couples to oversee agricultural projects to assist tribal members in gaining economic self-sufficiency through farming and ranching.[46] He secured $300,000 in government loans that funded Indian co-ops to purchase cattle to graze on the reservations. Dahl supervised the cattle buying and selling, with proceeds funding costs and repaying the loans. He did not receive money nor did any go to the Church. Several ranchers expressed interest in the Church for its teachings and for the cattle-buying program.[47]

The mission carried out reservation projects to irrigate cropland. Fort Yates Lakotas voted to irrigate 1,000 acres of their reservation so the Church helped them purchase motors, pumps, sprinklers, plows, and tractors. The tribe requested "good LDS men with experience in irrigation to help operate and direct this tribal project."[48] These projects opened doors and hearts. Joe Bear Come Out (Lakota) heard of the agricultural projects and invited the supervisors to his farm. They installed a pump in the Tongue River to help him irrigate his fields. With this new system installed, he planted barley, hay, potatoes, squash, and cantaloupe—and joined the Church. Seeing Bear Come Out's agricultural yields, other neighbors inquired about the Mormons and marveled at their generous works.[49] These agricultural projects provided a great service to the temporal well-being of reservation inhabitants and brought over 10,000 acres of Indian land into cultivation and agricultural production.[50]

Dahl believed public school and college education held the key to breaking the poverty cycle. On April 18, 1969 he called five missionaries into his office to launch the "Elders Five Mission Tour." He asked them to tour the mission and encourage Indian students of all grade levels to consider improving their access to education.[51] He sent missionaries to teach subjects and coach sports at local schools. "Elder Arrowgarp is helping with music at Fort Yates; Elder Hatch at Pine Ridge; Elder Tiutama and Elder Stokes are coaching and helping with athletic activities in Dupree and Pine Ridge."[52] Sister Hattie Bell Ross made one of the greatest contributions to reservation education in the mission. She was the only teacher in South Dakota who had a PhD in elementary education. She volunteered as a full-time missionary, donating her services to area schools helping children improve their skills at reading, writing, and speaking English. The children—but more especially their parents and grandparents—appreciated the alternative and supplemental educational opportunities programs like seminary and language instruction provided. Moreover, special emphasis for developing leadership among youth led to the establishment of programs for Indian children such as LDS seminary instruction, and youth missions of from one to three months, efforts designed to enable youth to receive public education, gain confidence, prepare them to attend college, and expose them to Church teachings.[53]

In 1954, the Church created a program to provide Indian youth with greater educational opportunities to attend public schools that would prepare them for college and for becoming future leaders in a changing, and increasingly urban world. Apostle Spencer W. Kimball established the Indian Student Placement Program (ISPP).[54] Each year, approximately 5,000 Indian students, ages 8 to 18, could opt to leave their reservation, live with an LDS family, and attend public schools instead of Bureau of Indian Affairs (BIA) schools. To qualify for the programs, Indian students agreed to uphold Church standards, maintain passing grades, and live with their designated LDS family. The foster parents, as volunteers, were responsible for providing financial assistance as well as emotional and spiritual support. The children lived with their foster families during the nine-month school year and returned to their biological families during the summer months. More than 50,000 American Indian children participated in ISPP.[55]

Elders Spencer W. Kimball, LeGrand Richards, A. Theodore Tuttle, and Stewart A. Durrant served on the Church Indian Affairs Committee in the 1960s while Elder John Longden supervised the Indian Missions. Kimball, in particular, served as an indefatigable advocate for causes he felt would benefit Indians and repeatedly expressed his sincere love for them. Patriarch Samuel Claridge blessed Kimball as a young man saying, "You will preach the Gospel to many people, but more especially to the Lamanites." As the head of the Church's Lamanite Committee, Kimball "was the driving force behind a number of Church and Brigham Young University programs to benefit 'the Lamanites,' usually targeting American Indians: Lamanite seminary, Lamanite Mutual Improvement Associations, Lamanite youth conferences, a BYU institute for Lamanite Research and Service (now American Indian Services), and most famously, the Indian (or Lamanite) Student Placement Program."[56] Kimball's efforts to serve as an "apostle to the Lamanites" stemmed from his understanding of fulfilling this promise he believed came directly from the Lord.[57] When he visited the reservations in the Dakotas, the Lakotas apparently greeted him and his message with enthusiasm, bestowing a new name upon him—Wom Dee Ho Wash Teh (Good Voice Eagle).[58]

These Church programs reflected a paternalistic view common at that time—that Indians needed to be redeemed. Redemption through federal programs often meant Indian dependency upon institutions and programs. The LDS Church differed in that they advocated Native self-sufficiency in order for Natives to achieve their bright future as "children of the promise."[59] In a form of noblesse oblige, the LDS Church and its members felt both a kinship toward the remnant of Israel and acted as if it was their inferred responsibility to act with generosity and nobility toward those less privileged. In many ways their

programs reflected the federal government's efforts to assimilate and accultur-
ate Indians into mainstream society through Christian instruction, educational
attainment, and agricultural pursuits. Yet, as sociologist Armand L. Mauss
noted, "white Mormons who tended to think of the Native Peoples primarily
as 'Lamanites' also tended to hold more sympathetic attitudes toward them than
did those regarding them primarily as 'Indians.'"[60]

The Church's programs differed significantly, however, in that Indigenous
people held all of the decision-making power: they could choose to accept all,
some, or none of what the Church offered; every decision was voluntary. Natives
participated in ISPP for a variety of reasons. Some appreciated the enhanced
educational opportunities, the religious components, or simply sought a new
experience. Others hoped to achieve better living conditions, became involved
when invited by friends or family, or hoped to get out of unsatisfactory situa-
tions. As Megan Stanton has pointed out in this anthology, these opportunities
made the ISPP "attractive even for students who did not believe the teachings of
the Church." Native families' and students' demands for placement consistently
"exceeded the supply of interested placement families" and students or parents
could "discontinue their participation in the program at any time." Moreover,
when the limited benefits of the program no longer met their needs, Natives
provided the rationale and reasoning for ending the ISPP altogether.[61]

Moreover, LDS Native Americans welded ultimate control to what degree
of syncretism of Native and cultural belief systems and practices they grafted
together. This cultural pluralism also benefited LDS communities and congregations, broadening their worldviews and appreciation for the Indigenous cultural
heritages of those they interacted with, although Native members still faced
naïveté, paternalism, and prejudice from some members. The Church generally
failed to study or appreciate the Indian point of view or build upon or adopt
Indigenous social forms. The Church often measured success by numbers of
converts, their commitment to the faith, and their ability to live within the
dominant society. In the conformity culture following World War II, prominent
Latter-day Saints both supported and opposed the government's termination
policy ending federal recognition of tribal sovereignty.[62]

The civil rights activism of the era—manifested by Indigenous voices such as
the American Indian Movement (AIM)—rejected settler colonialism and paternalism in favor of Indigenous self-determination, a notion that became reality
during the Nixon administration. Indigenous criticisms of what they viewed as

Mormonism's paternalistic programs such as the ISPP contributed to the Church modifying or eventually discontinuing them. The activism also had an influence on the reorganization of the NIM and SWIM missions during the 1970s.

AIM protesters led demonstrations targeting what they viewed as LDS colonialism when they marched on Temple Square in Salt Lake City during the early 1970s and requested $1 million annually to offset perceived colonialist practices.[63] Alternatively, the Church's emphasis on education and foster care may have contributed indirectly to the passage of legislation such as the Self-Determination and Education Act (1975), the Tribally Controlled Community College Assistance Act (1978), and the Indian Child Welfare Act (1978) to provide Indian alternatives to Mormon ones.[64]

Meanwhile, Elder Kimball and members of the Church Education System encouraged Brigham Young University to take an active interest in American Indian education and to help solve the perceived economic and social problems existing on reservations through education.[65] Dale Tingey, director of American Indian Services, oversaw reservation outreach to provide technical and financial assistance and adult education to Indian communities "to improve farming, foster economic development, and solve social problems."[66] The American Indian Services and Research Center and other reservation outreach programs served over four dozen reservations, providing adult education and technical and financial assistance to Indian communities, agricultural programs like fruit tree distribution, and opportunities for higher education at BYU.

BYU established scholarships for Indian students to attend the university and university programs to help them adjust to university life. During the Northern Indian Mission's heyday, as many as 550 Indian students representing 71 tribes enrolled at BYU.[67] School and Church officials reinforced the concept encouraging American Indians and Pacific Islanders to embrace Lamanite identify as descendants of Book of Mormon peoples. A BYU performing group known as the Lamanite Generation formed in 1971 and made their first international tour to Canada. Administrators formed an Indian Education Department, with courses in Native American Studies and formed a NAS minor in 1977 that subsequently became housed within the BYU Department of History in 1984, with Fred R. Gowans as the NAS Coordinator.[68]

American Indian students published a Native newspaper *The Eagle's Eye* to develop skills in art, photography, and journalism. Native students formed an all-Indian club called the Tribe of Many Feathers. They held an annual

Harold A. Cedartree Pow Wow and a Miss Indian BYU contest. Thousands of Indigenous students, including hundreds recruited on the reservations in the Northern Indian Mission, attended BYU. Between 1966 and 1974, BYU awarded 98 associate of arts degrees, 114 bachelor degrees, and 10 master degrees to Indian students.[69] News media lauded BYU's Indian program. A 1977 article in the *Deseret News* boldly proclaimed, "Indian Education at BYU is Finest in U.S."[70] Meanwhile, the *Christian Science Monitor* reported BYU spent more money on Indian scholarships than all other American universities combined and achieved an Indian graduation rate twice the national average.[71]

The Lamanite Generation performed its signature song, "Go My Son," at every performance. This song articulated the notion that Native students willing to receive an education could help solve the challenges of reservation life. Written by Native students Arlene Nofchissey Williams (Navajo) and Carnes Burson (Ute), the lyrics importune:

> Go my son, go and climb the ladder
> Go my son, go and earn your feather
> Go my son, make your people proud of you.
> Work, my son, get an education
> Work, my son, learn a good vocation
> Climb my son, go and take a lofty view.
> From on the ladder of an education
> You can see to help your Indian Nation
> Then reach, my son, and lift your people up with you.[72]

The NIM missionaries relayed the message about the educational possibilities through the seminary program, the ISPP, and Brigham Young University, and encouraged enrollment in all three. Traveling from reservation to reservation, missionaries told of the opportunities available to those who participated. They traveled over 8,500 miles in 7 weeks and said "their warmest receptions were at moments when we bore our testimony about the values of the placement program."[73] The Relief Society also helped to carry the word of the educational program to their people. Native women did much to encourage their children to "attend school, to take every opportunity to develop their talents, learn trades and skills, raise their standard of living, and find joy and satisfaction and friendship with all people."[74]

Eddie Cox (Lakota), a sixteen-year-old from Glasgow, Montana, was considered an ideal candidate for ISPP. Eddie's father struggled with alcohol and his mother had passed away. With minimal adult supervision, Eddie had committed minor violations resulting in his sentence to the state detention center in Miles City. The center released him early for good behavior. On November 7, 1968 Kenneth W. Finlinson (Poplar, Montana Area Coordinator) sent a letter to Reeve for help in getting Eddie to Utah where they could find a foster family willing to oversee his rehabilitation, which they did. Eddie's circumstances were not exceptional. Many young Natives accepted the proposal for placement, some adjusting to it, and others regretting their decision.[75] Nathan Halfe, a fourteen-year-old boy, said that the ISPP was "a great opportunity to come and live with people who treat you like their own children. It is much fun in MIA and going to Church and meeting many girls and boys at Church and school, who treat you very nice."[76]

Participation in the ISPP required numerous adjustments. Young Indian children and teenagers left their homes and went to unfamiliar places. Edouardo Zendejas (Omaha) recalled that his placement family was "the all-American family with a five-bedroom house, a den, three or four bathrooms around." I didn't have to worry about cockroaches crawling out of the cereal boxes and having clean sheets."[77] This sudden transition placed both challenges and opportunities before these Indian children. Donna Fifita (Sisseton-Wahpeton Sioux) recalled when she was 11 years old, "I knew nobody. I was the first and only person from my area to go on the Indian Placement Program. It was a decision I made on my own."[78] Whether or not participants enjoyed the experience often depended upon how their foster families treated them. Fifita "didn't get along at all with her [first] foster mom … they would let their kids get away with things. Even if it was the smallest thing, she would just yell at me and scold me." However, in later years she had foster families that she loved and that treated her kindly, and that made all the difference in her experiences. Although it was difficult, many who participated in ISPP graduated from high school and may have been better prepared for college than if they had attended a BIA school.[79]

"Recently we, in the Northern Indian Mission," said President Dahl, "have seen some of the fruits of Mormonism in the return of the placement students."[80] Some foster families provided the love, encouragement, and structure that appealed to the children. Others neglected or even abused the students in their care. In addition to the sacrifices made by the children, their biological parents and grandparents also made great sacrifices by placing their trust in others to care for those children they loved so much—even to the point of allowing them to travel far distances to live with strangers in another land during the school year to hopefully improve their educational experience.[81]

Roy Montclair (Sioux) recalled, "My mother spoke English to us. She was not allowed to speak her Native language while she attended school at Haskell Indian Institute in Kansas." He continued, "I attended a few pow-wows, but that was about the extent of my involvement in traditional Sioux ceremonies and activities." After moving in with his grandparents, he related, "My grandmother was a very strict Catholic, and she made us attend those services when we were small." After her death, two elders visited their home and told them about the foster care program. At age nine, Roy began his placement experience. "I realize it was a very difficult decision for my parents. My father was quiet, and my mother really made the decision. I believe she was prompted by the Holy Ghost to let us go. She had a vision and wanted us to break out from the reservation cycle of poverty, alcohol, drugs, and despair. It was a difficult but courageous decision."[82]

Flora Jane Dude (San Carlos Apache) served in the Northern Indian Mission. She remembered when she went on placement as a young girl, "At night I would get homesick and start crying. I cried until I went to sleep. I did this for two or three weeks until my foster parents said, 'You had better stop crying or we will send you home.' I didn't want to be sent home and make my parents feel bad, so I quit crying and started to enjoy new things and my new life."[83]

While some like Montclair and Dude thrived, for others "the Indian Placement Program became a secular solution (providing education) to a religious mandate (providing salvation)." In Elise Boxer's thoughtful study analyzing "how American Indian foster students constructed their social and religious identities, both in the LDS Church and in their tribal communities," she noted that "Mormon foster homes became sites of colonization and provided an intimate space for this process to take place." Moreover, the "Mormon home became an important tool to aid in the assimilation of Indian children. Indigenous minds and bodies could be transformed."[84]

Sometimes Natives took matters into their own hands, shaping mission policies and practices through their own initiative. Sixteen-year-old Donna Sitake (Sisseton-Wahpeton Sioux) attended placement for five years. She called President Reeve on the phone and asked him "Do you think you could go pray and ask Heavenly Father if it's ok if sisters could come to Sisseton?" He was taken by surprise. He said that he would talk to Heavenly Father and see what the Lord would like. So he prayed about it, and a couple days later, he called me back and said, "Donna, the Lord has told me that it's a good idea to put sister missionaries there." And so he did. The first sisters who served there were both Navajo sisters: Sister Marie Sandoval and Sister Pelanovy, who had both attended BYU before their missions. "I would spend every Friday night with them, and they would make a little bed on the floor for me. They would tell me about BYU, and what they went through, and what a wonderful program they had for Indian students at BYU. Through their inspiration, they talked me into wanting to go to BYU."[85]

This same sister missionary, Marie Sandoval (Navajo), remembers the excitement she had receiving her call. "And when the call came, I remember it was in October, and it said, you're going to serve among the Indians, your own people, and I thought, wow! You know, this is the Northern Indian Mission, of course, and all those are the Indians from the North. I always thought it would be interesting to see what their cultures were like." After arriving in the NIM, Sandoval loved serving on the reservations. She recalled that they were able to get into quite a few homes because they were Navajos. "We were teaching this young couple. The husband was a Presbyterian pastor. He didn't like that we were teaching his wife. When I left the area, my companion wrote me a letter and she said, 'He's going to be baptized.' The next summer he sent his wife to BYU to finish her schooling. He became the Branch President."[86]

Emphasis on Teaching Indian Women and Youth: President Rex C. Reeve, 1970–1973

The leaders of the Church called Rex C. Reeve Jr. as the Coordinator of Indian Seminaries in the Southwest Indian Mission where he served from 1964–1965. In 1965, he was transferred to Rapid City, South Dakota, where he served as Division Coordinator of Seminary and Institute, assistant to President Grant Farmer, counselor to the mission president, and Sunday school teacher (1965–1969). In 1970, Reeve became the third NIM president. His wife, Barbara, served as the mission's Relief Society president for about one and a half years and as its general secretary for six months, in addition to teaching Relief Society and Sunday school. President and Sister Reeve dedicated themselves to teaching Indian women and children. The Reeves firmly believed that the gospel would bring great blessings to Native women and children and would strengthen Indian families. "I think the Church really appealed to women," recalled Linda Uranga (Rosebud Sioux). "We had a lot of women in the Church. I think the message of family, wanting to keep their families together, wanting to make sure their kids did well, wanting to raise them in an environment that was healthy. I think that really appealed to them.... A lot of single mothers, some who were divorced, and some whose husbands weren't involved in the Church."[87]

The Relief Society actively worked to engage the Indian sisters in the gospel. Barbara Reeve adapted the Relief Society and Visiting Teaching messages for the women in the mission, emphasizing the history and importance of the Lamanite people, the Book of Mormon, and modern-day Lamanites and their specific circumstances. She posted these lessons in each month's *Relief Society Bulletin*. The sisters organized multiple activities for fellowship and fund-raising including picnics, quilting groups, luncheons, food sales, and rummage sales. These activities brought the sisters together, helped them make friends, and earned money for local charities. Occasionally, the Relief Society planned trips to take several Indian sisters to general conference in Salt Lake City. On one trip to Salt Lake, some of the sisters sang in a Relief Society choir at general conference. This became "a happy and unforgettable memory."[88]

The female Relief Society encouraged sisters to research their genealogy and serve as proxies in temple ordinances for their ancestors. They urged families to "go find this information or write to a friend and have them find it for you."[89] Individuals would have to visit the Tribal Enrollment and BIA Realty Offices on their respective reservation. The Relief Society advised them to record any missing names, dates, or locations before moving forward. Once they collected the information, family members were encouraged to take these names to the temple and perform baptisms for the deceased. As the numbers of members within the mission increased, Reeve held the first mission-wide Priesthood and Relief Society convention. It was a three-day meeting and lasted from October 19 to 21 in 1972.[90]

Reeve had established five seminaries at Cass Lake, Minnesota; Fort Yates, North Dakota; Pine Ridge, South Dakota; Wolf Point, Montana; and Hardin, Montana, in 1966. Student enrollment reached 1,200 by the end of May.[91] The mission organized a student seminary program for the youth and a home seminary program for families. Both programs attempted to gain the support of tribal officials with mixed results. The mission leaders and missionaries expressed the idea that by teaching the Indian children, they could eventually make their way into their homes to teach entire families. They also knew of the great spiritual influence that Indian children could have on their parents.[92] Leaders believed the Indian Seminary Program could help Indian children overcome what Church leaders viewed as the challenges of reservation life and prepare them to integrate into the dominant society.[93] Students expressed mixed reactions to this religious instruction, yet attendance continually increased. Buck Thomas, seminary area coordinator wrote that, "It is quite evident that we have better attendance and involvement on the part of the students in the Seminary Program than we do in any other auxiliary of the Church."[94]

Activities, of course, played a significant role in the Indian Seminary Program. To encourage seminary attendance, teachers required that students attend 50 percent of a month's seminary meetings in order to qualify for participation in activities. Seminary teachers and leaders organized movies, skating, swimming, hayrides, picnics, talent shows, and basketball games. The basketball tournaments aroused the most interest and enthusiasm.[95] Not only did these activities promote seminary attendance, they also brought the community together in a wholesome environment where they could grow physically and spiritually. The home seminary program brought families together one night a week for a religious devotional.[96]

Gaining the support of community and tribal officials proved challenging. "They seem to avoid any overt activity with the program," noted Buck Thomas, "We are able to get them involved somewhat from time to time but only as they see that their activity will be of some benefit to the students in a personal way."[97] Community members occasionally inquired about Church programs and activities on their own. Kenneth Finlinson summated, "Hardly a day passes that someone in the store, service station, barber shop, bank, post office, or on the street, don't inquire about the progress of our Seminary Program."[98]

Lawrence E. Cook (Omaha) remembers being transformed by the seminary program. Cook, a descendant of the famous Chief Little Cook, served in World War II in the Pacific and European theatres, spending four months at a German POW camp. Awarded the Bronze Star, Cook returned home and his people elected him to the tribal council where he helped manage every aspect of their 8,000 acres of real estate. He served on the reservation's board of education as well as serving as a delegate on an intertribal council constituted with members of three tribes in Nebraska. Cook's desire for educating youth drew him to the Latter-day Saints. Cook advocated for the seminary program and—after attending the All-Lamanite Youth Conference at BYU—he was so touched by the experience he sought baptism on May 31, 1969.[99]

Naomi Broken-Leg attended seminary before deciding to be baptized in August 1967, whereupon her former group of friends dissipated and her non-member parents and siblings opposed her decision. Broken-Leg bravely risked ostracization from her peers and rejection and disapproval from her family when she joined the LDS faith. Her example and vibrant testimony led to the conversion of at least nine people—including her parents, sister, and brother-in-law—within the next year. Four years after her baptism, Broken-Leg served as a missionary in the Southwest Indian Mission.[100]

Mary Jane Otter Robe's (Lakota) grandmother raised her after her parents separated. Because her grandparents had custody, "I needed their permission to be baptized. My grandfather wasn't really in favor, but he agreed because I really wanted to be baptized. I'll always remember the day I came home from school and found my baptism dress on the table," she recounted. "Grandfather had purchased the dress for me; it was his special way of saying that he was okay with my decision."[101]

Outreach to the Reservation Communities and Leaders

President Grant Farmer put forth great effort to establish the Church on the reservations. He spent countless hours with tribal officials and local residents working as an advocate for the LDS Church and for individual and collective improvement. Farmer encouraged the missionaries and mission leaders to embrace Native culture, both to appreciate it in and of itself as well as a means of teaching the people. Buck Thomas, Hardin Area coordinator, wrote, "I have been out hunting more this month than I have in any month of my life. I have had a lot of the Indian men come and ask me to go hunting with them. I am grateful for this because I feel that we are beginning to get into their hearts. I sometimes wonder if I have done more with the rifle than I have been able to do with the bible."[102] President Farmer advocated building trust and friendship with Native Peoples before proselytizing. For example, one missionary under Farmer's administration told a story of a woman that he had taught who had lived a raucous lifestyle before finding the Church. He said, "Have you ever felt the spirit of the Lord when one of these souls who has tasted much of the bitterness and evil of life repents, when confronted with the beauty of the Gospel.... With eyes brimming with testimonial tears of true heart-broken repentance, she confessed the sins of her youth and accepted our invitation to baptism for the remission of her sins."[103]

President Dahl encouraged education, agricultural advancement, and financial stability among the Indian Nations. On August 2, 1969, Dahl attended the Yankton Sioux Powwow at Lake Andes, South Dakota. Over 3,000 Natives from 26 different tribes were present as tribal chairman Percy Archambault (Yankton Sioux) gifted a peace pipe to Dahl with the words, "May peace be between us," bestowing this token of friendship for the Church's help in helping the Indian "to help himself."[104]

Some tribal councils could not agree on how to treat the Mormons. Members of various faiths, each of their religious traditions offered different courses of action. Some Presbyterian and Catholic leaders pressured council members to oppose the construction of Mormon chapels and seminary buildings and other Mormon activities. Tribal members who joined the LDS faith faced denied admittance in the parochial schools, and some prevented LDS members from being buried in their church cemeteries next to their relatives.[105]

Donna Gill Sitake (Sisseton-Wahpeton Sioux) remembered joining the Church often meant ostracization. "My dad's family were Jehovah Witnesses [sic], and of course, they really had bad feelings toward the Mormon Church. They thought it was the devil's Church. And, of course my mom's side, they resented it, because my dad was a lay-minister for the Episcopal Church, and they served together (my mom was the Lady's Aid) but they were very active on the Native American Episcopal Church on the reservation. They were really resented and ostracized by the family. It took time for the community to warm up and change toward my parents. My dad and mom eventually received respect from the community, but this distance with relatives still remains to this day."[106]

Despite potential repercussions, Carolyn Good Shield (Lakota) investigated and joined the Church. During her investigation, her pastor wrote her a letter advising her not to listen to the missionaries and sent her some anti-Mormon literature attempting to dissuade her from pursuing what he viewed as a devilish cult. She respectfully wrote back to the reverend and staunchly defended her newfound faith, even though she had only recently been baptized. She said,

"[The Mormons] are really sincere. All they do is ask us to pray to God and see if the things they teach us are true. I believe no matter what religion you are if you are sincere and humble and really want to know, God will answer your prayers. Is this a teaching of the devil? If they are from the devil why do they ask us to pray to God?"[107] Another woman joined the Church in order to "live a better life and take better care of her grandchildren." She loved the Church so much that she said she "would like to see the rest of my Indian people baptized in the Church."[108]

For others, conversion took more time. Tony Boxer (Sisseton-Wahpeton Sioux) recalled the missionaries began teaching his family, all of whom attended the Pentecostal Church. "I chose not to listen to the missionaries at first. They would come in one door and I would go out the other." Then, "later on, the sto-ries about the Book of Mormon kind of got to me." Soon, "I felt an impression to join the Church, which I did on December 18, 1965, I was baptized in Glasgow, Montana. I believe it was the story about the Lamanites and the Book of Mor-mon. . . . It had a kind of familiar ring to it, it was like I had known it before. But the Spirit that I felt from the missionaries—I guess it was the influence of the Holy Ghost, I didn't know it at the time—I felt that was very strong, and I liked that feeling. I liked the feeling that I got when I was around the missionaries: a warm fuzzy feeling as it were."[109]

Lacee Harris (Ute-Paiute) questioned why LDS teachings often remained bifurcated from LDS cultural practices. "My faith in Mormonism is still strong. It is important to me that both my Indian people and the Mormons believe that the earth was created spiritually before it was created physically, that the purpose of this life is to gain experience, that our lives are to be lived so that our Creator can be proud of us individually and as a people, that the Son of God came among us to teach us how to live. We have traditions around the numbers three, twelve, and thirteen, that are reminiscent of Mormon ways. Ceremonies allow those who are authorized to bless, marry, and heal. Fasting and prayer are ways to spiritual power in both cultures." Harris concluded many Indians "feel that the culture of the Mormons gets in the way of the teachings."[110]

Yet, the transformation of at least a part of LDS culture did require leaving some elements of Native culture behind. Andrea Little (Oglala Lakota) recalled that for most of her young life, she felt very conflicted about who she was as a person and how to mesh her Indian culture within mainstream society. She was still pondering this question when she got in an accident shortly after her nineteenth birthday that left her paralyzed from the waist down. She felt that she had been spared from death for some reason, but she did not know why. Two LDS missionaries knocked on her door and the message they shared was just what she was looking for. "I've gained a perpetual purpose, as the elders continued to extend their teachings with their humble Mormon sincerity and simplicity.... The Church was the missing piece of my life's purpose and the link between two cultures so desperately needed everywhere."[111] She was baptized and her fiancé joined the Church soon thereafter. The Church provided some Natives with comfort, peace, and meaning in their lives while presenting others with challenges, obstacles, and family and tribal opposition when they accepted the gospel. Assimilation or acculturation always involves choices and often comes at a cost, including the preferences of one set of ideals and cultural values over others.[112]

During the first decade of the Northern Indian Mission's existence, the teaching methods focusing on athletics, education, seminary instruction, and community service enabled the Northern Indian Mission to introduce the LDS faith to thousands of American Indians. Nearly 3,000 Indian converts joined during that ten-year period. Many others became active again and encouraged others to hear the gospel message. During one month, April 1971, five Indian converts went to the temple for the first time, nine more received patriarchal blessings, one entered the mission field, and several received priesthood ordinations.[113] During the 1970s, the NIM averaged 331 convert baptisms annually.[114] Programs like seminary and the ISPP benefited some students while others rejected the assimilationist overtures.[115] Some ISPP alumni continued their education at Brigham Young University and other local and tribal colleges. These converts made significant contributions in their local communities, strengthening economic and educational opportunities for youth, providing stability and leadership to local Church congregations and the Church in general.[116] Serving in Indian communities forced the Church to examine and determine "how the stakes could best serve Indian people. This effort helped members and leaders reach out to another culture with which they were generally unfamiliar and paved the way for more formal programs," as well as new curriculum, and a simplification of the complex Church organization to focus on the basics and enable Indigenous priesthood and auxiliary leaders the flexibility to move the Church forward more quickly and effectively.[117]

The Northern Indian Mission existed for a decade before being integrated within the South Dakota Rapid City and the Manitoba-Minnesota missions.

This was done so that missions would not overlap and were arranged geographically instead of ethnically. Missionaries' methods of working with tribal community leaders, building friendships and conducting community service, and providing youth programs like seminary and sporting activities established goodwill in several Indian communities and aided the establishment of Latter-day Saints congregations in Indian Country. Native converts strengthened and diversified the Church and grafted Mormons and Indians together in unique ways. Native men and women served in leadership positions. Natives voiced their concerns and needs. Natives modified Church and Mission policies and practices, both directly and indirectly. Native children received educational, social, recreational, and leadership opportunities. Yet Native individuals and families also faced heartache, challenges, ostracization, and exclusion from family and friends, and disruptions and separation from their tribal lives and cultural expressions. They endured prejudice, misguided assumptions, and hurtful comments from some members of the Church. Finally, LDS Natives constructed their own identities of Indigeneity, negotiating their own meanings even though the Church and its missions and programs were devised and run principally by non-Natives. Native Peoples continue to influence the policies and practices of the LDS Church and make their own important contributions.

10

The Indian Student Placement Program and Native Direction

MEGAN STANTON

The Indian Student Placement Program was a coordinated effort to improve the educational opportunities available to American Indian children in the United States in the twentieth century. The Church of Jesus Christ of Latter-day Saints (or LDS or Mormon Church) maintained that the program provided Indian children from reservations with educational opportunities, access to intercultural experiences, and a stable family life. From its informal start in 1947 to its end in 2000, the program placed American Indian children from their families of origin into LDS, generally white American, households. Students stayed with these placement (also known as foster) families throughout the nine-month school year, returning to their biological families and reservations over each summer. Up to 70,000 Indian students, a majority of them Navajo, participated in this program.[1]

The program influenced the trajectory not only of Indian students' lives but also of the LDS Church. It provided Latter-day Saints (or Saints or Mormons) with tangible opportunities to enact the promises described in the Book of Mormon regarding the redemption of the Lamanites.[2] It expanded LDS involvement in social services as predominantly white American men and women sought to improve Indian children's lives. Native children and families who participated in this program gained access to education and white Mormon culture, although often at the cost of Native cultural continuity and family integrity. However, Native Peoples were not passive recipients of the program. They voiced their needs and concerns to one another, to LDS leaders, and to state and federal officials. They left their mark on the program, indirectly fashioning its creation, many of its policy changes, and eventually its demise. This chapter reconsiders the role of Native Peoples in indirectly directing the placement program. American Indians sought to influence the program in order to protect themselves and their interests. This history is not simply a Mormon story or a Native Mormon story, but instead one of repeated conversations and contestations among Mormons, both white American and Native, and American Indians, both Mormon and not.

The placement program was a reaction to the fraught educational opportunities available to American Indians living on US reservations. From the 1880s, private institutions and the Bureau of Indian Affairs (BIA) sought to assimilate Indian children to white American culture through boarding schools. These schools limited students' access to their tribal cultures. Students spent months or years living away from their biological families and tribes. In many cases, the schools forbade use of Native languages. Such policies threatened the continuity of Indian families, cultures, and languages.[3] Educational opportunities for Navajo children remained bleak in the middle of the twentieth century.[4] The Senate Special Subcommittee on Indian Education found that, in 1969, many Navajo adults had received less than a sixth-grade education, with some unable to read, write, or speak English fluently. Navajo leaders had advocated for better schooling choices after World War II, but development was slow. Many Navajo children attended off-reservation boarding schools, often in different states. These schools kept children as young as six away from their families for months at a time.[5]

Some Navajo youth sought additional opportunities for education. Helen John (Navajo), an adolescent in 1947, instigated the creation of the placement program. Her family had migrated to Richfield, Utah to work in the beet fields owned by non-Native Mormons. She requested permission to live in the backyard of one family so that she might attend school. The family consulted with stake president Golden Buchanan, who in turn contacted Apostle Spencer W. Kimball. Kimball suggested that John should stay in Buchanan's home and receive the education she had requested. Soon thereafter, John and other young Navajo women were living in white-Mormon homes within Buchanan's stake.

John, after each placement, spent her summer in the beet fields with her family. She had succeeded in gaining educational access for herself and some kin. Significantly, her request also provided the impetus for the placement program.[6]

Kimball recognized an opportunity in such placements to expand the Church's interactions with American Indians. He drew the Saints' attention to the economic problems that the Navajo people faced in the late 1940s. Federal livestock reduction and the end of the World War II economic boom from war industries had harmed the Navajo economy, leaving many in search of itinerant agricultural work.[7] These problems, Kimball argued, were caused by a lack of education.[8] Although Kimball blamed the federal government for creating the limited opportunities that the Navajo faced, he also saw the Lord's hand in them. Through the Navajo's deprivation, the Lord was "bringing the Lamanites back to us ... in to the beet and cotton fields, on the railroads, and in the mines to find employment." These Navajo difficulties were a "great opportunity" for missionary work.[9] Kimball urged white American Saints to take advantage of this rare opportunity of Navajo proximity and vulnerability. He received approval from the First Presidency to formalize the placement program in 1954.[10]

Not all Indian parents and tribes approved of the placement program in its early years. Some voiced their opposition by discontinuing their children's participation in the program, but others too registered their complaints. Some Sioux and Assiniboine students enrolled in the program in 1956, for example, but none returned in 1957.[11] The Hualapai were more explicit about their concerns. They complained to workers in the Phoenix BIA office about baptisms of large groups of children. (Between 1954 and 1956, 66 children received mass baptisms before they entered the placement program.) BIA workers in turn forwarded these concerns to the LDS Church, together with inquiries about placement's effects on family unity.[12] It is significant that Indian parents and BIA workers already had identified as problems the recruitment practices of the program and its effects on Indian family continuity. Two of the primary complaints about the program had emerged within the first years of its history.

The concerns expressed by Hualapai and Navajo adults indirectly created changes within the program. The LDS Indian Placement Committee reviewed the concerns raised by Hualapai parents and other Native leaders. In 1957, the committee held a meeting concerning the Hualapai and BIA complaints. It invited no Hualapai people, instead receiving only representatives from state and federal agencies.[13] A subsequent meeting invited more direct Native input. In 1958, two representatives from the Navajo Tribe, in addition to the 1957 attendees, met. Samuel Billison (Navajo) requested that the minimum age for participation be raised from six to eight.[14] The following month, the committee decided that incoming participants in most cases should be no younger than eight.[15] Significantly, these first steps toward the professionalization of the program (through communication with governmental agencies and compliance with state and federal law), and the inclusion of only students in full membership in the Church, complied with conversations initiated by Hualapai and Navajo adults.

Placement and Church leaders sought to maintain good relations with the Navajo Nation. In 1959, chairman Paul Jones (Navajo) accepted an invitation to visit the reception center in Utah as placement officials processed incoming students. He voiced his support for elements of the program. The removal of children from the reservation by various programs remained a point of concern for the Navajo Nation, however.[16] In 1960, the Navajo Tribal Council passed a resolution preventing non-Navajo individuals from "remov[ing] any Navajo minor from the Navajo Reservation" without committee approval. The Tribal Council further authorized its chairman to investigate "missionaries and other non-Navajo persons" responsible for these removals.[17] Jones investigated the placement program again that year and visited a foster home in Sandy, Utah. He spoke with the foster family's young Navajo student, and was "satisfied" to learn of her pleasant stay and of her biological family's LDS membership. Soon thereafter, Kimball arranged for the Navajo Tribal Council and other Navajos to view *Upon Their Shoulders*, a 30-minute film produced by Brigham Young University students that promoted the program.[18]

Placement peaked in the early 1970s. Indian children participating during these years engaged with a bureaucratized program. From 365 students in the 1959–1960 school year, the program grew to its peak in the 1970–1971 school year with 4,997 students placed in several US states and Canada.[19] Although neither the program nor the Church tracked tribal affiliation, most of the students were Navajo.[20] The program required LDS membership, but did not distinguish between baptism in fact and belief in Mormonism. Mass baptisms of children blurred the boundaries between LDS and non-LDS students at least through the early 1960s. Although some of the students recruited were already LDS, others reported that their placements occurred almost immediately after LDS baptism.[21] LDS caseworkers handled recruitment until the early 1970s. Given that their job stability depended upon successful recruitment, caseworkers had reason to keep participation numbers high. When local LDS leaders took over recruitment in 1973, the number of students interested in participating began a slow decline. Many of the Native families who participated in the program did so in response to recruitment efforts but also because they considered placement "the least immediately painful solution" to financial difficulties and limited educational choices, according to the anthropologist Martin D. Topper.[22]

Placement parents typically participated in the program to aid Indian children or to fulfill their religious obligations. They underwent an application process that required their bishop's approval.[23] In the 1960s and 1970s, they received cultural training about Indian people in order to better understand their students.[24] The program required some financial sacrifice from foster parents, who financed Indian students' care just as they did with their own children. (Beginning in 1961, they also counted up to $50 in expenses per month per placement child as charitable contributions in their federal income tax deductions.)[25] Their commitment entailed welcoming Indian children into their families "not as guests nor as servants, but as sons and daughters without adoption."[26] Placement students living with foster families took part in all activities, including not only schooling but also social and religious functions. Students also participated in parties and conferences for placement students only, which were designed at least in part to prevent interracial dating with white American students.[27]

Native students reported mixed experiences in placement. Some struggled with their placement families. Ione Yellowjohn (Shoshone), who spent one year on placement in elementary school in the late 1960s, complained:

> They changed my hair. . . . It was hard at first to make up my hair because my foster mother didn't know how to curl hair. She cut my hair because she didn't want to curl it. It was kind of like a boy's hair. It was hard for me to have my hair get cut because I've always had it long.[28]

Other students enjoyed the program. For example, Emery Bowman (Navajo) participated for nine years in the 1970s–1980s. He considered his first placement family, which cared for his oldest brother for eight years before caring for him for five, to be part of his family. He recalled, "Most of my experiences on the Placement Program were happy. I remember there were some trials. There's ups and downs as with everything."[29] Stephanie Chiquito (Navajo), who participated for eight years in the 1970s–1980s, also reported positive experiences: "I think my foster family really tried to make me feel a part of the family." She acknowledged, however, that some families communicated disunity by, for example, taking family vacations without their students.[30] The unevenness of placement families—with some uncertain as to how to support cultural practices or physical bodies different from their own, and only some interested in incorporating students into family life—affected students' experiences in placement.

Indian students, as well as their parents, could discontinue their participation in the program at any time. Early departures were not uncommon. Between 15 and 30 percent of students who left the program before 1970 did so during the school year.[31] (Foster families and placement caseworkers also had authority to initiate the end of a student's stay.[32]) Participation could end because students were unhappy with placement, but they ended for other reasons as well. Ione and Carletta Yellowjohn (Shoshone), for example, participated in the program along with their brother for only one year in the late 1960s because their mother, newly widowed, "couldn't take care of us." By the end of the school year, their mother was prepared to care continuously for all seven of her children, so the three placement students said their goodbyes to their foster families.[33] Indian students and families began and ended placements according to their needs.

A significant number of students ended their participation in the program, with many of those discontinuing over the summer. Indian students' returns to the reservation in the summer were one of the most difficult aspects of placement. Each summer, students lost access to the material advantages of placement families, but gained access to their biological families. They also had to navigate families and communities that, in some cases, questioned their tribal identities. George P. Lee (Navajo) recalled that his older brothers complained after his first placement year, in the 1950s, that he was "no Navajo."[34] Anthropologist Martin D. Topper, after observing 25 Navajo placement students in the late 1960s and early 1970s, argued that a majority of placement students temporarily rejected, over the summer, the behavioral requirements of Mormonism, only to return to them at the start of the next placement. Such temporary rejections included, for Topper's subjects, drinking alcohol or participating in Navajo rituals. These temporary rejections of placement eventually became permanent, as 23 of Topper's 25 students refused to return by their high school years.[35] Although Topper's reported dropout rate is high, other studies have confirmed that between one third and 45 percent of students dropped out of the program before the beginning of a second placement year. A later study found that two-thirds of placement students discontinued participation prior to graduating from high school.[36] Indian students were not passive recipients of a placement program. Their decisions to continue or discontinue placement highlight their control of their educational trajectories and their ability to voice their needs to program caseworkers, placement families, and biological families.

Some students chose to complete the program. George P. Lee (Navajo) was the most well-known placement graduate. Lee, born in 1943, was baptized into the LDS Church in 1954 and entered the program in 1955. He later attended BYU, served a mission, married in the Salt Lake Temple, and earned graduate degrees in education.[37] In 1975, he became the first American Indian General Authority when he was called to the Quorum of the Seventy.[38] He repeatedly articulated his identity as a Lamanite: "I am proud to be a child of the Book of Mormon people. I have found my true heritage; I have found my true identity."[39] He encouraged younger American Indian Mormons to prepare "to transcend both [white and Indian] cultures, so that you can function well in both."[40] Lee's description of his identity echoes Matthew Garrett's analysis of students who internalized the goals of the program.[41]

Many students, however, were neither interested in nor capable of such transcendence. Instead, the program created feelings of distance from their tribal communities. Mabel Yazzie (Navajo), a legal administrator in the Navajo Tribe Legal Department, claimed comfort with both white and Native worlds. Nevertheless, she also told her interviewer, "Placement has made me lose touch with my culture. I respect it, but I don't really feel it's mine."[42] Similarly, John Benally (Navajo), explained, "I'll never be white; yet I don't have a sense of being Navajo.... I could never go back and live on the reservation. The only thing I know about Indians I learned from books."[43] Other sources too indicate that placement created distance between students and their tribal identities. A 1981 study conducted by BYU sociologists found that, as adults, placement students were less likely to feel that they fit in with other Indians.[44] Elise Boxer's analysis of Mormonism sets white and Indian interactions within the context of colonization. The placement program, as "a colonizing enterprise," created space in which LDS Americans and their Indian students grappled with the meaning of Lamanite and Indian identities. Although students chose their own identities, they did so through a program devised and run by white adults.[45] Other scholarship has likewise acknowledged that the program diminished students' relationships with their biological families and their tribes.[46]

The program and the Church were not separate from larger developments within Native America in the middle of the twentieth century. Just as the placement program arose as American Indians and federal officials grappled with questions surrounding access to education, so did the program coexist with other activist and governmental strategies developed by American Indians and white Americans. American Indians protested termination and relocation policies, advocated for self-determination, and created civil rights and red power organizations. Although these organizations had many priorities, some professionals and activists focused on families' abilities to keep their children. This work led to the Indian Child Welfare Act (1978) and to better educational opportunities on reservations.[47] The placement program, by tethering the Church to Indian children, brought Mormonism into national conversations taking place primarily among American Indians and white Americans in activist and federal capacities.

Some of these conversations criticized the premises and consequences of the placement program. Critics included those with personal or professional experience with the program or with Indian children and foster care more generally. One such critical discussion of the program occurred during a 1977 conference of the American Academy of Child Psychiatry held in Utah. Topper, the anthropologist who studied Navajo youth on placement, shared his findings at the conference. Conference attendees, nearly four-fifths of whom were Indian, then discussed their disapproval of the placement program. An employee of LDS Social Services in attendance at the conference spoke out in its defense. He also mentioned that the Church was "phasing out placement." His statement drew comment and applause twice the following day. This applause transformed into "an angry atmosphere," however, after he clarified that the Church planned to phase out the program only at some unknown future date.[48] Another critical discussion spurred federal review of the program. The Interstate Compact Secretariat commissioned a study of the program in 1976 without notifying the LDS Church.[49]

These professionals and activists were also concerned about the fate of Indian children more generally. Surveys conducted by the Association on American Indian Affairs (AAIA) in 1969 and 1974 concluded that a staggering 25 to 35 percent of Indian children were not living with their biological families. Some of these children were in institutions such as boarding schools, but others were lost more permanently through adoption and other custody arrangements. Some tribes were more affected than others. The surveys determined that nearly

90 percent of Navajo school-age children, for example, lived apart from their families in order to attend school.[50] These statistics point to significant disruptions in tribal life and cultural continuity. In hearings before Congress, Indians and concerned white Americans pled for on-reservation educational opportunities and custody policies that created less disruption in Indian families.[51] Senator James Abourezk of South Dakota, the chairman of the Senate Select Committee on Indian Affairs, worked with the AAIA to produce legislation limiting the removal of Indian children from families. The Indian Child Welfare Act (ICWA), which Abourezk submitted to Congress in 1977, augmented the authority of tribal governments in determining custody, placement, and adoption of Indian children. The legislation was premised on the argument that Indian tribes and families have important but previously unrecognized authority to determine the best interests of Indian children in custodial and familial hearings.[52]

Most American Indians and non-governmental agencies communicated their endorsement of ICWA. Indeed, "the only non-governmental witnesses to testify against the bill" during the Senate hearings of the legislation were representatives of the placement program and Mormon Church—most notably Harold C. Brown, then the LDS Social Services commissioner and a former placement coordinator, and George P. Lee.[53] Brown argued that ICWA would harm placement. Although he did not oppose ICWA as a whole, he objected to the specific wording of two sections. First, the law defined "child placement" to include not only state and federal placements of children, but also "voluntary" and "private" ones. Second, Brown worried that the program would, under ICWA, have to provide notice to each tribe's "chief executive officer or such other person as such tribe or tribes may designate" of any children from that tribe who participated in placement.[54] He proposed changes to the wording of ICWA that would prevent the law from affecting the program. For example, he requested an amendment revising the definition of "child placement" to specifically exclude the LDS program. The proposed revision identified any "temporary residence for a period of less than one year at a time ... for educational, spiritual, cultural or social opportunities for the child, and with terminable written consent of its parents or guardian" as not being subject to ICWA.[55] His opposition, in other words, focused on narrow provisions of ICWA.

The Saints lobbied the Senate committee to endorse the proposed revisions so that the placement program would not be affected by ICWA. Members of the Church, and particularly American Indian parents and students, were encouraged to sign petitions and write letters to congressional leaders to request these changes.[56] In Senate hearings held in 1977, Lee and Brown numbered among those speaking before the Select Committee on Indian Affairs. Although historian James Allen characterized Lee's testimony as "most persuasive," this testimony focused almost entirely on Lee's personal experience of the placement program rather than on the reasons that the Church was concerned with the wording of ICWA.[57] When Abourezk asked how ICWA legislation would harm the program, Lee asserted that the legislation would create "a lot of policies and red-tape, courts, procedures."[58] Brown outlined the Saints' specific concerns about how ICWA might affect the LDS program, commenting on the legislation's definition of "child placement." He also indicated that program officials would experience difficulties in reporting the removal of children to tribal authorities from smaller and less "well organized" tribes and for children with multiple tribal affiliations. His comments about the size and organization of tribes led to a disturbance in the hearing room, which Abourezk quashed. When Brown continued his testimony, he clarified that LDS Social Services was not "concerned about the information [regarding placement students] being in the hands of professional people or the tribe that would understand its use." He argued that he was concerned that not all tribal governments would use this information appropriately and respect the privacy of the placement children and foster families.[59]

This 1977 testimony did affect the wording of ICWA, at least temporarily. During the Senate hearing, Abourezk observed that the Mormons had their Utah "congressional delegation whipped into line"; both Representative Gunn McKay and Senator Orrin Hatch of Utah had conveyed their support.[60] The Senate committee revised the language of the proposed ICWA. Abourezk later acknowledged that his committee "exempted [the placement program] on purpose and out of necessity," for not doing so would have led to "one hell of a political fight."[61] The exemption defined placement to specifically exclude the LDS program, thereby preventing LDS Social Services from having to comply with the notification requirements of ICWA. The exemption itself proved temporary, however. Steven Unger, who worked with the AAIA when it helped to draft and pass ICWA, later noted that the House of Representatives completely rewrote the bill. The new, House-produced version used a definition of "placement" that removed the previous ambiguity and thus excluded placements such as those of the LDS program. Indeed, Unger argues that the final version of ICWA in 1978 contained no exemption specifically addressing the concerns of the LDS Church or the placement program. Neither he nor the other drafters of the original ICWA bill had intended to restrict LDS placement. The intent of ICWA was never to target the program, but instead to prevent "unwarranted, unjust and coerced child placements."[62] The Saints' interventions to protect the program were unnecessary, in Unger's view. Instead, these interventions only drew additional attention to the Church and the program. Many American Indians and white Americans claimed, after the 1977 hearing, that the Mormon Church received an exemption from legislation intended to protect Indian children.[63]

LDS lobbying in the ICWA hearings brought criticism from American Indian and white American voices. The *Navajo Times* devoted a significant portion of two issues to the Church and program in 1978. Although the first set of articles was generally more positive than the second, both stressed the potential linguistic or cultural costs of the program. *Akwesasne Notes*, a popular Native US newspaper, likewise featured articles criticizing the program and Church in 1978.[64] Don Reeves of the Friends Committee on National Legislation, speaking after Lee and Brown at the 1977 Senate hearing, read into oral testimony a 1976 resolution passed by the National Congress of American Indians that condemned the placement program. Months later, Faye LaPointe (Puyallup) testified before the 1978 House hearing on ICWA that the placement program was a "genocide on our people."[65] Goldie Denny (Quinault), the National Congress of American Indians' Child Welfare Committee chairperson, complained that white American Mormons attended all hearings and meetings about Indian education. Their presence was unwarranted, in her view, and equivalent to her "going to Chinatown in San Francisco and telling the resident [*sic*] there how to educate their children. It is just that ridiculous."[66] White Americans too used the program in their criticism of the LDS Church.[67]

The placement program and the Church's interventions in ICWA hearings led to increased public attention. LDS efforts to improve Indian children's lives through placement brought placement officials, including one General Authority, before Congress to lobby on behalf of their program. Indian Mormons wrote letters to Congress defending the program in an effort to supplement this lobbying work. The Church's placement policies became topics of conversation among members of Congress as well as Mormon and non-Mormon lobbyists. Journalists too brought attention to the LDS Church's participation in the hearing. This lobbying permitted the placement program to function without ICWA interventions, but it also brought criticism and increased the Church's interactions with government.

The placement program's activities, nonetheless, were diminishing. Fewer students enrolled by the late 1970s, and the Church implemented policy changes in the 1980s that further reduced enrollment. The activism that secured better educational opportunities on reservations, such as day schools, had reduced the raison d'être of the program. For example, the Rough Rock Demonstration School, founded in 1966 by the BIA, was transferred to private Navajos soon thereafter and offered bicultural education to students.[68] With the 1984–1985 school year, placement officials raised the minimum age of enrollment from eight to eleven because younger Indian students enjoyed on-reservation educational opportunities. Soon thereafter, the Church announced that the program's minimum age was raised another year, and that it would increase each year until it became, in 1988–1989, a program for high school students only.[69]

Other factors likely also contributed to reductions in the placement program. Studies from the 1970s suggested that the program was unsuccessful in its educational goals.[70] An additional study, conducted by BYU sociologists, reported mixed results. In comparison to a control group of Indian students who did not enter the program, placement students gained better educations. But these educations did not translate to improved work or economic success. The placement students also reported feeling more distant from other Indians than did their control group peers.[71] Thus, this study found that placement students received only limited benefit from the program. These findings added to the criticism voiced by some American Indians since the first years of the program, and indicated too that the program was failing its students.

Not all Saints were prepared for the reduction of the placement program, however. George P. Lee, as a member of the Quorum of the Seventy, argued that the reduction was one example of the Church's disengagement with American Indians in the 1980s. As had American Indian parents and children previously, Lee advocated for what he identified as Native Peoples' needs. Despite his prominent position in the Church, he was unable to strengthen the program. In defending it, he claimed that his fellow General Authorities were disinterested in the needs of American Indians. This criticism led to his excommunication in 1989 for apostasy and conduct unbecoming a member of the Church.[72] With his excommunication, the Church lost its only American Indian General

Authority. American Indian Mormons described Lee's excommunication as a disappointment.[73]

Given the placement program's reductions in enrollment age and its losses of Lee to excommunication and Spencer W. Kimball to death, it is not surprising that it eventually died away. The program might have lasted longer than it did, however, had another program for American Indians not filed a lawsuit against a school district in Utah. Raindancer Youth Services demanded the same free public education for its out-of-state students that placement students received. (Utah had absorbed the costs of educating out-of-state placement students throughout the history of the placement program.)[74] In 1989, however, the Washington County School District in Utah protested the costs of Raindancer, which enrolled troubled, out-of-state Indian teenagers in public school. In a letter to Raindancer, the Washington County School District asserted its ability to refuse admission of students or to require the payment of out-of-state tuition. Raindancer's director filed a lawsuit, noting that the state continued to provide free education to LDS placement students. Rather than help to fight the lawsuit, Church leaders decided to end the placement program. Students already enrolled in placement were permitted to continue until they graduated from high school, but the program and Utah would not provide free public education to additional out-of-state Indian students.[75] By 2000, the final placement student graduated from high school.[76]

American Indians from the placement program continue to affect the LDS Church's reputation and relationship to government, however. In 2016–2017, at least five Navajo adults filed four lawsuits in the Navajo Nation District Court against the LDS Church, alleging that caseworkers and placement policies enabled foster family members to sexually abuse them. Attorneys for the Navajo plaintiffs unsuccessfully sought a deposition of Thomas S. Monson, who served as the president of the LDS Church until his death in January 2018. The attorneys had argued that Monson, who became an apostle in 1963, knew about placement policies and institutional decisions regarding Indian children. (General Authorities with direct oversight of the program, such as Kimball, died before these lawsuits began.) Subpoenas to depose Monson in court were quashed in 2017. Attorneys representing both the plaintiffs and the LDS Church continue to battle over whether and where these lawsuits should proceed. As of May 2018, the lawsuits are expected to continue in the Navajo Nation District Court.[77]

These lawsuits provide insight into the history of the placement program. The charges underscore the vulnerability of young students who stayed in the homes of strangers with only monthly contact from caseworkers. In addition, these lawsuits again recall the power of the program to bring the LDS Church into contact with governmental bodies. These former participants began court proceedings that demanded that the president of the Church provide testimony about the placement program. In other words, the program continues to draw the LDS Church into contact with federal and tribal governments, as former participants advocate for themselves.

The placement program remains a significant episode in Native Mormon People's history. The program witnessed successes and disappointments. It provided many students with educational opportunities. It also exposed young people to environments and worldviews to which they might not otherwise have had easy access. The program was a living ecclesiastical institution, however, that responded to the praise and criticism it received from participants, their families, and others. Whether Mormon themselves or not, American Indians voiced their approval and concern about the program, and placement officials in many cases adapted the program to fit these needs. The placement program is thus not only a case study in Mormon and Native history—it also demonstrates Native Peoples' resilient efforts to improve their lives, both individually and collectively, even when faced with limited choices.

11

"Which Side of the Line?"

American Indian Students and Programs at Brigham Young University, 1960–1983

R. WARREN METCALF

In the late 1970s, a young employee of the Navajo Division of Education went to see a Navajo diagnostician, called a "hand trembler," to find out why she had been feeling ill. The old healer said to her, "Ernesteen, there's just one thing that is the matter with you. It's your heart. You're trying to decide if you want to walk the way of the white people or if you want to walk the way of a Navajo." Ernesteen replied, "How can you say that to me? I'm a Navajo." She said, "Of course, that's what you are, but you have to know it. You're never going to be anything else. That's what you are, and it's a great blessing for you to be it. You need to know it now. If you don't identify yourself now as Navajo, hold on to it, and consider it a blessing, you can possibly die of a broken heart in the future. Nothing will ever satisfy you in the white man's way. You must always have your touchstone as Navajo."[1]

For Ernesteen Bates Lynch, finding which side of the line upon which to stand meant examining her cultural roots as a Navajo, a Mormon convert, and as a graduate student. Her experience mirrored that of thousands of American Indian students at Brigham Young University who struggled to conform to the expectations of church and school. Beyond the strictures and pressures of student life, these Indian students found themselves torn between competing and sometimes conflicting identities. Many struggled to find accommodation and personal happiness in an environment of religious orthodoxy and expectation.

The American Indian program at Brigham Young University had many components and different names. From the decade of the mid-1960s to the mid-1970s it was one of the largest and most successful Indian education programs in the United States, at least in terms of producing graduates. It became a role model for a prototype of affirmative action—a program built around the need to provide unique courses and an extensive network of academic support for a select minority. It differed from the emerging Native Studies programs at other universities in significant ways, focusing on academic and spiritual growth of individual students while rejecting, or at least failing to support, concepts of indigeneity. With little concern for tribal needs or the cultural moorings of Native students, BYU administrators laid out a program that had assimilationist objectives. By the early 1980s, however, the program had run its course and leaders of the LDS Church abruptly dismantled it—not because it had failed academically or even in attaining the assimilationist goals that had been set for it. Church leaders abandoned the program ostensibly because it did not meet the spiritual expectations that they had intended for it.

Indian programs at Brigham Young University grew out of long associations between a few key Mormon leaders and their experiences with American Indians. The most important of these undoubtedly was Spencer W. Kimball, a member of the Quorum of the Twelve Apostles who had been called in 1946 by Church president George Albert Smith to head a committee to spread "the word of the Gospel among the Indians." Kimball's family connection to American Indians reached back well into the nineteenth century. His father, Andrew Kimball served as a missionary in Indian Territory in the mid-1880s. Released in 1887, he immediately received another call to serve as president of the Indian Territory Mission, a position which he filled for another decade.[2] Seemingly destined to live among Indians, when he returned to Utah he received yet another call to move his young family to the Arizona Territory and serve as stake president. Young Spencer grew up in Thatcher, Arizona, where Apaches and other Indians could be seen traveling through town atop freight trains from the nearby San Carlos Reservation. From his own exposure and his father's lengthy experiences, Spencer developed a lively interest in American Indians.[3]

Under Kimball's direction, Church programs for Indians expanded dramatically and did so at a time when Americans broadly supported the integration of

American Indians into American society. This new consensus on race relations owed much to a new ethos of civic nationalism that coalesced in opposition to fascist doctrines of racial supremacy in the years leading up to the Second World War. Civic nationalism held that America's core political beliefs, rooted in concepts of the equality of peoples and inalienable rights, represented a kind of democratic universalism that had great, transformative power.[4] The war generation, typified by men like Kimball, held fiercely to these ideals. In practical terms, this faith made them integrationists in matters of race. The old racially based nationalism of white supremacy and segregation had to give way.

In the area of Indian affairs, civil nationalism took the form of new federal policy initiatives that were intended to more fully integrate American Indians into modern society. The most contentious of these, a policy known as "termination," reached fruition in the early 1950s. The formulators of the policy believed that federal guardianship over Indian assets fostered dependency and that the antiquated Bureau of Indian Affairs perpetuated a reservation system that resulted in de facto segregation. The logical solution was to end, or "terminate," the trust relationship between the federal government and the tribes. So doing would remove the restrictions and allow Indians to attain the full benefits of citizenship and inclusion into American life.

Interestingly, in the unfolding debate over these initiatives, many of the leading advocates turned out to be Mormons, many were Utahans, and acquaintances to some degree of Spencer Kimball. The leading congressional advocate of termination policy, Senator Arthur V. Watkins, had been a stake president in Orem, Utah. As head of the Senate's Subcommittee on Indian Affairs, Watkins pushed relentlessly for what he called his "Indian Freedom Program" to liberate Indians from wardship status. Other key Mormon figures included John S. Boyden, the Ute tribal attorney who wrote the Ute Partitioning Act which terminated about a third of the members of the Ute Tribe; H. Rex Lee, a high-level bureaucrat in the BIA and close ally of Senator Watkins and most significantly with regard to Indian education; and Ernest Wilkinson, the Ute tribal claims attorney and president of Brigham Young University.[5]

One might argue that any group of policymakers and office holders from Utah in this era were apt to be Mormons, but the distinction misses an important point: Mormonism heavily influenced the way these individuals *thought* about Indians. Book of Mormon theology holds that contemporary American Indians are, in fact, the fallen and degraded descendants of a more enlightened, ancient, and

Christ-centered people who inhabited the Americas. In an important corollary to this doctrine, Mormons believe that they have a prophetic responsibility to elevate American Indians to their former status as members of the House of Israel. The upshot is, that in perceiving Indians as people in a fallen state, Mormons have never accepted the intrinsic legitimacy of Indigenous cultures. To "elevate" Indians in a Mormon context means to convert and assimilate them. Therefore, when noting that Mormon leaders such as Kimball, Watkins, Wilkinson, Boyden, and Lee were adherents to Mormon doctrine, one makes an important point about their perspectives on Indians. None of these men saw any particular value in the retention of Native culture. As a consequence, they were predisposed to support policies and programs that aimed to assimilate Indians into both society and the Church.

In February 1952, the LDS *Church News* reprinted an editorial from the Los Angeles *Herald Express* in support of Watkins's termination program:

> As we celebrate "Bill of Rights Week," shouldn't we also do something about providing a Bill of Rights for the American Indian? Shouldn't we free him from the virtual slavery imposed upon him by the grasping greediness of the Indian Bureau? ... Why don't we smash this bureau once and for all and give the Indian the chance to be proud of the fact that he is an American?[6]

Some Church leaders were more temperate than the editors of the *Church News*. In particular, Elder Kimball, through long association with Indian people in Arizona, Utah, and throughout the Southwest, saw value in programs that helped Indians. The Bureau of Indian Affairs, for all of its problems, existed primarily to provide services for them. But Kimball also had cause to question the efficacy of government programs on reservations. He had been particularly outraged by the destitution brought on by the terrible winter of 1947 on the Navajo Reservation. Learning the particulars of the crisis from his friend Golden Buchanan, Kimball wrote to Senator Watkins and encouraged support for an emergency federal appropriation to avert starvation. He also wrote an article about the crisis for the Church magazine, *Improvement Era*, and he persuaded the *Deseret News* to publish a front-page story that roused public opinion and produced a humanitarian food drive.[7] These and other experiences taught Kimball the value of programs, especially Church-sponsored ones, for Indians.

Elder Kimball had, in fact, a program of his own in the works. Rather than attacking the problem of Indian privation with broad, systemic efforts such as the emerging federal termination policy, Kimball had been experimenting with an Indian adoption program that operated on a much more intimate scale. In 1947, alerted to the condition of Navajo school-age children working seasonally in the beet fields around Richfield, Utah, Kimball acted on the suggestion of Golden Buchanan, a member of the Sevier Stake presidency, that these young Indians could be cared for by faithful Mormon families and educated in local public schools during the school year. Resembling the "outing system" pioneered by Richard Henry Pratt and other off-reservation boarding school administrators in the early twentieth century, the proposal to place Indian students in the homes of host families might yield a number of benefits. As Buchanan explained the idea to Kimball, "they could live in LDS homes and be treated exactly as sons and daughters. Not only would they be trained in scholastic affairs in the schools, they would learn to keep house, tend to a family, learn to manage a house and a farm." He went on to contend that, if placed in the homes of local Mormon leaders, "they could see the Church at work and learn the blessings of service to God and fellow men. I can see them going on missions, attending and graduating from college. After all this training what an immense help they would be to their people!" Blessings would accrue to the host families as well, since they would be fulfilling the prophetic mission of bringing the gospel to the Lamanites. "This ought to cut down the time it takes to restore this people to their former blessing by a generation or two," gushed Buchanan.[8]

Elder Kimball enthusiastically embraced the concept and asked Buchanan, much to the initial chagrin of his wife and one of his sons, to serve as host for a rather courageous young Navajo woman, Helen John. The experiment turned out so well that Helen later lived for a time in Elder Kimball's own home in Salt Lake City while she completed beauty school. Forging ahead without the approval of the Quorum of the Twelve, Kimball called other families to host Indian children while he coordinated and experimented with the program.[9] In 1954, after several years of development, the Church gave the program official approval and Indian Placement, as it became known, commenced operation. Early on, administrators placed relatively few Indian students, mostly Navajo children recently converted to the faith, into Mormon homes along the Wasatch Front. By the mid-1960s, however, the program had expanded considerably.

American Indian education programs at BYU grew naturally out of the Indian Placement Program. A Church Indian Committee of Spencer W. Kimball, LeGrand Richards, and Boyd K. Packer, worked to coordinate and expand Indian programs throughout the Church. Elder Kimball, in particular, felt that Indian high school graduates should continue their education at BYU, but he also understood that they needed more preparation. In 1958, following the recommendations of a report written by General Authorities A. Theodore Tuttle and Boyd K. Packer, the Church directed that all American Indian children with Church membership be identified and given access, whenever possible, to seminary courses. To help meet the needs of Indian students, educational specialists developed seminary programs specifically for Indian communities. Implemented first at the Intermountain Indian School in Brigham City, the Church won approval to establish LDS seminaries at Bureau of Indian Affairs schools around the country.[10]

Meanwhile, Elders Tuttle and Packer also recommended that the Church sponsor and support a research institute to study the needs of Indian members and to develop programs to resolve the social problems faced by American Indians. In 1960, the Institute of American Indian Studies and Research was established in the Division of Continuing Education at BYU under the direction of S. Lyman Tyler.[11]

Tyler and other scholars at BYU knew that Indian students transitioning into BYU faced a formidable academic challenge. More than half failed classes and dropped out of the program, statistics that mirrored national trends. In response to these dismal outcomes, in 1964 the BYU administration created an Office of Indian Affairs under the direction of Paul E. Felt. Felt instituted a system to track Indian students into vocational and technical fields if they lacked the necessary background for the traditional four-year curriculum. In the meantime, more rigorous efforts were undertaken to provide academic support for existing students. Dean Lester B. Whetten of the General College began a comprehensive assessment of Indian programs both on and off campus. He interviewed Indian students, analyzed course offerings, and visited other schools with successful Indian programs, including Arizona State University, Northern Arizona University, the University of New Mexico, the University of Minnesota, and Michigan State University.

Whetten found prototypes of emerging American Indian Studies programs at these schools. While most schools offered academic support to struggling

Indian students, invariably they treated American Indians as subjects of academic study that employed the traditional disciplines of history, language, literature, anthropology, and the arts. Such an approach seemed ill-suited to BYU, however, where the mission of the Church toward American Indians embraced Lamanite identity and promoted conversion. Whetton recognized that he needed a program that would emphasize Indian *students* rather than Indian Studies.[12]

At the end of his lengthy study, Dean Whetten settled on principles that offered a student-centered approach to education with no inclusion or awareness of the culturally specific needs of Native students. He defined Indian "success" in terms of becoming successful, like other students on campus. Indian students would be integrated into the mainstream with no effort to control or influence associations with other students. Given the cultural dominance of the overwhelmingly white LDS student body and the all-encompassing extent of LDS Church activities at BYU, no such limitations would be needed—Indian students would have few alternatives. Finally, in language that calls to mind the self-help rhetoric of assimilated boarding school graduates in earlier generations, Whetten insisted that Indians students should be "free to fail." All the help that the institution could conceivably offer would be available to provide assistance, but in the end, success or failure would depend on individual initiative.

In 1968, Church program specialists produced the *Lamanite Handbook of The Church of Jesus Christ of Latter-day Saints* to guide the efforts of Church leaders in administering Indian programs. The *Handbook* expressed typically ambiguous sentiments about the place of Indian students—referenced as Lamanites—within the context of Indian culture. Among the objectives was one that "encouraged active participation of Lamanite students in the full offerings the university," yet found room to "give opportunities for identification in all-Lamanite groups as the individual feels the need."[13]

The assimilationist subtext of the *Lamanite Handbook* reflected the same basic objectives of the General College, which housed the academically oriented Indian programs at BYU. The Department of General Curriculum provided remedial coursework in a number of subjects, including English, general science, biology, and history. All students could enroll in these courses and, in practice, they tended to divide equally between Indian and non-Indian students. The objectives had all shared the goals of overcoming academic deficiencies and transitioning Indian students into the mainstream colleges and departments.

But the American Indian students still faced formidable barriers. A study undertaken in 1972 found that Indian students entered BYU with a mean ACT score of only 12.77 and a composite GPA of only 1.85—scores so low that fully 87 percent entered the university on academic probation.[14] Moreover, many of the incoming freshmen, most of whom had been recruited through the Indian Placement Program, had no idea that they had been admitted at a comparative disadvantage to their non-Indian peers. Once enrolled, they struggled to compete for grades or even keep up in class.

Nevertheless, the commitment of the Church hierarchy to incoming Indian students remained very high and enrollments at BYU grew in parallel with the continued expansion of the Indian Placement Program throughout the 1960s. By the end of the decade, the university admitted more than 500 Indian students every year and might have admitted even more, except for cost factors, as the school provided matching funding for Indian students who received tribal and BIA funding.[15] By the early 1970s, approximately 5,000 Indian students participated annually in the placement program, most of them living with non-Native Mormon families in Utah, Arizona, California, Idaho, and Washington. These students typically attended local high schools, participated in LDS seminary programs, and were supervised by "specially assigned and trained LDS social workers." Most of these BYU alumni served as natural recruiters for the university.[16]

As Indian student enrollments increased, administrators at BYU hired more instructors for the General College and created the Indian Education Department with courses in mathematics, business, and history added to the existing curriculum. Even so, Indian students continued to struggle. As admissions requirements at the university became more rigorous, they found themselves competing against better and more qualified non-Indian students. Con Osborne, one of the original faculty members assigned to the program, held in-depth interviews with the most experienced instructors to try to comprehend the depths of the problem. Everyone agreed that incoming Indian students had "poor study habits, low reading skills, and minimal writing ability." Many came from BIA boarding schools or on-reservation boarding schools. A majority came from the Navajo, Hopi, Pueblo, or other Southwestern tribes where native languages still predominated. According to Osborne, only a "small percentage … came from homes where the parents had attained at least a high-school education and where standard English was the language of the home."[17]

Apart from academic struggles, Indian students also faced formidable cultural barriers. Few had any real grasp of the workings of the university and saw only, as Osborne put it, "myriads of strange faces running several different directions at once." According to William Fox, another of the original instructors, the majority of Indian students had "a limited concept of what was expected of them."[18]

In an attempt to soften the harsh realities of cultural disorientation, BYU educators increasingly placed Indian students into general curriculum courses restricted to other Indians. In so doing, advisors unwittingly created a segregated classroom experience for students and faculty alike. William Fox noted that "Indian students often felt estranged from the non-Indian students and kept largely to themselves in social functions." Many came to BYU at the urging of local Church leaders, university recruiters, or Church placement directors, and lacked a real appreciation of what a university degree might mean to their future prospects. They "keenly desired to be able to 'help their people' but had really no idea of how to go about that, or how a university degree could assist them in doing so."[19]

While the inadvertent segregation of Indian students grew out of attempts to ease the transition to academic life, the goals of Church and university leaders centered largely on Church attendance and spiritual growth. In the 1950s, the Church created a separate ward (58th Ward of the BYU 2nd Stake) solely for Indian students. Indian students were not required to attend it, but the majority did "in order to affiliate with other Indian students and to receive church leadership training." Later on, two other "Lamanite" wards, the 92nd and 97th, were created to meet the rising enrollments.[20] At various times the Church leadership closed and reopened the special "Lamanite" wards, depending on the attitudes of those in leadership at the time.

The policy shifts could be wrenching for the Indian students. Carletta Yellowjohn, a Shoshone from the Fort Hall Reservation in Idaho, experienced the integration first hand. She noted that "a few years ago they decided to have the whites go with the Indians. That was the hardest thing because we were seeing who were the strongest to be with the non-Indians." Yellowjohn had been on an LDS mission and possessed firm convictions, but even she found the social disruption challenging. "Being a Lamanite ward, we were together. We were bonded together. To not see that anymore kind of hurts. Yet we have to be out there existing and being as everyone else."[21]

Some felt that the wards segregated Indian students and stunted their integration in regular wards and stakes.[22] When in operation, though, the Lamanite
wards followed the same standard conventions as all student wards at BYU. Student wards created opportunities for male students to advance in the priesthood
and all students to gain experience through Church callings. As Carletta Yellowjohn put it, "They tried to tell us, 'you're going to be the next leaders ... Are
you going to be the example that we are to you? How are you going to help your
Indian people?'"[23]

Administrators at BYU made other efforts to accommodate Indian students,
especially during the peak years of Indian enrollment of the early 1970s. At the
time, BYU claimed to have the largest university enrollment of American Indians in the United States, with approximately 600 on campus. Indian students
had their own newspaper, the *Eagle's Eye*, which began publication in 1971 and
continued without interruption for more than a decade. As student newspapers
go, the *Eagle's Eye* filled a need for Native students by giving them a collective
voice and a sense that they had a special status on campus. Interest in the paper
waned in the early 1980s, however, and in 1983 the university administration cut
back production to a magazine format published only four times a year.[24]

Indian students also had their own on-campus club, the Tribe of Many
Feathers. Interestingly, the club welcomed not only American Indian students,
but also former Mormon missionaries who had served in Indian-centered mission fields. Among other things, "TMF," as the students called it, sponsored the
Miss Indian BYU Pageant. Starting in 1967, the pageant continued every year
until 1990, when it too fell victim to administrative reductions in Indian programs. One of the first winners, Jeanie Sekaquaptewa Groves (Hopi) explained
that the pageant brought Indians "to the same level as the other groups ... For
us, it was showing that we were good, faithful members of the Church, that
we had talents, and that we could get a college education."[25] Pageant winners
also served as unofficial representatives of TMF, as they had an opportunity to
address contemporary Indian-related issues. At times the spotlight proved less
than welcoming, as Miss Indian BYU Nora Mae Begay (Navajo) discovered in
1972, when she followed up on her success at BYU by winning the Miss Indian
America Pageant. Begay became a target of American Indian activists who criticized her success as a "product" of the LDS Indian Placement Program and
a poor role model for "true Indians." She responded in the manner typical of
beauty pageant contestants by calling for "cooperation and unity between the

different people of the world," which, she argued, would "result in a better future for all of us."[26]

Not all TMF leaders succumbed so easily to orthodoxy. A generation earlier, young Mel Thom, a Paiute from the Walker River Reservation in Nevada, served for three years as the organization's president. Afterward, he famously collaborated with Clyde Warrior and other student activists in founding the National Indian Youth Council. A thoroughgoing radical later in the 1960s, Thom no doubt toed the line very carefully while at BYU, especially given President Ernest Wilkinson's antipathy toward any form of radicalism or campus activism. Wilkinson held firm throughout the tumultuous 1960s, never permitting expressions of sympathy toward the emerging Red Power movement. In 1970, when TMF president Phillip Smith and other Indians wore red arm bands in a protest against San Jose State University's exclusion of Indian athletes, Wilkinson criticized them for resembling "activists" and associating with activist organizations such as the NIYC.[27]

Perhaps in an attempt to project a more compliant version of Mormon-Indian identity, in 1971 BYU students and faculty produced an all-Indian song and dance troupe called the "Lamanite Generation" at the suggestion of President Dale Tingey of the Southwest Indian Mission. Tingey envisioned using the group as a proselyting tool to draw attention to the Church's Indian programs and for a time they toured and traveled throughout the Southwest in pickup trucks. As the Lamanite Generation became more successful, their schedule expanded to include the Northern Indian Mission and Alberta-Saskatchewan Indian Mission.[28] Drawing on Native dances for inspiration, the group performed highly anglicized song and dance routines. Founder and artistic director Janie Thompson had a long career as a musician, talent scout, performer, and musical producer before accepting a faculty position at BYU. She directed thousands of shows during her early years at the university and knew how to produce an entertaining spectacle. Thompson sought to project an image of wholesomeness and inclusiveness while remaining respectful of Native culture, if not authentic to it. The goal was to expose audiences to the "richness of the Lamanite cultures, the talents of the performers, the colorful costumes, the beauty of the dances, and the uniqueness of the songs."[29]

Some Indian students seem to have been directly recruited to BYU as Lamanite Generation performers, occasionally without even knowing it. Milli Garrett, a Navajo and former Miss Indian BYU, remembered her invitation to "perform in some kind of talent show. You could enter in the dance, art, and some other category. I entered all three. I won in all three, first place. They said to me, 'since you won in all three, just choose the one that you want to go in.'" Then she learned that the prize for winning "was to come to BYU." Before she knew it, she and her friends had signed up for BYU orientation, despite the fact that she had no affiliation with the LDS Church. Thinking back on her innocence, she said, "We were just so dumb. My cousin didn't even know what we were doing ... We didn't have any plans for that summer, so we went."[30]

During the peak years of its existence in the 1970s and early 1980s, the Lamanite Generation became a highly coordinated road show with an extensive touring schedule. But as the performance regimen expanded, the emphasis on American Indians shifted to a more inclusive, emerging perspective of Lamanite identity. Performers became more "Lamanite" than Indian, with a third of the performers Latin Americans, a third Polynesians, and a third American Indians. The troupe functioned primarily as a proselyting tool for the Church and had little to do with the education objectives of the university. Sometimes the conversion process worked the other way around. Milli Garrett, who had still not joined the Church, found that what she had learned about the Book of Mormon came alive to her while touring South America. She said, "We would go right to the homes of these people up in the mountains, they reminded me so much of Navajos and some of the Indians. I saw them weaving. They would weave like my grandmother. I saw their designs on their rugs and on their pottery. It was so much like what we have here." Convinced that the Native people she observed shared her lineage, she converted. "I just felt like the Lord wanted me to see those things. It just made sense to me when I would sit there and look at those women and those men."[31]

The Church used other BYU performing groups for missionary work, but the Lamanite Generation seems to have been a primary tool for reaching out to Native Peoples. In North America, Indian communities became less receptive over time and questioned the legitimacy of the performances. They also criticized Mormon efforts to supplant authentic Indigenous culture with Lamanite identity. Church leaders responded by shifting Lamanite Generation performances to overseas venues with non-Indian audiences. By the 1980s, the original intent of Lamanites performing in American Indian communities became "subservient to the newer intent of world-wide exposure."[32]

Such criticisms reflected the emerging confidence of ethnic and racial groups in the United Status and elsewhere. The Black and Red Power movements of the late sixties, combined with the Vietnam anti-war protest movement and the rise of the counterculture, culminated in campus movements that embraced diversity and promoted multicultural studies. Although BYU remained relatively immune for a time, the LDS Church did not escape the notice of Indian activists. At the April 1973 general conference of the Church, a small group of protestors from the American Indian Movement gathered outside the gates of Temple Square, pounding on drums, singing, and demanding to be heard. Wendell Ashton, representing Church president Harold B. Lee, came out to meet the protestors, but he rebuffed their demand for $1 million of aid annually to support Indian programs. He told them that the Church already accomplished much more for American Indians with its existing programs than a million dollars might provide. In response, they presented Ashton with a box of flowers intended for President Lee and continued their singing. As Salt Lake City police officers looked on, Temple Square security personnel locked the gates to prevent the protestors from entering the grounds or disturbing the conference. Avid Hill, a Utah AIM member told the gathered news media, "We come in peace and brotherhood, and are met with militancy and locked gates."[33] They made an impact, but not a positive one. The protest "annoyed" Elder Kimball and other General Authorities. Many felt that Indian critics neither understood nor appreciated the extent of the Church's efforts on behalf of American Indians.[34]

During these turbulent years in the 1970s, many universities created African American and Native American Studies programs and began actively recruiting minority students. BYU recruiters suddenly found themselves competing with 15 to 30 other institutions for the best American Indian students and often did so at a disadvantage. In addition, the 1978 Tribally Controlled Community College Assistance Act created regional opportunities for Indian students at tribal colleges. Unlike the "student-centered" program at BYU, Native Studies programs at other institutions embraced tribalism, language retention, and promoted the preservation of Indigenous culture. From the mid-1970s on, with the explosion of NAS programs around the country, BYU lost its position of sponsoring one of the few university Indian education programs. Recruiting became more difficult.

In response to these social and academic trends, educators at BYU promoted the creation of a redesigned Native Studies program, one that would include courses in American Indian history, art, and literature, but the administration rejected their plans for a full-blown studies program or even an NAS major,

claiming that graduates would find few opportunities for employment. The educators achieved a partial victory in 1975 when school officials relented slightly by
allowing the implementation of a Native American Studies minor. It remained a
supplementary program, one designed specifically to enhance the undergraduate
educational experience of Indian students.[35]

Even the location reflected the second-rate status afforded the program. The
few offices devoted solely to Native Studies were located in the old Brimhall
Building on the historic lower end of campus. The Indian students called it "Fort
Brimhall." They shared a large study hall, arranged with tables and adorned with
portraits of Miss Indian BYU on the walls. Con Osborne remembered that "the
offices were dingy in appearance; the furniture old. In spite of many requests for
more attractive and functional facilities, only minor remodeling was authorized.
So one of the nation's leading university-Indian programs remained housed in
crowded, uncomfortable, unattractive offices."[36]

As a result of these developments, American Indian enrollments at BYU
tapered off somewhat by the middle 1970s. Navajo students still constituted
the vast majority of those enrolled, numbering 280 in 1973–1974. By way of
contrast, the next highest tribal enrollment came from Siouan Tribes, with
only 26 students combined. BYU administrators started shifting funding away
from Indians to "other" Lamanites. From 1973 to 1977, 1,014 Mexican American,
Latin American, and Polynesian students received grants from the Lamanite
Scholarship Fund.[37]

To provide a doctrinal justification for the increasing emphasis on a broader,
pan-ethnic focus and less emphasis on American Indians, the Institute of American Indian Services and Research at BYU published an eight-page booklet in
1979, titled "The Old and Modern Lamanite." The author, BYU sociology professor Arturo de Hoyos, declared, "A Lamanite is anyone who had any degree
of traditional connection with the ancient inhabitants of the American continent, whose origin is described in the Book of Mormon." After listing the many
peoples mentioned therein, de Hoyos concluded, "In modern times, therefore,
all those who have any degree or relationship to the people who came at the time
of Lehi, whether they are from the North, Central, or South America, or from
the islands of the Pacific, can legitimately be called Lamanites."

Given the nationwide emphasis on multiculturalism and the increased
competition from much more Native-centric programs at other universities,
one might have expected a more accommodating approach to tribal cultures,

but in this regard de Hoyos remained unapologetic. Demonstrating how little the objectives had changed since the establishment of the Research Institute in 1960, he asserted that "the challenge of every Lamanite now is really a great and marvelous challenge. For we must overcome the consequences of what wrong traditions have done to the people of Lehi ... among the Lamanites of North and South America and the South Pacific who have not yet accepted the gospel, there are many customs, ideas, ceremonies and other traditions that must be abandoned." Prospective recruits to the program must have been shocked to learn that the ceremonial practices of their Native cultures were "wrong," but de Hoyos offered only the compensation of a brighter future: "When these wrong cultural traditions are abandoned, and in their place Mormon culture, or the pure culture of the gospel is adopted, then the new Lamanites will blossom and the world will speak their name with respect and admiration." He foresaw the day when Indigenous Peoples would take their place as "scientists, teachers, statesmen, merchants—individuals of notable achievement and contribution in the nations of the world and the kingdom of God."[38]

Arturo de Hoyos stood out among Mormon scholars affiliated with the Indian Education Department for his willingness to express, unambiguously, the assimilationist underpinnings of Mormon doctrine. According to sociologist Armand Mauss, "The Mormons had had an extensive historical experience with Indians. Yet, unlike the other denominations, most Mormons continued to understand Indians as 'Lamanites' and therefore looked at them through the prism of the Book of Mormon story." In an echo of de Hoyo's sentiments, he noted that, "Such a view combined the negative attribution of a fallen and degraded people with the positive expectation of a people ready and willing to be redeemed and restored to greatness."[39] After nearly two decades of experience educating Indian students at BYU, an awareness of the inherent value of Indigenous cultures remained outside the conceptual boundaries of the program.

Yet it must be acknowledged that many Indian students accepted the transformative power of Lamanite identity and flourished in it. Those who grew up in the Indian Placement Program adapted more readily to Mormon culture. Garnet Comegan, an Ojibway from Ontario who served as president of TMF, had good friends who came through the program. He recalled, "Some of them are kind of so-so because they have been too mainstream into the Anglo culture. They don't go back to their roots at all. I know a girl who doesn't even care to associate with Indians anymore. She's always with her white buddies." Comegan was unsparing in his criticism: "I'm like, 'why?' There's something there for you. There's still a part of you over there ... Some don't speak their languages. They've lost a lot of the things they learned when they were kids. They carry with them more of what they learned from the placement program."[40] He believed in a more acculturative version of Indian identity, one that accepted the good in both the Mormon *and* the Indian.

Ernesteen Lynch had a similar perspective, one that drew on a wider range of experience than most American Indian students at BYU. She grew up on the Navajo Reservation and attended a boarding school in Farmington, New Mexico. Acculturated in the Methodist Church, she earned a bachelor's degree in history at the University of Oklahoma and became, as she put it, "more or less" a member of the American Indian Movement. Returning to the Navajo Reservation, she converted to Mormonism and later earned a graduate degree in history at BYU. Lynch experienced firsthand the ethnic cleavages that existed in Mormon wards on the Navajo Reservation. She said, "I don't think this problem of ethnic identity is going to go away magically. I think it has to be addressed. The Church is worldwide, and it's going to be even more worldwide in the future from all indications." Drawing on her own experiences, she wondered, "are they not going to let the blacks meet all together in Africa as a church? Are they going to import people from the outside to have callings? In communities where they are all one ethnic [group], are they going to stop them from practicing their culture?" She believed that it could not be done. "It's stepping on some of their God-given rights to practice the gospel within their culture. Many cultures are very good."[41]

Oral histories conducted with American Indian students at BYU reveal a pattern of difficult choices that they had to make in deciding "which side of the line" they would live on. Most found it impossible to stay always on one side or the other. In practical terms, the process of acculturation forced them to make eclectic choices, drawing what worked from both sides of the cultural line.[42] Even after she converted to Mormonism and married a non-Indian returned missionary while at BYU, Milli Garrett insisted on a traditional Navajo wedding ceremony, because, as she put it, "that is what she always wanted." Almost immediately she discovered the challenge of bridging two worlds. At her wedding reception a woman came through the line and told her, "My son is on a mission in South Dakota, and I just pray that he won't bring back an Indian girl." Incredulous, Milli and her new husband just looked at each other. She wondered, "Does she know what she's saying? We just shook hands with her and she went on her way. She was the bishop's wife."[43]

Other Indian students encountered difficulties with non-Indian students at BYU. Tonia Halona, a Navajo, found it difficult to establish friendships with white LDS students. She recalled that her roommate asked questions that revealed ignorance and condescension toward her people. "She asked if Indians have cheese and stuff down there. She asked if they have a church … They [roommates and other students] ask about living conditions. They ask us if we have running water—which I don't have. They totally freak out about that. They can't understand why we live that way."[44]

More unfortunate Indians found intolerance on both sides of the line. Lucinda McDonald, a Navajo, joined the Mormon Church at age 10, the only member of her family to do so. She entered the Indian Placement Program while in the fifth grade but returned home because of homesickness. Shortly afterward her father died and she felt compelled to stay on the reservation. When she reached high school age her mother, in difficult financial straits and near death herself, insisted that she reenter the placement program. Lucinda knew that after her mother's passing she had to find a way to succeed in the broader world, but found the transition difficult. "[The] first day in seminary I was so lost. I was thinking, 'why am I here?' I thought it was so stupid for me to be there or to even be a member of the Church. I just did not grow up in the Church. My parents didn't have religion. They didn't want it that way." A native Navajo speaker, she felt lonely and isolated in her school, where she was the only American Indian. "Sometimes I just felt like talking to someone in Navajo. There was nobody there to talk to in Navajo." She found that when she did speak her native language people made fun of her. "They just try and copy me. They laugh about me." Fortunately, McDonald found a much more welcoming environment at BYU, where her roommates appreciated her background and expressed interest in learning more about her culture. When she returned to the reservation, however, she had a "hard time" with some of her own people who, she said, would "make fun of the Mormons. A lot of Native Americans, my friends and my cousins that aren't members, asked me all of these questions."[45]

By the end of the 1970s, American Indian students at BYU had gained much, but had lost even more. They came to the University better prepared and possessing higher degrees of acculturation. Many had attended good high schools. But they still fell behind other incoming freshmen because the qualifications and standards had increased for *all* students. Indian Education Department chair Con Osborne noted, "BYU, although no one wanted to admit it, was fast becoming an elite school where the under-prepared, less academically gifted, student had little chance."[46] Faced with an impossible choice, the department became more restrictive with admissions and many Indian students chose to go elsewhere. Enrollments declined even further.

The administration requested a lengthy series of program evaluations and self-studies. Hoping to survive through expansion and inclusion, Osborne, along with the dean of Student Life, David Sorenson, formally requested a reorganization that transformed the Indian Education Department into the Multicultural Education Department. The change, as Osborne put it, "was a signal to the university and especially to all minority students that the services of the department were available to them." Continuing a process that had been underway for more than a decade, Latin American, Polynesian, Asian, African American, and other minority students sought assistance from the new department even as enrollments for American Indian students continued to fall.[47]

By the early 1980s, the program had attained impressive achievements. The Multicultural Education Program had tenured faculty and staff, ample funding from the LDS Church, and a specialized curriculum that faculty had developed through a long process of trial and error. Tremendous efforts had been made to facilitate student retention. And in large measure, these efforts succeeded. Between 1950 and 1985, close to 600 American Indians received degrees at BYU with more than 1,500 listed on school records as alumni. Tempered by the fact that fully 80 percent of the Indians who attended the university failed to earn a degree, BYU still had a graduation rate five times higher than the national average for American Indians.[48]

Then, amazingly, the Church leaders, or perhaps one leader in particular, Elder Boyd K. Packer, reached the decision to terminate the program. The process took a number of years but undoubtedly began in 1979, when Packer insisted on delivering the keynote address for the Indian Week awards banquet in place of the scheduled speaker, George P. Lee, a member of the Quorum of the Seventy and president of the Arizona Holbrook Mission.[49] As an original member of the Lamanite Committee of the Church that instituted many of the programs at BYU, Packer had come to believe that Indian students had not lived up to the investment that the Church had made in them. As he addressed the gathering, he pointed out that the one million or so Indians of Lamanite lineage in North

America were numerically dwarfed by the many millions of people of Mexico, Yucatan, Guatemala, and the nations of South America, "of whom 31,990,000 are pure Indians." These words slightly shocked the Indian students, just as Packer had intended. He added, "If it sounds like I'm scolding you just a little, it will be because I am." Continuing the reprimand, he informed the students that the Lamanites of North America had failed in their duty to carry the gospel to those in Latin America. "Those millions to the south are waiting for redemption. They're waiting for you. You can do more to redeem them than I can do … [and] have so much power that I do not have, and so much affiliation and affinity with these people that I could never have, that it pains me to see being wasted." Honing in more particularly on the successful BYU Indian students, he chided them, saying, "If all you come away with is a degree, and the ability to make a living, if all you have come here for is to get [that], then you may well have failed."[50]

Osborne and other faculty members in the Indian Education Department understood the implicit threat in Packer's remarks. The signs were already in place. The number of students in the Indian Placement Program had declined to about 2,500 per year, half of what it had been in the mid-1970s. The Church Education System had begun phasing out seminary programs in Indian communities and withdrawing instructors. Lamanite branches in the mission fields were integrated into existing wards. Helan Taosoga, an Omaha from Nebraska, remembered that "just before I came out to BYU in 1970 there were a lot of Indians back home getting baptized into the LDS Church … we even had our own branch, and I knew the Native American branch president … The gospel was just blooming." She returned later, after the branch had been shuttered, and found that "all of the sudden there was no meeting place. I remember seeing my Indian president friend again … He broke down and told me that the reason a lot of the Indians quit the Church was because they were pushed into a basement of an all-white chapel." Her former branch president described how the Indians "tried real hard to clean themselves up because they wanted to go to church," but they had been relocated to a ward on the west side of Omaha in a wealthy neighborhood. He said, "First they let us stay in their ward. Gradually we got pushed further and further to the point where they really didn't want you in their ward. Pretty soon the white ward started another branch [for us], and they put the Indians in the basement. That didn't hold good for any of them back home. So they quit." All of the Indians that had converted in 1970 had left the Church. Helan Taosoga said, "It's sad because it started out so good."[51]

Even before they completed the reorganization of the Indian Education Department into the Multicultural Education Department, administrators at BYU detected the shifting attitudes of the Church hierarchy. In correspondence with university leaders, Dean Maren Mouritsen noted that "there appears to be some questions and even far reaching interests coming from Salt Lake with regard to the Church's overall concern for our Indian Services and the Programs."[52] Her concerns were not misplaced. The end of the Indian Education Program was at hand.

After authorizing numerous internal audits and studies, including a detailed report compiled at the Church offices by the Lamanite Coordinating Committee, Elder Packer created an ad hoc committee to review the status of Church Lamanite programs. The members included several General Authorities, with Elder Carlos Asay serving as committee chair. In language reminiscent of the termination advocates of the 1950s, Asay encouraged his fellow members to heed Packer's wish and end the "pattern of dependency that Church programs had created for Indian people." Others noted that these programs cost four times as much as resources devoted to other members.[53] In May 1983, after the findings were conveyed to Packer, he abruptly disbanded the committee.

Mandated changes followed shortly afterward. In early 1984, the BYU administration requested specific recommendations for the closure of the Multicultural Education Department and the transfer of faculty, courses, and resources to regular academic departments. After years of study, assessment, review, and discussion, the American Indian program at BYU came to an end with sudden swiftness. Campus administrators replaced it with a solitary campus office to provide academic and financial support for minority students.

Indian students at BYU felt demoralized by the changes. Garnet Comegan reflected on the transformation, noting that at the end of the 1980s, "There are not as many Indians. That's gone way down. I work with the Tribe of Many Feathers now, and there are not hardly any Indians on campus. Even then there's not really any particular closeness." He remembered the way it used to be, continuing, "It's just a feeling I felt when I first arrived at BYU. There was a big closeness at BYU. There was a big push for Lamanites, and there were special programs for them here. Now they're just being integrated back into the main stream again."[54]

Why did the BYU Indian program, once the largest and, in terms of academic achievement, arguably the most successful in the United States, fail?

In part because of the rise of tribal colleges and the multicultural programs at other institutions that created an alternative model of Indian education, one more favorable to Indigenous culture. These programs not only provided Indian students with more options, they coincided with a growing awareness of Native American rights and a new-found respect for tribalism. The student-centered, assimilationist model employed for decades at BYU seemed strikingly at odds with both the world of higher education and an increasingly pluralistic society. But such an assessment overlooks the fact that the Indian Education Department at BYU hewed closely to the goals that had been set for it by the Church leadership, and by that criteria, the program succeeded beyond what anyone outside of those circles might have expected. Education administration at BYU did not pull the plug on the Indian program, nor did it result from disapproval that the program engendered in various quarters outside of the Church. The LDS Church hierarchy, for reasons never fully articulated, made that decision.

A more logical explanation for the demise of the program might be found in the shifting cultural patterns of the second half of the twentieth century. In the 1950s, when the LDS Church conceived and implemented the Indian Placement Program, the prevailing winds of integration and assimilation favored its success. In the 1960s, when the postwar baby boom generation came of age and institutions of higher education expanded rapidly in the sheer number of students and campuses, as well as the greater inclusion of women and minorities, the trends favored the growth of a highly specialized program for American Indians. The Church investment in Indian Placement initially gave BYU a significant advantage in the recruitment and retention of Indian students. From the mid-1970s onward, however, the social and cultural patterns became much less favorable to the Church's Indian proselyting efforts and educational programs. The Red Power movement, the reassertion of Indian sovereignty, and increasing pride American Indians took in their cultural identity all dimmed the attraction of the Church's gospel message to Lamanites.

In the end, the promise of multicultural society held a far greater appeal for American Indians. Elder Packer's message that the Lamanites of North America had failed to attain their prophetic destiny seemed rooted in a deeper truth: that American Indians would reclaim their place in American society, but they would do it on their own terms.

12

"A Candid Investigation"

Concluding Observations and Future Directions

BRENDEN W. RENSINK

On July 10, 1832, LDS missionary Samuel Smith was in Boston, Massachusetts, ministering to Church members, preaching to interested parties, and struggling against numerous challenges. That day, he recorded an intriguing experience in his journal of visiting with none other than William Apess, a well-known Pequot Methodist minister, poet, and one of the earliest recorded Indigenous North American authors.[1] Smith indicated that Apess was skeptical of his message, but eventually expressed interest and invited Smith to preach to his congregation. Smith wrote that Apess concluded to give Mormonism "a candid investigation."[2] The missionaries left for Providence, Rhode Island, indicating they would return to preach for Apess. Unfortunately, either the return visit did not occur or they made no record of it.

Their encounter is instructive for this volume of essays and the position in which it places us, the readers—whether American Indian, Mormon, or general interested public. These essays represent a number of "candid" investigations, intersecting writings, histories, and experiences of American Indians and Mormons. How will we respond? Interests piqued, will we vow to return to these topics and engage further, only to drift away to more familiar or comfortable intellectual pursuits? I advocate that we take these candid investigations, sit with them, struggle with them, and then take steps to inquire further. Let this not be the last entry in scholarly and public discussion about how American Indian and Mormon worlds have been, and often still are, intertwined.

Toward this end, I offer summaries and syntheses of this volume's chapters, highlighting their unique insights, and pointing toward promising avenues for ongoing future study and discussion. We must recognize that many chapters represent authors' initial forays into these fields. Others draw from long-germinating ideas and ponderings. None position themselves as the definitive last words on their given topics. Quite to the contrary, readers have likely found that these essays open as many doors and pose as many unanswered questions as they do resolve existing ones. This may be the product of a scholarly field that is, in many ways, still in its infancy. Few of our authors benefited from fully developed and robust literatures upon which to build. Excusing fraught and loaded terminologies, our authors stand on the frontiers of inquiry—pioneering new paths for other scholars to follow. Staking out claims on such precarious ground is daunting. Oversights, mistakes, unconsidered possibilities no doubt abound. In reviewing these authors' arguments and explorations, however, I am confident that the value of their work far outweighs any nagging issues we might identify.

Introductions

We began this volume with four pieces from individuals who identify as both Native and Mormon, an introduction co-authored by P. Jane Hafen (Taos Pueblo), a selection of poetry from Tacey Atsitty (Diné), a childhood reflection from Michalyn Steele (Seneca), and a thought piece on historical memory and community from Darren Parry (Shoshone).[3] The significance of these pieces is multifold. First, we should take note of whom they represent. With the exception of Parry, who does speak broadly for a community, the other three are individual voices. Together, their individual perspectives offer at least a glimpse into the variety of contemporary *lived* Native Mormon experience. The general worlds of Mormon and Native discourse intersect irregularly. When they do, the voices of Natives are often not privileged in Mormon circles and the voices of Mormons are often not privileged in Native circles. Hafen, Atsitty, Steele, and Parry make no pretense to speak for Mormon Indians, but listening to them can help direct our thoughts and questions down productive paths. With intimate inquiries—whether seeking insight into faith communities or Indigenous communities—learning how to listen is a skill too often ignored. These four voices tune our ears to *listen* better.

Hafen and I were direct in our introduction chapter and confront readers with major problems and dilemmas in the overlapping histories and experiences of American Indians and Mormons. The questions we pose will likely make many readers uncomfortable on one point or another. That is a good thing. These topics are wrapped up, shielded, and at times obscured by the intimate nature of faith, identity, tradition, and family. Attempts to understand them, no matter how well intentioned, may cause discomfort and even pain. Perhaps this is why so few have attempted extended forays into the field. Thus, simply opening topics for view—unpacking and shining light on interconnected Mormon-Indian histories—is a major task. We attempt to shoulder some of this work by the questioning of settler colonialism, Mormon tradition and doctrine, ethnic and racial issues, and Native histories broadly. We do not provide easy answers, but point toward the questions we should be asking. Following up will require humility, sincerity, and courage. In emulating those very attributes, Hafen certainly offers us an example to follow.

Atsitty evokes imagery, intimacy, and experience where the Navajo and Mormon seem inseparable. They represent fully integrated facets of her being, and while possible incongruities and tensions exist, she weaves them together as inherent and organic parts of her whole. When Atsitty graced our 2016 Redd Center seminar with a reading of her work, the sincerity and gravity of her words left a deep impression on the audience, as if we had witnessed something rare, something sacred. I hope the printed word conveys that spirit here. Michalyn Steele also joined our summer seminar to offer a reading of her piece. Most contemporary work in Mormon-Indian studies skews West, so her personal New York history of Seneca Mormons offers a welcomed eastern perspective. She recalls little incongruity in her family's Indigeneity and Mormon faith. Indeed, the Corn Soup Social hosted by the Seneca congregation brought the two communities together, serving both. What an inspiring example of intercommunity sacrifice and service, a sacrament of sorts through which all participants are bound together in shared values and experience. Surely, this is a concept to be modeled where Native and Mormon communities overlap and coexist elsewhere. Darren Parry offers us an exercise in historical memory, trauma, and recovery. He grounds this in personal and community histories of horrific loss on the one hand, and the regenerative and sustaining powers of community and faith on the other. In this, Parry suggests a path that draws from the best of both Indian and Mormon worlds.

Part One, "Native Experience with the Early LDS Church, Interpretation of Mormon Scripture, and Literary Representations"

The Church of Jesus Christ of Latter-day Saints situates Joseph Smith and his translation (or transcription) of the Book of Mormon at the center of belief and testimony. Asked in 1842 to explain the Church's beliefs, Joseph Smith offered 13 "Articles of Faith," the eighth of which unequivocally asserted "we believe the Book of Mormon to be the word of God."[4] This clear declaration that the Book of Mormon contains God's word, however, is not necessarily a cut-and-dry claim of Book of Mormon inerrancy, that Joseph Smith was infallible, nor that the book's revealed text represented God's last word. These ideas are relevant to the first three chapters of Part One, and merit exploration.

Joseph Smith stated "the Book of Mormon was the most correct of any book on earth, and the keystone of our religion, and a man would get nearer to God by abiding by its precepts, than by any other book."[5] Neither Smith, nor the Book of Mormon's text, propose doctrines of *prima scriptura, sola scriptura,* or Biblical-styled inerrancy. Mormon, the historian chronicler who is presented as the author and compiler of the Book of Mormon source text prefaced the tome by stating, "And now, if there are faults they are the mistakes of men."[6] He later lamented of his poor writing, crying, "Lord, the Gentiles will mock at these things, because of our weakness in writing ... And thou hast made us that we could write but little, because of the awkwardness of our hands ... wherefore, when we write we behold our weakness, and stumble because of the placing of our words; and I fear lest the Gentiles shall mock at our words."[7] The Book of Mormon is, intriguingly, revered by followers of the LDS faith but acknowledged by the same to be an imperfect distillation of eternal truth—sullied by the weaknesses and foibles inherent in all mortal endeavors.

Mormons couple this complicated view of scripture with a proclaimed belief that the Church is led by a prophet and apostles, inspired by continuing revelation from God. However, even in this belief, the LDS Church does not claim infallibility of its leaders. Members are urged to place faith in leaders and their words, but commanded to appeal directly to their Creator for personal revelation and confirmation of teachings. Speaking of Latter-day Saints' follow-ing their prophet, LDS Church president Brigham Young stated his fear that Mormons "have so much confidence in their leaders that they will not inquire for themselves of God whether they are led by Him."[8] Apostle Dallin H. Oaks com-mented more recently, "Revelations from God—the teachings and directions of the Sprit—are not constant. We believe in continuing revelation, not contin-uous revelation. We are often left to work out problems without the dictation or specific direction of the Spirit."[9] This dualistic belief in revelation through prophets and the need for personal revelation is a unique and powerful aspect in the spiritual lives of Latter-day Saints.

These doctrines make Mormon faith simultaneously rooted in divinely revealed knowledge (via prophetic and personal means) *and* anticipatory of continued revelation as mortal understanding of God's doctrines evolve. This opens the Mormon scriptural cannon and doctrine to innumerable potential interpretations and questions. The promise that God "will yet reveal many great and important things" and prophecy that "other books" would be revealed in the last days deepen Latter-day sense that more is yet to come.[10] How then, might this anticipation intersect with Indigenous readings or interpretations of Mor-mon scripture or its founding?

Broadly, the first three chapters in Part One all approach this question. Their musings and analyses will likely prove the most challenging in this volume for some Latter-day Saint readers. Thomas Murphy and Lori Taylor both push Mormon readers to set aside traditional beliefs of the Church founding and its scriptures and invite them to explore Indigenous perspectives, alternatives, and interpretations. Rather than viewing these as challenges to their faith, LDS read-ers might approach these in the spirit of listening and deepening understanding, knowledge, and faith—regardless of whether they agree with the authors' con-clusions. Challenging thought exercises might spur new introspection.

Elise Boxer (Dakota) examines the Book of Mormon and settler colonialism in ways that may likewise be uncomfortable for LDS readers, but not because she offers unconventional interpretations of scripture or the Church's founding. Rather, Boxer forwards an unconventional (by Mormon standards) exploration into the historical context of Mormon-Indian relations and how certain readings of the Book of Mormon play into those interactions. Mainstream Mormon instruction via Sunday school and other curriculums, biannual Church-wide general conference addresses, or local congregations rarely approach thorny and challenging settler-colonial topics such as Native dispossession, violence, coercive assimilation, and how their legacies continue to impact Native communities. Taking pause to consider these new questions may help frame future productive dialogs between Mormons and Native Peoples, imbuing them with a greater understanding of the unseen implications or unintended consequences of Mormon views of American Indians. Max Perry Mueller also reaches into the history of Mormon-Indian interaction to explore when Ute Chief Wakara produced a written document—highlighting a unique moment of Native agency and action. The written word has potency often denied to oral traditions or community memory. Surely, other moments of Native agency in the history of Mormon-Indian interactions that did *not* produce a textual artifact would benefit from similar renewed investigation.

Lastly, Michael P. Taylor's foray into Native literary representations of Mormons opens readers to a wide world of unconsidered possibilities. A striking product of Taylor's chapter is the revelation of Native writers depicting Mormons— the inverse of the more familiar Mormon writers depicting Natives. The power of Taylor's call for readers to "humbly listen … reciprocally repair, remake, and retain these crucial relationships" cannot be overstated. This unexpected opportunity for American Indians and Mormons to use literary exploration as a means to further real-world dialog should not be dismissed. What other literary (or historical) texts wait to be created if more Native authors were to consider Mormon subjects? This is a field rich with possibilities. Taylor's examination of Cruz Smith's *The Indians Won*, an entertaining venture into "what if" counterfactual history, should not be brushed off as solely entertaining. Such exercises in creative imaginings of possible alternate timelines show us the innumerable possible ways that history *could* have unfolded. Our world is full of contingency. Reminding ourselves of historical contingency should remind us of our present ability to shape and contour our world and relationships—an opportunity we would be remiss to ignore.

Part Two. Native Mormon Experiences in the Twentieth Century

Whereas Part One considered Native Peoples and the founding of the LDS Church, its scriptural record, and early history, the six chapters of Part Two pull from more recent twentieth-century histories and experiences. Readers likely find these chapters easier to contextualize and digest, but they should grapple and wrestle with their findings and implications with as much care and humility as was required in Part One. While there exist many global Indigenous-Mormon connections, Hafen and I planned this volume to highlight exclusively those within the continental United States. The unique history of US territorial expansion, nation-to-nation treaty relationships, American Indian sovereignty, and other issues unique to the United States as described in this volume's introduction explain this scope. However, I hope that many of the twentieth-century "American" topics explored in these chapters resonate with parallel studies of Indigenous Peoples, Mormons, other faith traditions, and colonial enterprises across the globe.

Elise Boxer's chapter on the Book of Mormon and settler colonialism hinted at the complexities of joint Indian-Mormon identities, and this plays out through many of the chapters in Part Two. Stan Thayne's ethnographic work within the Catawba Indian Nation explores the legacy of mass-conversion to the LDS Church. He reveals remarkable examples of syncretic identities, where Native Peoples have consciously and subconsciously interwoven Mormon belief with their personal sense of Indigeneity. Is this the product of the large-scale Catawba community conversion or did these intimate issues unfold along purely personal lines? One is left with the question of how specific these personal navigations of identity are to the Catawba people, or if similar patterns are widespread among Native Mormons.

Farina Noelani King (Diné) and Jay Buckley, Kathryn Cochran, Taylor Brooks, and Kristen Hollist echo some of these issues. King uncovers multiple Indigenous Peoples negotiating Mormon terrains as Hawaiian missionaries worked among Navajo converts. The complexity of overlapping and competing identities—both Indigenous and religious—is remarkable and the revelation of unique Indigenous relationships and cooperation is fascinating. King's coverage treads familiar Southwestern ground, but Buckley and his student co-authors offer the first broad history of *northern* mission efforts of the LDS. They reveal equally fascinating interplay between Indigenous and religious identities. Their sources offer glimpses of the challenge Native converts faced in reconciling new Mormon culture with existing family and community traditions, language, and society. They also offer unique perspectives of how Natives viewed Mormon proselyting efforts. Both of these essays explore unique Native-specific missionizing efforts and the richness of the sources they uncover promises there is much more here to research and understand.

Erika Bsumek's work intersects not only the histories of American Indians and Mormons, but contextualizes them via environmental, labor, and economic histories. This is revelatory work and stands as an exemplary case study in how Native and Mormon histories can provide new insight into old topics. Reclamation, environmental contest, and the politics thereof in the American Southwest boast rich and well-developed historiographies. Bsumek approaches these topics from the new Indian and Mormon angles, and unsurprisingly, demonstrates how much more we need to reexamine these familiar topics. The content of her chapter is worthy of consideration on its own merit. Unwittingly, perhaps, Bsumek also succeeds in calling attention to this broader historiographic point—there is no shortage of seemingly well-trodden Western history topics that can be revived and reinvigorated with new wrinkles and insights when previously unconsidered Indian, Mormon, and Mormon-Indian actors or perspectives are employed as vectors for or subjects (not objects) of inquiry.

Finally, Megan Stanton and Warren Metcalf tackle a pair of connected topics—the LDS Indian Student Placement Program and the concurrent or subsequent prevalence of American Indian students at the LDS Church's flagship Brigham Young University. Church programs to move Native children into LDS homes for secondary education (and later college) is one of the topics that *has* received significant attention by scholars and the public.[11] Exploring these topics requires care and caution. Participant experiences and program outcomes varied widely and it easy to overgeneralize what were, indeed, personal and intimate matters.[12] In the individual family and student's stories we find joy in positive experiences and educational successes, and pain and struggle in the tensions between Indigenous and religious identities, ethnic and cultural misunderstanding, suspicion, and prejudice. These are delicate matters. Stanton and Metcalf are unflinching in asking difficult questions, but treat them with requisite care. They provide a model in how others might approach similarly fraught topics.

Looking Forward

In 2015, the summer before the Charles Redd Center for Western Studies hosted the American Indians and Mormons seminar to workshop these essays, we hosted a similarly structured seminar intersecting the fields of Mormon and environmental studies. The resulting volume, *The Earth Will Appear as the*

Garden of Eden: Essays on Mormon Environmental History, established a pattern that this volume has followed.[13] Two fields—often disparate and unconnected—were brought into conversation and the subsequent scholarship shed light on myriad topics. This approach allows scholars and readers to take familiar stories and ask new questions of them. If done with care, new insights should reveal that our previous understandings of individual topics were, in fact, incomplete. Be it environmental and Mormon studies, or American Indian and Mormon studies, once joined by scholarly inquiry we should discover integral knowledge of each subject—ideas and concepts never before understood because the questions raised by joint study had never been asked. We hope this volume has accomplished a similar feat.

This volume may potentially open Mormon eyes to a host of unexplored ideas that might enrich belief through challenging study and thought of Native subjects. Conversely, it should also serve to enlarge Native understandings of the Mormon world with which Native ancestors have interacted, or in which they themselves currently do. If these goals are realized, this collection has met one of its primary aims. Through thoughtful and provoking study, these essays highlight ground upon which fruitful dialog, joint exploration, and constructive debate can be held between Mormons, Indians, Mormon-Indians, and the general interested public.

Mormons and many American Indians share considerable history and experience. Latter-day Saint doctrine and history cannot be divorced from the Native (or Lamanite) worlds. Conversely, the recent histories and experiences of Native Americans living in the West—particularly the Intermountain West—often overlap Mormon worlds. With such intertwined history and experience there exists opportunity for continued and meaningful interaction. These chapters posed questions, both intentional and unintentional. Many questions were left unanswered and I hope this volume has provided a foundation for productive future scholarship and conversation. Such "candid investigation" promises to set the tone for relationships between American Indians, Mormons, and other interested parties—if approached with goodwill, humility, and rigor.

Notes

Introduction

1. Associated Press, "Archaeologist: Idaho site of Bear River Massacre pinpointed," *The Salt Lake Tribune*, May 23, 2016, http://archive.sltrib.com/article.php?id=3924071&itype=CMSID; Dan Bammes, "Shoshone Mark 150 Years Since Bear River Massacre," *All Things Considered and KUER Local News*, January 13, 2013, http://www.kuer.org/post/shoshone-mark-150-years-bear-river-massacre#stream/0; Sean Dolan, "Honoring their ancestors: Bear River Massacre interpretive center in the works, fundraising kicking off," *The Herald Journal News*, April 7, 2018, https://www.hjnews.com/logan_hj/honoring-their-ancestors-bear-river-massacre-interpretive-center-in-the/article_811d0cf-09e1-5153-9c0b-08550d36efd4.html; Brigham Madsen, *The Shoshoni Frontier and the Bear River Massacre* (Salt Lake City: University of Utah Press, 1985); Darren Parry, "The Tragedy of the Bear River Massacre, and Miracles of Forgiveness that Followed," Talk at Pleasant Valley Stake, South Ogden, Utah, July 29, 2018.

2. Robert Gehrke, "Its 2017, but people in Utah still put on 'redface' for an inaccurate re-creation of an American Indian vs. Mormon battle," *The Salt Lake Tribune*, September 6, 2017, http://www.sltrib.com/news/2017/09/06/gehrke-historically-inaccurate-and-wildly-offensive-a-utah-town-should-end-its-annual-sham-battle-between-cowboys-and-indians/; Matthew Piper, "Northwest Shoshone want American Indian vs. Mormon 'Sham Battles' to stop, but Wellsville mayor hopes for 'compromise,'" *The Salt Lake Tribune*, September 9, 2017, http://www.sltrib.com/news/politics/2017/09/09/hoping-to-end-american-indian-vs-mormon-sham-battles-northwest-shoshone-plan-meeting-with-wellsville-leaders/; Courtney Tanner, "Wellsville leaders pledge to revise 'Sham Battle' with rising tensions over depiction of American Indians," *The Salt Lake Tribune*, September 18, 2017, http://www.sltrib.com/news/politics/2017/09/18/wellsville-leaders-pledge-to-revise-sham-battle-with-rising-tensions-over-the-depiction-of-american-indians/; Courtney Tanner, "As divide grows among residents, Wellsville council votes to examine how American Indians are depicted in annual Sham Battle," *The Salt Lake Tribune*, September 21, 2017, http://www.sltrib.com/news/politics/2017/09/21/as-divide-grows-among-residents-wellsville-council-votes-to-form-a-committee-to-examine-how

-american-indians-are-depicted-in-annual-sham-battle/; and Courtney Tanner, "Redface will no longer be part of annual Wellsville 'Sham Battle,' committee decides," *The Salt Lake Tribune*, October 12, 2017, http://www.sltrib.com/news /politics/2017/10/12/committee-decides-dressing-up-as-native-americans-will -no-longer-be-part-of-annual-wellsville-sham-battle/.

3. Book of Mormon, Introduction. While many Church members historically interpreted Book of Mormon Lamanites to be the ancestors of all American Indians, the LDS Church has recently pushed back against this interpretation. Prior to 2006, the introduction to the Book of Mormon stated that Lamanites were the "principal" ancestors of American Indians. In 2006 this was changed to "among the ancestors." More recently, the LDS Church published a provocative essay exploring the complexities of Native American DNA and their relation to the Book of Mormon. See "Book of Mormon and DNA Studies," https://www .lds.org/topics/book-of-mormon-and-dna-studies.

4. *Native Historians Write Back: Decolonizing American Indian History*, (Lubbock, Texas: Texas Tech University Press, 2011), 2.

5. Parallel relations of First Nations Peoples with Canada exist. Some tribal Nations like the Blackfeet and Ojibwe groups cross the Canadian border or Medicine Line and are separated merely by national political divisions.

6. US Constitution, art. 1, sec. 4 and sec. 8.

7. *Johnson v. M'Intosh*, 21 US 543 (1823); *Cherokee Nation v. Georgia*, 30 US 1 (1831); and *Worcester v. Georgia*, 31 US 515 (1832).

8. For recent scholarship on the politics of blood quantum, genetic science, and tribal identity, see Kimberly TallBear, *Native American DNA: Tribal Belonging and the False Promise of Genetic Science* (Minneapolis: University of Minnesota Press, 2013). Identifying Native American markers through a DNA test does not, by itself, establish tribal identity.

9. Charles Eastman, *Indian Heroes and Great Chieftains* (New York: Little, Brown, and Company, 1918), 11–12.

10. Juanita Brooks, *The Mountain Meadows Massacre* (Norman: University of Oklahoma Press, 1950).

11. Ronald R. Walker, Richard E. Turley Jr., and Glen M. Leonard, *Massacre at Mountain Meadows* (New York: Oxford University Press, 2008), 265–70.

12. See https://www.lds.org/topics/mountain-meadows-massacre.

13. Logan Hebner, *Southern Paiute: A Portrait*. Photographs by Michael L. Plyler. (Logan: Utah State University Press, 2010).

14. See Benjamin Wood, "'Forgotten' massacre of Utah Paiute group recalled with new monument," *The Salt Lake Tribune*, April 22, 2016, http://archive.sltrib .com/article.php?id=3808340&itype=CMSID; and Utah Division of State History "Circleville Massacre Memorial Dedication," https://heritage.utah.gov /history/circlevillemassacre.

15. Gordon B. Hinckley, "The Need for Greater Kindness," *LDS Church General Conference*, April 2006, https://www.lds.org/general-conference/2006/04 /the-need-for-greater-kindness. The Church reaffirmed this more recently in

August 2017. See "Church Issues Statements on Situation in Charlottesville, Virginia," https://www.mormonnewsroom.org/article/church-statement-charlottesville-virginia

16. One scholar writes, "More than 100 years ago, American sociologist W.E.B. Du Bois was concerned that race was being used as a biological explanation for what he understood to be social and cultural differences between different populations of people. He spoke out against the idea of "white" and "black" as discrete groups, claiming that these distinctions ignored the scope of human diversity. Science would favor Du Bois. Today, the mainstream belief among scientists is that race is a social construct without biological meaning." Megan Gannon, "Race is a Social Construct, Scientists Argue," *Scientific American*, February 5, 2017, https://www.scientificamerican.com/article/race-is-a-social-construct-scientists-argue.

17. For recent LDS Church essay on race, see https://www.lds.org/topics/race-and-the-priesthood.

18. Paula Gunn Allen, *The Sacred Hoop: Recovering the Feminine in American Indian Traditions*, (Boston: Beacon Press, 1992).

19. The term "Two Spirit" is also problematic and evolved to contrast misunderstandings of application of some terms of colonization, such as *berdache*. See Sue-Ellen Jacobs, Wesley Thomas, and Sabine Lang, eds. *Two-Spirit People: Native American Gender Identity, Sexuality and Spirituality*, (Urbana: University of Illinois Press, 1997).

20. Tacey M. Atsitty, *Rain Scald: Poems* (Albuquerque: University of New Mexico Press, 2018).

Chapter 1

1. Albert R. Lyman, *A Voice Calling: From the Hills of America to the Children of its Ancient People*, (Salt Lake City: The Church of Jesus Christ of Latter-day Saints, 1947), 2.

2. P. Jane Hafen, "Afterword," in *Decolonizing Mormonism: Approaching a Postcolonial Zion*, eds. Gina Colvin and Joanna Brooks, (Salt Lake City: University of Utah Press, 2018), 266.

3. Ibid.

4. James Riding In and Susan A. Miller, *Native Historians Write Back: Decolonizing American Indian History* (Lubbock: Texas Tech University Press, 2011), 2.

5. Waziyatawin Angela Wilson and Michael Yellowbird, eds., *For Indigenous Eyes Only: A Decolonization Handbook*, (Santa Fe, NM: School of American Research, 2005), 2.

6. Ibid.

7. Patrick Wolfe, "Settler Colonialism and the Elimination of the Native," *Journal of Genocide Research* 8, no. 4 (2006): 387.

8. Ibid., 388.

9. Ibid.
10. Ibid.
11. Adria Imada, "Aloha 'Oe:" Settler-Colonial Nostalgia and the Genealogy of a love song," *American Indian Culture and Research Journal* 37, no. 2 (2014): 35.
12. Michael Omi and Howard Winant, *Racial Formations in the United States: From the 1960s to the 1980s* (New York: Routledge & Kegan Paul, 1986), 61.
13. Ibid., 64.
14. Introduction to the Book of Mormon.
15. Ibid.
16. Ibid.
17. Carrie A. Moore, "Debate renewed with change in Book of Mormon introduction," *Deseret News*, November 8, 2007.
18. Hafen, 264.
19. Gwen Westerman and Bruce White, *Mni Sota Makoce: The Land of the Dakota.* (Minneapolis: Minnesota State Historical Society Press, 2012), 3.
20. Barbara Deloria, Kristen Foehner, and Sam Scinta eds., *Spirit & Reason: The Vine Deloria Jr., Reader,* (Golden, CO: Fulcrum Publishing, 1999), 80.
21. Ibid.
22. Ibid, 6.
23. Ibid.
24. Ibid., 13.
25. Ibid., 15.
26. Ibid.
27. Ibid.
28. Ibid., 19.
29. Ibid.
30. The Neal A. Maxwell Institute for Religious Scholarship provides a comprehensive discussion regarding the geographic location of the Book of Mormon. Recent scholarship by LDS scholars and scholars of the Book of Mormon favor a "limited geography theory" that the Book of Mormon homeland extends from southern Mexico to Guatemala. The Neal A. Maxwell Institute provides an extensive reading list on four major topics: archaeology, civilization, geography, and geology concerning this topic available on their website: http://farms.byu .edu/display/topical.php?cat_id=62.
31. 2 Nephi 5:6 (Book of Mormon).
32. 2 Nephi 5:20–23 (Book of Mormon).
33. Mormon scholars defend racialized language in the Book of Mormon, arguing that it has been misinterpreted. John A. Tvedtnes turns to the Book of Mormon for clarification by stating the Lord made clear distinctions between "curse" and "mark" using the Book of Mormon as a point of reference; "Behold, the Lamanites have I cursed, and I will set a mark on them that they and their seed maybe separated from thee and they seed," the curse sets "Lamanites" apart as the "Other." This curse was designed to prevent "Lamanites" from intermarriage with "Nephites" and their incorrect traditions. Tvedtnes further proclaims that

pejorative terms assigned to "Lamanites" does not reference "one's skin color but are cultural traits." This division "wicked" versus "righteous" became an important demarcation between Lamanite/Indigenous and Nephite/Mormon whiteness. See John A. Tvedtnes, "The Charge of 'Racism' in the Book of Mormon," *FARMS Review* 15/2 (2003): 186.

34. 4 Nephi 1:17 (Book of Mormon).
35. Matthew J. Grow, Ronald K. Esplin, Mark Ashurst-McGee, Gerrit J. Dirkmaat, et al., eds., *The Joseph Smith Papers: Administrative Records, Council of Fifty, Minutes, March 1844–January 1846* (Salt Lake City: The Church Historian's Press, 2016), xxvi.
36. Joseph Smith, *American Revivalist and Rochester Observer* 7/6, February 2, 1833.
37. Matthew J. Grow, et al., eds., xxvi.
38. Matthew C. Godfrey, et al., *The Joseph Smith Papers: Documents: Volume 4: April 1834-September 1835* (Salt Lake City: The Church Historian's Press, 2016), 288.
39. Ibid., 289.
40. Ibid., 288.
41. John-Charles Duffy, "The Use of 'Lamanite' in Official LDS Discourse," *Journal of Mormon History* 34, no. 1 (Winter 2008): 118–67. Duffy carefully explores the use of "hemispheric Lamanite identification" meaning that Indigenous People in North and South America, including Pacific Island Peoples were taught they were direct blood descendants of Book of Mormon peoples and "limited Lamanite identification" to specifically reference a new trend that the Book of Mormon peoples lived as a small colony in Mesoamerica and due to intermarriage with other peoples, no longer survive as a distinct people.
42. Matthew J. Grow, et al., eds. xxvii.
43. Smith, Joseph Jr., *Doctrine and Covenants of the Church of Jesus Christ of Latter-day Saints* (Salt Lake City: The Church of Jesus Christ of Latter-day Saints, 1957).
44. Ibid., 49:24.
45. Please see Armand L. Mauss, *All Abraham's Children: Changing Mormon Conceptions of Race and Lineage* (Urbana: University of Illinois, 2003) for information regarding the connections between US federal policies and shifting Mormon ideas about race and American Indians.
46. Paul E. Felt, "Remnants of Israel: Who? When Gathered?" in *Sidney B. Sperry Symposium on The Book of Mormon*, January 24, 1981 (Provo, UT: Brigham Young University, 1981), 86.
47. James R. Clark, ed., *Messages of the First Presidency of the Church of Jesus Christ of Latter-day Saints*, 6 vols. (Salt Lake City: Bookcraft, 1965–75), 1:252–66.
48. Wolfe, 388.
49. Lane Johnson, "Who and Where are the Lamanites?" *Ensign*, December 1975, 15.
50. Johnson, "Who and Where are the Lamanites?" Both the Lane and Mormon historian Gordon C. Thomasson articles highlight that confusion regarding the term "Lamanite" by LDS Church membership was evident. There was a series

of articles published to help clarify "Lamanite." Thomasson highlights this flu-idity concerning "Lamanite" identity. His answer to a general query submitted to the LDS Church magazine, *Ensign*, "What exactly does the word Lamanite mean?" depends on the "place and the individuals involved. At different times in history the word has had distinctly different meanings, and like all labels, the word *Lamanite* should be used with extreme care, even when discussing Book of Mormon history." Thomasson's answer highlights the fluidity of "Lamanite" identity. To be "Lamanite" means to be a person "who rejects the gospel" or later in the nineteenth century, Indigenous People who reject Mormonism. Thomas-son explores how diverse the term "Lamanite" might also include what is com-monly called, "nationality, on other occasions to ancestry, and at still other times to pattern to believe, life-styles, or conduct." Thomasson asserts that the term *Lamanite* must be used with "extreme care" because of the various meanings and uses ascribed to "being Lamanite." The very nature of its fluidity makes it diffi-cult to define clearly "Lamanite" unless looking at a specific historical moment in the Book of Mormon.

51. C. Thomasson, "What exactly does the word Lamanite mean?" *Ensign*, Septem-ber 1977, 39.
52. 2 Nephi 30:6 (Book of Mormon).
53. Ibid.
54. Spencer W. Kimball, "The Day of the Lamanites," *Improvement Era*, December 1960, 922–23, 925.
55. Spencer W. Kimball, "Of Royal Blood," *Ensign*, July 1971, 7.
56. Elise Boxer, "'Lamanites Shall Blossom as the Rose': Indian Student Placement Program, Mormon Whiteness, and Indigenous Identity," *The Journal of Mor-mon History* 41, no. 4 (October 2015): 132–76.
57. Spencer W. Kimball, "Our Paths Have Met Again, *Ensign*, December 1975, 2.

Chapter 2

1. 3 Nephi 23:6 (Book of Mormon).
2. Helaman 14:1; and 3 Nephi 26:6 (Book of Mormon).
3. Joseph Smith Jr., *Book of Mormon* (Palmyra: E. B. Grandin, 1830). See also, Thomas W. Murphy, "Sin, Skin, and Seed: Mistakes of Men in the Book of Mormon," *Journal of the John Whitmer Historical Association* 25 (2004): 36–51.
4. 2 Nephi 31:3 (Book of Mormon).
5. Some of the earliest Latter-day Saint missions targeted the Seneca at Cat-taraugus near Buffalo, New York and minutes from a meeting of the Twelve Apostles in 1835 suggest that early Church leaders made distinctions between eastern Indians who live "among the gentiles" and those farther west. Orson Hyde, "Minutes, 12 March 1835," in *Documents, Vol. 4, The Joseph Smith Papers*, ed. Mathew C. Godfrey, Brenden W. Rensink, et al. (Salt Lake City: The Church Historian's Press, 2016), 287.

6. C. Stanley Banks, "The Mormon Migration into Texas," *The Southwestern Historical Quarterly* 49, no. 2 (1945): 238. See also, John A. Price, "The Book of Mormon vs. Anthropological Prehistory," *Indian Historian* 7, no. 3 (Summer 1974): 35–40.

7. Edmund Wilson, *Apologies to the Iroquois* (Syracuse, NY: Syracuse University Press, 1992[1959]), 123.

8. Bruce E. Johansen, *Forgotten Founders: Benjamin Franklin, the Iroqouis and the Rationale for the American Revolution* (Ipswich, MA: Gambit Publishers, 1982), 121.

9. Lori Elaine Taylor, "Telling Stories About Mormons and Indians," PhD diss. (State University of New York at Buffalo, 2000), 321–22.

10. Phil Deloria, *Playing Indian* (New Haven: Yale University Press, 1998), 219; and Clyde R. Forsberg Jr., *Equal Rites: The Book of Mormon, Masonry, Gender, and American Culture* (New York, NY: Columbia University Press, 2004), 55.

11. Rick Grunder, *Mormon Parallels: A Bibliographic Source*, (Lafayatte, NY: Rick Grunder Books, 2014). 361–64, 1120–29, 33–37, 492–517, 892–94; John Larsen and Christopher Smith, *The Iroquois as the Lamanite: An Argument for a Contemporary Reading of the Book of Mormon*, podcast audio, 2012, https://www.sunstonemagazine.com/the-iroquois-as-the-lamanite-an-argument-for-a-contemporary-reading-of-the-book-of-mormon/; and Lindsay Hansen Park, Gina Colvin, and Thomas W. Murphy, *Lamanite DNA with Thomas Murphy*, Color of Heaven, podcast audio, 2016.

12. Peter Manseau, *One Nation under Gods: A New American History* (New York: Little, Brown, and Company, 2015), 299–300.

13. Linda Tuihiwai Smith, *Decolonizing Methodologies: Research and Indigenous Peoples*, 2nd ed. (New York: Zed Books, 2012); Susan A. Miller and James Riding In, *Native Historians Write Back: Decolonizing American Indian History* (Lubbock, TX: Texas Tech University Press, 2011); Joanna Brooks and Gina Colvin, *Decolonizing Mormonism: Towards a Postcolonial Mormonism* (Salt Lake City: University of Utah Press, 2018); Gina Colvin, "Theorizing Mormon Race Scholarship," *Journal of Mormon History* 41, no. 3 (2015); Michael Yellow Bird and Angela Waziyatawin Wilson, *For Indigenous Minds Only: A Decolonization Handbook* (School of American Research Press, 2012); and Angela Waziyatawin Wilson and Michael Yellow Bird, *For Indigenous Eyes Only: A Decolonization Handbook* (School of American Research, 2005).

14. Margaret E. Kovach, *Indigenous Methodologies: Characteristics, Conversations, and Contexts* (Toronto: University of Toronto Press, 2010); and Shawn Wilson, *Research Is Ceremony: Indigenous Research Methods* (Winnipeg, Manitoba: Fernwood Publishing, 2008).

15. Thomas W. Murphy, "Decolonization on the Salish Sea: A Tribal Journey Back to Mormon Studies," in *Decolonizing Mormonism: Towards a Post-Colonial Mormonism*, ed. Joanna Brooks and Gina Colvin (Salt Lake City: University of Utah Press, In Press), 47–66; Thomas W. Murphy, Jessyca B. Murphy, and Kerrie S. Murphy, "An Indian Princess and a Mormon Sacagawea:

Decolonizing Memories of Our Grandmothers," in *Race, Gender, and Power on the Mormon Borderlands*, ed. Andrea Radke-Moss Dee Garceau, and Sujey Vega (Forthcoming).

16. Tom Porter, *And Grandma Said ... Iroquois Teachings as Passed Down through the Oral Tradition* (Bloomington, IN: Xlibris Corporation, 2008). I came across and was deeply impressed by the work of Sakokweniónkwas, who had led a group of Kanienkehaka (Mohawk) back to neighboring site of Kanatsiohareke, as I had prepared for a recent visit to Tiononderoge (now called Fort Hunter) in the Mohawk Valley in search of more information about my ancestors.; *Kanatsiohareke: Traditional Mohawk Indians Return to Their Ancestral Home-land* (Greenfield Center, New York: Bowman Books, 2006).

17. Barbara Alice Mann, *Native Americans, Archaeologists, & the Mounds* (New York, NY: Peter Lang, 2003); *Iroquoian Women: The Gantowisas* (New York: Peter Lang, 2011). Her work is valuable for its emphasis on women's voices and for balancing Mohawk narratives with those from Seneca.

18. Murphy, "Decolonization on the Salish Sea: A Tribal Journey Back to Mormon Studies"; John G. Neihardt, *Black Elk Speaks: Being the Life Story of a Holy Man of the Oglala Sioux* (Lincoln, NE: Bison Books, 1988 [1932]); Dennis Tedlock, *Popol Vuh: The Definitive Edition of the Mayan Book of the Dawn of Life and the Glories of Gods and Kings*, trans. Dennis Tedlock, revised and expanded ed. (New York: Touchstone, 1996); Taylor; Jerry Johnston, "LDS Shoshone is a Visionary of 2 Cultures," *Deseret News*, 24 July 1999; Lori Taylor, "Joseph Smith in Iroquois Country: The Handsome Lake Story," *The Juvenile Instructor* (2010), http://juvenileinstructor.org/joseph-smith-in-iroquois-country-the-handsome-lake-story/; Thomas W. Murphy, "Reinventing Mormonism: Guatemala as a Har-binger of the Future?" *Dialogue: A Journal of Mormon Thought* 29, no. 1 (1996): 177–92; Raymond J. DeMallie, *The Sixth Grandfather: Black Elk's Teachings Given to John G. Neihardt* (Lincoln, NE: University of Nebraska Press, 1984); William Powers, "When Black Elk Speaks, Everybody Listens," *Social Text* 24 (1990): 43–56; Clyde Holler, *Black Elk's Religion: The Sun Dance and Lakota Cathol-icism* (Syracuse, New York: Syracuse University Press, 1995); and Arthur C. Parker, "Code of Handsome Lake, the Seneca Prophet," in *Parker on the Iroquois*, ed. William N. Fenton (Syracuse, NY: Syracuse University Press, 1968).

19. Nosmelone, "Black Elk's Vision and Lehi's Dream," http://inthecavityofarock.blogspot.com/2015/05/black-elks-vision-and-lehis-dream.html; Gary P. Gil-lum, "Written to the Lamanites: Understanding the Book of Mormon through Native Culture and Religion," *Interpreter: A Journal of Mormon Scripture* 6 (2013): 31–48; B. H. Roberts, *New Witnesses for God*, Vol. II (Salt Lake City: Deseret News, 1909), 420–27; Louis E. Hills, *A Short Work on the Geography of Mexico and Central America from 2234 B.C. To 421 A.D.* (Independence: Louis E. Hills, 1917); *Historical Data from Ancient Records and Ruins of Mexico and Central America* (Independence: Louis E. Hills, 1919); and Allen J. Chris-tenson, ed. *Popol Vuh: The Mythic Sections-Tales of First Beginnings from the Ancient K'iche'-Maya* (Provo, UT: Foundation for Ancient Research and Mor-mon Studies, 2000), 24–34.

20. Jared Hickman, "The Book of Mormon as Amerindian Apocalypse," *American Literature* 80, no. 3 (2014): 429–61.

21. Richard Twiss, *Rescuing the Gospel from the Cowboys: A Native American Expression of the Jesus Way* (Downers Grove, IL: IVP Books, 2015), 60.

22. Murphy, "Reinventing Mormonism: Guatemala as a Harbinger of the Future?"; and Murphy, "Decolonization on the Salish Sea: A Tribal Journey Back to Mormon Studies."

23. C. Jess Groesbeck, "The Book of Mormon as a Symbolic History: A New Perspective on Its Place in History and Religion," *Sunstone* 131 (March 2004): 35–45; Thomas W. Murphy, "Imagining Lamanites: Native Americans and the Book of Mormon," PhD diss. (University of Washington, 2003). For a thoughtful but broader reflection on the topic of self-determination through "Indigenous ontological logics and religious lifeways" see Natalie Avalos Cisneros, "Indigenous Visions of Self-Determination: Healing and Historical Trauma in Native America," *Global Societies Journal* (2014): 1–14.

24. Porter, *And Grandma Said*, 1–4.

25. Barbara Alice Mann, "Epilogue: Euro-Forming the Data," in *Debating Democracy: Native American Legacy of Freedom*, ed. Bruce E. Johansen (Santa Fe, NM: Clear Light Publishers, 1998), 171.

26. 1 Nephi 8:2 (Book of Mormon); Porter, *And Grandma Said*, 56.

27. 1 Nephi 5:15 (Book of Mormon); Susan Easton Black, "Behold, I Have Dreamed a Dream," in *First Nephi, the Doctrinal Foundations*, ed. Monte S. Nyman and Charles D. Tate Jr. (Provo, UT: Religious Studies Center, Brigham Young University, 1988), 113–24. While here I am emphasizing the different social approaches to dreams and vision Lori Taylor finds "many common elements" between content of Lehi's vision, that of Joseph Smith Sr., and of Handsome Lake. See Taylor, 378–83.

28. Porter, *And Grandma Said*, 89.

29. Ibid., 182.

30. In Alma 19:16 we encounter an alternative story of a "Lamanitish woman," named Abish, who believes her father's vision and becomes an instrument in rallying Lamanites to come see the Nephite missionary Ammon. In her belief and support Abish, too, validates a patriarchal culture and plays no apparent leadership role after this incident.

31. Porter, *And Grandma Said*, 116.

32. Ibid., 41, 116–17.

33. Ibid., 43.

34. "History, Circa Summer 1832," in *Joseph Smith Papers: Histories, Vol. 1, 1832–1844*, Karen Lynn Davidson, David J. Whittaker, Mark R. Ashurst-McGee, and, Richard L. Jensen, eds. (Salt Lake City: The Church Historian's Press, 2012), 14.

35. Daniel K. Richter, *The Ordeal of the Longhouse: The Peoples of the Iroquois League in the Era of European Colonization* (Chapel Hill, NC: University of North Carolina Press, 1992), 28.

36. Thomas W. Murphy and Angelo Baca, "Rejecting Racism in Any Form: Latter-Day Saint Rhetoric, Religion, and Repatriation," *Open Theology* 2, no. 1 (August

2016): 707; Mann, *Native Americans, Archaeologists, & the Mounds*, 233–38; and Henry Timberlake, *Memoirs of Lieut. Henry Timberlake* (London: J Ridley and C. Henderson, 1765), 48.

37. Mark Ashurst-McGee, "A Pathway to Prophethood: Joseph Smith Junior as Rodsman, Village Seer, and Judeo-Christian Prophet," MA thesis (Utah State University, 2000), 163–69; Murphy and Baca; D. Michael Quinn, *Early Mormonism and the Magic World View, Revised and Enlarged* (Salt Lake City: Signature Books, 1998), 242–55; and Warren K. Moorehead, *Stone Ornaments Used by Indians in the United States and Canada* (Andover, MA: The Andover Press, 1917), 52–55, 201–12, 364.

38. Susan Alt, "Spindle Whorls and Fiber Production at Early Cahokian Settlements," *Southeastern Archaeology* 18 (Winter 1999): 124–34; Quinn, 242–55; and Murphy and Baca.

39. 2 Nephi 27:9 (Book of Mormon).

40. Mann, *Native Americans, Archaeologists, & the Mounds*; Devon Mihesuah, ed. *Repatriation Reader Who Owns American Indian Remains?* (Lincoln: University of Nebraska Press, 2000); and Murphy and Baca.

41. Taylor; Manseau.

42. Taylor, 311.

43. Parker, 13.

44. Mann, *Iroquoian Women: The Gantowisas*, 49.

45. Ibid., 49–50; Anthony F.C. Wallace, *The Death and Rebirth of the Seneca* (New York: Vintage Books, 1972); and David Swatzler, *A Friend among the Seneca: The Quaker Mission to Cornplanter's People* (Mechanicsburg, PA: Stackpole Books, 2000).

46. Mann, *Iroquoian Women: The Gantowisas*, 50.

47. In the Book of Mormon see 1 Nephi 13:30–31, 15:14; 2 Nephi 4:37; Ether 13:5–8; and Mormon 7:1–5 (Book of Mormon). See also Parker, 45.

48. Porter, *And Grandma Said*, 54–77. For a version of this story recorded prior to the publication of the Book of Mormon see John Norton, "The Creation of the World," in *Early American Writings*, ed. Carla Mulford (New York: Oxford University Press, 2002[1816]).

49. See entries for Nephi and Laman in: "The Guide to the Scriptures," The Church of Jesus Christ of Latter-day Saints, https://www.lds.org /scriptures/gs/laman.p2.

50. 2 Nephi 2:11 (Book of Mormon).

51. Mann, *Iroquoian Women: The Gantowisas*, 71–74, 138.

52. Ibid., 72.

53. *Native Americans, Archaeologists, & the Mounds*, 172. For Book of Mormon references see Alma 18–22.

54. *Iroquoian Women: The Gantowisas*, 72.

55. Swatzler, 27–29.

56. 2 Nephi 5:11–24 (Book of Mormon).

57. Mann, *Native Americans, Archaeologists, & the Mounds*, 53.

58. Alan Taylor, *William Cooper's Town: Power and Persuasion on the Frontier of the Early American Republic* (New York: Vintage Books, 1995), 39.

59. Robert Wauchope, *Lost Tribes and Sunken Continents: Myth and Method in the Study of American Indians* (Chicago: University of Chicago Press, 1962); Robert Silverberg, *Mound Builders of Ancient America: The Archaeology of a Myth* (Greenwich: New York Graphic Society, 1968); Murphy, "Imagining Lamanites: Native Americans and the Book of Mormon"; Thomas W. Murphy and Angelo Baca, "Science, Settlers, and Scripture: Native Perspectives on DNA and the Book of Mormon," in *The Mormon Church and Its Gospel Topics Essays: The Scholarly Community Responds*, ed. Matthew L. Harris and Newell G. Bringhurst (Salt Lake City, UT: University of Utah Press, forthcoming); and Cyrus Thomas, "Report on the Mound Explorations of the Bureau of Ethnology" (Washington, D. C.1985 [1894]).

60. Mann, *Native Americans, Archaeologists, & the Mounds*, 117, 36–37. Mann does suggest that Iroquois may have been lighter skinned than other Natives but discourages the racialization of such observations from early accounts. See: *Iroquoian Women: The Gantowisas*, 256–58.

61. Ethan Smith, *View of the Hebrews: Or the Tribes of Israel in America*, 2nd ed. (Poultney: Smith and Smith, 1825). Religious scholar Jace Weaver (Cherokee) has objected to the Book of Mormon for its embrace "of the old slur that Native Americans were descendants of the Ten Lost Tribes of Israel, a belief perpetuated by those who could not accept that indigenous peoples could develop any degree of civilization without fertilization from the Old World." See Jace Weaver, "Missions and Missionaries," in *Native America in the Twentieth Century: An Encyclopedia* (New York: Garland Publishing, 1994), 348.

62. Thomas W. Murphy, "Lamanite Genesis, Genealogy, and Genetics," in *American Apocrypha: Essays on the Book of Mormon*, ed. Dan Vogel and Brent Lee Metcalfe (Salt Lake City: Signature Books, 2002), 47–77; Simon G. Southerton, *Losing a Lost Tribe: Native Americans, DNA, and the Mormon Church* (Salt Lake City: Signature, 2004); D. Jeffrey Meldrum and Trent D. Stephens, *Who Are the Children of Lehi? DNA and the Book of Mormon* (Salt Lake City, UT: Greg Kofford Books, 2007); Ugo A. Perego, "The Book of Mormon and the Origin of Native Americans from a Maternally Inherited DNA Standpoint," *The FARMS Review* 22, no 11 (2010): 171–217; Jennifer A. Raff and Deborah A. Bolnick, "Does Mitochondrial Haplogroup X Indicate Ancient Trans-Atlantic Migration to the Americas? A Critical Re-Evaluation," *PaleoAmerica* 1, no. 4 (November 2015): 297–304; and Thomas W. Murphy, "Simply Implausible: DNA and a Mesoamerican Setting for the Book of Mormon," *Dialogue: A Journal of Mormon Thought* 36: 4 (2003): 109–31.

63. "Book of Mormon and DNA Studies," The Church of Jesus Christ of Latter-day Saints, https://www.lds.org/topics/book-of-mormon-and-dna-studies; Peggy Fletcher Stack, "Single Word Change in Book of Mormon Speaks Volumes," *Salt Lake Tribune*, November 8, 2007; "New Mormon Scriptures Tweak Race, Polygamy References," ibid., March 19, 2013; Murphy and Baca,

"Science, Settlers, and Scripture: Native Perspectives on DNA and the Book of Mormon"; and "Rejecting Racism in Any Form: Latter-Day Saint Rhetoric, Religion, and Repatriation."

64. A de-historicized hermeneutic for the Book of Mormon would be more compatible with prominent Indigenous approaches to sacred narratives. As described by Standing Rock Dakota scholar, Vine Deloria Jr., Native traditions typically do not require that a particular event took place in the past. "The western preoccupation with history and a chronological description of reality was not a dominant factor in any tribal conception of either time or history." Most oral traditions are prefaced by "the way I heard it" or "it was a long time ago," indicating that "the story itself is important, not its precise chronological location." According to Deloria, tribes do not present their "history as having primacy over the accounts of any other tribe." Sharing stories is a "social event embodying civility" and differing accounts receive credence because it is "not a matter of trying to establish power over others to claim absolute truth." Vine Deloria Jr., *God Is Red: A Native View of Religion, the Classic Work Updated* (Golden: Fulcrum Publishing, 1994), 98–100.

65. Mann, *Iroquoian Women: The Gantowisas*, 89.

66. Ibid.

67. Ibid., 90.

68. 2 Nephi 26:33 (Book of Mormon).

69. This statement marks a change from my previous position that no people, places, or events in the Book of Mormon have been substantiated by reliable external sources. My previous position, which was hardly unique to me and had become pretty standard in Book of Mormon studies, needs to be reconsidered in light of the evidence from Haudenosaunee oral tradition outlined in this article. For examples of my previous perspective and for its prevalence in the field see: Joel Kramer and Jeremy Reyes, "DNA vs. The Book of Mormon," (Brigham City, Utah: Living Hope Ministries, 2003); Scott Johnson and Joel Kramer, "The Bible vs. The Book of Mormon," (Brigham City, Utah: Living Hope Ministries, 2005); Terryl L. Givens, *By the Hand of Mormon: The American Scripture That Launched a New World Religion* (Oxford and New York: Oxford University Press, 2002), 155; and Paul C. Gutjahr, *The Book of Mormon: A Biography* (Princeton: Princeton University Press, 2012), 146.

70. 3 Nephi 23:6 (Book of Mormon).

71. Porter, *And Grandma Said*, 161–90. There are other interesting accounts of the Peacemaker's visit to the Old World. T'hohahoken, "Organizing Indigenous Governance to Invent the Future," in *For Indigenous Eyes Only: A Decolonization Handbook*, ed. Waziyatawin Angela Wilson and Michael Yellow Bird (Santa Fe, NM: School of American Research, 2005); Brian Rice, *The Rotinonshonni: A Traditional Iroquoian History through the Eyes of Teharonhhia:Wako and Sawiskera* (Syracuse, NY: Syracuse University Press, 2013), 183; and Jacob Thomas and Terry Boyle, *Teachings from the Longhouse* (Toronto, Canada: Stoddart, 1994), 29, 117–18.

72. Porter, *And Grandma Said*, 191–92.
73. Ibid., 195–96.
74. Ibid., 164.
75. Parker, 67–68.
76. Mann, *Iroquoian Women: The Gantowisas*, 314–16.
77. Ibid., 126.
78. Ibid. See also: Dean R. Snow, *The Iroquois* (Cambridge, MA: Blackwell, 1996).
79. Barbara Alice Mann and Jerry L. Fields, "A Sign in the Sky: Dating the League of the Haudenosaunee," *American Indian Culture and Research Journal* 21, no. 2 (1997): 114.
80. Ibid., 146. The Book of Mormon also appears to exaggerate the length of the darkening of the sun. The actual eclipse from 1142 was a remarkable three and a half minutes long, but not three days.
81. Ibid.
82. Porter, *And Grandma Said*, 274. Intriguingly, the Book of Mormon (Moroni 9:8–10) also discusses cannibalism but places it at the end of the narrative rather than just before the Great Peace.
83. Ibid., 275–90.
84. Mann, *Iroquoian Women: The Gantowisas*, 127; and Pete Jemison, "Mother of Nations—the Peace Queen, a Neglected Tradition," *Northeast Indian Quarterly* (*Akwe:kon*) 5 (1988): 68–70.
85. Mann, *Iroquoian Women: The Gantowisas*, 130, 61.
86. Ibid., 161.
87. Ibid., 163. Iroquois oral tradition is pretty clear about the connections between the United States, the United Nations, and the League of the Haudenosaunee but the extent of "Iroquois influence" is hotly debated by scholars. Donald A. Grinde Jr. and Bruce E. Johansen, *Exemplar of Liberty: Native America and the Evolution of Democracy* (Los Angeles, CA: American Indian Studies Center Unviersity of California, Los Angeles, 2008); Akwesasne Notes, ed. *Basic Call to Consciousness* (Summertown, TN: Native Voices, 2005); Bruce E. Johansen, ed. *Debating Democracy: Native American Legacy of Freedom* (Santa Fe, NM: Clear Light Publishers, 1998); and Eric Hinderaker, *The Two Hendricks: Unraveling a Mohawk Mystery* (Cambridge, MA: Harvard University Press, 2010).
88. Mann and Fields, 107, 28.
89. Mann, *Iroquoian Women: The Gantowisas*, 185–237; and Murphy, Murphy, and Murphy; *Journals of the Military Expedition of Major General John Sullivan against the Six Nations of Indians in 1779* (Glendale, NY: Benchmark Publishing Company, 1970 [1887]).
90. Arthur C. Parker, *An Analytical History of the Seneca Indians*, Researches and Transactions of the New York State Archaeological Association (Rochester, NY: Lewis H. Morgan Chapter, 1926), 126.
91. Mann, *Iroquoian Women: The Gantowisas*; Audra Simpson, *Mohawk Interruptus: Political Life across the Borders of Settler States* (Durham, North Carolina: Duke University Press, 2014).

92. 2 Nephi 31:3 (Book of Mormon).
93. For more background on this struggle see the following. Wallace; and Swatzler; Mann, *Iroquoian Women: The Gantowisas*.
94. Christopher Densmore, *Red Jacket: Iroquois Diplomat and Orator* (Syracuse, NY: Syracuse University Press, 1999), xiii; and Arthur C. Parker, *Red Jacket: Seneca Chief* (Lincoln, NE: University of Nebraska Press, 1998 [1952]).
95. Red Jacket, "Reply to Rev. Jacob Cram, November 1805," in *The Collected Speeches of Sagoyewatha, or Red Jacket*, ed. Granville Ganter (Syracuse, NY: Syracuse University Press, 2006 [1809]), 138–43.
96. Parker, *Red Jacket: Seneca Chief*, 110; Mathew Dennis, *Seneca Possessed: Indians, Witchcraft, and Power in the Early American Republic* (Philadelphia: University of Pennsylvania Press, 2012), 105; and Mann, *Iroquoian Women: The Gantowisas*, 167–68.
97. "Seneca Indians," *Palmyra Herald*, July 31, 1822; Taylor, 343; Taylor; Manseau, 297–98; and Jana Riess, "New Theory Connects a Native American Prophet with Joseph Smith and the Book of Mormon," *Flunking Sainthood, Religion News Service*, February 5, 2015, http://religionnews.com/2015/02/05/new -theory-connects-native-american-prophet-joseph-smith-book-mormon/.
98. Murphy, "Sin, Skin, and Seed: Mistakes of Men in the Book of Mormon."

Chapter 3

1. This article is based on a chapter from my doctoral dissertation. Lori Elaine Taylor, "Telling Stories about Mormons and Indians," PhD diss. (University at Buffalo, 2000).
2. Nicholas Vrooman is a folklorist, historian, Executive Director of the Northern Plains Folklife Resources and author of *"The Whole Country was . . . 'One Robe'": The Little Shell Tribe's America* (Helena, MT: Drumlummon Institute, 2012).
3. I have heard shorter versions from others, versions falling into two categories: young Joseph comes into contact with Haudenosaunee (Iroquois) farmhands or Joseph spends time in Indian country.
4. Nicholas Vrooman taped this story November 7, 1994 for me but without me present. He titled it "Handsome Lake, Joseph Smith, and the Word," on the cassette cover. Audio tape in my possession. The full version is available in Taylor, "Telling Stories about Mormons and Indians."
5. This is not a creation story in the sense of the origin of the universe as in scientific and religious cosmogonies. For discussion of "Cosmogony and Mormon Creation Narratives" see Erich Robert Paul, *Science, Religion, and Mormon Cosmology* (Urbana: University of Illinois Press, 1992), 103–4, 170–73. This deals not so much with narratives as with quickly acknowledged derivatives.
6. I refer specifically to this story with details of Iroquois influence. I have heard secondhand of Mormon Natives making a connection between Iroquois and

the Book of Mormon, and I refer to published speculation below. It is certainly possible there are more stories and more versions of this story to be heard and a richer fabric of connections to be told.

7. Nicholas Vrooman to Lori Taylor, personal correspondence, October 7, 1999.

8. In 1967, a group of LDS historians determined to find primary materials and promote secondary analysis of the New York period of Mormon history formed "Mormon Origins in New York" with Truman G. Madsen as chair. For more information, see James B. Allen and Leonard J. Arrington, "Mormon Origins in New York: An Introductory Analysis," *BYU Studies* 9, no. 3 (Spring 1969): 241–73. This whole issue, guest edited by Madsen, is devoted to their findings. Other than two brief mentions of the idea of Indians being Israelites, there is no mention that they found (or even looked for) the presence of American Indians among the settlers during the time of Mormon history in New York. Why no search among the Iroquois? How is it that the possibility and all investigation of early Mormons and Indians slipped through extensive, even seemingly exhaustive, research on Mormons in New York?

9. For the fullest studies of the Handsome Lake religion, see Anthony F.C. Wallace, *The Death and Rebirth of the Seneca* (New York: Alfred A. Knopf, 1970); and Arthur C. Parker, *The Code of Handsome Lake, the Seneca Prophet*, New York State Museum Bulletin 163 (Albany, New York, 1912): 5–148. Also in *Parker on the Iroquois*. Marilyn L. Haas lists 18 other studies of Handsome Lake or the Handsome Lake religion in *The Seneca and Tuscarora Indians: An Annotated Bibliography*, Native American Bibliography Series, no. 17 (Metuchen, New Jersey: Scarecrow Press, 1994): 76–82. These are in addition to general works on the Seneca or Iroquois which discuss Handsome Lake. Wallace estimated that in 1969, 5,000 of the approximately 20,000 Iroquois were followers of the Longhouse (3), but membership census may not be a fair way of measuring Longhouse affiliation since the vast majority of people's participation is somewhere between always and never.

10. Sources for Handsome Lake's vision are *Parker on the Iroquois*, 62–76; and Anthony F.C. Wallace, *Death and Rebirth*, 242–48. Lehi's vision: 1 Nephi 8: 5–35, 11: 1–36, and 12: 1–18 (Book of Mormon).

11. The buried weapons of the Confederacy are shown in symbols of the Confederacy in many places, including the cover of the Haudenosaunee passport, as a war club under a white pine. The burial of weapons is mentioned in Paul A. W. Wallace, *White Roots of Peace* (Philadelphia: University of Pennsylvania Press, 1946), 8. The Anti-Nephi-Lehies' burial of weapons: Alma 24: 17–19.

12. Some printed reports of Handsome Lake's visions and teachings were available during Joseph Smith's youth, as were a few reports of the origin and structure of the Iroquois Confederacy, so one could try to make a case for Joseph Smith meeting these stories in print and molding them to his purposes in his new religion, but that approach makes assumptions that clash with the sacred nature of the Joseph Smith story among Mormons. Among the early mass-printed reports of Handsome Lake and his teachings are Timothy Alden,

An Account of Sundry Missions Performed Among the Senecas and Munsee; in a series of letters. With an appendix (New York: J. Seymour, 1827); "Prophet of the Alleghany," *Portfolio* 5, no. 1 (1811): 58–64; and Dorothy Ripley, *The Bank of Faith of Works United* (Philadelphia: J.H. Cunningham, 1819). One of the earliest printed reports of the formation of the Confederacy can be found in *David Cusick's Sketches of Ancient History of the Six Nations: comprising first a tale of the foundation of the Great Island (now North America), the two infants born, and the creation of the universe. Second a real account of the early settlers of North America, and their dissentions. Third origin of the kingdom of the Five Nations which was called a long house: the wars, fierce animals, etc.* (Tuscarora Village, Lewiston, New York: 1826 or 1827; reprint, Lockport, New York: Niagara County Historical Society, 1961). If the questions a prophet asks are influenced by what a prophet knows in his life, I do not see that seeking out Joseph Smith's early influences necessarily questions his status as a prophet.

13. Joseph Smith was 10 years old when his family moved to New York, 24 years old when he published the Book of Mormon and organized his new church.

14. Joseph Smith wrote at least four accounts of early Mormonism in 1832, 1835, 1838, and 1842. These were used by the compilers of the "Manuscript History of the Church," which was published 1842–46 in the *Times and Seasons* (Nauvoo, Illinois) and 1851–58 in the *Deseret News* (Salt Lake City, Utah); this was later reedited by B. H. Roberts as *The History of the Church of Jesus Christ of Latter-day Saints: Period I. History of Joseph Smith the Prophet* (Salt Lake City, Utah: Deseret Press, 1902–1912). The original accounts have also been published in *An American Prophet's Record: The Diaries and Journals of Joseph Smith,* ed. Scott H. Faulring (Salt Lake City, Utah: Signature Books in association with Smith Research Associates, 1989); and *The Personal Writings of Joseph Smith,* ed. Dean C. Jessee (Salt Lake City, Utah: Deseret Book, 1984). For 1832, see Faulring, 3–8; 1835, Faulring, 50–52; and 1838 and 1842, Jessee, 196–220.

15. "During our evening conversations, Joseph would occasionally give us some of the most amusing recitals that could be imagined. He would describe the ancient inhabitants of this continent, their dress, mode of traveling, and the animals upon which they rode; and also their religious worship. This he would do with as much ease, seemingly, as if he had spent his whole life among them." Lucy Mack Smith, *Biographical Sketches of Joseph Smith, the Prophet, and His Progenitors for Many Generations* (Liverpool: S.W. Richards, 1853): 85. If she told her stories in chronological order, then the dates of these recitals would be 1823 or 1824.

16. One of the first scholars to make a case for broadening the scope of Joseph Smith's influences was Fawn M. Brodie in *No Man Knows My History: The Life of Joseph Smith the Mormon Prophet* (New York: Alfred A. Knopf, 1945). Since then, we've seen scholarship on early Mormonism touch on early settlement experiences, transportation, growing manufacture and mercantilism, religious revivals, landscape, interest in popular antiquities. Find the case for folk magic among early Mormons in D. Michael Quinn, *Early Mormonism and the Magic*

World View. Rev. and enlarged (Salt Lake City: Signature Books, 1998); and Seekers in Dan Vogel, *Religious Seekers and the Advent of Mormonism* (Salt Lake City: Signature Books, 1988). Seventeenth-century hermeticism in John L. Brooke, *The Refiner's Fire: The Making of Mormon Cosmology, 1644–1844* (Cambridge: Cambridge University Press, 1994).

17. One feeble attempt to ask questions of American Indian—not specifically Iroquois—influence on Mormons appeared in a Finnish publication in 1969. In order to "draw attention to a whole series of items where earliest Mormonism differs from Christianity but is in accord with Red Indian religion," the author compares Mormon and Delaware ideas and, by misunderstanding aspects of each, finds similarities (128). I have found no response to this article. Åke B. Ström, "Red Indian Elements in Early Mormonism," *Temenos: Studies in Comparative Religion* 5 (1969): 120–68. Fawn Brodie wrote of Joseph Smith as a sort of amateur archaeologist who discovered information to mine for his book, but she stretched circumstantial evidence and literal interpretations into a personal history for Joseph Smith, something that would not hold up today (if, indeed, it did in 1945). Fawn M. Brodie, *No Man Knows My History*, 34–37. Another 1945 publication claimed Iroquois influence specifically without citation. C. Stanley Banks, "The Mormon Migration into Texas," *The Southwestern Historical Quarterly* 49, no. 2 (1945): 238. Banks is maddeningly vague in saying, "Tradition has it that the prophet Joseph Smith, in his authorship of the Book, was greatly influenced by his study of the beliefs of the Iroquois Indians of New York." Thanks to Thomas Murphy for pointing this out.

18. My statement is mild when compared to other scholars pressing for a reevaluation of the roles of American Indians in US history. Consider the words of John Mohawk: "The tendency of the classical historians to overlook or understate the significance of certain groups in history has pervaded practically all historical writing in the West. . . . For example, the history of the origins of American democratic traditions was written during the nineteenth century when the ideology of Aryanism was at its zenith. This is the most significant explanation of why American Indians were not cited as influential in the formation of the ideas of democracy or in inspiring the United States Constitution. To most of these historians, it is unacceptable that Indians might have played a role in the democratic tradition." John C. Mohawk, "Indians and Democracy: No One Ever Told Us," in *Exiled in the Land of the Free: Democracy, Indian Nations, and the U.S. Constitution*, ed., Oren Lyons, et. al. (Santa Fe: Clear Light Press, 1992), 62.

19. For a discussion of breaking down Indian-white relations—as a written form and as vulnerable to challenge, see Taylor, "Telling Stories of Mormons and Indians."

20. There were certainly interesting people during this period with some ability to move between Iroquois and settler groups. Just a few of the people who moved between Iroquois and white cultures during this period are: Horatio Hale, Jasper Parrish, and Joseph Smith ("captives" who later acted as interpreters);

Mary Jemison ("The White Woman," a captive who lived her life as a Seneca, and who late in life provided an articulate report of Seneca life); Henry O'Bail (a literate Seneca who acted as interpreter); Red Jacket (a diplomat, non–English speaking; a celebrity, known for being known); General Israel Chapin (Indian agent); Griffith Cooper (Quaker, along with many other Quakers); and Rev. Samuel Kirkland and Asher Wright (missionaries).

21. Arthur Caswell Parker, "Ancient Land of the Genesee," in *History of the Genesee Country*, ed. Lockwood R. Doty (Chicago: S. J. Clarke Publishing, 1925): 111.

22. Helen Hornbeck Tanner, ed., *Atlas of Great Lakes Indian History* (Norman: University of Oklahoma Press for the Newberry Library, 1987): 71. In the raids of August 1779 under the command of General John Sullivan and General James Clinton, 5,000 men destroyed 40 villages in retaliation for the Iroquois alliance with the British in the Revolutionary War, despite the fact that not all Iroquois allied with the British. There were battles in the Revolutionary War between members of the same nation, fighting a proxy battle for the Americans and British. After the destruction of so many of their villages, Senecas, understandably, had some difficulty adjusting to new lives.

23. Among the ten Seneca Reservations were six on the Genesee River, a large tract at Buffalo Creek, and three more (those that remain today) at Tonawanda, Allegany, and Cattaraugus. Indian Agent Erastus Granger wrote to George Graham, Acting Secretary of War, 20 January 1817: "The situation of the Indians is truly deplorable. They have exerted themselves for the year past in trying to raise crops, but have failed in their expectations. Their prospects have failed. Their hunting ground is gone. They have availed themselves of their money arising from their public funds, but they fall short. They are in fact in a state of starvation." Charles M. Snyder, ed., *Red and White on the New York Frontier: A Struggle for Survival. Insights from the Papers of Erastus Granger, Indian Agent, 1807–1819* (Harrison, New York: Harbor Hill Books, 1978): 85.

24. Red Jacket dictated a letter to Jasper Parrish, the Indian Sub-agent, in 1819 or 1820 complaining about white people near the reservations stealing timber, horses, and game, and of Indians being thrown into jail for "trifling causes." William L. Stone, *The Life and Times of Red Jacket, or Sa-go-ye-wat-ha; being the sequel to the history of the Six Nations* (New York: Wiley and Putnam, 1841): 324–25. Parrish had written in his report to the Secretary of War, December 3, 1818, of "frequent depredations, petty thefts, and trespasses committed on each other by whites and Indians; most frequently commencing on the part of the former." In Jedediah Morse, *A Report to the Secretary of War of the United States, on Indian Affairs* (New Haven, CT: S. Converse, 1822): A78.

25. De Witt Clinton, "Legislature of New-York. Governor's Speech," *Palmyra Register*, February 18, 1818, 2 [speech delivered January 27, 1818]. Reply in "Indian Letter," *Palmyra Register*, March 24, 1818, 2 [letter dated February 14, 1818]. David Ogden, of the Ogden Land Company, asked the Secretary of War to concentrate the Seneca at Allegany; March 27, 1819 the Secretary wrote to a local agent that he was to examine the feasibility of this arrangement. A collection of

several related letters can be found in *Message from the President of the United States Transmitting a Report of the Secretary of War, Containing the Information Required by the Resolution of the House, Respecting the Negotiations with the Six Nations of Indians in the State of New York* (Washington: Gales and Seaton, 1821).

26. Of the six Haudenosaunee or Iroquois nations, five lived in and around western and central New York at this time: Seneca, Tuscarora, Cayuga, Onondaga, and Oneida. Mohawks lived farther east and northeast of the Finger Lakes. Most Tuscaroras moved to the Tuscarora Village in Niagara County by 1788. The Onondagas did not move; they stayed on their own land, on a reservation established in 1788, south of present-day Syracuse. Helen Hornbeck Tanner, ed., *Atlas of Indian History* 165. Until 1807 the Cayugas still held three tracts of land near the head of Cayuga Lake; the last of their homeland, the Fishcarrier grant, was not sold until 1841, but most of the Cayugas left long before. Fishcarrier himself had moved to the Grand River Reserve in Ontario shortly after the other two tracts were sold. Marian E. White, William E. Engelbrecht, and Elisabeth Tooker, "Cayuga," in *Handbook of North American Indians*, vol. 15, *Northeast*, ed. Bruce G. Trigger (Washington, DC: Smithsonian Institution, 1978): 502. In 1824 and 1827 90 Cayugas still lived at Buffalo Creek. During removals, many of this group rejected lands in Kansas and moved to the Grand River in Ontario in 1832. Marian E. White, William E. Engelbrecht, and Elisabeth Tooker, "Cayuga," in *Handbook of North American Indians*, vol. 15, 502. Christian Oneidas began making arrangements to move to Wisconsin in the 1820s; by 1837, 600 Oneidas lived in Wisconsin. Another group of Oneidas moved in 1839 and after to Ontario on the Thames, near the Grand River. Helen Hornbeck Tanner, ed., *Atlas of Indian History*, 129.

27. In 1816 Indian Agent Erastus Granger counted 4,492 Iroquois in New York, which included 1,879 Senecas. Charles M. Snyder, *Papers of Erastus Granger*, 30. New York State officials made several attempts to remove the Senecas, and eventually they were moved from most of their Western New York reservations, including six on the Genesee River. Between 1826 and 1831 all of the reservations on the Genesee River were sold. These were not necessarily voluntary sales. Helen Hornbeck Tanner, ed., *Atlas of Indian History*, 165.

28. According to a Secretary of War report. Thomas Donaldson, *Extra Census Bulletin. Indians. The Six Nations of New York* (Washington, DC: Government Printing Office, 1892): 6.

29. Oliver Phelps opened his land office in Canandaigua in 1789 and began to sell township lots; ten towns in the Phelps and Gorham Purchase were opened for settlement in 1789. Lockwood R. Doty, ed., *Genesee Country*, 552. In the first year after sale of township lots, 1,075 settlers moved to Ontario County. Ontario County then covered the whole of the Genesee country east of Seneca lands.

30. Data for 1800 is estimated. Barbara Shupe, Janet Steins, and Jyoti Pandit, eds., *New York State Population: A Compilation of Federal Census Data* (New York: Neal-Schuman Publishers, 1987).

31. Between June 1812 and July 1815 there were more than 30 battles in the Niagara frontier area; the closest battle to the Finger Lakes had been at Oswego on Lake Ontario, May 6, 1814. Helen Hornbeck Tanner, ed., *Atlas of Indian History*, 107.

32. Barbara Shupe et al., *New York State Population*. The 1830 figure is after the old Ontario County was divided into Ontario, Wayne, and Monroe counties.

33. The author names the Seneca residents: "Hot-bread, a worthy chief, with Tommy-jemmy, Captain Thompson, Blackbird, and some other red men of note, spent part of their time here." Henry O'Reilly, *Settlement in the West. Sketches of Rochester; with incidental notices of western New-York* (Rochester: William Alling, 1838): 249.

34. This Iroquois trail and highway was later paved as Routes 5 and 20, just south of the present New York State Thruway. The Iroquois trails between the main settlements on the Finger Lakes were widened by Oliver Phelps in 1789, but pioneers remarked that a widened trail was not so different from an Indian trail. A four-rod road was built from Syracuse to the Genesee in 1800 and a turnpike from Canandaigua to Bath in 1803. Margaret Schmitt McNab, Katherine W. Thompson, and Shirley Cox Husted, *Northfield on the Genesee* (Rochester, New York: Monroe County Historian's Office, 1981): 23–4. A road was built across the Genesee and to Lake Erie in 1815. Jedediah Morse, *Report to the Secretary of War*, 174–75. The *Palmyra Register* published in 1811 a notice that a petition to build a turnpike road from Canandaigua through Gorham, Farmington, Palmyra, and on to Pultneyville would be presented at the next legislature. See January 8, 1811, 3.

35. Handsome Lake died of a quick illness at 80 years old in 1815. He was at Onondaga, where he stopped on his annual circuit.

36. In September 1826 the women Faithkeepers of Tonawanda called on Handsome Lake's grandson Sosheowa, Jimmy Johnson, to recall the words of the teacher; from these recollections they created the Handsome Lake Code. Tooker, "Iroquois Since 1820," 452. Jimmy Johnson at Tonawanda and another follower at Allegany (Handsome Lake's Nephew Governor Blacksnake, according to Anthony F.C. Wallace, *Death and Rebirth*, 11; Owen Blacksnake, according to A.C. Parker, *Parker on the Iroquois*, 14; and Handsome Lake's son-in-law, identified by Parker as Htgwi'yot [23], according to John Mohawk) each preached versions of what has come to be known as Gaiwiio (the Good Word), which is still the central text of the Longhouse religion recited at certain points in the ceremonial year. At Six Nations meetings in the fall, every year at Tonawanda and every other year at the other longhouses, Handsome Lake preachers recite the Gaiwiio in full over three (or four) days. The circuit remains, but I believe the preachers drive rather than walk.

37. Lewis H. Morgan, *League of the Ho-dé'-no-sau-nee, Iroquois* (Rochester, New York: Sage & Brothers, 1851), 469. Morgan called his book *The League of the Iroquois*, but his primary informants were Tonawanda Seneca. Some of the detail he assigns to the whole Confederacy actually reveals his Tonawanda sources.

38. See report of Dr. Ludlow for a list of "the diseases of the Genesee country." Settlements along creeks "were sickly as late as 1821" with chills and fever. "The attacks of this disorder were incessant and very severe along Mud creek." In Lockwood R. Doty, ed., *Genesee Country*, 31–32.

39. O[rasmus] Turner, *History of the Pioneer Settlement of Phelps and Gorham's Purchase, and Morris' Reserve* (Rochester, New York: William Alling, 1851): 263.

40. Charles B. Herendeen, "Indians," in *Pioneers of Macedon, and other papers of the Macedon Center Historical Society*, comp. Mary Louise Eldredge (Macedon Center, New York: [Macedon Center Historical Society], 1912): 105–6. Article dated April 13, 1896.

41. Horace Eaton, *A Thanksgiving Sermon, delivered at Palmyra, N.Y., Nov. 26, 1857* (Rochester: A. Strong, 1858), 8–9.

42. O[rasmus] Turner, *Phelps and Gorham*, 383. Stephen Durfee was the son of Palmyra pioneer and Quaker Gideon Durfee and brother of Lemuel Durfee, who occasionally helped Joseph Smith Sr., by employing his sons (including Joseph Jr.) and once by attempting to stop a foreclosure on the Smith's farm.

43. Ibid., 209.

44. Ibid., 222. It is possible that memories of close association with this Joseph Smith were transferred to the prophet Joseph Smith and embellished with justifications.

45. Charles F. Milliken, *History of Ontario County, New York, and Its People* (New York: Lewis Historical Publishing, 1911): 27. Jasper Parrish spoke five of the six Haudenosaunee languages.

46. O[rasmus] Turner, *Phelps and Gorham*, 311–14.

47. Ibid., 310–11.

48. W. H. McIntosh, *History of Wayne County, New York* (Philadelphia: Everts, Ensign & Everts, 1877): 19.

49. O[rasmus] Turner, *Phelps and Gorham*, 230.

50. Ibid., 172.

51. Ibid., 392.

52. Ibid., 264–66. All of these are reports of the first generation, probably between 1790 and 1812 (though not all are dated). It is possible that because Orasmus Turner, whose history is the source of most of these reports, focused on second-generation memories of the first-generation settlers (the pioneers), he did not attempt to collect stories and histories of the second generation. Rather than consider this a problem, I have chosen to see how the familiarity with which some of Turner's informants tell of their acquaintance with the Iroquois implies not the fear of hostility or the nostalgia of distance but the casual reporting of ordinary life.

53. W.H. McIntosh, *Wayne County*, 134. This is the earliest version of the story I have found. It also appears in "A. E. Benjamin Tells the Palmyra Story: History of Palmyra," *Palmyra Courier-Journal*, April 23, 1964, 2.

54. Charles B. Herendeen, "Indians," 101–9.

55. Ibid., 107. John Mohawk, a Seneca speaker, confirmed that "scat" is one, "tickine" two, and "was" five, but the rest does not look to him like numbers. The words

"ski" and "sky" between numbers may have meant something like "Boo!" Still, for a witness to remember these words for so long implies either familiarity through repetition or a very good memory.

56. Another John Sky also signed several treaties in the 1830s. Francis Jennings, ed., *Iroquois Indians: A Documentary History of the Diplomacy of the Six Nations and their League. Guide to the Microfilm Collection* (Woodbridge, Connecticut: Research Publications, 1985), 446, 658.

57. Anthony F.C. Wallace, *Death and Rebirth*, 266.

58. "Red Jacket, Cornplanter and Blue Sky demanded satisfaction as a price for their continued support of the war." Charles M. Snyder, *Papers of Erastus Granger*, 16.

59. Timothy Alden, *Account of Sundry Missions*, 58–60.

60. Charles B. Herendeen, "Indians," 108. John Mohawk says "sago" is a greeting but not exactly "good morning," and "de-qua" is something like "how are you."

61. Quaker missionaries set up working farms as examples of skills and ways of life they hoped Senecas would follow. Quakers on a model farm at Allegany recorded the first written witnesses to Handsome Lake's first visionary experiences and the beginning of his ministry.

62. A Quaker pioneer, Charles Williamson, for whom the township was named, chose Sodus Bay as a commercial depot. He cut roads from there to Palmyra and Phelpstown in 1794. O[rasmus] Turner, *Phelps and Gorham*, 249, 263. Sodus Bay had already been a gathering place for Iroquois; and it was the port of the Cayuga. Lockwood R. Doty, ed., *Genesee Country*, 1319; W.H. McIntosh, *Wayne County*, 38.

63. Mary B. Durfee, diary (from typescript), June 15, 1838, Wayne County Historian's Office, Lyons, New York.

64. Mary B. Durfee, diary, April 26, 1840.

65. Mary B. Durfee, diary, June 17, 1840.

66. Orasmus Turner was going to include in his *Phelps and Gorham's Purchase* "something of the history of our immediate predecessors, the Senecas. It was mainly abandoned however, on learning that a local author, quite competent for the task ... was preparing for the press, a work which would embrace much of the interest in their history." Turner, vii. He writes of Lewis H. Morgan's *League of the Iroquois*, which was published the same year as Turner's book. It is a shame that Turner did not write a history of the Seneca; his style of attributed anecdote (he was a journalist) would have been more historically informative than Morgan's unattributed specifics used to construct generalizations.

67. For a thorough biography of Red Jacket, see Christopher Densmore, *Red Jacket: Iroquois Diplomat and Orator*. The Iroquois and their neighbors, series ed. Laurence Hauptman (Syracuse: Syracuse University Press, 1999).

68. Blue Sky was the same man remembered to have teased a child in Macedon. Twenty Canoes had been present at councils as early as 1789. Francis Jennings, *Iroquois Indians*, 453.

69. An early biographer of Red Jacket wrote of the difficulty of translating Red Jacket's speech July 5, 1819 at Buffalo Creek when the Ogden Land Company

negotiated for Seneca land: "The only liberty taken in transcribing [the speeches], has been to omit the repetitions for which both Red-Jacket's and Pollard's speeches were remarkable. The interpreter stated that he could not translate some of Red-Jacket's figurative flights—they were too wild and difficult to appear in English—and he did not attempt it. Should his speech be improved by omitting its tautology, it has no doubt lost much of its most characteristic beauty and interest from the acknowledged omissions of the interpreter." William L. Stone, *Red Jacket*, 308–309n.

70. *Lyons Advertiser*, Friday, August 2, 1822, 2, 4–5. The date of the speech would have been Monday, July 29 or 22, 1822 (depending on what the writer meant by "last week"). Also reference: *Herald* (Palmyra) July 31, 1822 [original—I have not been able to see this]; *Gazette* (Geneva), August 7, 1822: 2; and *Ontario Repository* (Canandaigua), August 20, 1822.

71. A biographer claims that he did understand English very well but did not speak it well. William L. Stone, *Red Jacket*, 359n. An Indian view of contact, from a specific cultural and individual context, is seldom hinted in works on Indian-white relations or on Iroquois-white relations. Even the frequently recorded speeches and letters of Red Jacket were translations, dictations, and approximations by interpreters and editors. I point this out not to lament the fact but merely to make it clear that even the words and ideas of one so familiar were in the nineteenth century and remain now managed wholly within white understandings.

72. O[rasmus] Turner, *Phelps and Gorham's Purchase*, 214.

73. The *Western Farmer* of January 23, 1822 announced a meeting "at the school house near Mr. Billings' on Friday next." John Phillip Walker, ed., *Dale Morgan on Early Mormonism: Correspondence and a New History* (Salt Lake City, Utah: Signature Books, 1986): 224, 365n27.

74. Barbara Shupe et al., *New York State Population*.

75. Stephen S. Harding was governor of Utah Territory June 1862–July 1863. These recollections were originally published in Thomas Gregg, *The Prophet of Palmyra* (New York, 1890). Reprinted as "Governor Harding's Recollection," *Among the Mormons: Historic Accounts by Contemporary Observers*, eds. William Mulder and A. Russell Mortensen (New York: Alfred A. Knopf, 1958), 41–46.

76. Horace Eaton, *A Thanksgiving Sermon*, 8–9.

77. O[rasmus] Turner, *Phelps and Gorham's Purchase*, 383.

78. The fact that he referred to them as "Senecas" and "Cayugas" rather than just "Indians" is remarkable given how seldom Iroquois people of the area were recorded by settlers as individuals with specific biographies. Charles B. Herendeen, "Indians," 107.

79. For Joseph Smith as a field hand, see Richard L. Bushman, *Joseph Smith and the Beginnings of Mormonism* (Urbana: University of Illinois Press, 1984), 59; and Larry Porter, "The Church in New York and Pennsylvania, 1816–1831," *The Restoration Movement: Essays in Mormon History*, eds F. Mark McKiernan,

Alma R. Blair, and Paul M. Edwards. Rev. ed. (Independence, Missouri: Herald Publishing House, 1992), 31.

80. John L. Brooke, *The Refiner's Fire*, 152, 363n12. He cites June S. Parfitt, *A Genealogy of the Walter Family* (Manchester, New Hampshire, 1986), 3–10, 62, 71, 109–10, 128, 246. D. Michael Quinn discusses Luman Walters at length in *Early Mormonism and the Magic World View*.

81. September 19, 1821, *Western Farmer*, ed. Timothy C. Strong. Also quoted in Fawn M. Brodie, *No Man Knows My History*, 35.

82. Perhaps we could make these connections if archaeologists could get past the idea that "proto-Iroquois" meant something other than ancestors of the Iroquois. And if we could, would they fit the descriptions of the plates Joseph Smith translated? Emma Smith, wife of Joseph Smith Jr., described feeling the plates: "They seemed to be pliable like thick paper, and would rustle with a metallic sound when the edges were moved by the thumb." "Last Testimony of Sister Emma," *Saints' Advocate* 2/4 (Plano, Illinois, October 1879), 50–52; and *Saints' Herald* 26/19 (Plano, Illinois, October 1, 1879), 290. Quoted in John W. Welch and Tim Rathbone, "The Translation of the Book of Mormon: Preliminary Report on the Basic Historical Information," 1986. Paper & Reprint WRR-86 (Provo, Utah: F.A.R.M.S., 1986), 14.

83. Philip Cook does not seem to have heard the story of Handsome Lake followers and Joseph Smith, since Wilson does not mention it. The *New Yorker* articles were published as Edmund Wilson, *Apologies to the Iroquois*, intro. William N. Fenton (1959, 1960; Syracuse: Syracuse University Press, 1991), 123.

84. According to Vine Deloria, Mad Bear Anderson's travels as merchant seaman to ports throughout the world allowed him contact with Native Peoples in Mexico and Central America, which laid the foundation for closer ties between Indians of the North and Indians of the South. Vine Deloria Jr., *Behind the Trail of Broken Treaties: An Indian Declaration of Independence* (New York: Delacorte Press, 1974), 233.

85. Leslie A. Fiedler, *The Return of the Vanishing American* (New York: Stein and Day, 1968), 12.

86. Edmund Wilson, *Apologies to the Iroquois*, 163–68.

87. Peter Manseau, *One Nation Under Gods: A New American History* (New York: Little Brown, 2015).

88. Jana Riess, "New theory connects a Native American prophet with Joseph Smith and the Book of Mormon." Interview with Peter Manseau, February 5, 2015, Religion News Service.

89. Thomas W. Murphy, "Other Scriptures: Restoring Voices of Gantowisas to an Open Canon," in this volume. Murphy cites several sources that hint at connection. Even more interesting is one earlier source that doesn't cite a source but specifically claims Iroquois influence on Mormonism: Banks, "The Mormon Migration into Texas." I don't dismiss these, but they offer rumors and hints. I'm assuming the need for more solid research and citation before we can see this as historical scholarship, as more than amplification of other rumors, hints, and scholarship. Show me the sources!

Chapter 4

1. Thomas Kane, *The Mormons* (Philadelphia: King and Baird, 1850), 72. Part of this this essay is drawn from Max Perry Mueller, *Race and the Making of the Mormon People* (The University of North Carolina Press, forthcoming).

2. Jared Farmer, *On Zion's Mount: Mormons, Indians, and the American Landscape* (Cambridge, MA: Harvard University Press 2008), 54–104.

3. Thomas Bullock, Meeting with Utes, May 22, 1850, Box 74, Folder 42, Brigham Young Papers, CR 1234 1, LDS Church History Library (CHL), Salt Lake City, Utah (here after abbreviated as BYP); See also, George W. Bean to Brigham Young, May 1, 1854, Box 23, Folder 10, BYP. After Wakara's death, another Timpanogos leader Highforehead (Ton-om-bu-gah) repeated Wakara's rejection of the Mormons' offer to buy land outright. See Ton-om-bu-gah or Highforehead, the Indian Chief, at the Bowery at Provo, July 15, 1855, CR 100 137, Box 3, Folder 13, CHL. For a precedent of Mormon-Ute reciprocity as a way to "mitigate levels of violence," see a discussion of the Spanish-Ute alliance in Ned Blackhawk, *Violence over the Land: Indians and Empire in the Early American West* (Cambridge, MA: Harvard University Press, 2008), 56–80.

4. Thomas Bullock, "Weight, size, etc. of Indians," August 2, 1852, Box 74, Folder 46, BYP; Paul Dayton Bailey, *Wakara, Hawk of the Mountains* (Los Angeles: Westernlore Press, 1954), 14, 79. On Bullock as a record keeper and historian, see Jerald F. Simon, "Thomas Bullock as an Early Mormon Historian, *BYU Studies* 30 no. 1 (Winter 1990): 71–88.

5. "Walker's writing" could be considered occupying a space between the forms of precontact Native literacies that, as Brigit Brander Rasmusssen has argued, have long been excluded from American literary studies because of the privileging of alphabetized writing, and the Native American alphabetized print culture that emerged in the late eighteenth century as a literary weapon that Native Peoples used, as Philip Round has written, in their own "battles against relocation, allotment, and cultural erasure." Phillip H. Round, *Removable Type: Histories of the Book in Indian Country, 1663–1880* (Chapel Hill: University of North Carolina Press, 2010), 5; Birgit Brander Rasmussen, *Queequeg's Coffin: Indigenous Literacies & Early American Literature* (Durham: Duke University Press, 2012), 3–4.

6. Toni Morrison, *Playing in the Dark* (New York: Random House, 2007) xii.

7. I further theorize about the "paper Indian" and its place within the "Mormon archive" in *Race and the Making of the Mormon People.*

8. Robert Berkhofer, *The White Man's Indian: Images of the American Indian from Columbus to the Present* (New York: Vintage, 1979) 134–36; Roy Harvey Pearce, *Savagism and Civilization: A Study of the Indian and the American Mind* (Berkeley: University of California Press, 1988), 135–68.

9. Revelation to Oliver [Cowdery], September 1830 [*D&C* 28:8], *RT* vol. 1, 53. On this first mission to the Lamanites, see Warren A. Jennings, "The First Mormon Mission to the Indians," *Kansas Historical Quarterly* 37 (Fall 1971): 288–99.

10. Levi Jackman, Journal, July 28, 1847; Farmer, *On Zion's Mount*, 60.

11. D. B. Huntington to Brigham Young, May 18, 1849, Box 21, Folder 16, BYP; D. B. Huntington to BY, April 19, 1849, Box 21, Folder 16, BYP.

12. Special Order No. 2, issued by Daniel H. Wells to G. D. Grant January 31, 1850, Utah Territorial Militia Records, 1849–1877, Utah State Archives and Records, Series 2210, accessed June 23, 2014, https://familysearch.org/pal:/MM9.3.1 /TH-1951-22024-3922-55?cc=1462415&wc=14229733.

13. Special Order No. 2, issued by Daniel H. Wells to G. D. Grant, January 31, 1850.

14. John Williams Gunnison. *The Mormons* (Philadelphia: Lippincott, Grambo & Company, 1852), 146–47; Farmer, *On Zion's Mount*, 74–75.

15. Gunnison, *The Mormons*, 146–47.

16. Farmer, *On Zion's Mount*, 54–140. As Anne Hyde has argued, like other white Americans in the American West during the mid-nineteenth century, the Mormons were not a nation of laws, but instead "a nation of squatters who used violence to establish rights and to dispossess other people." Anne Hyde, *Empires, Nations, Families: A History of the North American West, 1800–1860* (Lincoln: University of Nebraska Press, 2012), 484.

17. Gunnison also took note of the irony "that those whose *mission* [emphasis in original] it is to convert these aborigines by the sword of the spirit, should thus be obliged to destroy them." Gunnison, *The Mormons*, 147.

18. General Church Minutes, February 10, 1850, Box 2, Folder 17, GCM; Farmer, *On Zion's Mount*, 73.

19. General Church Minutes, January 31, 1850, Box 2, Folder 17, GCM.

20. John Gunnison to Martha Gunnison, March 1, 1850, quoted in Farmer, *On Zion's Mount*, 76.

21. Wells, "Daniel H. Wells' Narrative," 126; Farmer, *On Zion's Mount*, 77.

22. As Brigit Rasmussen has argued, alphabetized literacy had long been used in colonial settings as "a marker of racial difference" as well as epistemological infrastructure through which colonialism was imposed on (supposedly) illiterate and thus inferior Indigenous Americans. Rasmussen, *Queequeg's Coffin*, 29, 1.

23. As the cartographer for the Domínguez-Escalante Expedition, Bernardo de Miera described it in a 1777 letter to the Spanish Crown, the "Lake of the Timpanogos" region "is the most pleasant, beautiful and fertile in all of New Spain," capable of supporting "a city with as large a population as that of Mexico City." Farmer, *On Zion's Mount*, 30.

24. Warner, *Domínguez-Escalante Journal*, 33, 38–41, 63–72; Blackhawk, *Violence over the Land*, 94.

25. Bailey, *Wakara*, 13.

26. Daniel Jones, *Forty Years among the Indians* (Salt Lake City: Juvenile Instructor's Office, 1890), 49; Blackhawk, *Violence over the Land*, 70–80.

27. William Clayton, *The Journals of William Clayton*, edited by George D. Smith (Salt Lake City: Signature Books, 1995), 348–53; Juanita Brooks, "Indian Relations on The Mormon Frontier." *Utah Historical Quarterly* 12, no. 1–2 (1944): 3.

28. In fact, even on July 24, 1847—now celebrated annually in Utah as "Pioneer Day," marking the arrival of the first Mormons to their Rocky Mountain Zion—Wakara was probably on Brigham Young's mind. Three days earlier on July 21, Apostles Willard Richards and George A. Smith sent word to the Vanguard Company's advance party to bear north "toward the region of the Salt Lake" on their approach out of the Wasatch Mountain Range. "Young gave us his views concerning a stopping place in the Basin," wrote Richards and Smith. "He felt inclined for the present not to crowd upon the Utes until we have a chance to get acquainted with them." Quoted in Arrington, *Brigham Young: American Moses* (New York: Knopf, 1985) 144.

29. Kane, *The Mormons*, 72.

30. Brigham Young to Chief Walker, November 22, 1849, Box 16, Folder 18, BYP.

31. Big Chief Brigham Young to Pe-tete-net, Walker, Tow-ee-ette, Blackhawk, Tab-bee, and other good Indian chiefs, May 6, 1850, quoted in Coates, "A History of Indian Education by the Mormons," 73–79.

32. Brigham Young to Chief Walker, November 22, 1849, Box 16, Folder 18, BYP.

33. Dimick Huntington, Minutes of Meeting with Indians, Fort Utah, May 14, 1849, Box 16, Folder 17, BYP.

34. Howard A. Christy, "Open Hand and Mailed Fist: Mormon-Indian Relations in Utah, 1847–52." *Utah Historical Quarterly* 46 (Summer 1978): 221–22.

35. Farmer, *On Zion's Mount*, 65–66.

36. Lawrence Coates has described Manti as Brigham Young's "peace corps" for Wakara's Indians. Coates, "Brigham Young and Mormon Indian Policies: The Formative Period, 1836–1851," *BYU Studies* 18, no. 3 (1978): 440. Yet because Young and other Mormon leaders were always prepared to use force to quell Indian resistance to Mormon settlement expansion, the better modern analogy might be that Manti was part of the Mormons' "counterinsurgency" efforts. Sarah Sewell, "A Radical Field Manual," in *The U. S. Army/Marine Corps Counterinsurgency Field Manual* (Chicago: University of Chicago Press, 2006), xxi–xlx.

37. Isaac Morley to Brigham Young, March 15, 1850, BYP. See also Ronald Walker, "Wakara Meets the Mormons, 1848–52: A Case Study in Native American Accommodation," *Utah Historical Quarterly* 70 (Summer 2002): 226.

38. The Presidency to Isaac Morley and the Saints in Sanpete, March 24, 1850, quoted in Ibid.

39. Ibid.

40. Young put a particular Mormon spin on what would become the dictum of the late nineteenth century "friends of the Indian" movement—kill the Indian and save the man. "The Indians would dwindle away, but let a remnant of the seed of Joseph be saved." "History of Brigham Young," *Millennial Star*, May 13, 1851, quoted in Brooks, "Indian Relations," 6. As Andrés Reséndez has recently written, despite cutting off the trade of New Mexican traffickers, "the American occupation of the West," including the Mormons, "did not reduce the enslavement of Indians. In fact, the arrival of American settlers rekindled the traffic in

humans." Reséndez, *The Other Slavery: The Uncovered Story of Indian Enslavement in America* (New York: Houghton Mifflin Harcourt, 2016), 266.

41. Ibid.

42. Brigham Young, "Testimony Given in First District Judicial Court," quoted in Sandra Jones, *The Trial of Don Pedro León Luján* (Salt Lake City: The University of Utah Press, 1999), 49–50.

43. On the trial of Luján, its irregularities and Mormon biases, see Ibid., 86–92.

44. Yet while working to pay off their debt, the law stipulated that their Mormon parents/masters were required not only to clothe and feed their children/servants, but also to ensure that the children received three months of schooling per year. "An Act for the Relief of Indian Slaves and Prisoners," March 7, 1852, in *Acts, Resolutions and Memorials, Passed at the Annual Sessions of the Legislative Assembly of the Territory of Utah* (Salt Lake City: Brigham H. Young, 1852), 92–94.

45. Jones, *Forty Years among the Indians.* 52–53. In June 1853, Young wrote to the federal commissioner of Indian Affairs, "One of Waker's [sic] brothers, lately killed an Indian prisoner child, because the traders would not give him what he asked for it." Quoted in Blackhawk, *Violence over the Land,* 240. The Utah territory, which then included parts of Nevada, Colorado, and Wyoming, was too vast for the Mormons to police completely. So the slave trade with New Mexico went underground. Census records indicate that Luján had Paiute children in his household as late as 1870. Jones, *The Trial of Don Pedro León Luján,* 95.

46. Blackhawk, *Violence over the Land,* 70–80.

47. James F. Brooks, *Captives and Cousins: Slavery, Kinship, and Community in the South West Borderlands* (Chapel Hill: The University of North Carolina Press, 2002), 364, 244.

48. Peter Gottfredson, *Indian Depredations in Utah* (Salt Lake City: Skelton Publishing CO, 1919), 44–58. For a "Gentile" perspective on the "Walker War" published in the 1850s, see Gwinn Harris Heap and E. F. Beale, *Central Route to the Pacific* (Philadelphia: Lippincott, Grambo & Company, 1854), 91–93. Recent scholarship has questioned how much Wakara directly orchestrated the war that bears his name. *On Zion's Mount,* 131–32.

49. See Nauvoo Legion Papers, July-August 1853, MS 17208, CHL; Adelia Almira Wilcox Kimball, *Memoirs of Adelia Almira Wilcox* (New York: Stanley Kimball, 1956) 34.

50. William Hubbard, *A Narrative of the Troubles with the Indians* (London: Printed for Tho. Parkhurst, 1677) 71; Jill Lepore, *The Name of War: King Philip's War and the Origins of American Identity* (New York: Vintage, 1999), 41, 105.

51. Gottfredson, *Indian Depredations in Utah,* 44–58.

52. Lepore, *The Name of War,* xviii.

53. On the theatric performance of this "inverted conquest," see Richard White, "Frederick Jackson Turner and Buffalo Bill," in *The Frontier in American Culture,* edited by James R. Grossman (Berkeley: University of California Press, 1994), 7–66; Farmer, *On Zion's Mount,* 137.

54. Blackhawk, *Violence over the Land*, 120. On slave traffic between Utah and New Mexico, see chart 13, "Number of Ute/Paiute Captives in New Mexico, 1730–1870," in Jones, *Trial of Don Pedro León Luján*, 97.

55. "Remarks by Tow-om-bw-gah or High Forehead, the Indian Chief, at the Bowery at Provo." At the same meeting, Wilford Woodruff acknowledged the same change to the land. "Before the whites came, there was [*sic*] plenty of fish and antelope, plenty of game of almost every description," noted the future Church president. "But now the whites have killed off these things, and there is scarcely anything left for the poor natives to live upon." Wilford Woodruff, "Preaching the Gospel to, and Helping the Lamanites," July 15, 1855, *Journal of Discourses* IX: 227, accessed April 15, 2016, http://jod.mrm.org/9/221. See also, Farmer, *On Zion's Mount*, 93–94.

56. Brigham Young, "Indian Hostilities," July 31, 1853, *Journal of Discourses* I: 171, accessed April 15, 2016, http://jod.mrm.org/1/162. See Richard W. Stoffle, Kristine L. Jones and Henry F. Dobyns. "Direct European Immigrant Transmission of Old World Pathogens to Numic Indians during the Nineteenth Century." *American Indian Quarterly* 19, no. 2 (Spring, 1995): 181–203. Suzanne Alchon has argued that Old World disease was just one factor of European colonialism that dissimilated Native populations. *A Pest in the Land: New World Epidemics in a Global Perspective* (Albuquerque: The University of New Mexico Press, 2003).

57. During the early 1850s, the Mormon-Paiute alliance formed to stop Ute aggression and slaving, as well as the Mormons' efforts to buy and adopt Paiute children, suggest that the Mormons also learned to differentiate between Utah's Indian tribes. Knack, Martha C. *Boundaries Between: The Southern Paiutes, 1775–1995* (Reno: University of Nevada Press, 2004) 30–36, 54–59.

58. For an analysis of Brigham Young's views on the theological and political justifications of legalizing "African" slavery in the Utah Territory, see W. Paul Reeve. *Religion of a Different Color: Race and the Mormon Struggle for Whiteness* (New York: Oxford University Press, 2015), 148–60.

59. Ibid., 57. For the precipitous decline of the Indian slave trade in and out of Utah between the 1840s and 1850s, see chart 13, "Number of Ute/Paiute Captives in New Mexico, 1730–1870," in Jones, *Trial of Don Pedro León Luján*, 97.

60. Jacob E. Holeman to Luke Lea, Commissioner of Indian Affairs, September 12, 1851; Jacob E. Holeman to Luke Lea, Commissioner of Indian Affairs, March 29, 1852. Quoted in Lawrence G. Coates, "A History of Indian Education by the Mormons, 1830–1900," PhD diss. (Ball State University, 1969), 88.

61. H. R. Day to Luke Lea, Commissioner of Indian Affairs, January 2, 1851, MS 16773, CHL.

62. "Meeting with Utes in Utah," May 22, 1850, Box 74, Folder 42, BYP; Brooks, "Indian Relations," 6.

63. Wakara to George A. Smith, n.d., quoted in Heap and Beale, *Central Route to the Pacific*, 92. What Martha C. Knack has suggested in terms of later Mormon-Paiute agreements in the southern settlements of the Sanpete Valley can

perhaps be applied to Mormon-Ute agreements in the late 1840s and early 1850s. "By cooperating with local bishops or even Brigham Young himself, Paiutes need not have been acknowledging white supremacy in wisdom or power or submitting themselves to political subordination; they may have been trying to manipulate the Mormon wealth by placing the Mormons under the kind of obligations Paiutes assumed would result: to share reciprocally in exchange for natives' initial gift of the very land Mormons occupied." Knack, *Boundaries Between*, 61.

64. Walker Statement, M. S. Martenas, interpreter, July 6, 1853, Box 58, Folder 14, BYP.

65. Ibid.; Farmer, *On Zion's Mount*, 85.

66. See Solomon Nunes Carvalho's description of the peace parley in Carvalho, *Incidents of Travel and Adventure in the Far West* (New York: Derby & Jackson, 1859), 180–94. See also, Thomas Bullock, Minutes, May 3–11, 1854, Box 2, Folder 52, 100, 318, CHL; Scott Kenney, *Wilford Woodruff's Journal*, IV (Midvale, UT: Signature Books, 1983), 262–74.

67. Here follow Ann Laura Stoler's method of examining the archives not (necessarily) as a collection of biased sources, but instead as sites of "epistemic anxieties" about the colonial power's categories of ethnological classifications, including, or especially, racial ones. *Along the Archival Grain: Epistemic Anxieties and Colonial Common Sense* (Princeton, NJ: Princeton University Press, 2010) 19–20, 36–40.

68. Kenney, *Wilford Woodruff's Journal*, 273–74.

69. While an all-Mormon jury found three Paiutes guilty of manslaughter, none were convicted of murder. The Pahvant leader Kanosh, Young's most trusted Indian ally who had been accused of orchestrating the attack, was exonerated completely. Blackhawk, *Violence over the Land*, 234–35, 244.

70. George A. Smith to Franklin D. Richards, *Millennial Star*, April 28, 1855. Later retellings elaborated on the account. The horses were not killed, but buried alive. So were "an Indian boy and girl," wrote Peter Gottfredson. The captives were "secured near the corpse of the Chief at the bottom of a deep pit … and left until death brought them relief." Two Indians who passed by the pit heard the boy begging to be freed. "The boy said that Walker was beginning to stink." The Indians ignored the boy's pleas. Gottfredson, *Indian Depredations in Utah*, 84.

71. Henry C. Yarrow, "A Further Contribution to the Study of the Mortuary Customs of the North American Indians," *First Annual Report of the Bureau of Ethnology* (Washington, DC: Government Printing Office, 1881), 141; See also, Ann Fabian, *The Skull Collectors: Race, Science, and America's Unburied Dead* (Chicago: University of Chicago Press, 2010), 197–203.

72. See among dozens of others, Susa Young Gates, "The Courtship of Kanosh: A Pioneer Indian Love Story," in *Improvement Era*, 9:21–38. Salt Lake City: General Board, Y.M.M.I.A., 1906; Howard Christy, "The Walker War: Defense and Conciliation as Strategy," *Utah Historical Quarterly* 47 (1979): 395–420. Walker, "Wakara Meets the Mormons."

73. "Indians, 1850–1865," in CR 1234 1: Brigham Young office files 1832–1878, CHL, accessed April 13, 2016, https://dcms.lds.org/delivery/DeliveryManagerServlet ?dps_pid=IE4489793

74. I have now shown the letter to a dozen scholars who have studied Ute-Numic languages. But no one has been able to identify the writing as anything legible.

75. Round, *Removable Type*, 121–40.

76. Max Perry Mueller, "Playing Jane," *Journal of Africana Religions* 1, no. 4 (2013): 513–61.

77. There are distinct limits, however, to this new era of openness. Max Perry Mueller, "Review: *The Columbia Sourcebook on Mormons in the United States,*" *Mormon Studies Review* (forthcoming).

78. Michel Foucault, *The Archeology of Knowledge* (New York: Vintage, 1982), 130–31; Sara Morais, "Archive Practice and Digital Humanities," The Centre for the Internet & Society, accessed April 13, 2016, http://cis-india.org/raw/digital -humanities/archive-practice-and-digital-humanities.

Chapter 5

1. W. W. Phelps, "O stop and tell me, Red Man," in *A Collection of Sacred Hymns, for the Church of the Latter Day Saints*, ed. Emma Smith (Kirtland, OH: F. G. Williams & co., 1835), 83–84.

2. Larry Echo Hawk was sustained on March 31, 2012 as the Church's second ever American Indian General Authority, the first being Elder George P. Lee (Navajo).

3. Larry Echo Hawk, "Come unto Me, O Ye House of Israel," *Ensign* (Salt Lake City: The Church of Jesus Christ of Latter-day Saints, Nov. 2012).

4. Joseph Smith Jr., *The Doctrine and Covenants*, (Salt Lake City: The Deseret News Office, 1876), 140.

5. Richard Dilworth Rust, "A Mission to the Lamanites," *Revelations in Context* (February 2013), accessed May 13, 2016, https://history.lds.org/article/doctrine -and-covenants-lamanite-mission?lang=eng.

6. Daniel Walker Howe, *What Hath God Wrought: The Transformation of America, 1815–1848* (New York: Oxford University Press, 2007), 317.

7. Gary P. Gillum, "Written to the Lamanites: Understanding the *Book of Mormon* through Native Culture and Religion," *Interpreter: A Journal of Mormon Scripture* 6 (2013): 37–46.

8. "The Iroquois Great Law of Peace" *The Book of Mormon is True*, March 3, 2016, http://thebookofmormonistrue.com/tag/arthur-c-parker.

9. Stuart Kirsch, "Lost Tribes: Indigenous People and the Social Imaginary," *Anthropological Quarterly* 70 (1997): 58.

10. See Lori Elaine Taylor's "Telling Stories about Mormons and Indians" (2000) for a more in-depth analysis of the intertwining of historical and doctrinal Mormon stories about American Indians.

11. Zitkala-Ša (Gertrude Bonnin) and Hanson debuted *The Sun Dance Opera* in 1913. See Zitkala-Ša's *American Indian Stories, Legends, and Other Writings* (2003) and *Dreams and Thunder: Stories, Poems, and the Sun Dance Opera* (2005).

12. From the American literary canon, as represented by *The Norton Anthology of American Literature* (2011) edited by Nina Baym and *The Heath Anthology of American Literature* (2013) edited by Paul Lauter, as well as the many other widely accessible American Indian writers not represented within the current canon, I have been able to locate eight American Indian writers who addressed Mormonism in some form between 1830–1930.

13. Gina Colvin and Joanna Brooks, eds., *Decolonizing Mormonism*. See also Angelo Baca's documentary films "In Laman's Terms" (2008) and "Into America" (2013), as well as the published work of those within this collection.

14. See Alexander Posey's *The Fus Fixico Letters* (Lincoln: University of Nebraska Press, 1993). See Will Rogers's *More Letters of a Self-Made Diplomat*, ed. Steven K. Gragert (Stillwater: Oklahoma State U Press, 1982); *Radio Broadcasts of Will Rogers*, ed. Steven K. Gragert (Stillwater: Oklahoma State University Press, 1983); *Will Rogers' Daily Telegrams*, ed. James M. Smallwood, Vol. 1 (Stillwater: Oklahoma State University Press, 1978); and *Will Rogers' Weekly Articles*, ed. James M. Smallwood, Vols. 1–5 (Stillwater: Oklahoma State University Press, 1980–1982). There are also American Indian and Indigenous Mormons such as Margarito Bautista (Nahua), Samuel Taylor Blue (Catawba), Chief Walkara (Ute), Penina Cotton (Cherokee), William McCary (Choctaw), Anthony Navarre (Potawatomi), Chief Washakie (Shoshone), and others who were speaking and/or writing about Mormonism throughout the early 1900s, but I have chosen to focus this essay specifically on American Indian writers who have come to represent nineteenth- and early twentieth-century American Indian intellectual, political, and literary discourse. See Lori Elaine Taylor's "Elder Nigeajasha and Other Mormon Indians Moving Westward" (2004).

15. Silko, Leslie Marmon, *Gardens in the Dunes* (New York: Simon & Shuster, 1999), 16.

16. Ibid., 31, emphasis added.

17. Ibid., 33–34.

18. Ibid., 20.

19. Ibid., 39.

20. Ibid., 40.

21. Ibid., 47.

22. Ibid., 464.

23. 3 Nephi 20:14–17.

24. Matthew J. Grow et al., eds., *The Joseph Smith Papers: Administrative Records, Council of Fifty, Minutes, March 1844–January 1846* (Salt Lake City: The Church Historian's Press, 2016), 296.

25. Ibid.

26. John G. Turner, *Brigham Young: Pioneer Prophet* (Cambridge, MA: Harvard U. Press, 2012), 131.

27. *The Joseph Smith Papers.*, xx–xxi, xlii.

28. Ibid., 73–75.

29. Ibid., 76 n191.

30. Ibid., 58 n139, 252.

31. Ibid., 410. For a more comprehensive history of early motivations for and accusations of American Indian–Mormon alliance, see W. Paul Reeve, *Religion of a Different Color: Race and the Mormon Struggle for Whiteness* (New York: Oxford University Press, 2015).

32. Martin Cruz Smith, *The Indians Won* (New York City: Belmont Books, 1970), 61.

33. Ibid., 99.

34. Ibid., 100.

35. Ibid., 100.

36. Ibid., 101.

37. Ibid., 104.

38. Ibid., 155.

39. Ibid., 191.

40. Ibid., 195.

41. Ibid.

42. Joseph Smith, "Articles of Faith," *The Pearl of Great Price*, The Church of Jesus Christ of Latter-day Saints, accessed November 1, 2016, https://www.lds.org /scriptures/pgp/a-of-f/1.1-13?lang=eng#1.

43. Jack Hicks, James D. Houston, Maxine Hong Kingston, and Al Young, *The Literature of California: Native American Beginnings to 1945* (Berkeley, CA: University of California Press, 2000), 163.

44. John Rollin Ridge, "John Rollin Ridge Goes West," *Northwest Arkansas Times*, March 11–14, 1973, accessed May 2, 2016, http://www.fayettevillehistory.com /primary/2009/06/john-rollin-ridge-goes-west.html.

45. Sarah Winnemucca, *Life among the Piutes; Their Wrongs and Claims* (New York: G. P. Putnam's Sons, 1883), 76–105.

46. Some interesting context that Winnemucca does not describe in *Life Among the Piutes* is the fact that she also traveled to Salt Lake City to avoid Nevada's antimiscegenation law and marry her first husband, First Lieutenant Edward C. Bartlett.

47. James W. Parins, *John Rollin Ridge: His Life and Works* (Lincoln: University of Nebraska Press, 1991), 128.

48. Winnemucca, *Life among the Piutes*, 5.

49. Rudyard Kipling, "The White Man's Burden," in *The White Man's Burdens: An Anthology of British Poetry of the Empire*, ed. Chris Brooks and Peter Faulkner (Exeter: The University of Exeter Press, 1996), 307–8.

50. Stanley P. Hirshon, *The Lion of the Lord: A Biography of Brigham Young* (New York: Knopf, 1969); and Ted J. Warner, "Nevada, Pioneer Settlements in,"

Encyclopedia of Mormonism, ed. Daniel H. Ludlow (New York: Macmillan Publishing Company, 1992), 1006–7.

51. Winnemucca, *Life Among the Piutes*, 59.

52. Warner, "Nevada," 1007.

53. Ned Blackhawk, *Violence over the Land: Indians and Empires in the Early American West* (Cambridge, MA: Harvard University Press, 2006), 226–66.

54. Winnemucca, *Life among the Piutes*, 61.

55. Ibid., 62.

56. Kiara A. Vigil, *Indigenous Intellectuals: Sovereignty, Citizenship, and the American Imagination, 1880–1930* (New York: Cambridge University Press, 2015), 7.

57. Simon Pokagon, "The Future of the Red Man," *Forum* 23 (1897): 698.

58. Ibid., 708.

59. Ibid., 700–705.

60. Ibid., 703.

61. For a comprehensive history of the Mountain Meadows Massacre, see Ronald W. Walker, Glen M. Leonard, and Richard E. Turley Jr.'s *Massacre at Mountain Meadows: An American Tragedy* (Oxford: Oxford University Press, 2008).

62. "Lesson 151: The Utah War and the Mountain Meadows Massacre." *Doctrine and Covenants and Church History Seminary Teacher Manual* (Salt Lake City, UT: The Church of Jesus Christ of Latter-day Saints, 2013), accessed April 18, 2016, https://www.lds.org/manual/doctrine-and-covenants-and-church-history-seminary-teacher-manual-2014/section-7/lesson-151-the-utah-war-and-the-mountain-meadows-massacre?lang=eng.

63. Henry B. Eyring, "Remarks at the Mountain Meadows Massacre Sesquicentennial" (Washington County, 2007), accessed April 18, 2016, http://www.mormonnewsroom.org/article/150th-anniversary-of-mountain-meadows-massacre.

64. Charles Alexander Eastman, *Indian Heroes and Great Chieftains* (Mineola, NY: Dover Publications, 1997 [1918]), 6.

65. Ibid., 5.

66. Ibid., 13.

67. Ibid., 86.

68. "The Problem of Old Harjo" was originally published in the April 1907 issue of Hampton Institute's *Southern Workman* journal.

69. John Milton Oskison, *The Tales of the Old Indian Territory*, ed. Lionel Larré (Lincoln: University of Nebraska Press, 2012), 248–54.

70. Cristina Stanciu, "An Indian Woman of Many Hats: Laura Cornelius Kellogg's Embattled Search for an Indigenous Voice," *American Indian Quarterly* 37 (2013).

71. Laura Cornelius Kellogg, *Our Democracy and the American Indian and Other Works*, eds. Kristina Ackley and Cristina Stanciu (Syracuse, NY: Syracuse University Press, 2015), 149.

72. Ibid., 97.

73. Ibid., 149–52.

74. Ibid., 190.
75. Ibid., 79.
76. Daniel Heath Justice, "'Go Away Water!': Kinship Criticism and the Decolonization Imperative," in *Reasoning Together: The Native Critics Collective* (Norman: University of Oklahoma Press, 2008), 148.

Chapter 6

1. The Northwestern Band of the Shoshone Nation also converted to Mormonism en masse in the late nineteenth century. See Scott Christensen, *Sagwitch: Shoshone Chieftan, Mormon Elder 1822–1887* (Logan, UT: Utah State University Press, 1999).
2. Frank Speck, "Catawba Religious Beliefs, Mortuary Customs, and Dances," *Primitive Man* 12.2 (April 1939): 21–28.
3. Speck, "Catawba Religious Beliefs," 21–22.
4. Change and adaptation have always been features of Indigenous identity on the Carolina Piedmont, as elsewhere. According to an anthropological model of coalescence, the Catawba Confederacy, the forerunner of the Catawba Indian Nation, coalesced in the 1700s in the Lower Catawba Valley after the shattering of three larger "chiefdoms" that dominated the Carolina Piedmont, due to incursions from Spanish colonialism. Robin A. Beck, "Catawba Coalescence and the Shattering of the Carolina Piedmont, 1540–1675," in *Mapping the Mississippian Shatter Zone*, ed. Robbie Ethridge and Sheri M. Shuck-Hall (Lincoln: University of Nebraska Press, 2009). However, as historian James Merrell explains, this does not mean that the Catawba Nation constituted a "new tribe" that only became a coherent entity after the 1700s. There is continuity with a "core" or "nucleus" of a Catawba polity and people that extends far prior to the 1700s—a point that is crucial to the Catawba Indian Nation's legal standing as a federally recognized American Indian Nation. James H. Merrell, *The Indians' New World: Catawbas and Their Neighbors from European Contact through the Era of Removal* (Chapel Hill: Published for the Omohundro Institute of Early American History and Culture, Williamsburg, Virginia, by the University of North Carolina Press, 2009), xvi–xvii. Thus, in this sense, by adopting Mormonism—and later, for some, by also abandoning it—Catawba people are continuing to adapt to changing circumstances to assure their csurvival as a people.
5. See James Clifford, *The Predicament of Culture: Twentieth-Century Ethnography, Literature, And Art* (Cambridge, MA: Harvard University Press, 1988).
6. Hokulani Aikau, *A Chosen People, A Promised Land: Mormonism and Race in Hawai'i* (Minneapolis and London: University of Minnesota Press, 2012), 173–74.
7. Any unattributed quotations or observations are taken from recordings and field notes I produced during ethnographic field work in the Catawba Indian Nation and among Catawba citizens and descendants between 2012–15.

8. Life of Chief Samuel T. Blue, July 28, 1955, p. 2, qtd. in Mikaela Adams, *Who Belongs? Race, Resources, and Tribal Citizenship in the Native South* (New York: Oxford University Press, 2006), 66.

9. Columbia South Carolina Stake, Columbia South Carolina Stake Fortieth Anniversary, 199–200, qtd. in Liestman, "We Have Found What We Have Been Looking For!" 235.

10. James Clifford, "Introduction: Partial Truths," in *Writing Culture: The Poetics and Politics of Ethnography*, ed. James Clifford and George E. Marcus (Berkeley: University of California Press, 1986).

11. This chapter is a condensed and revised version of a chapter in my dissertation, "The Blood of Father Lehi: The Book of Mormon and Indigenous Peoples," PhD diss. (University of North Carolina at Chapel Hill, 2016).

12. "In 1851 a remnant band [of Catawba people] reached the Choctaw Nation, Indian Territory, where they were later granted citizenship. By 1950 an unknown number were counted among the Choctaw, Creek, and Cherokee populations of Oklahoma." Jon D. May, "Catawba," Encyclopedia of Oklahoma History and Culture, accessed April 7, 2016, www.okhistory.org.

13. See Adams, *Who Belongs?*, 63.

14. According to Willey's diary, the first five to be baptized were Lucy Wats, James Harvey Wats, Mary Jane Wats, James Patterson, and Taylor George. Jerry D. Lee, "A Study of the Influence of the Mormon Church on the Catawba Indians of South Carolina, 1882–1975," MA thesis (Brigham Young University, 1976), 39.

15. Liestman, "We Have Found What We Have Been Looking For," 229–30.

16. Quoted in Judy Canty Martin, *Genealogy of the Western Catawba* (n.p., 1998), 3.

17. Patrick Mason, *The Mormon Menace: Violence and Anti-Mormonism in the Postbellum South* (New York: Oxford University Press, 2011).

18. Liestman, "We Have Found What We Have Been Looking For!," 237.

19. This may be true, as most branches established prior to this in the West among American Indian Peoples were typically presided over by missionaries or "white" branch presidents. Lee, "Influence of Mormon Church on the Catawba Indians," 51.

20. Ibid. Lee also makes this claim, stating that the Catawba Branch/Ward it is the "oldest Indian branch in the church," by which he presumably means the oldest branch that is still organized as such (though it is now the Catawba First and Second Wards), because he also notes that the Washakie Ward was established in 1877 but closed in 1965. This claim thus rests on definitional technicalities by ruling out wards with an earlier claim if they were eventually closed, and presumably not counting wards that were not exclusively Lamanite units (though the Catawba Branch/Ward never has been *exclusively* Lamanite either). For example, the Papago Ward was organized by 1883, if not earlier, among Tohono O'odham and Maricopa Peoples and is still in existence and, as far as I know, has been continually meeting since then (the earliest recorded bishop for this ward was white, but he assigned at least one O'odham-Papago bishopric

counselor). Thus, the Papago Ward may beat the Catawba Ward's claim by at least two years. See D. L. Turner, "Akimel Au-Authm, Xalychidom Piipaash, and the LDS Papago Ward," *Journal of Mormon History* 39.1 (Winter 2013): 170.

21. Liestman, "We Have Found What We Have Been Looking For!," 232–36.

22. Journal of Pinkney Head, as quoted in Martin, *Genealogy*, 88. Mission President John Morgan stated regarding these missionaries: "During our visit two of their number quite intelligent young men, were called and sent on a mission to a remnant of the Cherokee Native in North Carolina, numbering about 1500, and it was trusted that through their acquaintance with the Cherokees, formed in previous visits that access could be obtained to their hearts and confidence, and that in due season Elders could follow after and much good be done in their midst." John Morgan to Pres. John Taylor, Charlotte, NC, October 7, 1885, in Morgan Papers, Marriott Library Special Collections, University of Utah, Salt Lake City, Utah.

23. Morgan noted in his journal entry for October 4, 1885, regarding a visit to the Spartanburg branch: "The greater part of the congregation were Lamanites of the Cauoluba [*sic*] tribe." He also noted that he stayed that night "at bro. James Pattersons, a Lamanite, with a wife and eight daughters." John H. Morgan papers, box 1, fd 8, Marriott Library Special Collections, University of Utah, Salt Lake City, Utah.

24. John Morgan to Pres. John Taylor, Charlotte, NC, October 7, 1885, in Morgan Papers, Marriott Library Special Collections, University of Utah, Salt Lake City, Utah.

25. Scaife, "History and Condition of the Catawba Indians of South Carolina," 9; "Catawba Indians," *Liahona: The Elders Journal* 3 (1905): 181. Jerry D. Lee, who is skeptical of these numbers, states that it is impossible to accurately state with any certainty exactly how many Catawba people migrated westward with the Mormon gathering, but it constituted a significant portion of the small nation at the time. Lee, "Influence of Mormon Church on the Catawba Indians."

26. JM to JT, Manassa, Colo., December 23, 1886.

27. JM to JT, Manassa, Colo., December 10, 1886; JM to JT, Manassa, Colo., December 23, 1886; JM to JT, Salt Lake City, UT, January 11, 1887; JM to JT, January 26, 1887, Salt Lake City, UT; Morgan Papers.

28. JM to JT, Manassa, Colo., December 10, 1886; JM to JT, Manassa, Colo., December 23, 1886; JM to JT, Salt Lake City, UT, January 11, 1887; JM to JT, anuary 26, 1887, Salt Lake City, UT; Morgan Papers.

29. JM to JT, Chattanooga, TN, February 11, 1887, Morgan Papers.

30. Interview, Cortez, CO, May 26, 2012. Martin has not been able to find any baptism records for Hillery Harris or for his mother, Nancy Harris, and concludes that these two may not have ever formally joined the church, despite migrating to the Mormon colonies in Colorado.

31. Adams, *Who Belongs?*, 66.

32. For a fuller treatment of this issue, see Adams, *Who Belongs?*; and Thayne, "Blood of Father Lehi," chapter 2.

33. This memory of conflict between Danish and Southern States settlers is cor-
    roborated by EchoHawk, "Struggling to Find Zion," 5–6, which suggests that
    conflicts arose between the Danish and Southern settlers because, among other
    reasons, Danish Saints were placed in leadership positions, yet the Southern
    converts complained that these Danish leaders were lax in observing Mormon
    laws such as the Word of Wisdom (proscribing alcohol and tobacco), they
    swore, and were difficult to understand. EchoHawk suggests that Catawba
    migrants "kindled no similar strife in the already growing communities."

34. Obituary: "Mrs. Martha Head Dead at Age 102," clipping in private collection.
    I thank Dana EchoHawk for sharing this source with me.

35. See Armand Mauss, *All Abraham's Children: Changing Mormon Conceptions
    of Lineage and Race* (Urbana: University of Illinois Press, 2003); and Thayne,
    "Blood of Father Lehi," chapter 4.

36. "First Lamanite Patriarch," in Martin, *Genealogy of the Western Catawba*, 108.

37. "Sanford Celebration Holds Memories," in Martin, *Western Catawba Gene-
    alogy*, 109-a. The 24th of July Pioneer Day celebration commemorate the
    entrance of Mormon pioneers into the Salt Lake Valley in 1847. In places like
    Sanford and neighboring towns it also seems to double as a celebration of the
    Mormon colonization of the San Luis Valley.

38. See Thomas Blumer, *The Catawba Indian Nation of the Carolinas* (Charleston,
    SC: Arcadia Publishing, 2004), 57–58. Similar pictures depict Elbert Garce
    (a Patterson descendant) riding in 4th of July parades decked out in a head-
    dress and Native garb.

39. Kyle Canty also sees his identity as tribe of Manasseh as deeply significant.

40. My use of the term *affiliation* is intentional; as Liestman points out, scholars
    such as Speck, James Merrell, and Tom Blumer question whether Catawba
    people had really "converted" to Mormonism, maintaining, rather, that, as Liest-
    man summarizes their position, "the Catawba have a syncretic belief system
    combining their traditional beliefs with Mormonism." Liestman, "We Have
    Found What We Have Been Looking For!" 242. A term such as *affiliation*
    allows for such hybridity and obviates the need of total adherence and the
    elimination of all other ideological commitment. Of course, such a model of
    conversion does not really apply to most humans, who are typically influenced
    by multiple ideological formations—religion, science, health, etc.—at one time.
    On religious *affiliation* and *engagement* see Linford Fisher, *The Indian Great
    Awakening* (New York: Oxford University Press, 2012).

41. Jerry D. Lee, "A Study of the Influence of the Mormon Church on the Catawba
    Indians of South Carolina, 1882–1975 (MA thesis, Brigham Young University,
    1976), 55.

42. Liestman, "We Have Found What We Have Been Looking For," 240–41.

43. LDS Institutes of Religion are local, Church-run organization that provide
    religious education for college-age young adults between ages 18–30.

44. See Ruth Y. Wetmore, *First on the Land: The North Carolina Indians* (Winston-
    Salem, NC: John F. Blair, 1975), 52–53; and Hudson, *Catawba Nation*, 102.

45. Individuals of African descent were barred from priesthood ordination in The Church of Jesus Christ of Latter-day Saints prior to 1978.

46. Charles M. Hudson, *The Catawba Nation* (Athens, GA: University of Georgia Press, 1970), 53, 80–81, 114–17.

47. Aikau, *A Chosen People, A Promised Land*, 174.

48. From a newspaper article, probably *Church News*, included in Judy Canty Martin, *My Father's People: A Complete Genealogy of the Catawba Nation* (self-published, 1999), photocopy of article preceding p. 136.

49. Peter M. Judge, "Catawba Mormons hold services in new church," *Rock Hill Herald*, August 31, 1985.

50. The Catawba Nation was "terminated" in 1959 as a part of broader termination policy effort by the United States in the 1940s-1960s. In the name of assimilating Natives as "normal" Americans, the policy dissolved tribal governments and ended formal nation-to-nation treaty relations. Results were disastrous. Many tribes, including Catawbas, subsequently petitioned for reinstated recognition. The Catawbas initiated recognition efforts in 1973 and finally secured federal tribal recognition in 1993. Many tribes are still fighting for recognition. For a general overview of termination programs see Donald L. Fixico, *Termination and Relocation: Federal Indian Policy, 1945–1960* (Albuquerque: University of New Mexico Press, 1990). For an overview of some tribal recognition efforts see Bruce Granville Miller, *Invisible Indigenes: The Politics of Nonrecognition* (Lincoln: University of Nebraska Press, 2003); and Mark Edwin Miller, *Forgotten Tribes: Unrecognized Indians and the Federal Acknowledgment Process* (Lincoln: University of Nebraska Press, 2006).

51. Hudson, *Catawba Nation*, 103.

52. Mormon prayer language is distinctive and marked by several stylistic features children learn when they are young, both through hearing others and through actual instruction. For a prescriptive example of such instruction, see Dallin H. Oaks, "The Special Language of Prayer," *New Era* (January 2006).

53. Lucile C. Tate, *LeGrand Richards: Beloved Apostle* (Salt Lake City: Bookcraft, 1982), 169.

54. According to a table in Douglas Summer Brown, *The Catawba Indians: The People of the River* (Columbia: South Carolina University Press, 1966), 340–48, Blue served from 1931–1938, 1941–1943; and 1956–1958.

55. The story relates an incident that occurred in the Catawba Nation when Chief Blue's son was shot, ostensibly by accident, by two tribal members who were reportedly known to be his political opponents. Chief Blue felt an urge to avenge his son's death but instead knelt in prayer and pled for the power to forgive them until he was able to. The story was included in Marion G. Romney, *The Power of God unto Salvation*, Brigham Young University Speeches of the Year, Provo, February 3, 1960, 6–7, and has been reproduced in a number of Church publications and talks since then, often citing that source. Its inclusion, for example, in the Church's *Family Home Evening Resource Book* (1997), under the topic "Forgiving," means that the story is likely recited as part of family home evening lessons in Mormon homes throughout the world.

56. Doctrine and Covenants 38:39. This verse is perhaps most associated with Church president Ezra Taft Benson's landmark address "Beware of Pride," *Ensign*, May 1989.

57. Interview with anonymous Catawba community member, in possession of author.

58. Interview with anonymous Catawba community member, in possession of author.

59. Interview with David Garce, in possession of author.

60. From a newspaper article, probably *Church News*, included in Judy Canty Martin, *My Father's People: A Complete Genealogy of the Catawba Nation* (self-published, 1999), photocopy of article preceding p. 136.

Chapter 7

1. Stewart Udall, "Glen Canyon Dam Dedication Ceremony," September 22, 1966, item display 75977, Cline Library (CL), Northern Arizona University (NAU).

2. Lady Bird Johnson, "Glen Canyon Dam Dedication Ceremony," September 22, 1966, item display 75982, CL, NAU.

3. Elder Theodore Burton, "Glen Canyon Dam Dedication Ceremony," September 22, 1966, item display 75984, CL, NAU.

4. Termination is technically known as House Concurrent Resolution 108 and Public Law 280. Paul Rosier, "They Are Ancestral Homelands: Race, Place, and Politics in Cold War Native America, 1945–1961," *Journal of American History*, (March 2006), 1300–1326; Thomas Cowager, "'The Crossroads of Destiny': The NCAI's Landmark Struggle to Thwart Coercive Termination," *American Indian Culture and Research Journal*, 20:4 (1996): 121–144.

5. Russell Martin, *A Story that Stands like a Dam: Glen Canyon and the Soul of the West* (Salt Lake City: UT, University of Utah Press, 2017); Norris Hundley Jr., *The Great Thirst: Californians and Water, 1770s–1990s* (Berkley: University of California Press, 1992); Donald Worster, *Rivers of Empire*; and Mark Harvey, *A Symbol of Wilderness: Echo Park and the American Conservation Movement* (Seattle: University of Washington Press, 2000).

6. Raymond Nakai, "Dedication of Glen Canyon Dam," "Equality of Opportunity," September 22, 1966, item display 77978, CL, NAU.

7. Ibid.

8. Raymond Nakai, "Glen Canyon (Lake Powell) Speech," June 19, 1969, Nakai Papers, CL, NAU.

9. On the Sierra Club's efforts to fight the Echo Park Dam see Harvey, *A Symbol of Wilderness*.

10. Howard Stambor, "Manifest Destiny and American Indian Religious Freedom: Sequoya, Badoni, and Drowned Gods," *American Indian Law Review*, 10:1 (1982): 59–89.

11. Stambor, 59–89; Brian Edward Brown, "Native American Religions, the First Amendment, and the Judicial Interpretation of Public Land," *Environmental*

History Review, 15:4 (Winter 1991): 19–44; Scott K. Miller, "Undamming Glen Canyon: Lunacy, Rationality, or Prophecy?" *Stanford Environmental Law Journal,* 19 (January 2000): 151.

12. Rainbow Bridge was made a National Monument in 1910. The monument consists of 160 acres in southern Utah, entirely surrounded by the Navajo Indian reservation. Karl W. Luckert, *Navajo Mountain and Rainbow Bridge Religion* (Flagstaff, AZ: Museum of Northern Arizona, 1977); Peter Nabokov, *Where Lightening Strikes: The Lives of American Indian Sacred Places* (London: Penguin, 2006), 97–104.

13. Howard Stambor, "Manifest Destiny and American Indian Religious Freedom: Sequoya, Badoni, and Drowned Gods," *American Indian Law Review,* 10: 1 (1982): 59–89.

14. Karl W. Lukert, "Rainbow Mountain and Rainbow Bridge Religion," *American Tribal Religions,* vol. 1, (Flagstaff: Museum of Northern Arizona, 1977).

15. David Kent Sproul, *A Bridge Between Cultures: An Administrative History of Rainbow Bridge National Monument"* (Washington: GPO, 2001).

16. Klara B. Kelly and Francis Harris, *Navajo Sacred Places,* (Bloomington, Indiana University Press), 1994; Sproul, *Bridge Between Cultures.*

17. Karl W. Lukert, "Rainbow Mountain and Rainbow Bridge Religion," 1977; Paul G. Zolbrod, *Diné bahané: The Navajo Creation Story* (Albuquerque: University of New Mexico Press, 1984).

18. Charles S. Peters, *Take up your Mission: Mormon Colonizing Along the Little Colorado River, 1870–1900* (Tucson: The University of Arizona Press, 1973); Brent Rogers, "A Distinction Between Mormons and Americans: Mormon Indian Missionaries, Federal Indian Policies, and the Utah War," *Utah Historical Quarterly* 82:4 (2014): 251–72; Susan E. Woods and Robert S. McPherson, editors, *Along Navajo Trails: Recollections of a Trader* (Logan, UT: Utah State University Press, 2005), 3; William S. Abruzzi, "Ecology, Resource Redistribution, and Mormon Settlement in Northeastern Arizona," *American Anthropologist* (September 1989): 642–59.

19. Abruzzi, "Ecology, Resource Redistribution, and Mormon Settlement," 91.

20. Quote on "agents of God's great plan," from Mark Fiege, *Irrigated Eden: The Making of an Agricultural Landscape in the American West* (Seattle: University of Washington Press, 1998), 23; Jared Farmer, *On Zion's Mount: Mormons, Indians, and the American Landscape* (Boston: Harvard University Press, 2008). On the desert blossoming as a rose see Isaiah, 35:1.

21. William Lyon, "The Navajos in the Anglo-American Historical Imagination, 1807–1870," *Ethnohistory* (Summer 1996): 504.

22. Steve Pavlik, "Of Saints and Lamanites: An Analysis of Navajo Mormonism," *Wicaso Sa Review* (Spring 1992): 21–22.

23. Traders like Hamblin, along with Ira Hatch, Joseph Foutz, Thales Haskell and Will Evans all fit into this category Woods and McPherson, *Along Navajo Trails,* 10.

24. While the Church did not set up a formal mission to the Navajos until relatively late, they did establish numerous missions to the area to work with Indians in

general and specific groups, such as the Paiutes, Utes, Zuni, and Hopi earlier in the nineteenth century. See Erastus Snow to Jacob Hamblin, September 24, 1869. Jacob Hamblin Papers, Huntington Library, San Marino, California.

25. Pavlik, 22. On the Indian Placement Program see Matthew R. Garrett, *Making Lamanites: Mormons, Native Americans, and the Indian Student Placement Program, 1947–2000* (Salt Lake City: University of Utah Press, 2016); and Megan Stanton, "The Indian Student Placement Program and Native Direction," herein. Arthur V. Watkins influenced Navajo education policy, was a key supporter of the Indian Placement Program, and was instrumental in getting funding for the construction of a Navajo boarding school in Brigham City, Utah. Arthur V. Watkins, "Speech to President given by Watkins," File 4/9/1951, Watkins Papers, Brigham Young University.

26. George Dewey Clyde, "History of Irrigation in Utah," *Utah Historical Quarterly* (January 1959): 27. Clyde ignored the fact that many Mormon and US government irrigation efforts relied on Indigenous knowledge, resources, and in some cases, the previous irrigation efforts of Native Americans.

27. Interview with Senator Arthur V. Watkins, January 4, 1968, p. 10, *Eisenhower Administration Project*, Oral History Research Office, Columbia University, 1970.

28. Charles F. Wilkenson and Eric Biggs, "The Evolution of the Termination Policy," *American Indian Law Review*, vol. 5, No. 1 (1977): 139–184.

29. On termination see Parker M. Nielson, *Cultural Genocide of the Mixed-Blood Utes: An Advocates Chronicle* (Norman: University of Oklahoma Press, 1982), 203.

30. *House Concurrent Resolution 108*, 83rd Cong., 1st sess. (1953); Kenneth R. Philp, "Dillion S. Meyer and the Advent of Termination, 1950–1953," *Western Historical Quarterly* (January 1988): 37–59; Donald Fixico, *Termination and Relocation, 1945–1960* (Albuquerque, NM: University of New Mexico Press, 1990).

31. Daniel Cobb, *Native Activism in Cold War America* (Lawrence, KS: University Press of Kansas, 2008); Parker Neilson, *The Dispossessed*, 203.

32. Mark Reisner, *Cadillac Desert: The American West and its Disappearing Water* (New York: Penguin Books, 1993), 231. In fact, some of the most influential engineers working on Western water issues were Mormon including Ellis L. Armstrong, who served as commissioner of the Bureau of Reclamation from 1969–1973; Laurence Armand French, *Legislating Indian Country: Milestones in Transforming Tribalism*, 105.

33. R. Warren Metcalf, *Termination's Legacy: The Discarded Indians of Utah* (Lincoln, NE: University of Nebraska Press, 2002), 35. Quote on political strategy, p.27.

34. Arthus V. Watkins, "Oral History, January 4, 1968," p.16. Interview by Ed Edwin. Eisenhower Administration Project, Oral History Research Office, Columbia University, 1970. Watkins used similar language in other speeches. See W. A. Dawson Collection, A. V. Watkins, "The Last Water Hole," Box 5, book 2, section 20. Marriott Library, University of Utah.

35. Aqualante Speakers Kit, "What is the project?" document. Ernest Untermann Collection (EUC), Marriott Library, University of Utah, n.d. On membership numbers see Mark Harvey, *A Symbol of Wilderness: Echo Park and the American Conservation Movement* (Seattle: University of Washington Press, 1994), 200.

36. Don Shannon, "River Storage Project Lobbyists Get Top Fee," *Los Angeles Times*, January 13, 1957, p. 27.

37. "Aqualante materials," (EUC). See also "Colorado River Storage Project," reports, B. H. Stringham Collection, Box 12, Folder 14 Utah State University.

38. "What are Aqualantes?" document M-5, (EUC). Many environmental historians contend, for example, that to "understand the history of modern environmentalism . . . one has to understand the debate over Echo Park." Mark Harvey, *A Symbol of Wilderness: Echo Park and the American Conservation Movement* (Seattle, WA: University of Washington Press, 2000).

39. Scott K. Miller, "Undamming Glen Canyon: Lunacy, Rationality, or Prophecy," *Stanford Environmental Law Journal*, 19 (January, 2000): 148.

40. Quote from Aqualante Speakers Kit, "A 3 minute Talk on the Colorado River Storage Project," Document 1, p. 2, (EUC).

41. Ibid.

42. Richard White, *The Roots of Dependency: Subsistence, Environment, and Social Change among the Choctaws, Pawnee, and Navajos* (Lincoln: University of Nebraska Press, 1983).

43. Marsha Weisiger, *Dreaming in Sheep in Navajo Country* (Seattle, WA: University of Washington Press, 2008).

44. Aqualante Speakers Kit, Document 1, p. 2, (EUC). Coincidentally, though, the Mr. Yellowman in question may have been Jake Yellowman, one the Navajos who had vehemently fought stock reduction, and in all likelihood may have even evaded it by hiding his sheep. Weisiger, *Dreaming,* 217.

45. Aqualante Speakers Kit, Document 1, p. 2, (EUC).

46. Emmons/Watkins exchange, "Termination of Federal Supervision Over Certain Tribes of Indians," *Joint Hearing before the Subcommittees of the Committees on Interior and Insular Affairs Congress of the United States,* 83rd Congress, second session on S. 2670 and H.R. 7674 (Washington: Government Printing Office, 1954), 45.

47. Aqualante material, Press Release, n.d., (EUC).

48. Sam Akheah, "Statement of Sam Ahkeah, chairman, Navajo Tribal Council, Accompanied by Norman M. Littell, General Council, Navaho Tribe," 83rd Congress, 2nd Session, Senate, Published Hearing, 1954, Colorado River Storage Project.

49. Ibid.

50. Ibid.

51. Ibid.

52. Paul Jones, "Reclamation and the Indian," *Utah Historical Quarterly* (January 1959): 56.

53. George Clyde to Dawson, January 31, 1957, Dawson Papers (DP) Special Collections, University of Utah.

54. According to scholars Tamara Mix and Kirsten Waldo, "Astroturf endeavors are clever public relations campaigns supported by large private public relations budgets. Also referred to as false grassroots, faux grassroots, and synthetic grassroots, these public relations campaigns are designed to suggest to their audience that a grassroots coalition is involved." Mix and Waldo, "Knowing your Power: Risk Society, Astroturf Campaigns, and the Battle over Red Rock Coal-Fired Plant," *The Sociological Quarterly* 56: (2015): 125–26.

55. Donald Worster, *Rivers of Empire: Water, Aridity, and the Growth of the American West*, (New York: Pantheon Book, 1985); Donald C. Jackson, *Big Dams of the New Deal Era: A Confluence of Engineering and Politics* (Norman: University of Oklahoma Press, 2006).

56. Jones, *Utah Historical Quarterly*, 54.

57. Ibid, 54.

58. Gerald Nash reports that Navajos tried to obtain jobs at Glen Canyon Dam but of the 6,000 workers affiliated with the dam, only 1,000 were Navajos. He notes that it took several decades before the dam provided Navajos with any economic benefit. Gerald Nash, *The Federal Landscape: An Economic History of the Twentieth Century West*, (Tucson: University of Arizona Press, 1999), 111–12.

59. US Statutes at Large, Public Law, 485, 70 Stat 106, April 11, 1956; Sproul, "A Bridge Between Cultures," 149; Brown, "Native American Religions, the First Amendment, and the Judicial Interpretation of Public Land," *Environmental History Review*, (Winter, 1991), 22–23.

60. Jared Farmer, *Glen Canyon Dammed: Inventing Lake Powell and the Canyon Country* (Tucson: Arizona University Press, 1999), 166–68; Joern Gerdts, "Lake Powell: A Controversial Reservoir in Glen Canyon Opens Magnificent Scenery for Sportsmen," in *Los Angeles Times*, September 11, 1966, W13; Michele and Tom Grimm, "Lake Powell a Popular Play Place," in *Los Angeles Times*, September 2, 1979, L2. The Grimm's report that "the most relaxing [trip] is the all-day trip to Rainbow Bridge."

61. *Bandoni v. Higgenson*, 638 F.2d 172, 177 (1980).

62. Ibid.

63. Brian Edward Brown, "Native American Religions, the First Amendment, and the Judicial Interpretation of Public Land," 23.

64. 638 F2nd, *Bandoni v. Higgeninson*, decided November 3, 1980 by Tenth Circuit Court of Appeals. *Badoni vs. Higginson* (1977, 1981).

65. Ibid.

Chapter 8

1. I use Navajo and Diné interchangeably since Navajos apply both terms synonymously.

2. The Indian Self-Determination and Education Act of 1960 marked this era by shifting Native American and federal government relations especially regarding

education. The legislation bestowed greater power in the Navajo Nation to determine their own educational systems and schooling.

3. Mitchell Kalauli became the principal of Whitehorse High School when Hector Tahu was the assistant principal. Farina McCarty-Stonex, personal conversations with author, October 2016. Farina and the author have talked several times between September and October 2016 through telecommunications. Tahu later became the Tuba City Unified School District Superintendent, living among Navajos and Hopis for over thirty years. See "Hector Tahu," Obituaries, February 21, 2007, *Arizona Daily Sun*, accessed September 22, 2016, http://azdailysun.com/news/local/obituaries/hector-tahu/article_a90d5db9 -843e-5700-a8bd-b3260b945449.html.

4. JoAnn Smith, personal conversation with author, September 16, 2016.

5. JoAnn Smith.

6. John Farella focuses on *hózhǫ́* and *S'ah naaghai bik'eh hózhǫ́ǫ* in *The Main Stalk*. See John R. Farella, *The Main Stalk: A Synthesis of Navajo Philosophy* (Tucson: University of Arizona Press, 1984). For a Navajo perspective of *hózhǫ́ǫ*, see Herbert J. Benally, "Hózhǫ́ǫgo Naasháa Doo: Toward a Construct of Balance in Navajo Cosmology," PhD diss. (California Institute of Integral Studies, 2008), 60, 69. *Si'ąh Naagháí Bik'eh Hózhǫ́* also has different spellings and diacritical marks depending on the literature. I use the same spelling as the Division of Diné Education in their publications from the late 1990s. Navajo researchers use its acronym, SNBH.

7. Mo'olelo o na Po Makole, an oral history as told by Kaili'ohe Kame'ekua of Kamalo, cited in Koko Willis and Pali Jae Lee, *Tales from the Night Rainbow* (Honolulu: Night Rainbow Publishing, 1990), 19.

8. Albert Smith (the author's uncle) cited by Deborah O'Grady, "Navajo Code Talkers," *Deborah O'Grady*, accessed September 24, 2016, http://www .deborahogrady.com/portfolio-items/navajo-code-talkers/.

9. Davianna Pomoaikai McGregor, "Recognizing Native Hawaiians: A Quest for Sovereignty," in *Pacific Diaspora: Island Peoples in the United States and Across the Pacific*, ed. Paul R. Spickard, Joanne L. Rondilla, and Debbie Hippolite Wright (Honolulu: University of Hawaii Press, 2002), 348.

10. For more about aloha and giving, see Elizabeth Nihipali, Lessa Kanani'opua Pelayo, Christian Hanz Lozada, Lorelie Santonil Olaes, and Cheryl Villareal Roberts, *Hawaiians in Los Angeles* (Charleston, South Carolina: Arcadia Publishing, 2012), 83.

11. David Kay Flake, "History of the Southwest Indian Mission" (n.p., 1965), 117.

12. Several Kanaka Maoli missionaries and my father told me that Navajos called Native Hawaiian missionaries *bilasáanaa diwozhí* with humor.

13. For studies that trace definitions and appropriations of Lamanites, see Armand L. Mauss, *All Abraham's Children: Changing Mormon Conceptions of Race and Lineage* (Urbana: University of Illinois Press, 2003), 10; Hokulani K. Aikau, *A Chosen People, A Promised Land: Mormonism and Race in Hawai'i* (Minneapolis: University of Minnesota Press, 2012); Marjorie Newton, *Tiki*

and Temple: The Mormon Mission in New Zealand, 1854–1958 (Draper, Utah: Greg Kofford Books, 2012); Thomas W. Murphy, "Other Mormon Histories: Lamanite Subjectivity in Mexico," Journal of Mormon History 26 (Fall 2000): 179–214; Max Perry Mueller, Race and the Making of the Mormon People (Chapel Hill: University of North Carolina Press, 2017); and S. Lyman Tyler, Modern Results of the Lamanite Dispersion: The Indians of the Americas (Provo, Utah: Extension Publications, Division of Continuing Education, Brigham Young University, 1965).

14. For examples relating to Mormon Indigenous studies, see Gina Colvin and Joanna Brooks, eds. Decolonizing Mormonism: Approaching a Postcolonial Zion (Salt Lake City: University of Utah Press, 2018); and Stanley Thayne, "The Blood of Father Lehi: Indigenous Americans and the Book of Mormon," PhD diss. (University of North Carolina, 2016). For studies concerning transnational and global "Indigenous" identities, see Maximilian C. Forte, Who is an Indian? Race, Place, and the Politics of Indigeneity in the Americas (Toronto: University of Toronto Press, 2013), 4–5; Robert Warrior, ed., The World of Indigenous North America (New York: Routledge, 2014); Jane Carey and Jane Lydon, eds., Indigenous Networks: Mobility, Connections and Exchange (New York: Routledge, 2014), 4; Zoe Laidlaw and Alan Lester, eds., Indigenous Communities and Settler Colonialism: Land Holding, Loss and Survival in an Interconnected World (New York: Palgrave Macmillan, 2015), 4–5.

15. Hokulani Aikau, "Indigeneity in the Diaspora: The Case of Native Hawaiians at Iosepa, Utah," American Quarterly vol. 62, no. 3 (September 2010): 480.

16. Aikau, "Indigeneity in the Diaspora," 477.

17. For more studies addressing "Lamanites," see Matthew Garrett, Making Lamanites: Mormons, Native Americans, and the Indian Student Placement Program, 1947–2000 (Salt Lake City: University of Utah Press, 2016); and John-Charles Duffy, "The Use of 'Lamanite' in Official LDS Discourse," Journal of Mormon History 34, no. 1 (Winter 2008): 118–67. See also the special edition of the Journal of Mormon History on race and Mormonism, Journal of Mormon History 41, no. 3 (July 2015). Some of these works also address why LDS officials moved away from publicly emphasizing Amerindians and Indigenous Pacific Islanders as "Lamanites" and the waning "Lamanite Cause" after President Spencer W. Kimball's passing in 1985.

18. Lane Johnson, "Who and Where are the Lamanites? Worldwide Distribution of Lamanites," Ensign, December 1975, accessed May 6, 2016, https://www.lds .org/ensign/1975/12/who-and-where-are-the-lamanites?lang=eng.

19. Aikau, A Chosen People, A Promised Land, 42; and Mauss, 2.

20. See Maile Renee Arvin, "Pacifically Possessed: Scientific Production and Native Hawaiian Critique of the 'Almost White' Polynesian Race," PhD diss. (University of California, San Diego, 2013).

21. For more information about the recent discourse of related genetic research, see John Noble Wilford, "Pacific Islanders' Ancestry Emerges in Genetic Study," The New York Times, January 18, 2008; "Book of Mormon and DNA Studies,"

The Church of Jesus Christ of Latter-day Saints, accessed October 11, 2016, https://www.lds.org/topics/book-of-mormon-and-dna-studies?lang=eng; Joel B. Groat, "Lamanites No More: DNA and Lost Ties to Father Lehi," Institute for Religious Research, published July 1, 2011, accessed October 11, 2016, http://mit.irr.org/lamanites-no-more-dna-and-lost-ties-father-lehi.

22. For more about these arguments and evidence, see Hannah Korevaar, "This is the Place: Race, Space, Religion and Law in Salt Lake City" (BA honors thesis, Wesleyan University, 2014), 71. See also, Gina Colvin, "Introduction: Theorizing Mormon Race Scholarship," *Journal of Mormon History* 41, no. 3 (July 2015): 11–21; and Max Perry Mueller, *Race and the Making of the Mormon People* (Chapel Hill: University of North Carolina Press, 2017).

23. Colvin, "Introduction: Theorizing Mormon Race Scholarship," 11.

24. See Stanley Thayne, "Wandering Significance: Hagoth and the Many Migrations of Latter-day Lamanite/Nephite Identity," *Juvenile Instructor Blog*, December 5, 2013, accessed September 12, 2016, http://www.juvenileinstructor.org/wandering-significance-hagoth-and-the-many-migrations-of-latter-day-lamanitenephite-identity/; Thomas W. Murphy, "Imagining Lamanites: Native Americans and the Book of Mormon," PhD diss. (University of Washington, 2003), 3; and Thomas Murphy, "From Racist Stereotype to Ethnic Identity: Instrumental Uses of Mormon Racial Doctrine," *Ethnohistory* 46, no. 3 (Summer 1999): 452.

25. For example, see Murphy, "From Racist Stereotype to Ethnic Identity," 451; César Ceriani Cernadas, *Nuestros hermanos lamanitas: Indios y fronteras en la imaginación mormona* (Buenos Aires: Editorial Biblos, 2008); and Stuart Parker, "Queso y gusanos: The Cosmos of Indigenous Mormon Intellectual Margarito Bautista," in *Just South of Zion: The Mormons in Mexico and Its Borderlands*, ed. Jason H. Dormady and Jared M. Tamez (Albuquerque: University of New Mexico Press, 2015), 115.

26. Mary Louise Pratt, "Arts of the Contact Zone," *Profession* 91 (1991): 33–40.

27. Thomas Murphy, "From Racist Stereotype to Ethnic Identity," 453.

28. Pratt, 35.

29. Ibid., 35.

30. Aikau, *A Chosen People, A Promised Land*, 42.

31. "Ned Kaili Aikau," Obituaries, *Daily Herald*, June 28, 2010, accessed May 3, 2016, http://www.heraldextra.com/lifestyles/announcements/obituaries/ned-kaili-aikau/article_8f94384d-3b40-5e69-81b7-813850b90074.html.

32. Aikau, *A Chosen People, A Promised Land*, xii.

33. Harvard C.S. Kim, email to Farina King, May 20, 2013, printout in possession of author.

34. Mary Pine, informal conversation with author, Fort Wingate, New Mexico, June 3, 2018.

35. *Lamanite Israel*, February 1966, Southwest Indian Mission Papers, 1961–1965, John Edwin Baird (1908–2003), MS 20569, LDS Church Archives, Salt Lake City, Utah. The LDS Church established the Northern Indian Mission by 1964. Armand Mauss claims: "By 1965, there were more than three hundred

missionaries and perhaps as many as fifteen thousand Indian LDS members in those two missions [the Southwest Indian Mission and the Northern Indian Mission]." See Mauss, 81.

36. Julius Ray Chavez, interview by Odessa Neaman, Provo, Utah, June 27, 1990, 32–33, LDS Native American Oral History Project, MSS OH 1180, Tom Perry Special Collections and Manuscripts, Harold B. Lee Library, Brigham Young University, Provo, Utah (hereafter cited as LDS NAOHP).

37. Milli Cody Garrett, interview by Odessa Neaman, Provo, Utah, June 12, 1990, MSS OH 1173, LDS NAOHP.

38. Scholars have mostly addressed colorism in cases of African Americans and Mexican Americans. For more on colorism, the discrimination based on skin color, see Margaret L. Hunter, *Race, Gender, and the Politics of Skin Tone* (New York: Routledge, 2005); and Kimberly Jade Norwood, ed., *Color Matters: Skin Tone Bias and the Myth of a Postracial America* (New York: Routledge, 2013).

39. Gabriel Holyan Cinniginnie, interview by Malcolm T. Pappan, Provo, Utah, April 9, 1990, MSS OH 1171, LDS NAOHP.

40. Tiyarra Roanhorse, cited in Rachel Reed, "Tiyarra Roanhorse: Bringing Native American Culture to Hawaii," *Ke Alaka'i* (Fall 2016): 63.

41. Some Navajo oral traditions differentiate between Changing Woman and White Shell Woman, identifying them as sisters. See Paul G. Zolbrod, *Diné Bahane': The Navajo Creation Story* (Albuquerque: University of New Mexico Press, 1987), 192.

42. "Ch'ahádiniini' Binálí," cited in *Stories of Traditional Navajo Life and Culture/ Ałk'idą́ą́'yę́ę́k'ehgo Diné Kéédahahat'íné̗e̗ Baa Nahane'*, ed. Broderick H. Johnson (Tsaile, Arizona: Navajo Community College Press, 1977), 220.

43. Julius Ray Chavez, interview.

44. Zenobia Kapahulehua Iese, interview by author, July 6, 2013, telephone communication, recording of interview in possession of author.

45. Iese, interview.

46. See Noenoe K. Silva, *Aloha Betrayed: Native Hawaiian Resistance to American Colonialism* (Durham: Duke University Press, 2004); J. Kēhaulani Kauanui, *Hawaiian Blood: Colonialism and the Politics of Sovereignty and Indigeneity* (Durham: Duke University Press, 2008); Jennifer Nez Denetdale, *Reclaiming Diné History: The Legacies of Navajo Chief Manuelito and Juanita* (Tucson: University of Arizona Press, 2007); Lloyd L. Lee, ed., *Diné Perspectives: Revitalizing and Reclaiming Navajo Thought* (Tucson: University of Arizona Press, 2014); and Lloyd L. Lee, ed., *Navajo Sovereignty: Understandings and Visions of the Diné People* (Tucson: University of Arizona Press, 2017).

47. Iese, interview.

48. Ibid.

49. Ibid.

50. Dennis Little, personal telephone conversation with Farina King, October 12, 2016.

51. Dennis Little.

52. Deborah Pe'a Tsinnijinnie, interview by Farina King, Salt River Pima-Maricopa Indian Community, Arizona, January 23, 2013.

53. See 2 Nephi 5: 21 in the Book of Mormon; and Mauss, 130–31.

54. Dennis Little, personal conversation with author.

55. William Keoniana Kelly, interview by Rachel Nathan, Orem, Utah, February 6, 1994, LDS Polynesian American Oral History Project, MSS OH 1880, Tom Perry Special Collections and Manuscripts, Harold B. Lee Library, Brigham Young University, Provo, Utah.

56. *Navajo Times*, January 9, 1969, vol. 10, issues 1–8, p. 22.

57. Chavez interview.

58. Dennis Little.

59. Ibid.

60. See John P. Livingstone, "Chapter 6: American Indian Services," in *Same Drum, Different Beat: The Story of Dale T. Tingey and American Indian Services* (Provo, Utah: Religious Studies Center, Brigham Young University, 2003), 79–92, accessed October 13, 2016, https://rsc.byu.edu/archived/same-drum-different -beat-story-dale-t-tingey-and-american-indian-services/chapter-6#_ednref19. See also Mauss, 92.

61. Harvard C.S. Kim, email to Farina King, May 20, 2013, printout in possession of author. Kim began his mission on the Navajo Reservation in 1972.

62. Ibid.

63. Harvard Kim, interview by Farina King, May 27, 2013, telephone communication, recording in possession of author.

64. Iese, interview.

65. "Church explains excommunication to Navajos as Lee seeks a rebirth," *Deseret News*, September 10, 1989, accessed October 11, 2016, http://www.deseretnews .com/article/62992/CHURCH-EXPLAINS-EXCOMMUNICATION-TO -NAVAJOS-AS-LEE-SEEKS-A-REBIRTH.html?pg=all. Other scholars discuss Lee as a former student and advocate of the LDS Indian Student Placement Program. See, for example, Lynette A. Riggs, "The Church of Jesus Christ of Latter-day Saints' Indian Student Placement Service: A History," PhD diss. (Utah State University, 2008), 133; and Matthew Garrett, *Making Lamanites.* See also George P. Lee, *Silent Courage: An Indian Story, The Autobiography of George P. Lee, a Navajo* (Salt Lake City: Deseret Book Company, 1987). Lee's autobiography ends with his calling as an LDS General Authority.

66. Phillip L. Smith, personal telecommunication conversation with author, September 28, 2016.

67. Thomas Tsinnijinnie, personal interview by Farina King, LDS Papago Ward building, Salt River Pima-Maricopa Indian Community, Arizona, September 12, 2012, recording in author's possession.

68. Mitchell Davis Kapuni Kalauli, interview by Matthew Heiss, Tuba City, Arizona, April 28, 1992, OH 1524, LDS Church Archives. The LDS Church organized the Chinle Stake in 1990 and the Tuba City Stake in 1995. A stake is an organizational unit, which consists of several wards (local congregations).

69. Fred Talker, public talk, The Church of Jesus Christ of Latter-day Saints chapel, Monument Valley, Utah, February 14, 2016, author in attendance of this talk and took personal notes. Author received permission from Fred Talker to refer to his talk.

70. Fred Talker.

71. Harvey Leon Gardner, interview by Matthew Heiss, Page, Arizona, May 1, 1992, OH 1225, LDS Church Archives.

72. Edwin Tano, interview by Farina King, January 13, 2013, telephone communication, transcription in author's possession.

73. LDS Church officials established the Polynesian Cultural Center, employing Polynesian students from the Church College of Hawai'i (later renamed Brigham Young University-Hawaii). See Craig Ferre, "A History of the Polynesian Cultural Center's 'Night Show,' 1963–1983," PhD diss. (Brigham Young University, 1988); and Aikau, "In the Service of the Lord: Religion, Race, and the Polynesian Cultural Center," in *A Chosen People, A Promised Land*, 123–56.

74. Tano interview, 2013.

75. See Sarah Begay of Tuba City, "Dear Editor: Thank you, Coach Ed Tano," *Navajo-Hopi Observer*, published December 14, 2006, accessed October 11, 2016, http://m.nhonews.com/news/2006/dec/26/thank-you-coach-ed-tano/. Sarah Begay thanks Tano for "being a male role model (being there) to help guide [her son] down the right path" as his football coach at Greyhills Academy High School in Tuba City, Arizona. In 2016, Tano was the Dean of Students at Greyhills Academy High School.

76. Chinle and Tuba City became the first and only two centers of LDS stakes on the Navajo Reservation. Tano was appointed the first president of each of these stakes.

77. Edwin I. Tano cited by Ruth Ann Brown McCombs, Chinle Stake Annual Report, 1992, LDS Church History Library, used by permission.

78. Edwin I. Tano, interview by Matthew Heiss, Kayenta, Arizona, May 4, 1991, OH 1073, LDS Church Archives.

79. Chinle Stake Annual Report, 1992, LDS Church Archives.

80. Tano interview, 1991.

81. Personal conversations with my father, Phillip L. Smith, who is the bishop of the Monument Valley Ward on the Navajo Reservation as of June 2018. My father's congregation was recently transferred to a predominately Navajo stake, the Tuba City Stake, from a predominantly white stake in San Juan County, Utah. See Romero Brown, interview with Farina King, February 17, 2008, St. Michaels, Arizona, 9, LDS NAOHP.

82. See Matthew Garrett, *Making Lamanites*.

83. Mitchell Davis Kapuni Kalauli, interview by Matthew Heiss, Tuba City, Arizona, April 28, 1992, OH 1524, LDS Church Archives.

84. Dan K. Smith, interview by Matthew Heiss, Chinle, Arizona, April 30, 1992, OH 1609, LDS Church Archives.

85. Victor Black (pseudonym because of interviewee's request), interview by Farina King, Tuba City, Arizona, April 21, 2012, LDS NAOHP.

86. Edwin Tano, email correspondence with author, November 11, 2013.
87. Harvey Gardner cited by Edwin Tano, email correspondence with author, November 14, 2013.
88. Tano email, November 11, 2013.
89. Iese interview.

Chapter 9

1. Jay H. Buckley, associate professor of history at Brigham Young University and Native American Studies minor coordinator, is grateful to BYU student co-authors Taylor Brooks, Kathryn Cochran, and Kristen Hollist; as well as student researchers Dylan Beazer and Rosemary Larkin. Since no published Northern Indian Mission history exists, this initial mission history conveys the viewpoints of mission presidents, missionaries, and Native converts. I thank Rex C. Reeve Jr., for entrusting me to donate his Northern Indian Mission collection to BYU's L. Tom Special Collections and for John M. Murphy cataloguing it and making it available to the public. The Charles Redd Center for Western Studies has shown tremendous support throughout. Thanks, too, for helpful reviewer comments from James Allen, John Alley, Erika Bsumek, Jessie Embry, Jane Hafen, Farina King, Warren Metcalf, Jeff Nokes, Rex Reeve, Brenden Rensink, and outside reviewers.
2. Rex C. Reeve Jr., "Message from President Reeve," *The Lamanite* (January 1972), Rex C. Reeve Jr., Northern Indian Mission Collection, Box 1, MSS 8816, L. Tom Perry Special Collections, Harold B. Lee Library, Brigham Young University, Provo, Utah.
3. Darrell Jensen, interview by Taylor Brooks, May 14, 2013.
4. Elise Boxer, "'To Become White and Delightsome': American Indians and Mormon Identity," PhD diss. (Arizona State University, 2009); David J. Whittaker, "Mormons and Native Americans: A Historical and Bibliographical Introduction," *Dialogue: A Journal of Mormon Thought* 18 (Winter 1985): 33–64.
5. Genesis 49:22 described Joseph as "a fruitful bough, even a fruitful bough by a well; whose branches run over the wall," indicating to Latter-day Saints that the Book of Mormon chronicled God's dealings with the tribe of Joseph in America just like the Bible chronicled God's dealings with the tribe of Judah in the Holy Land (Ezekiel 37:16–19; John 10:16). Larry Echo Hawk (Pawnee), an LDS General Authority, recently delivered a worldwide address on this theme. Larry Echo Hawk, "Come Unto Me, O Ye House of Israel," *Ensign* (November 2012), 32. A scripture from the Book of Mormon, 2 Nephi 9:2, reinforces this notion of the Abrahamic Covenant and being gathered home to lands of their inheritance.
6. Doctrine and Covenants 49:24.
7. For an example of the MTC curriculum, see "Culture for Missionaries: Sioux Indian," (Salt Lake City: The Church of Jesus Christ of Latter-day Saints, 1984).

8. Jay Smith, interview by Kristen Hollist, September 29, 2016.

9. 2 Nephi 30:5–6, *The Book of Mormon: Another Testament of Jesus Christ*. Elder Larry Echo Hawk, a Pawnee LDS general authority put it this way: "On the title page I read that it is 'written to the Lamanites, who are a remnant of the house of Israel; and also to Jew and Gentile.' In the introduction of the Book of Mormon: Another Testament of Jesus Christ, it says that the Lamanites are 'among the ancestors of the American Indians.' As I read the Book of Mormon, it seemed to me that it was about my American Indian ancestors." Larry Echo Hawk, "Come Unto Me, O Ye House of Israel," *Ensign* (November 2012), 32. For a discussion of the notion of Lamanite identity see: Michael R. Ash, "Lamanite Identity and the Book of Mormon," *Shaken Faith Syndrome: Strengthening One's Testimony in the Face of Criticism and Doubt* (2nd ed., Redding, CA: FairMormon, 2013), 195–207; John-Charles Duffy, "The Use of 'Lamanite' in Official LDS Discourse," *Journal of Mormon History* 34, no. 1 (Winter 2008): 118–67; Brent L. Metcalfe, Reinventing Lamanite Identity," *Sunstone* 131 (March 2004): 20–25; John A. Tvedtnes, "Reinventing the Book of Mormon," *Mormon Studies Review* 16, no. 2 (2004): 91–106.

10. According to the Book of Mormon, Jesus Christ led the first mission to the Americas (some of his other sheep spoken of in KJV John 10:16) with his visitation and ministry to the American Indians after his resurrection, recorded in 3 Nephi, the entire population of the land became converted and intertribal peace lasted several hundred years before factionalism and apostasy returned. In May 1830, the US Congress created a permanent Indian Territory in the present states of Nebraska, Kansas, and Oklahoma through the passage of the Indian Removal Act. A number of publications address this first LDS Indian Mission. Some of the more important include: *The Joseph Smith Papers: Documents*, vol. 1 (July 1828–June 1831), edited by Michael H. MacKay and Grant Underwood, et al. (Salt Lake City: The Church Historian's Press, 2013), 197–205, 268–73, 290–96. Leland H. Gentry "Light on the 'Mission to the Lamanites,'" *Brigham Young University Studies* 36 no. 2 (1996–97): 226–34; Warren A. Jennings, "The First Mormon Mission to the Indians," *Kansas Historical Quarterly* 37 (August 1971): 288–99; Max H. Parkin, "Lamanite Mission of 1830–31," *Encyclopedia of Mormonism*, 802–4; Keith Parry, "Joseph Smith and the Clash of Sacred Cultures," *Dialogue: A Journal of Mormon Thought* 18 (Winter 1985): 65–80; Ronald E. Romig, "The [1831] Lamanite Mission," *John Whitmer Historical Association Journal* 14 (1994): 25–33; Grant Underwood, "The Mission to the Lamanites," in *Joseph: Exploring the Life and Ministry of the Prophet*, eds. Susan Easton Black and Andrew Skinner, (Salt Lake City: Deseret Book, 2005): 144–55; Ron Walker, "Seeking the 'Remnant': The Native American During the Joseph Smith Period," *Journal of Mormon History* 19, no. 1 (Spring 1993): 1–33. Other sources on Indian missions include: Danny L. Jorgensen, "Building the Kingdom of God: Alpheus Cutler and the Second Mormon Mission to the Indians, 1846–1853," *Kansas History* 15 (Autumn 1992): 192–209; Henry W. Miller, "Missionaries of the Latter-day Saints Church in

Indian Territory," *Chronicles of Oklahoma* 13 (June 1935): 196–213; Emma R. Olsen, compiler, "Mission to the Indians," *An Enduring Legacy* 12 (1989): 353–400. For an alternative view, see Smith's directive to Brigham Young to preach to the Indians, March 12, 1835, *The Joseph Smith Papers: Documents*, vol. 4 (April 1834–September 1835), edited by Matthew C. Godfrey and Brenden W. Rensink, et al., (Salt Lake City: The Church Historian's Press, 2016), 287–89.

11. Parley P. Pratt, *Autobiography of Parley P. Pratt* (Salt Lake City: Deseret Book, 1963), 54–55; (Doctrine and Covenants 28:8; 32:1–3).

12. Missions included those in Indian Territory, as well as throughout the Intermountain West. Howard A. Christy, "Mormon-Indian Relations," in *Mapping Mormonism: An Atlas of Latter-day Saint History*, edited by Brandon S. Plewe (2nd ed., Provo: BYU Studies, 2014), 98–101. Elder Wilford Woodruff said on January 12, 1873: "The Lamanites will blossom as the rose on the mountains. I am willing to say here that, though I believe this, when I see the power of the nation destroying them from the face of the earth, the fulfillment of that prophecy is perhaps harder for me to believe than any revelation of God that I ever read. It looks as though there would not be enough left to receive the Gospel; but notwithstanding this dark picture, every word that God has ever said of them will have its fulfillment, and they, by and by, will receive the Gospel." Wilford Woodruff in *Journal of Discourses* (Liverpool: F. D. Richards, 1855–1886), 15:282.

13. Church leaders faced persecution and prosecution from congressional legislation and federal officials, a protracted battle for Utah statehood (granted in 1896), and endeavored to incorporate within the American mainstream during this awkward transitional period of Mormon history. Thomas G. Alexander, *Mormonism in Transition: A History of the Latter-Day Saints, 1890–1930* (Urbana: University of Illinois Press, 1986); Charles S. Peterson and Brian Q. Cannon, *The Awkward State of Utah: Coming of Age in the Nation, 1896–1945* (Salt Lake City: University of Utah Press/Utah State Historical Society, 2016). The Bureau of Indian Affairs assigned Protestant and Catholic denominations to almost all Indian reservations but refused to grant Latter-day Saints access to any. Francis P. Prucha, *The Great Father: The United States Government and the American Indians*, 2 vols. (Lincoln: University of Nebraska Press, 1984), 524–27. The following Church groups operated among the following reservation agencies: Methodists (Blackfeet; Milk River, Crow); Episcopalians (Shoshone and Bannock; Fort Berthold; Cheyenne River; Upper Missouri; Whetstone; Yankton; Ponca); Catholic (Devil's Lake; Grand River); Congregational (Leech Lake); Society of Friends (Santee Sioux; Omaha); American Board (Sisseton). Francis P. Prucha, *Atlas of American Indian Affairs* (Lincoln: University of Nebraska Press, 1990), 59.

14. The Church in the SWIM grew from 94 Native converts in 1945 to 4,600 Native Latter-day Saints in 1955, with 15 chapels and 10 branches, some presided over by Native men and women. The mission established Mutual Improvement Associations for the youth, Sunday schools, primary children's

groups, and female Relief Societies. Doyle L. Green, "The Southwest Indian Mission," *The Improvement Era*, April 1955, 233–34; David Kay Flake, "History of Southwest Indian Mission, 1965."

15. Douglas Baird (son of Edwin Baird), correspondence with author, June 2, 2015.

16. Missionaries began proselyting on the following reservations: Fort Peck (MT); Northern Cheyenne/Crow (MT); Wind River (WY); Fort Berthold (ND); Turtle Mountain (ND); Fort Totten (ND); Standing Rock (ND); Cheyenne River (SD); Pine Ridge (SD); Rosebud (SD); Crow Creek (SD), as well as others in Minnesota and Nebraska.

17. Rex C. Reeve Jr., "Tribute to the Northern Indian Mission," Northern Indian Mission Collection, Box 2, MSS 8816.

18. "Quarterly Historical Report for the Northern Indian Mission" (for the three months ending June 30, 1964). *Manuscript History and Historical Reports*. Microfilm, Church History Library, Salt Lake City.

19. Rex C. Reeve Jr., "Tribute," 1–2, Northern Indian Mission Collection, Box 2, MSS 8816. Some of the first LDS Native converts in the area occurred in the early 1900s with Sitting Eagle and Chief Moses White Horse joined the Church and helped establish the Sully Lake branch on the Fort Berthold Reservation. The construction of the Garrison Dam on the Missouri River buried the LDS Church building under Lake Sakakawea. R. Janet Kruckenberg, "The Church in the Dakotas," *Church News*, November 30, 1996.

20. Rex C. Reeve Jr., "Tribute," 2, Northern Indian Mission Collection, Box 2, MSS 8816.

21. Clarence R. Bishop, "Indian Placement: A History of the Indian Placement Program of the Church of Jesus Christ of Latter-day Saints," MA thesis, (University of Utah, 1967), 12; George L. Scott, "Lamanites Teach One Another," *Deseret News*, January 14, 1967, 9.

22. Keith Parr, "'To Raise These People Up': An Examination of a Mormon Mission to an Indian Community as an Agent of Social Change," PhD diss. (University of Rochester, 1972); Edward B. Preece, "Mormon Missionary Work among the Indians of North America in the Twentieth Century," L. Tom Perry Special Collections, Harold B. Lee Library, Provo, Utah, 1965.

23. Rex C. Reeve Jr., "Tribute," 2, Northern Indian Mission Collection, Box 2, MSS 8816.

24. Rex C. Reeve Jr., "Grant Farmer as President, 1964–1967," Rex C. Reeve Jr., Northern Indian Mission Collection, Box 2, MSS 8816.

25. Reeve Jr., "Grant Farmer as President, 1964–1967," 2, Rex C. Reeve Jr., Northern Indian Mission Collection, Box 2, MSS 8816.

26. Reeve Jr., "Grant Farmer as President, 1964–1967," 2–3, Rex C. Reeve Jr., Northern Indian Mission Collection, Box 2; Charles T. Powers, "The Indian Today: One Leader Has the Answer," *Deseret News*, May 8, 1968, A19.

27. "Indian Tribal Leaders See Church in Action," *Deseret News*, July 29, 1967, 10. Many tribal leaders expressed they would like to see the same types of programs and opportunities among their people. Reeve Jr., "Grant Farmer as

President, 1964–1967," 7, Rex C. Reeve Jr., Northern Indian Mission Collection, Box 2, MSS 8816.

28. Spencer W. Kimball articulated his thoughts on the term *Lamanite*: "The Indian is a Lamanite. There are South American, Central American, Mexican, Polynesian and other Lamanites, running into millions. Many are not specifically called 'Indians,' though they are related [to] Lamanites.... This [Lamanite] is an honorable name. It was the Lord who so designated them, and every descendent of Lehi should proudly say, 'I am a Lamanite, and I am proud of my heritage.'" Spencer W. Kimball, "The Lamanite: Their Burden, Our Burden," address given to BYU Student body, April 25, 1967, in *The Lamanites: In the Words of the Prophets*, edited by John R. Maestes and Jeff Simons (Provo: Brigham Young University, 1980). During Kimball's tenure, discourse about Lamanites was emphasized and disseminated more than at any other time in LDS history. Within this discourse, "Lamanites" were broadly defined as Native Americans in both North and South America, as well as the Natives in the Pacific Islands. See Melvin A. Lyman, *Out of Obscurity into Light* (Salt Lake City: Albany Book, 1985); Eugene England, "'Lamanites' and the Spirit of the Lord," *Dialogue: A Journal of Mormon Thought* 18, no. 4 (Winter 1985): 25–32.

29. *The Lamanite*, May 1965, Northern Indian Mission Collection, MSS 8816.

30. Grant R. Farmer to Northern Indian Mission Missionaries, January 1965, *The Lamanite*, Harold B. Lee Library Special Collections, Provo,

31. John Lines, interview by author, May 30, 2013. Elder Lines played the trombone and toured the mission with the band.

32. Alvin Watchman and Edna Crane Watchman, "Finding Destiny through the Holy Ghost," in *The Blossoming: Dramatic Accounts in the Lives of Native Americans in the Foster Care Program of the Church of Jesus Christ of Latter-day Saints*, edited by Dale and Margene Shumway (Dale and Margene Shumway, 2002): 203–8, esp. 206–7.

33. Donald and Mary Jane Otter Robe Pine biographies in *The Blossoming II: Dramatic Accounts in the Lives of Native Americans*, edited by Dale and Margene Shumway (Dale and Margene Shumway, 2007): 82–101, esp. 90.

34. "Work Among Indians Pleases Authorities," *Deseret News*, July 8, 1967, 11.

35. George L. Scott, "Lamanites Teach One Another," *Deseret News*, January 14, 1967, 9.

36. Rex C. Reeve Jr., "Tribute," 2, Northern Indian Mission Collection, Box 2, MSS 8816.

37. "The Mission President is a Cowboy's Cowboy." *The Deseret News*, May 10, 1969, 5.

38. R. Janet Kruckenberg, "The Church in the Dakotas," *Church News*, November 30, 1996.

39. Harvey Dahl, "President's Message, March 1969," Rex C. Reeve Jr., Northern Indian Mission Collection, Box 2, MSS 8816.

40. "We would go into an area to get set up and find a place that we could hold meetings. We would rent a building or a room or basement somewhere.

And, then we would start from scratch. We would contact the local newspaper, let them know what we were doing, and get some publicity on our activities and our service projects. If we had a Polynesian show, we would do a big luau: dig a pit and put several pigs in it. You could feed the whole community really or at least as many as would come out. They would perform, and we got some recognition with that, it helped draw in people to want to come to church." Dean Jensen, interview by Kristen Hollist, September 28, 2016.

41. Linda Uranga, interview conducted by Kristen Hollist, October 4, 2016.

42. Jay Smith, interview conducted by Kristen Hollist, September 29, 2016.

43. Elder Randy DeMars, interview conducted by Taylor Brooks, May 24, 2013; Reeve, interview by author, June 12, 2013.

44. Roy Montclair and Charla Roberts Montclair, "The Saga of an Honest Sioux Lawyer," in *The Blossoming: Dramatic Accounts in the Lives of Native Americans in the Foster Care Program of the Church of Jesus Christ of Latter-day Saints*, edited by Dale and Margene Shumway (Dale and Margene Shumway, 2002): 209–17, esp. 210.

45. Flora Jane Dude Shorten biography, in *The Blossoming II: Dramatic Accounts in the Lives of Native Americans*, edited by Dale and Margene Shumway (Dale and Margene Shumway, 2007): 42–52, esp. 48.

46. Harvey Dahl, "President's Message," March 1969, Northern Indian Mission Collection, Box 2, MSS 8816.

47. Reeve Jr., "North Central State District Evaluation, 1967–1968," 2, Northern Indian Mission Collection, Box 2, MSS 8816. See also, "Elders Assist in Bringing Water to Indian Land," *Deseret News*, December 18, 1971.

48. Reeve Jr., "North Central State District Evaluation, 1967–1968" 2, Northern Indian Mission Collection, Box 2, MSS 8816.

49. Elder and Sister Anderson, "Farm Projects," Rex C. Reeve Jr., Northern Indian Mission Collection, Box 2, MSS 8816.

50. Webb, "American Indian Education Program at Brigham Young University," 66.

51. "Elders Five Mission Tour," 1969, Rex C. Reeve Jr., Northern Indian Mission Collection, Box 2, MSS 8816.

52. Dahl, "President's Message," 1, Northern Indian Mission Collection, Box 2, MSS 8816.

53. For discussion of the Indian seminary program see: *The Church of Jesus Christ of Latter-day Saints Indian Seminary Program, Manual of Instructions* (Provo: Department of Education, Brigham Young University, 1961). Reeve noted that one year they rented a camping area in the Black Hills and held a weekend there as a final thank-you for the youth missionaries. After playing games and enjoying good food, they held a testimony meeting, wherein a sweet spiritual feeling overcame him. "As I was sitting there ... I had the distinct feeling Father Lehi was there. I knew exactly where he was, I didn't ever see him but I knew he was there, and I knew he was pleased ... to hear some of his grandkids bear witness of the Lord and the gospel.... The feeling was so strong. I knew he was there enjoying those testimonies." Rex C. Reeve Jr., interview by author, June 12, 2013.

54. For information on the LDS Indian Placement Program, see Megan Stanton, herein; Matthew Garrett, *Making Lamanites: Mormons, Native Americans, and the Indian Student Placement Program, 1947–2000* (Salt Lake City: University of Utah Press, 2016); James B. Allen, "The Rise and Decline of the LDS Indian Student Placement Program, 1947–1996," in *Mormons, Scripture, and the Ancient World: Studies in Honor of John L. Sorenson,* David Bitton, ed., (Provo, UT: Foundation for Ancient Research and Mormon Studies, 1998), 85–119; Clarence R. Bishop, "Indian Placement: A History of the Indian Placement Program of the Church of Jesus Christ of Latter-day Saints," MA thesis (University of Utah, 1967); J. Neil Birth, "Helen John: The Beginnings of Indian Placement," *Dialogue: A Journal of Mormon Thought* 18 (Winter 1985):119–29; Elise Boxer, "The Lamanites Shall Blossom as the Rose": The Indian Student Placement Program, Mormon Whiteness, and Indigenous Identity," *Journal of Mormon History* 41, no. 4 (October 2015): 132–76; Tona J. Hangen, "A Place to Call Home: Studying the Indian Placement Program," *Dialogue: A Journal of Mormon Thought* 30 (1997): 53–69; Brandon Morgan, "Educating the Lamanites: A Brief History of the LDS Indian Student Placement Program," *Journal of Mormon History* 35, no. 4 (Fall 2009): 191–217.

55. "The Placement Program: How Interested Families Can Help," *The Ensign,* August 1972. Jessie Embry, "Indian Placement Program Host Families: A Mission to the Lamanites," *Journal of Mormon History* 40, no. 2 (Spring 2014): 235–76.

56. Duffy, "Lamanite," 139.

57. Spencer W. Kimball served as an apostle from 1943 to 1973 and as the twelfth President of the Church from 1973 to 1985. Edward L. Kimball and Andrew E. Kimball Jr., "Apostle to the Indians" in *Spencer W. Kimball: The Early and Apostolic Years* (Salt Lake City: Deseret Book, 1977): 236. Elder LeGrand Richards recalled "when President George Albert Smith became the President of the Church, one of the things that he said to me was, 'Bishop, I don't think Father Lehi is going to be satisfied with the way we've neglected his posterity.' And he appointed Brother Kimball to do the work with the Indians. I served on his committee and I don't think any man in the church has ever been more devoted to a calling than Brother Kimball has been from that day on." LeGrand Richards, interview, Winter 1980, quoted in Edward L. Kimball, "Spencer W. Kimball and the Lamanite Cause," *Brigham Young University Studies* 25, no. 4 (Fall 1985): 73–76.

58. Mentioned in "Culture for Missionaries: Sioux Indian," (Salt Lake City: The Church of Jesus Christ of Latter-day Saints, 1984), 110.

59. Many Church leaders such as David O. McKay, Joseph Fielding Smith, Hugh B. Brown, Gordon B. Hinckley, Mark E. Peterson, and Boyd K. Packer supported these same views of Lamanite identification. See, for example, Mark E. Petersen, *Children of the Promise: The Lamanites, Yesterday and Today* (Salt Lake City: Bookcraft, 1981). In 1981, Bruce R. McConkie's new introduction to the Book of Mormon asserted that the Lamanites are *among* "the principal ancestors of the

American Indians." This lineage-based identification has largely been replaced
by the more inclusive invitation for all to come unto Christ.

60. Armand L. Mauss, "Mormonism's Worldwide Aspirations and its Changing
Conceptions of Race and Lineage," *Dialogue: A Journal of Mormon Thought*, 34,
no. 3 and 4 (Fall–Winter 2001), 116. Mauss, *All Abraham's Children: Changing
Mormon Conceptions of Race and Lineage* (Urbana: University of Illinois Press,
2003).

61. Megan Stanton, herein.

62. Ernest L. Wilkinson, a future Brigham Young University president, provided
legal counsel for Utes, Paiutes and other nations seeking compensation through
the Indian Claims Commission. Arthur V. Watkins, a Latter-day Saint serving
as chair of the Senate Subcommittee on Indian Affairs was a proponent of
House Concurrent Resolution 108, terminating federal recognition of Indian
Nations. Secretary of Interior Stewart Udall, another Latter-day Saint, played a
significant role in ending termination, promoting the self-determination policy
adopted by Nixon's administration as well as restitution of federal recognition
for some terminated tribes.

63. "Indians Plan to March Against Mormon Event," *Los Angeles Times*, April 8,
1973; "Locked Gates Meet March on Temple," *Salt Lake Tribune*, April 9, 1973;
"Indians Ask for $1 Million Annually," *Los Angeles Times*, April 9, 1973; The
Church of Jesus Christ of Latter-day Saints, "Press Release: Statement on Indi-
ans, April 8, 1973," Armand Mauss Papers, Utah State Historical Society, Salt
Lake City, Utah.

64. Stanley Snake (Winnebago) an LDS student at BYU and the son of AIM
leader Reuben Snake, was elected president of the National Indian Youth
Council in 1972 and saw himself "as a buffer between the Mormon Church and
certain segments of the Red Power movement." Dennis Banks, Scott Momaday,
and others even came to speak at BYU. "Stanley Snake elected NIYC President," *Eagle's Eye* 2, no. 5 (March 1972). George P. Castile, *To Show Heart: Native
American Self-Determination and Federal Indian Policy, 1960–1975* (Tucson: University of Arizona Press, 1998).

65. Boyd K. Packer, called as an LDS apostle in 1970, wrote his 1962 dissertation
on the "Manual of Policies and Procedures for the Administration of the
Indian Seminaries of The Church of Jesus Christ of Latter-day Saints," PhD
diss. (Brigham Young University, 1962). Meanwhile, efforts to develop Indian
youth into effective tribal leaders resulted in publications like: "The Church of
Jesus Christ of Latter-day Saints, 'Indian Leadership Program to Salvation,'"
(undated manuscript), copy from the Northern Indian Mission in the Harold B. Lee Library.

66. Bruce C. Chadwick and Stan L. Albrecht, "Mormons and Indians: Beliefs,
Policies, Programs, and Practices," in *Contemporary Mormonism: Social Science
Perspectives*, edited by Marie Cornwall, Tim B. Heaton, and Lawrence A. Young
(Urbana: University of Chicago Press, 1994): 287–309, quote from 291; For the
role of Dale Tingey with AIS, see John P. Livingstone, *Same Drum, Different*

Beat: The Story of Dale T. Tingey and American Indian Services (Provo: Religious Studies Center, 2003): 79–92; Melvin A. Lyman, *Out of Obscurity into Light* (Salt Lake City: Albany Book, 1985): 194–205.

67. L. Robert Webb, "An Examination of Certain Aspects of the American Indian Education Program at Brigham Young University," (Provo: Brigham Young University, February 1972); Ernest L. Wilkinson and Lenard J. Arrington, eds., "Education of Native Americans," in *Brigham Young University: The First One Hundred Years* (Provo: Brigham Young University Press, 1976), 3:503–35; Virgus C. Osborne, "Indian Education at Brigham young University, 1965–1985," unpublished manuscript, 1993, L. Tom Perry Special Collections, Harold B. Lee Library, Provo, Utah.

68. Native Americans employed by BYU's Department of Indian Education in 1973 included Dr. John R. Maestas (Tewa Pueblo), Dr. Janice White Clemmer (Wasco-Shawnee-Delaware), Kenneth Sekaquaptewa (Hopi), Darlene Monteaux Herndon Oliver (Rosebud Lakota), Howard Rainer (Taos/Tewa) and John R. Rainer Jr. (Taos-Muscogee/Creek). Janice White Clemmer, "Native American Studies: A Utah Perspective," *Wicazo Sa Review* 2, no. 2 (1986): 17–23.

69. Virgus C. Osborne, "An Appraisal of the Education Program for Native Americans at Brigham Young University, 1966–1974," PhD diss. (University of Utah, 1975), 60–61.

70. Lynne Hollisten, "Indian Education at BYU is finest in U.S.," *Deseret News*, June 4, 1977.

71. Mark Stevens, "Utah University Gives American Indians a Chance to Learn," *Christian Science Monitor*, February 25, 1980.

72. Arlene Nofchissey Williams (Navajo) and Carnes Burson (Ute), *Go My Son*, audio recording, Provo, Utah: Blue Eagle Records, 1970. P. Jane Hafen, "'Great Spirit Listen': The American Indian in Mormon Music," *Dialogue: A Journal of Mormon Thought* 18 (Winter 1985): 133–42, esp. 140–41.

73. "Elders Five," 1969, Northern Indian Mission Collection, Box 2, MSS 8816.

74. "The Indians and the Mormon Pioneers," *Relief Society Bulletin* 2, no. 2 (February 1967), Northern Indian Mission Collection, Box 2, MSS 8816.

75. Kenneth W. Finlinson letter to Rex C. Reeve, November 7, 1968, Northern Indian Mission Collection, Box 2, MSS 8816.

76. Nathan Halfe, *The Lamanite* 3, no. 3 (March 1966).

77. Edouardo Zendejas interview by Malcolm T. Pappan on April 7, 1990, *Oral History Transcript*, 3, Charles Redd Center for Western Studies, L. Tom Perry Special Collections, Harold B. Lee Library, Provo, Utah.

78. Donna Fifita interview by Odessa Neamen on June 5, 1990, *Oral History Transcript*, 7, Charles Redd Center for Western Studies, L. Tom Perry Special Collections, Harold B. Lee Library, Provo, Utah.

79. Donna Fifita interview by Odessa Neamen on June 5, 1990, *Oral History Transcript*, 10.

80. Harvey A. Dahl, "President's Page," 1969, Northern Indian Mission Collection, Box 2, MSS 8816.

81. Dahl, "President's Page," 1969, Northern Indian Mission Collection, Box 2, MSS 8816.

82. Roy Montclair and Charla Roberts Montclair, "The Saga of an Honest Sioux Lawyer," in *The Blossoming: Dramatic Accounts in the Lives of Native Americans in the Foster Care Program of the Church of Jesus Christ of Latter-day Saints*, edited by Dale and Margene Shumway (Dale and Margene Shumway, 2002): 211. Montclair later served in the Arizona-Holbrook Mission. He attended BYU, received a law degree, and worked for Dale Tingey at BYU's Institute of American Indian Services. Montclair said of his educational experiences, "I empowered myself with knowledge." He continued, "My sister and I were the only ones of us five siblings to stick with the Placement program, graduate from high school, and attend college. So I am extremely grateful to those 2 elders who came to our home over 30 years ago and the 3 foster families who helped me along the way." Ibid., 216.

83. Flora Jane Dude Shorten biography, in *The Blossoming II: Dramatic Accounts in the Lives of Native Americans*, edited by Dale and Margene Shumway (Dale and Margene Shumway, 2007): 42–52, esp. 44.

84. Elise Boxer, "The Lamanites Shall Blossom as the Rose," 135.

85. Donna Gill Sitake, interview by Kristen Hollist, October 3, 2016. Gill Sitake participated in the Lamanite Young Conference, served a youth mission, and attended BYU before serving a mission to Louisiana Baton Rouge. Then, through a miraculous series of events, she was transferred to serve in the Northern Indian Mission.

86. Marie Sandoval Little, interview by author, October 3, 2016.

87. Linda Uranga, interview conducted by Kristen Hollist, October 4, 2016.

88. "A Message to the Relief Society" *The Lamanite* (November 1969), Northern Indian Mission Collection, Box 1, MSS 8816.

89. Verna S. Carter, "A Family Tree," Relief Society Bulletin 1, no. 2 (April 1966), Northern Indian Mission Collection, Box 1, MSS 8816.

90. Rex E. Reeve Jr., "Northern Indian Mission Scrapbook, 1964–1972," microfilm, Church History Library, Salt Lake City.

91. "History," Rex C. Reeve Jr., Northern Indian Mission Collection, Box 2, MSS 8816.

92. Kenneth W. Finlinson, "A Synopsis of the Relationships and Acceptance of the Seminary Program by School Administration, Community, and Tribal Officials, Year End Analysis: High Line District, 1967–68," 2, Rex C. Reeve Jr., Northern Indian Mission Collection, Box 2, MSS 8816. For a similar objective among Mexican immigrants, see, George J. Sanchez, "Go After the Women: Americanization and the Mexican Immigrant Woman, 1915–1929," in *Mothers and Motherhood: Readings in American History*, edited by Rima D. Apple and Janet Golden (Columbus: Ohio State University Press, 1997), 475–94.

93. "Evaluation of the Pine Ridge Indian Seminary, 1966–68," 1, Northern Indian Mission Collection, Box 2, MSS 8816.

94. Thomas, "Evaluation of the Indian Seminary Program," 2, Northern Indian Mission Collection, Box 2, MSS 8816.

95. Thomas, "Evaluation of the Indian Seminary Program," 5, Northern Indian Mission Collection, Box 2, MSS 8816.

96. "Pine Ridge Indian Seminary," 1, Northern Indian Mission Collection, Box 2, MSS 8816.

97. Thomas, "Evaluation of the Indian Seminary Program," 1, Northern Indian Mission Collection, Box 2, MSS 8816; "An Evaluation of the Indian Seminary Program for the School Year 1967–1968," Rex C. Reeve Jr., Northern Indian Mission Collection, Box 2, MSS 8816.

98. Finlinson, "A Synopsis," 2, Northern Indian Mission Collection, Box 2, MSS 8816.

99. Rex C. Reeve Jr., "A Lamanite Dedicated to His Fellow Man," 1969, Northern Indian Mission Collection, Box 2, MSS 8816.

100. Rex C. Reeve Jr., *The Lamanite* 8, no 9, (September 1971), Northern Indian Mission Collection, Box 1, MSS 8816.

101. Donald and Mary Jane Otter Robe Pine biographies in *The Blossoming II: Dramatic Accounts in the Lives of Native Americans*, edited by Dale and Margene Shumway (Dale and Margene Shumway, 2007): 82–101, esp. 94.

102. Buck Thomas to Rex Reeve, November 3, 1968, Northern Indian Mission Collection, Box 2, MSS 8816.

103. *The Lamanite*, 2, no. 5 (May 1965), Rex C. Reeve Jr., Northern Indian Mission Collection, Box 1, MSS 8816.

104. James D. Mathews, "Three Thousand Honor LDS Church (1969)," Northern Indian Mission Collection, Box 2, MSS 8816.

105. Sometimes, tribal councils could be very helpful. Victor Scarpino recalled that at 6:00 a.m. in the morning, someone knocked on his door. The tribal council president told him to get in the car. "We have gone around our reservation, and we have picked out five different locations. We would like you to look at them." He picked out the spot he thought best on a little knoll. They said, "Okay, it's yours if you will talk your Church into building there." And they did. Victor Scarpino, interview by Kristen Hollist, September 27, 2016.

106. Donna Gill Sitake, interview by Kristen Hollist, October 3, 2016.

107. *The Lamanite* (June 1965), Rex C. Reeve Jr., Northern Indian Mission Collection, Box 1, MSS 8816.

108. *The Lamanite* (July 1966), Rex C. Reeve Jr., Northern Indian Mission Collection, Box 1, MSS 8816.

109. Tony Boxer, personal interview, October 3, 2016. Boxer served in the Southwest Indian Mission, attended BYU, married, had five children, and several of his children have earned PhDs. Randy DeMars, interview by Taylor Brooks, May 24, 2013. Elder DeMars helped teach and baptize the Boxer family.

110. Lacee A. Harris, "To Be Native American—and Mormon," *Dialogue: A Journal of Mormon Thought* 18 (Winter 1985): 143–52, esp. 151. For a wonderful account of what is means to be Indigenous and LDS, see P. Jane Hafen, "The Being and Place of a Native American Mormon," in *New Genesis: A Mormon Reader on Land and Community*, edited by Terry Tempest Williams, William B. Smart, and Gibbs M. Smith (Salt Lake City: Gibbs Smith, 1998): 35–41.

111. Andrea Little, *Scrapbook,* 1972. Rex C. Reeve Jr., Northern Indian Mission Col-
      lection, Box 1, MSS 8816.

112. Negotiating this tension between Indian and white worlds is not easy. See,
      P. Jane Hafen, "The Being and Place of a Native American Mormon," in *New
      Genesis: A Mormon Reader on Land and Community,* Terry T. Williams, ed.,
      (Salt Lake City: Gibbs Smith Publisher, 1998): 35–41; Clem Bear Chief,
      "Plucked from the Ashes," *Dialogue: A Journal of Mormon Thought* 25 no. 4
      (1992): 140–49; Lacee A. Harris, "To Be Native American—and Mormon,"
      Dialogue: A Journal of Mormon Thought 18 (Winter 1985): 143–52; Steve Pav-
      lik, "Of Saints and Lamanites: An Analysis of Navajo Mormons," *Wicazo Sa
      Review* 8, no. 1 (Spring 1992): 21–30; Larry Echo Hawk, personal biography,
      in *Why I am a Mormon,* 108–15, edited by Joseph A. Cannon (Stevens Point,
      WI: Worzalla Publishing Company, 2012); Linda Sillitoe, "Who We Are,
      Where We Come From," *Dialogue: A Journal of Mormon Thought* 25 no. 3
      (1992): 9–18.

113. Barbara Reeve, *The Lamanite* 8, no 5 (May 1971), Rex C. Reeve Jr., Northern
      Indian Mission Collection, Box 1, MSS 8816. Northern Indian Mission mem-
      bers and missionaries viewed these occurrences as manifestations of works
      indicative that the LDS faith was having a positive influence in people's lives.

114. R. Janet Kruckenberg, "The Church in the Dakotas," *Church News,* Novem-
      ber 30, 1996.

115. From 1947 to 2000, over 50,000 Indian children left their reservations to live
      with Mormon foster families and attend public schools in a program known
      as the Indian Student Placement Program. Garrett, *Making Lamanites,* intro-
      duction; See also, Alysa Landry, "Assimilation Tool or a Blessing? Inside the
      Mormon Indian Student Placement Program," *Indian Country Today,* January 7,
      2016; Landry, "How Mormons Assimilated Native Children," *Indian Country
      Today,* January 11, 2016; Landry, "From Very Good to Tragic: What the Mor-
      mons Did for Native Children," *Indian Country Today,* January 15, 2016.

116. In 1975, George P. Lee, a full-blooded Navajo and an early ISPP participant,
      was appointed as the first Native General Authority, a position he faithfully
      fulfilled. Over the next decade, he courageously defended the LDS Church and
      this educational program before Native peers and Congress, while detractors
      pointed to the ISPP as another form of colonialism. George P. Lee, *Silent Cour-
      age, an Indian Story: The Autobiography of George P. Lee, a Navajo* (Salt Lake
      City: Deseret Book Co., 1987).

117. John P. Livingstone, "Establishing the Church Simply," *BYU Studies* 39, no. 4
      (2000): 127–60; Jessie L. Embry, "Ethnic Groups and the LDS Church," *Dia-
      logue: A Journal of Mormon Thought* 25 no. 4 (1992): 81–97; Embry, "Speaking
      for Themselves: LDS Ethnic Groups Oral History Project," *Dialogue: A Journal
      of Mormon Thought* 25 no. 4 (1992): 99–110; Embry, "Lamanite Relief Societ-
      ies: The Relief Society and Its Relationship with Native Americans," (paper
      presented at the sesquicentennial Relief Society celebration, Brigham Young
      University, Provo, Utah, 1992).

Chapter 10

1. For comprehensive histories of the Indian Student Placement Program, see Matthew Garrett, *Making Lamanites: Mormons, Native Americans, and the Indian Student Placement Program, 1947–2000* (Salt Lake City: University of Utah Press, 2016); and Lynette A. Riggs, "The Church of Jesus Christ of Latter-day Saints' Indian Student Placement Service: A History," PhD diss. (Utah State University, 2008). Garrett focuses on the Indian students "who internalized the message presented by the LDS Church and foster families" in the placement program and constructed "a new identity" for themselves. The placement program proved integral to their construction of a Lamanite identity (8, 10). Riggs examines the accommodation and resilience of the Indian students in the program.

2. For examples of discussions of the placement program in relation to the Book of Mormon, see Spencer W. Kimball, talk, September 30, 1950, in "One Hundred Twenty-first Semi-Annual Conference of The Church of Jesus Christ of Latter-day Saints, Held in the Tabernacle, Salt Lake City, Utah, September 29, 30, and October 1, 1950, With Report of Discourses" (Salt Lake City: The Church of Jesus Christ of Latter-day Saints, 1950), 69; and Spencer W. Kimball, talk, October 6, 1956, in "One Hundred Twenty-seventh Semi-Annual Conference of The Church of Jesus Christ of Latter-day Saints, Held in the Tabernacle, Salt Lake City, Utah, October 5, 6 and 7, 1956, With Report of Discourses" (Salt Lake City: The Church of Jesus Christ of Latter-day Saints, 1956), 52.

3. For the history of American Indian education, see David Wallace Adams, *Education for Extinction: American Indians and the Boarding School Experience, 1875–1928* (Lawrence: University of Kansas Press, 1995); Margaret D. Jacobs, *White Mother to a Dark Race: Settler Colonialism, Maternalism, and the Removal of Indigenous Children in the American West and Australia, 1880–1940* (Lincoln: University of Nebraska Press, 2009); and Margaret D. Jacobs, *A Generation Removed: The Fostering and Adoption of Indigenous Children in the Postwar World* (Lincoln: University of Nebraska Press, 2014).

4. Lewis Meriam, et al, *The Problem of Indian Administration* (Baltimore: Johns Hopkins Press, 1928), chap. 9; and Spec. Subcomm. on Indian Education, "Indian Education: A National Tragedy—A National Challenge," S. Rep. No. P-91-501 (Washington, DC: US Government Printing Office, 1969), ix, 9–14, 67–71, 89.

5. Peter Iverson, *Diné: A History of the Navajos* (Albuquerque: University of New Mexico Press, 2002), 190–97; S. Rep. No. P-91-501, at 89, 68. The Arizona Employment Security Commission reported their findings about the consequences of Navajo educational access to the 1969 Senate Special Subcommittee on Indian Education. In the commission's work with over 20,000 unemployed Navajo adults, the commission determined that 63 percent had less than a sixth-grade education, resulting in a population in which nearly half of unemployed adults could not speak, write, or read English fluently.

6. For discussions of Helen John, see Clarence R. Bishop, "Indian Placement: A History of the Indian Student Placement Program of The Church of Jesus Christ of Latter-day Saints," (master's thesis, University of Utah, 1967), 30–34, 37; and J. Neil Birch, "Helen John: The Beginnings of Indian Placement," *Dialogue* 18, no. 4: 119–29.

7. For the economy on the Navajo Reservation and the work opportunities available to the Navajo between the 1930s and the 1950s, see Iverson, *Diné*, chap. 5; and Evon Z. Vogt with Malcolm J. Arth, "Intercultural Relations," in *People of Rimrock: A Study of Values in Five Cultures*, ed. Evon Z. Vogt and Ethel M. Albert (Cambridge: Harvard University Press, 1966), 71–72.

8. Edward L. Kimball and Andrew E. Kimball Jr., *Spencer W. Kimball: The Early and Apostolic Years* (1977; Salt Lake City: Deseret Book, 2006), 236; Spencer W. Kimball, "The Navajo ... His Predicament: The First of Two Articles," *The Improvement Era* 51, no. 2 (February 1948): 67–78; and Spencer W. Kimball, "The Navajo ... His Predicament: Part II," *The Improvement Era* 51, no. 4 (April 1948): 210–12, 252–53, 255.

9. Kimball, talk, September 30, 1950, 66.

10. Bishop, "Indian Placement," 43.

11. Ibid., 68n25.

12. Garrett, *Making Lamanites*, 70–72; and Bishop, "Indian Placement," 57–58.

13. Bishop, "Indian Placement," 59–61; and Center for Social Research and Development, "Indian Child Welfare: A State-of-the-Field Study," Denver Research Institute, University of Denver, 1976, 259.

14. Bishop, "Indian Placement," 63; Garrett, *Making Lamanites*, 72–73; and Christopher Reed, "Samuel Billison: Navajo Code Talker Whose Complex Native Language Baffled Wartime Japanese Cryptographers," obituary, *Guardian*, December 6, 2004. Samuel Billison, a WWII Navajo code talker and tribal council member, likely conveyed the concerns of the tribal council in his comments.

15. Bishop, "Indian Placement," 63–64. The increased minimum age for program participation from six to eight meant that all students who participated in the program were old enough to be baptized members of the Church.

16. Ibid., 66; and Garrett, *Making Lamanites*, 80, 79. The Indian Committee had also invited Jones to attend the reception center in 1958, but Billison attended in his stead. For the Indian Adoption Project, sponsored by the Bureau of Indian Affairs and the Child Welfare League from 1958 to 1967, see Steven Unger, "The Indian Child Welfare Act of 1978: A Case Study," (DPA diss., University of Southern California, 2004), 167–85; Jacobs, *A Generation Removed*, 47–50. Jacobs considers the placement program and the Indian Adoption Project to be comparable: "Both programs had the similar goal of changing Indian culture and assimilating Indian people through the removal of Indian children from their families and their placement in non-Indian families."

17. Navajo Tribal Council, "Tribal Policy on Adoption of Navajo Orphans and Abandoned or Neglected Children," in *The Destruction of American Indian Families*, ed. Steven Unger, (New York: Association on American Indian Affairs, 1977), 85–86.

18. Kimball and Kimball, *Spencer W. Kimball*, 321–23; and Bishop, "Indian Placement," 73.

19. Bishop, "Indian Placement," 77–78; and Bruce A. Chadwick, Stan L. Albrecht, and Howard M. Bahr, "Evaluation of an Indian Student Placement Program," *Social Casework: The Journal of Contemporary Social Work* 67, no. 9 (November 1986): 515.

20. Bishop, "Indian Placement," Table 6; and Genevieve De Hoyos and Arturo De Hoyos, "Indian Placement Program of The Church of Jesus Christ of Latter Day Saints: A Statistical and Analytical Study (First Draft)," (unpublished manuscript, Brigham Young University, 1973), 41–42, 56, 58, in Brigham Young University Library (hereafter BYU Library), Provo, Utah. Bishop notes that over 63 percent of the students participating in 1966–1967 were affiliated with the Navajo Nation. De Hoyos and De Hoyos found that Navajo students comprised 48 percent of a random sampling of student files in 1973.

21. De Hoyos and De Hoyos, "Indian Placement Program," 63–64; "North Carolina Lumbee—Not a Real Indian? Edward Clark and Helen Sloan Clark," in *The Blossoming: Dramatic Accounts of the Lives of Native Americans in the Foster Care Program of The Church of Jesus Christ of Latter-day Saints*, ed. Dale Shumway and Margene Shumway (published by the authors, 2002), 179–80; Elise Boxer, "'The Lamanites Shall Blossom as the Rose': The Indian Student Placement Program, Mormon Whiteness, and Indigenous Identity," *Journal of Mormon History* 41, no. 4 (October 2015): 154; and Pat Begay, "The Making of a Mormon Convert," *Navajo Times*, July 27, 1978. De Hoyos and De Hoyos explain that a random sampling of students who graduated from the program or dropped out indicated that anywhere between 26 to 75 percent of parents were not LDS. These numbers are not representative of all placement students; the low 26 percent from the 1955–1959 period included both graduates of the program and those who had dropped out, whereas the high 75 percent from the 1970 data included almost entirely placement students who had dropped out of the program. Most of those students who dropped out in 1970 had parents who were not members of the LDS Church. Edward Clark (Lumbee) recounted his baptism in North Carolina (which occurred in approximately 1962), when missionaries "baptized about 700 Indian children" in a "kiddy dip" without securing parental permission (179). Elise Boxer argues that, in the context of placement, "Baptism was more than just conversion to Mormonism. Baptism represented economic and educational opportunity off the reservation" (154).

22. Bishop, "Indian Placement," 108; Kimball, talk, October 6, 1956, 54–56; Indian Student Placement Program, "Foster Parent Guide," April 1965, BYU Library; Garth L. Mangum and Bruce D. Blumell, *The Mormons' War on Poverty: A History of LDS Welfare, 1830–1990* (Salt Lake City: University of Utah Press, 1993), 194; and Martin D. Topper, "'Mormon Placement': The Effects of Missionary Foster Families on Navajo Adolescents," *Ethos* 7, no. 2 (Summer 1979), 145 (hereafter cited as Topper, "Effects of Missionary Foster Families").

23. Jessie Embry, "Indian Student Placement Program Host Families: A Mission to the Lamanites," *Journal of Mormon History* 40, no. 2 (Spring 2014): 237; Indian

Student Placement Program, "Foster Parent Guide," 4; Bishop, "Indian Placement," 104–5 and Appendix IV: "Foster Home Application."

24. See, for example, Indian Student Placement Program, "Foster Parent Guide"; and Indian Student Placement Service, "Cultural Contrast: A Hand Out, February 1968," unpublished manuscript, 1970, BYU Library. The "Cultural Contrast" document closely follows the publication of James E. Chapman, "A Modest Contrast between Some of the Personal Life-Values of the Utah American Indian, and the Urban Middle-Class Utahn," *Utah Public Welfare Review: Professional Journal of the County Welfare Directors Association of Utah* 1, no. 5 (Summer 1966): 8–12.

25. "Collector Explains Regulations on Missionaries' Contributions," *Salt Lake Times*, February 24, 1961, 8; Indian Student Placement Program, "Foster Parent Guide," 19; and Bishop, "Indian Placement," 74–75. Bishop notes that "concentrated effort on the part of Utah Congressmen" led the federal government to loosen the terms of this tax benefit so that placement foster families might benefit from it (74).

26. Spencer W. Kimball letter to George Albert Smith, August 25, 1949, excerpted in Bishop, "Indian Placement," 37. See also Kimball, talk, September 30, 1950, 67.

27. For a history of legislation against interracial marriage, which was changing by the early 1960s in Utah and other states in the American West in the face of judicial activism and the civil rights movement, see Peggy Pascoe, *What Comes Naturally: Miscegenation Law and the Making of Race in America* (New York: Oxford University Press, 2009), 235, 240–43. For reports of dating (or lack thereof) on the placement program and efforts to increase placement students' access to one another, see "Red and Delightful," *Time* 74, no. 16 (September 7, 1959); "All-Lamanite Youth Conference," *Indian Liahona* 7, no. 4 (July-August 1970): 29–33; "Southwest Indian Mission Youth Conference," *Indian Liahona* 7, no. 6 (November-December 1970): 32; Bishop, "Indian Placement," 70–71; and Spencer W. Kimball letter "to all Indian workers," May 19, 1963, in James D. Mathews, "A Study of the Cultural and Religious Behavior of the Navaho Indians which Caused Animosity, Resistance, or Indifference to the Religious Teachings of the Latter-day Saints," (master's thesis, Brigham Young University, 1968), Appendix.

28. Ione Yellowjohn, interview by Odessa Neaman, March 1, 1990, transcript, LDS Native American Oral History Project, BYU Library.

29. Emery Bowman, interview by Deborah Lewis, January 27, 1990, transcript, LDS Native American Oral History Project, BYU Library. Bowman's interview, and several others used in this chapter, was collected in 1990 and 1991 by the Charles Redd Center for Western Studies under the direction of Jessie L. Embry. For more information about this collection, see Jessie L. Embry, "Speaking for Themselves: LDS Ethnic Groups Oral History Project," *Dialogue* 25, no. 4 (Winter 1992): 99–110.

30. Stephanie Chiquito, interview by Jim M. Dandy, April 11, 1991, transcript, LDS Native American Oral History Project, BYU Library.

31. De Hoyos and De Hoyos, "Indian Placement Program," 68.
32. Indian Student Placement Program, "Foster Parent Guide," 18–19; and "Mormons Use Program to Aid Indian Students," *Garfield County [UT] News*, November 6, 1969: 1.
33. Ione Yellowjohn ("couldn't take care of us"); and Carletta O. Yellowjohn, interview by Odessa Neaman, July 10, 1990, transcript, LDS Native American Oral History Project, BYU Library.
34. George P. Lee, *Silent Courage: An Indian Story* (Salt Lake City: Deseret Book, 1987), 161 ("no Navajo"), 162–67.
35. Topper, "Effects of Missionary Foster Families," 153–58. Topper found that, eventually, 23 of the 25 students rejected the program and refused to continue participating. Most of these rejections occurred during students' high school years.
36. De Hoyos and De Hoyos, "Indian Placement Program," 51, 49, 52; and Chadwick, Albrecht, and Bahr, "Evaluation of an Indian Student Placement Program," 517. De Hoyos and De Hoyos analyzed data across tribal affiliations. Chadwick, Albrecht, and Bahr focused on Indians from the Four Corners region, including the Navajo.
37. Lee, *Silent Courage*, 157, 94–96, 103–4, 119, 207–8, 246–47, 269, 279, 281, 297, 321.
38. Ibid., 343–44.
39. George P. Lee, "My Heritage Is My Choice," *Ensign*, November 1975.
40. Robert Raleigh, "Elder George P. Lee: Navajo General Authority Speaks on Self-Image, Discipline," *Eagle's Eye* 18, no. 2 (Winter 1985–1986): 20–21.
41. See Garrett, *Making Lamanites*, chap. 6.
42. Mabel Yazzie quoted in Beth Wood, "The LDS Indian Placement Program: An Educational System that Works," *Navajo Times*, September 28, 1978: B6, B8 ("Placement"). See also Beth Wood, "LDS Indian Placement Program: To Whose Advantage?" *Akwesasne Notes* 10, no. 5 (Winter 1978): 18.
43. John Benally quoted in Wood, "Educational System that Works," B10. See also Wood, "To Whose Advantage," 18.
44. Chadwick, Albrecht, and Bahr, "Evaluation of an Indian Student Placement Program," 521. This 1981 study was published in 1986.
45. Boxer, "'Lamanites Shall Blossom as the Rose,'" 136 ("a colonizing enterprise"), 139–41.
46. See Brandon Morgan, "Educating the Lamanites: A Brief History of the LDS Indian Student Placement Program," *Journal of Mormon History* 35, no. 4 (Fall 2009): 217.
47. For histories of American Indian activism in the second half of the nineteenth century, see Bradley G. Shreve, *Red Power Rising: The National Indian Youth Council and the Origins of Native Activism* (Norman: University of Oklahoma Press, 2011); Daniel M. Cobb, *Native Activism in Cold War America: The Struggle for Sovereignty* (Lawrence: University Press of Kansas, 2008); and Charles Wilkinson, *Blood Struggle: The Rise of Modern Indian Nations* (New York: W. W. Norton, 2005), esp. 258–61.

48. Martin Topper, "Mormon Placement: Survival Strategy or a Finger in the Dyke?" in "Supportive Care, Custody, Placement and Adoption of American Indian Children: Special Questions and New Answers," American Academy of Child Psychiatry conference proceedings, April 19–22, 1977, Bottle Hollow, UT, ed. Janet P. Swenson, 49, 9 ("some 150"), 50 ("phasing out"), 51 ("an angry"). See also Topper, "Effects of Missionary Foster Families," 143; Select Comm. on Indian Affairs, *Indian Child Welfare Act of 1977: Hearings on S. 1214*, 95th Cong. (1977), Appendix D, 431. Lyle Cooper, the attendee from LDS Social Services at the 1977 conference, also worked with Stewart Durrant, Harold C. Brown, and Bob Barker in proposing changes to the language of the Senate's proposed ICWA legislation.

49. Harold C. Brown, statement, in Select Comm. on Indian Affairs, *Indian Child Welfare Act of 1978*, 212–13; and Robert E. Leach to Maureen Herman, letter and research summary, 15 February 1977, in Select Comm. on Indian Affairs, *Indian Child Welfare Act of 1977*, 435–41. Harold C. Brown, then the LDS Social Services commissioner and a former placement coordinator, complained the following year about the 1976 study taking place without his knowledge in his statement to the Select Committee on Indian Affairs. Leach, the Interstate Compact administrator in South Dakota, characterized the findings of his study, which focused on 50 Indian parents with children placed in Idaho, as "relatively positive" (435).

50. William Byler, "The Destruction of American Indian Families," in *Destruction of American Indian Families*, 1. Byler's chapter was delivered as testimony to the Senate in 1974.

51. See, for example, the 1967 testimony of Daniel J. O'Connell, the executive secretary of the national Committee on Indian Health, and a 1968 publication of psychiatrist Robert Bergman, both of whom spoke out about the negative effects of elementary-age boarding schools on Navajo children and families, in Rep. No. P-91-501, at 67–71.

52. Indian Child Welfare Act of 1978, Pub. L. No. 95-608, 92 Stat. 3069 (1978). Early legal criticism of the law suggested that the final version of ICWA created ambiguities that would limit its effectiveness; see Russel Lawrence Barsh, "The Indian Child Welfare Act of 1978: A Critical Analysis," *Hastings Law Journal* 31 (1979–1980): 1287–88.

53. "Senate Child Welfare Hearings," *Indian Family Defense* 8 (November 1977): 1, 2 ("the only").

54. S. 1214, Rep. No. 95-597, in Select Comm. on Indian Affairs, *Indian Child Welfare Act of 1977*, 7 ("child placement," "voluntary," and "private"), 37 ("the chief"), 206; and Herm Olsen to Patty Marx, memo, October 7, 1977, in Select Comm. on Indian Affairs, *Indian Child Welfare Act of 1977*, 431–32 ("small band").

55. Ibid., 431; "[Proposed] Amendment to Section 4(g) of S. 1214, 95th Congress, 1st Session," in Select Comm. on Indian Affairs, *Indian Child Welfare Act of 1977*, 434 ("temporary residence").

56. Brown, testimony, in Select Comm. on Indian Affairs, *Indian Child Welfare Act of 1977*, 205; and Appendix D, in Select Comm. on Indian Affairs, *Indian*

Child Welfare Act of 1977, 433. Evelyn Blanchard provides a close summary of the hearings in Evelyn Lance Blanchard, "To Prevent the Breakup of the Indian Family: The Development of the Indian Child Welfare Act of 1978," PhD diss. (University of New Mexico, 2010).

57. James B. Allen, "The Rise and Decline of the LDS Indian Student Placement Program, 1947–1996," in *Mormons, Scripture, and the Ancient World: Studies in Honor of John L. Sorenson*, ed. Davis Bitton (Provo, UT: Foundation for Ancient Research and Mormon Studies, 1998), 118n62.

58. Lee, testimony, 195, in Select Comm. on Indian Affairs, *Indian Child Welfare Act of 1977*, 195.

59. Harold C. Brown, testimony, in Select Comm. on Indian Affairs, *Indian Child Welfare Act of 1977*, 206–7.

60. James Abourezk in Select Comm. on Indian Affairs, *Indian Child Welfare Act of 1977*, 193. Lee presented several hundred petition signatures and letters to the Senate Select Committee on Indian Affairs himself, during his testimony.

61. James Abourezk quoted in Molly Ivins, "Mormons' Aid to Indian Children Preserved by New Law," *New York Times*, December 26, 1978: A16.

62. Unger, "Indian Child Welfare Act of 1978," 284 ("unwarranted"), 285. In the 1970s, Unger was the editor of the newsletter *Indian Family Defense* for the Association on American Indian Affairs (AAIA). He succeeded William Byler as the executive director of AAIA in 1980.

63. See, for example, Ivins, "Mormons' Aid to Indian Children," A16; Barsh, "Indian Child Welfare Act of 1978," 1313n142; and "Is the Placement Program Legal? Doing the LDS Sidestep," *Akwesasne Notes* 10, no. 5 (Winter 1978): 16–17.

64. See Jerome and Belinda Dubois, "The LDS Placement Service: 'It's Not a Form of Kidnapping,'" *Navajo Times*, July 27, 1978: A5; Wood, "Educational System that Works," B6-B10; Wood, "To Whose Advantage," *Akwesasne Notes* 10, no. 5 (Winter 1978): 16–18; "Is the Placement Program Legal?"; and "Busy as Bees Around the Beehive: Mormons and the Navajo Nation," *Akwesasne Notes* 10, no. 5 (Winter 1978): 19.

65. Don Reeves and Barbara Reeves, testimony, Select Comm. on Indian Affairs, *Indian Child Welfare Act of 1977*, 218–19; Faye LaPointe, testimony, February 9, 1978, in Subcomm. on Indian Affairs and Public Lands of the Comm. on Interior and Insular Affairs, House of Representatives, *Indian Child Welfare Act of 1977: Hearings on S. 1214*, 95th Cong. (1978), at 310. LaPointe, as the Coordinator of Social Services for Child Welfare of the Puyallup Tribe, may have been familiar with the placement program's activities in Washington state. Her comments also followed the testimony of Robert W. Barker, then special counsel to the LDS Church, about the placement program.

66. Goldie Denny quoted in Wood, "Educational System that Works," B6. See also Wood, "To Whose Advantage," 17.

67. See, for example, Bob Gottlieb and Peter Wiley, "The Kids Go Out Navaho, Come Back Donny and Marie: The Mormons' Controversial Save-Our-Indians Program," *Los Angeles Magazine*, December 1979, 138–46; Jon Stewart

and Peter Wiley, "Cultural Genocide: The American Indians' Two Greatest
Resources—Their Children and Their Land—Are Threatened by the Mormon
Church," *Penthouse* 12, June 1981, 80–84, 152–54, 163–64; and Robert Gottlieb
and Peter Wiley, *America's Saints: The Rise of Mormon Power* (New York:
G.P. Putnam's Sons, 1984), chap. 6.

68. Iverson, *Diné*, 232–36; Lee, *Silent Courage*, 282, 284–85; and S. Rep. No. P-91-
501, at 130. Lee taught at the Rough Rock Demonstration School in 1968. The
following year, the Senate Special Subcommittee on Indian Education identified Rough Rock as "a successful school under tribal control" (130).

69. "Indian Student Placement Policy Changed," *Ensign*, May 1984; and "A Conversation about Changes in the Indian Student Placement Service," *Ensign*, October 1985.

70. See, for example, Bert P. Cundick, Douglas K. Gottfredson, and Linda Willson, "Changes in Scholastic Achievement and Intelligence of Indian Children
Enrolled in a Foster Placement Program," *Developmental Psychology* 10, no. 6
(1974): 815–20; and Topper, "Effects of Missionary Foster Families," 142–60.
Cundick, Gottfredson, and Willson found, in their analysis of students from
the Four Corners area who spent at least five years in placement in Utah, that
students did not realize "the hoped-for educational outcomes" of the program;
their standardized test scores instead decreased over time. Cundick was a BYU
psychology professor.

71. Chadwick, Albrecht, and Bahr, "Evaluation of an Indian Student Placement
Program," 517, 519, 521. Although the study was conducted in late 1981, it was
not published until 1986.

72. "The Lee Letters," *Sunstone* 13, no. 4 (August 1989): 50; and "Press Coverage of
Lee's Excommunication Ambivalent," *Sunstone* 13, no. 4 (August 1989): 47.

73. Oral history interviews conducted by the Charles Redd Center captured many
Indian Mormons' reactions to the excommunication. See, for example, Embry,
"Speaking for Themselves," 100; Antoinette Dee, interview by Jim M. Dandy,
November 15, 1990, transcript, LDS Native American Oral History Project,
BYU Library; and Tonia Halona, interview by Jim M. Dandy, April 10, 1991,
transcript, in LDS Native American Oral History Project. Halona notes that
some Native American Mormons resigned from the Church in protest.

74. Garrett, *Making Lamanites*, 229–31; Allen, "Rise and Decline of the Placement
Program," 119n68; and Bishop, "Indian Placement," 109.

75. Garrett, *Making Lamanites*, 229–31.

76. Ibid., 231–32.

77. Bill Donovan, "Lawsuit Filed on Behalf of Navajo Children Abused in Mor-
mon Placement Program," *Navajo Times*, March 31, 2016; Suzette Brewer,
"'I Am X': Mormon Church Faces Growing Sex Abuse Scandal, Pt. 1," *Indian
Country Today*, October 19, 2016; Lilly Fowler, "Why Several Native Ameri-
cans Are Suing the Mormon Church: Participants in the Church-Sponsored
Indian Student Placement Program Have Filed at Least Three Sexual-Abuse
Lawsuits," *Atlantic Monthly*, October 23, 2016; Bill Donovan, "Fifth Navajo Files

Sex Abuse Lawsuit against Mormon Church," *Navajo Times*, February 2, 2017;
Ben Winslow, "Judge Quashes Deposition Subpoena of LDS Church President
Thomas S. Monson," *Fox13 Salt Lake City*, February 25, 2017; "Navajo Nation
Judge Weighs Jurisdiction of Mormon Church," *Navajo-Hopi Observer*, April 17,
2018; and Ben Winslow, "Judge Won't Dismiss Lawsuit against LDS Church
over Sex Abuse Claims," *Fox13 Salt Lake City*, May 31, 2018.

Chapter 11

1. Ernesteen B. Lynch, Oral history interview, conducted by Jesse Embry, May 17,
   1990. Harold B. Lee Library (HBLL) Special Collections, Brigham Young University, Provo, Utah.
2. Edward L. Kimball and Andrew E. Kimball Jr., *Spencer W. Kimball: Twelfth
   President of the Church of Jesus Christ of Latter-day Saints* (Salt Lake City, UT:
   Bookcraft, Inc., 1977), 15–17.
3. Ibid., 236–37.
4. Gary Gerstle, *American Crucible: Race and Nation in the Twentieth Century*
   (Princeton, NJ: Princeton University Press, 2001), 4.
5. For the broader story of the termination of Utah Indians, see R. Warren Metcalf, *Termination's Legacy: The Discarded Indians of Utah* (Lincoln: University of
   Nebraska Press, 2002).
6. "Let's Give Indians a Bill of Rights," *Deseret News*, 6 February 1952, Church
   News Section, 10.
7. Kimball and Kimball, 244–45.
8. J. Neil Birch, "Helen John: The Beginnings of Indian Placement," *Dialogue:
   A Journal of Mormon Thought*, 18 (Winter 1985): 124–25. There have been a
   number of studies of the Indian Placement Program and the subject is complex—and beyond the scope of this essay. For a brief overview of the scholarly
   issues, see Tona J. Hangen, "A Place to Call Home: Studying the Indian Placement Program," *Dialogue: A Journal of Mormon Thought*, 30 (Spring 1997):
   53–69.
9. Ibid., 126.
10. Virgus C. Osborne, "Indian Education at Brigham Young University 1965–
    1985," Typescript. Harold B. Lee Library Special Collections, Brigham Young
    University, 9.
11. Ibid.
12. Ibid, 11.
13. *Lamanite Handbook of The Church of Jesus Christ of Latter-day Saints* (Salt Lake
    City, UT: The Church of Jesus Christ of Latter-day Saints, 1968), 16–17.
14. L. Robert Webb, "The American Indian Education Program at Brigham Young
    University: a Report to Interested Publics," (Provo, UT: Brigham Young University, 1972).
15. Osborne, 18–20.

16. Ibid., 59.
17. Ibid., 22.
18. William Fox interview, 1991. Cited in Osborne, 23.
19. Ibid.
20. Osborne, 39.
21. Carletta Yellowjohn oral history interview, conducted by Odessa Neaman, July 10, 1990. HBLL Special Collections, 18.
22. Armand Mauss, *All Abraham's Children: Changing Mormon Conceptions of Race and Lineage* (Urbana and Chicago: University of Illinois Press, 2003), 81.
23. Yellowjohn Interview, 18.
24. Osborne, 119.
25. Farina King, "Miss Indian BYU: Contestation over the Crown and Indian Identity," *Journal of the West,* 52 (Summer 2013): 11.
26. "Miss Indian America Begay travels extensively, seeks unity," *Eagle's Eye,* January 1972, cited in King, 13.
27. King, 14.
28. Osborne, 44–45.
29. Ibid., 84.
30. Milli Cody Garrett oral history interview, conducted by Odessa Neaman, June 12, 1990. HBLL Special Collections, 6.
31. Ibid., 10.
32. Osborne, 123–24.
33. "Mormons Assure Indian Militants On Aid by Church," *New York Times,* April 9, 1973.
34. Mauss, *All Abraham's Children,* 101; and Kimball and Kimball, *Spencer W. Kimball,* 404–5.
35. Osborne, 54–55.
36. Ibid., 51.
37. Ibid., 61, 71.
38. Arturo de Hoyos, "The Old and the Modern Lamanite," (Provo, Utah: Institute of American Indian Services and Research, 1979), LDS Church History Library Archives, Salt Lake City, Utah.
39. Mauss, 84.
40. Garnet Wayne Comegan oral history interview, conducted by Deborah Lewis, December 9, 1989. HBLL Special Collections.
41. Lynch interview, 42.
42. Jessie L. Embry, "Ethnic Groups and the LDS Church," and "Speaking for Themselves: LDS Ethnic Groups Oral History Project," *Dialogue: A Journal of Mormon Thought* 25 (Winter 1992): 104–5.
43. Garrett interview, 6.
44. Tonia Halona oral history interview, conducted by Jim M. Dandy, April 10, 1991. HBLL Special Collections.
45. Lucinda McDonald oral history interview, conducted by Jim M. Dandy, March 19, 1991. HBLL Special Collections.

46. Osborne, 107.
47. Ibid., 137.
48. Mauss, 90.
49. Lee held the distinction of becoming the first American Indian called as a General Authority of the LDS Church in 1975. His story is entwined with the demise of Church programs for American Indians, as he became deeply disillusioned by the termination of Indian programs within the Church and what he called the "spiritual extermination of Indians and other Lamanites" by Church leaders. Lee was excommunicated for apostasy in 1989.
50. Boyd K. Packer, Untitled address to Indians students during BYU Indian Week, February 1979. Two versions of this speech are known to exist, one published in *Eagle's Eye* 11 [3]: 2–3, and a draft in the possession of Armand L. Mauss and largely quoted in *All Abraham's Children*, 96–97. The material cited herein is from Mauss.
51. Helan Wells Grady Taosoga oral history interview, conducted by Jesse Embry, May 17, 1990. HBLL Special Collections, 10.
52. Mouritsen, Maren. "Campus Memorandum to Con Osborne," December 4, 1980, quoted in Osborne, 137.
53. Osborne, V. C. "Notes on Meeting of the Ad Hoc Lamanite Committee," 1983, quoted in Osborne, 138.
54. Comegan Interview, 16.

Chapter 12

1. For the writings of Apess, see William Apess and Barry O'Connell, *On Our Own Ground: The Complete Writings of William Apess, a Pequot* (Amherst: University of Massachusetts Press, 1992). For broader histories of Apess's life, see Philip F. Gura, *The Life of William Apess, Pequot* (Chapel Hill: The University of North Carolina Press, 2015), and Drew Lopenzina, *Through an Indian's Looking-Glass: A Cultural Biography of William Apess, Pequot* (Amherst: University of Massachusetts Press, 2017).
2. Samuel Smith Diary, July 10, 1832. MS 4213. LDS Church History Library, Salt Lake City.
3. I co-authored the Introduction with Hafen, and have deferred throughout our collaborative process to her voice as the senior scholar between us and as a Native elder whose perspective I greatly respect.
4. Article of Faith Nr. 8 (Pearl of Great Price).
5. Introduction (Book of Mormon).
6. Title Page (Book of Mormon).
7. Ether 12:23–25 (Book of Mormon).
8. "Remarks by President Brigham Young, Tabernacle, January 12, 1862." *The Deseret News*, February 12, 1862.
9. Dallin H. Oaks, "Teaching and Learning by the Spirit." *Ensign*, March 1997.

10. Article of Faith Nr. 9 (Pearl of Great Price); and 1 Nephi 13:39 (Book of Mormon).
11. Review of conference programs over the past decade from various academic associations reveals multiple presentations on these programs, as do popular and academic blogs. Also, consider Matthew Garrett's recent full-length monograph. Matthew Garrett, *Making Lamanites: Mormons, Native Americans, and the Indian Student Placement Program, 1947–2000* (Salt Lake City: University of Utah Press, 2016).
12. The variety of experiences are well represented in the LDS Native American Oral History Project produced by the BYU Charles Redd Center for Western Studies and a subsequent article published by then center associate director, Jessie Embry. Casual discussion with host families or Native students likewise reveal a variety of experiences, positive and negative, casual and inconsequential to transformative. See LDS Native American Oral History Project transcripts and case files, MSS 7752, Series 20, Brigham Young University Harold B. Lee Library Special Collections, Provo, UT; and Jessie L. Embry, "Indian Placement Program Host Families: A Mission to the Lamanites," *Journal of Mormon History* 40:2 (Spring 2014): 235–76.
13. Jedediah S. Rogers and Matthew C. Godfrey, eds. *The Earth Will Appear as the Garden of Eden: Essays on Mormon Environmental History* (Salt Lake City: The University of Utah Press, 2019).

Bibliography

"A. E. Benjamin Tells the Palmyra Story: History of Palmyra." *Palmyra Courier-Journal*, April 23, 1964, 2.

"All-Lamanite Youth Conference." *Indian Liahona* 7, no. 4 (July-August 1970): 29–33.

Abruzzi, William S. "Ecology, Resource Redistribution, and Mormon Settlement in Northeastern Arizona." *American Anthropologist* (September 1989): 642–659.

Acts, Resolutions and Memorials, Passed at the Annual Sessions of the Legislative Assembly of the Territory of Utah. Salt Lake City: Brigham H. Young, 1852.

Adams, David Wallace. *Education for Extinction: American Indians and the Boarding School Experience, 1875–1928.* Lawrence: University of Kansas Press, 1995.

Adams, Mikaela. *Who Belongs? Race, Resources, and Tribal Citizenship in the Native South.* New York: Oxford University Press, 2006.

Aikau, Hokulani K. *A Chosen People, A Promised Land: Mormonism and Race in Hawai'i.* Minneapolis: University of Minnesota Press, 2012.

———. "Indigeneity in the Diaspora: The Case of Native Hawaiians at Iosepa, Utah," *American Quarterly* vol. 62, no. 3 (September 2010): 477–500.

Akheah, Sam. "Statement of Sam Ahkeah, chairman, Navajo Tribal Council, Accompanied by Norman M. Littell, General Council, Navaho Tribe." 83rd Cong., 2nd sess., Senate, Published Hearing, 1954, Colorado River Storage Project.

Albrecht, David A. "A Conversation about Changes in the Indian Student Placement Service." *Ensign*, October 1985.

Alchon, Suzanne. *A Pest in the Land: New World Epidemics in a Global Perspective.* Albuquerque: The University of New Mexico Press, 2003.

Alden, Timothy. *An Account of Sundry Missions Performed Among the Senecas and Munsee; in a series of letters. With an appendix.* New York: J. Seymour, 1827.

Alexander, Thomas G. *Mormonism in Transition: A History of the Latter-Day Saints, 1890–1930.* Urbana: University of Illinois Press, 1986.

Allen, James B. "The Rise and Decline of the LDS Indian Student Placement Program, 1947–1996." In *Mormons, Scripture, and the Ancient World: Studies in Honor of John L. Sorenson*, edited by Davis Bitton (Provo, UT: Foundation for Ancient Research and Mormon Studies, 1998), 85–120.

Allen, James B. and Leonard J. Arrington. "Mormon Origins in New York: An Introductory Analysis." *BYU Studies* 9, no. 3 (Spring 1969): 241–73.

Alt, Susan. "Spindle Whorls and Fiber Production at Early Cahokian Settlements." *Southeastern Archaeology* 18, no. 2 (Winter 1999): 124.

Apess, William, and Barry O'Connell. *On Our Own Ground: The Complete Writings of William Apess, a Pequot.* Amherst: University of Massachusetts Press, 1992.

Aqualante Speakers Kit, "What is the project?" document. Ernest Untermann Collection (EUC), Marriott Library, University of Utah, n.d.

Arrington, Leonard. *Brigham Young: American Moses.* New York: Knopf, 1985.

Arvin, Maile Renee. "Pacifically Possessed: Scientific Production and Native Hawaiian Critique of the 'Almost White' Polynesian Race." PhD diss., University of California, San Diego, 2013.

Ash, Michael R. "Lamanite Identity and the Book of Mormon." *Shaken Faith Syndrome: Strengthening One's Testimony in the Face of Criticism and Doubt,* 195–207. 2nd ed. Redding, CA: FairMormon, 2013.

Ashurst-McGee, Mark. "A Pathway to Prophethood: Joseph Smith Junior as Rodsman, Village Seer, and Judeo-Christian Prophet." Utah State University, 2000.

B. H. Stringham Collection, Box 12, Folder 14 Utah State University.

Bailey, Paul Dayton. *Wakara, Hawk of the Mountains.* Los Angeles: Westernlore Press, 1954.

Bandoni v. Higgenson, 638 F.2d 172, 177 (1980).

Banks, C. Stanley. "The Mormon Migration into Texas," *The Southwestern Historical Quarterly* 49, no. 2 (1945): 233–44.

Barsh, Russel Lawrence. "The Indian Child Welfare Act of 1978: A Critical Analysis." *Hastings Law Journal* 31 (1979–1980): 1287–1336.

Baym, Nina, ed. *The Norton Anthology of American Literature.* New York: W. W. Norton & Company, 2011.

Bear Chief, Clem. "Plucked from the Ashes." *Dialogue: A Journal of Mormon Thought* 25 no. 4 (1992): 140–49.

Beck, Robin A. "Catawba Coalescence and the Shattering of the Carolina Piedmont, 1540–1675," in *Mapping the Mississippian Shatter Zone,* ed. Robbie Ethridge and Sheri M. Shuck-Hall. Lincoln: University of Nebraska Press, 2009.

Begay, Pat. "The Making of a Mormon Convert." *Navajo Times* 27, July 1978.

Begay, Sarah. "Dear Editor: Thank you, Coach Ed Tano." *Navajo-Hopi Observer,* December 14, 2006, accessed October 11, 2016. http://m.nhonews.com/news/2006/dec/26/thank-you-coach-ed-tano/.

Benally, Herbert J. "Hózhǫ́ǫgo Naasháa Doo: Toward a Construct of Balance in Navajo Cosmology." PhD diss., California Institute of Integral Studies, 2008.

Benson, Ezra Taft. "Beware of Pride," *Ensign,* May 1989.

Berkhofer, Robert. *The White Man's Indian: Images of the American Indian from Columbus to the Present.* New York: Vintage, 1979.

Birch, J. Neil. "Helen John: The Beginnings of Indian Placement," *Dialogue: A Journal of Mormon Thought,* 18 (Winter 1985): 119–30.

Bishop, Clarence R. "Indian Placement: A History of the Indian Placement Program of the Church of Jesus Christ of Latter-day Saints." MA thesis, University of Utah, 1967.

Black, Susan Easton. "Behold, I Have Dreamed a Dream." In *First Nephi, the Doctrinal Foundations,* edited by Monte S. Nyman and Charles D. Tate Jr., 113–24. Provo, UT: Religious Studies Center, Brigham Young University, 1988.

Blackhawk, Ned. *Violence over the Land: Indians and Empire in the Early American West*. Cambridge, MA: Harvard University Press, 2008.

Blanchard, Evelyn Lance. "To Prevent the Breakup of the Indian Family: The Development of the Indian Child Welfare Act of 1978." PhD diss., University of New Mexico, 2010.

Blumer, Thomas. *The Catawba Indian Nation of the Carolinas*. Charleston, SC: Arcadia Publishing, 2004.

"Book of Mormon and DNA Studies." The Church of Jesus Christ of Latter-day Saints, accessed October 11, 2016. https://www.lds.org/topics/book-of-mormon-and-dna-studies?lang=eng.

Book of Mormon is True Blog, The. "The Iroquois Great Law of Peace." Accessed March 3, 2016. http://thebookofmormonistrue.com/tag/arthur-c-parker.

Book of Mormon. 2018. The Church of Jesus Christ of Latter-day Saints.

Bowman, Emery. Interview by Deborah Lewis, January 27, 1990, transcript. LDS Native American Oral History Project. Brigham Young University Library, Provo, Utah.

Boxer, Elise. "'Lamanites Shall Blossom as the Rose': Indian Student Placement Program, Mormon Whiteness, and Indigenous Identity." *The Journal of Mormon History* 41, no.4 (October 2015): 132–76.

———. "'To Become White and Delightsome': American Indians and Mormon Identity." PhD diss., Arizona State University, 2009.

Brewer, Suzette. "'I Am X': Mormon Church Faces Growing Sex Abuse Scandal, Pt. 1." *Indian Country Today*, October 19, 2016.

Brigham Young Papers, CR 1234 1, LDS Church History Library (CHL), Salt Lake City, Utah.

Brodie, Fawn M. in *No Man Knows My History: The Life of Joseph Smith the Mormon Prophet*. New York: Alfred A. Knopf, 1945.

Brooke, John L. *The Refiner's Fire: The Making of Mormon Cosmology, 1644–1844*. Cambridge: Cambridge University Press, 1994.

Brooks, James F. *Captives and Cousins: Slavery, Kinship, and Community in the South West Borderlands*. Chapel Hill: The University of North Carolina Press, 2002.

Brooks, Joanna, and Gina Colvin. *Decolonizing Mormonism: Towards a Postcolonial Mormonism*. Salt Lake City: University of Utah Press, 2018.

Brooks, Juanita. "Indian Relations on The Mormon Frontier." *Utah Historical Quarterly* 12, no. 1–2 (1944): 1–48.

Brown, Brian Edward. "Native American Religions, the First Amendment, and the Judicial Interpretation of Public Land." *Environmental History Review*, 15:4 (Winter 1991): 19–44.

Brown, Douglas Summer. *The Catawba Indians: The People of the River*. Columbia: South Carolina University Press, 1966.

Brown, Victor L. "An Overview of Church Welfare Services." *Ensign*, November 1975.

Burton, Elder Theodore. "Glen Canyon Dam Dedication Ceremony," item display 75984, Cline Library, Northern Arizona University.

Bushman, Richard L. *Joseph Smith and the Beginnings of Mormonism*. Urbana: University of Illinois Press, 1984.

"Busy as Bees Around the Beehive: Mormons and the Navajo Nation." *Akwesasne Notes* 10, no. 5 (Winter 1978): 19.

Carey, Jane and Jane Lydon, eds. *Indigenous Networks: Mobility, Connections and Exchange.* New York: Routledge, 2014.

Carvalho, Solomon Nunes. *Incidents of Travel and Adventure in the Far West.* New York: Derby & Jackson, 1859.

Castile, George P. *To Show Heart: Native American Self-Determination and Federal Indian Policy, 1960–1975.* Tucson: University of Arizona Press, 1998.

"Catawba Indians," *Liahona: The Elders Journal* 3 (1905): 181.

Center for Social Research and Development. "Indian Child Welfare: A State-of-the-Field Study." Report, Denver Research Institute, University of Denver, 1976.

Cernadas, César Ceriani. *Nuestros hermanos lamanitas: Indios y fronteras en la imaginación mormona.* Buenos Aires: Editorial Biblos, 2008.

Chadwick, Bruce A., Stan L. Albrecht, and Howard M. Bahr. "Evaluation of an Indian Student Placement Program." *Social Casework: The Journal of Contemporary Social Work* 67, no. 9 (November 1986): 515–24.

Chadwick, Bruce A. and Stan L. Albrecht. "Mormons and Indians: Beliefs, Policies, Programs, and Practices." In *Contemporary Mormonism: Social Science Perspectives,* 287–309. Edited by Marie Cornwall, Tim B. Heaton, and Lawrence A. Young. Urbana: University of Chicago Press, 1994.

Chapman, James E. "A Modest Contrast between Some of the Personal Life-Values of the Utah American Indian, and the Urban Middle-Class Utahn." *Utah Public Welfare Review: Professional Journal of the County Welfare Directors Association of Utah* 1, no. 5 (Summer 1966): 8–12.

Chiquito, Stephanie. Interview by Jim M. Dandy, April 11, 1991, transcript. LDS Native American Oral History Project. Brigham Young University Library, Provo, Utah.

Christensen, Scott. *Sagwitch: Shoshone Chieftan, Mormon Elder 1822–1887.* Logan, UT: Utah State University Press, 1999.

Christenson, Allen J., ed. *Popol Vuh: The Mythic Sections-Tales of First Beginnings from the Ancient K'iche'-Maya.* Provo, UT: Foundation for Ancient Research and Mormon Studies, 2000.

Christy, Howard A. "Mormon-Indian Relations." In *Mapping Mormonism: An Atlas of Latter-day Saint History,* 98–101. Edited by Brandon S. Plewe. 2nd ed. Provo: BYU Studies, 2014.

———. "Open Hand and Mailed Fist: Mormon-Indian Relations in Utah, 1847–52." *Utah Historical Quarterly* 46 (Summer 1978): 216–35.

———. "The Walker War: Defense and Conciliation as Strategy," *Utah Historical Quarterly* 47 (1979): 395–420.

"Church explains excommunication to Navajos as Lee seeks a rebirth." *Deseret News,* September 10, 1989, accessed October 11, 2016. http://www.deseretnews.com /article/62992/CHURCH-EXPLAINS-EXCOMMUNICATION-TO -NAVAJOS-AS-LEE-SEEKS-A-REBIRTH.html?pg=all.

Cisneros, Natalie Avalos. "Indigenous Visions of Self-Determination: Healing and Historical Trauma in Native America." *Global Societies Journal* 2 (2014): 1–14.

Clark, James R., ed. *Messages of the First Presidency of the Church of Jesus Christ of Latter-day Saints*. Vol. I. Salt Lake City: Bookcraft, 1965–75.

Clayton, William. *The Journals of William Clayton*, edited by George D. Smith. Salt Lake City: Signature Books, 1995.

Clemmer, Janice White. "Native American Studies: A Utah Perspective." *Wicazo Sa Review* 2, no. 2 (1986): 17–23.

Clifford, James. "Introduction: Partial Truths," in *Writing Culture: The Poetics and Politics of Ethnography*, ed. James Clifford and George E. Marcus. Berkeley: University of California Press, 1986.

———. *The Predicament of Culture: Twentieth-Century Ethnography, Literature, And Art*. Cambridge, MA: Harvard University Press, 1988.

Clinton, De Witt. "Legislature of New-York. Governor's Speech," *Palmyra Register*, February 18, 1818, 2.

Clyde, George Dewey. "History of Irrigation in Utah." *Utah Historical Quarterly* (January 1959): 26–36.

Coates, Lawrence G. "A History of Indian Education by the Mormons, 1830–1900." PhD diss., Ball State University, 1969.

———. "Brigham Young and Mormon Indian Policies: The Formative Period, 1836–1851," *BYU Studies* 18, no. 3 (1978): 425–52.

Cobb, Daniel. *Native Activism in Cold War America*. Lawrence, KS: University Press of Kansas, 2008.

Colvin, Gina and Joanna Brooks, eds. *Decolonizing Mormonism: Approaching a Postcolonial Zion*. Salt Lake City: University of Utah Press, 2018.

Colvin, Gina. "Theorizing Mormon Race Scholarship," *Journal of Mormon History* 41, no. 3 (July 2015): 11–21.

Comegan, Garnet Wayne. Oral history interview, conducted by Deborah Lewis, December 9, 1989. Harold B. Lee Library Special Collections, Brigham Young University.

Cowager, Thomas. "'The Crossroads of Destiny': The NCAI's Landmark Struggle to Thwart Coercive Termination." *American Indian Culture and Research Journal*, 20:4 (1996): 121–44.

Cruz Smith, Martin. *The Indians Won*. New York: Leisure Books, 1981.

Cusick, David. *Sketches of Ancient History of the Six Nations*. Tuscarora Village, NY: 1826 or 1827; reprint, Lockport, NY: Niagara County Historical Society, 1961.

Dawson Papers, Special Collections, University of Utah.

de Hoyos, Arturo. "The Old and the Modern Lamanite." Provo, UT: Institute of American Indian Services and Research, 1979. LDS Church History Library Archives, Salt Lake City, Utah.

De Hoyos, Genevieve and Arturo De Hoyos. "Indian Placement Program of the Church of Jesus Christ of Latter Day Saints: A Statistical and Analytical Study (First Draft)." Unpublished manuscript, Brigham Young University, 1973. Brigham Young University Library, Provo, Utah.

Dee, Antoinette. Interview by Jim M. Dandy, November 15, 1990, transcript. LDS Native American Oral History Project. Brigham Young University Library, Provo, Utah.

Deloria, Barbara, Kristen Foehner, and Sam Scinta eds. *Spirit & Reason: The Vine Deloria" Reader.* Golden, CO: Fulcrum Publishing, 1999.

Deloria, Phil. *Playing Indian.* New Haven: Yale University Press, 1998.

Deloria, Vine, Jr. *Behind the Trail of Broken Treaties: An Indian Declaration of Independence.* New York: Delacorte Press, 1974.

———. *God Is Red: A Native View of Religion, the Classic Work Updated.* Golden: Fulcrum Publishing, 1994.

DeMallie, Raymond J. *The Sixth Grandfather: Black Elk's Teachings Given to John G. Neihardt.* Lincoln, NE: University of Nebraska Press, 1984.

Denetdale, Jennifer Nez. *Reclaiming Diné History: The Legacies of Navajo Chief Manuelito and Juanita.* Tucson: University of Arizona Press, 2007.

Dennis, Mathew. *Seneca Possessed: Indians, Witchcraft, and Power in the Early American Republic.* Philadelphia: University of Pennsylvania Press, 2012.

Densmore, Christopher. *Red Jacket: Iroquois Diplomat and Orator.* Syracuse, NY: Syracuse University Press, 1999.

Doctrine and Covenants of the Church of Jesus Christ of Latter-day Saints. Salt Lake City: The Church of Jesus Christ of Latter-day Saints, 1957.

Donaldson, Thomas. *Extra Census Bulletin. Indians. The Six Nations of New York.* Portion of the 1890 US Census reports, 1892.

Donovan, Bill. "Fifth Navajo Files Sex Abuse Lawsuit against Mormon Church." *Navajo Times*, February 2, 2017.

———. "Lawsuit Filed on Behalf of Navajo Children Abused in Mormon Placement Program." *Navajo Times*, March 31, 2016.

Dubois, Jerome and Belinda. "The LDS Placement Service: 'It's Not a Form of Kidnapping.'" *Navajo Times*, July 27, 1978: A4-A5.

Duffy, John-Charles. "The Use of 'Lamanite' in Official LDS Discourse." *Journal of Mormon History* 34, no. 1 (Winter 2008): 118–67.

Durfee, Mary B. Diary (from typescript). Wayne County Historian's Office, Lyons, New York.

Eastman, Charles Alexander. *Indian Heroes and Great Chieftains.* Mineola, NY: Dover Publications, 1997 [1918].

Eaton, Horace. *A Thanksgiving Sermon, delivered at Palmyra, N.Y., Nov. 26, 1857.* Rochester, NY: A. Strong, 1858.

Echo Hawk, Larry. "Come unto Me, O Ye House of Israel." *Ensign* (November 2012), 32–33.

———. Biography. In *Why I am a Mormon*, 108–15. Edited by Joseph A. Cannon. Stevens Point, WI: Worzalla Publishing Company, 2012.

Embry, Jessie L. "Ethnic Groups and the LDS Church," and "Speaking for Themselves: LDS Ethnic Groups Oral History Project," *Dialogue: A Journal of Mormon Thought* 25, no. 4 (Winter 1992): 81–112.

———. "Indian Placement Program Host Families: A Mission to the Lamanites" *Journal of Mormon History* 40:2 (Spring 2014): 235–76.

———. "Lamanite Relief Societies: The Relief Society and Its Relationship with Native Americans," Paper presented at the sesquicentennial Relief Society celebration, Brigham Young University, Provo, Utah, 1992.

England, Eugene. "'Lamanites' and the Spirit of the Lord." *Dialogue: A Journal of Mormon Thought* 18, no. 4 (Winter 1985): 25–32.

Eyring, Henry B. "Remarks at the Mountain Meadows Massacre Sesquicentennial." Washington County, UT, 2007. Accessed April 18, 2016. http://www .mormonnewsroom.org/article/150th-anniversary-of-mountain-meadows -massacre.

Fabian, Ann. *The Skull Collectors: Race, Science, and America's Unburied Dead.* Chicago: University of Chicago Press, 2010.

Farella, John R. *The Main Stalk: A Synthesis of Navajo Philosophy.* Tucson: University of Arizona Press, 1984.

Farmer, Jared. *Glen Canyon Dammed: Inventing Lake Powell and the Canyon Country.* Tucson: Arizona University Press, 1999.

———. *On Zion's Mount: Mormons, Indians, and the American Landscape.* Cambridge, MA: Harvard University Press, 2008.

Faulring, Scott H. *An American Prophet's Record: The Diaries and Journals of Joseph Smith.* Salt Lake City: Signature Books in association with Smith Research Associates, 1989.

Felt, Paul E. "Remnants of Israel: Who? When Gathered?" in *Sidney B. Sperry Symposium on The Book of Mormon*, January 24, 1981. Provo, UT: Brigham Young University, 1981.

Ferre, Craig. "A History of the Polynesian Cultural Center's 'Night Show,' 1963–1983." PhD diss., Brigham Young University, 1988.

Fiedler, Leslie A. *The Return of the Vanishing American.* New York: Stein and Day, 1968.

Fiege, Mark. *Irrigated Eden: The Making of an Agricultural Landscape in the American West.* Seattle: University of Washington Press, 1998.

Fisher, Linford. *The Indian Great Awakening.* New York: Oxford University Press, 2012.

Fixico, Donald. *Termination and Relocation, 1945–1960.* Albuquerque, NM: University of New Mexico Press, 1990.

Flake, David Kay. "History of the Southwest Indian Mission." N.p., 1965.

Forsberg, Clyde R., Jr. *Equal Rites: The Book of Mormon, Masonry, Gender, and American Culture.* New York: Columbia University Press, 2004.

Forte, Maximilian C. *Who is an Indian? Race, Place, and the Politics of Indigeneity in the Americas.* Toronto: University of Toronto Press, 2013.

Foucault, Michel. *The Archeology of Knowledge.* New York: Vintage, 1982.

Fowler, Lilly. "Why Several Native Americans Are Suing the Mormon Church: Participants in the Church-Sponsored Indian Student Placement Program Have Filed at Least Three Sexual-Abuse Lawsuits." *Atlantic Monthly*, October 23, 2016.

Gardner, Harvey Leon. Interview by Matthew Heiss, Page, Arizona, May 1, 1992, OH 1225, LDS Church Archives.

Garrett, Matthew. *Making Lamanites: Mormons, Native Americans, and the Indian Student Placement Program, 1947–2000.* Salt Lake City: University of Utah Press, 2016.

Garrett, Milli Cody. Oral history interview, conducted by Odessa Neaman, June 12, 1990. Harold B. Lee Library Special Collections, Brigham Young University.

Gates, Susan Young. "The Courtship of Kanosh: A Pioneer Indian Love Story," in *Improvement Era*, 9:1 (1096): 21–38.

Gentry, Leland H. "Light on the 'Mission to the Lamanites.'" *Brigham Young University Studies* 36 no. 2 (1996–97): 226–34.

Gerdts, Joern. "Lake Powell: A Controversial Reservoir in Glen Canyon Opens Magnificent Scenery for Sportsmen." *Los Angeles Times*, September 11, 1966, W13.

Gerstle, Gary. *American Crucible: Race and Nation in the Twentieth Century*. Princeton, NJ: Princeton University Press, 2001.

Gillum, Gary P. "Written to the Lamanites: Understanding the Book of Mormon through Native Culture and Religion." *Interpreter: A Journal of Mormon Scripture* 6 (2013): 31–48.

Givens, Terryl L. *By the Hand of Mormon: The American Scripture That Launched a New World Religion*. Oxford and New York: Oxford University Press, 2002.

Godfrey, Matthew C. and Brenden W. Rensink, et.al, eds. *The Joseph Smith Papers: Documents*, vol. 4 (April 1834–September 1835). Salt Lake City: The Church Historian's Press, 2016.

Gottfredson, Peter. *Indian Depredations in Utah*. Salt Lake City: Skelton Publishing Co, 1919.

Gottlieb, Robert and Peter Wiley. "The Kids Go Out Navaho, Come Back Donny and Marie: The Mormons' Controversial Save-Our-Indians Program." *Los Angeles Magazine*, December 1979, 138–46.

———. *America's Saints: The Rise of Mormon Power*. New York: G.P. Putnam's Sons, 1984.

Green, Doyle L. "The Southwest Indian Mission." *The Improvement Era* (April 1955), 233–34.

Gregg, Thomas. *The Prophet of Palmyra*. New York, 1890. Reprinted as "Governor Harding's Recollection," *Among the Mormons: Historic Accounts by Contemporary Observers*, eds. William Mulder and A. Russell Mortensen. New York: Alfred A. Knopf, 1958.

Grimm, Michele and Tom Grimm. "Lake Powell a Popular Play Place," in *Los Angeles Times*, September 2, 1979, L2.

Grinde, Donald A., Jr., and Bruce E. Johansen. *Exemplar of Liberty: Native America and the Evolution of Democracy*. Los Angeles, CA: American Indian Studies Center Unviersity of California, Los Angeles, 2008.

Groat, Joel B. "Lamanites No More: DNA and Lost Ties to Father Lehi," Institute for Religious Research, July 1, 2011, accessed online October 11, 2016. http://mit.irr .org/lamanites-no-more-dna-and-lost-ties-father-lehi.

Groesbeck, C. Jess. "The Book of Mormon as a Symbolic History: A New Perspective on Its Place in History and Religion." *Sunstone*, no. 131 (2004): 35–45.

Grow, Matthew J., Ronald K. Esplin, Mark Ashurst-McGee, Gerrit J. Dirkmaat, et al., eds. *The Joseph Smith Papers: Administrative Records, Council of Fifty, Minutes, March 1844–January 1846*. Salt Lake City: The Church Historian's Press, 2016.

Grunder, Rick. *Mormon Parallels: A Bibliographic Source*. Lafayatte, NY: Rick Grunder Books, 2014.

Gunnison, John Williams *The Mormons*. Philadelphia: Lippincott, Grambo & Company, 1852.

Gura, Philip F. *The Life of William Apess, Pequot*. Chapel Hill: The University of North Carolina Press, 2015.

Gutjahr, Paul C. *The Book of Mormon: A Biography*. Princeton: Princeton University Press, 2012.

Haas, Marilyn L. *The Seneca and Tuscarora Indians: An Annotated Bibliography*, Native American Bibliography Series, no. 17, Metuchen, New Jersey: Scarecrow Press, 1994, 76–82.

Hafen, P. Jane, "Afterword," in *Decolonizing Mormonism: Approaching a Postcolonial Zion*, eds. Gina Colvin and Joanna Brooks. Salt Lake City: University of Utah Press, 2018.

———. "'Great Spirit Listen': The American Indian in Mormon Music." *Dialogue: A Journal of Mormon Thought* 18 (Winter 1985): 133–42.

———. "The Being and Place of a Native American Mormon." In *New Genesis: A Mormon Reader on Land and Community*, 35–41. Edited by Terry Tempest Williams, William B. Smart, and Gibbs M. Smith. Salt Lake City: Gibbs Smith, 2008.

Halona, Tonia. Oral history interview, conducted by Jim M. Dandy, April 10, 1991. Harold B. Lee Library Special Collections, Brigham Young University.

Hangen, Tona J. "A Place to Call Home: Studying the Indian Placement Program," *Dialogue: A Journal of Mormon Thought*, 30 (Spring 1997): 53–69.

Harris, Lacee A. "To Be Native American—and Mormon." *Dialogue: A Journal of Mormon Thought* 18 (Winter 1985): 143–52.

Harvey, Mark. *A Symbol of Wilderness: Echo Park and the American Conservation Movement*. Seattle: University of Washington Press, 1994.

"Hector Tahu." Obituaries. *Arizona Daily Sun*, February 21, 2007, accessed September 22, 2016. http://azdailysun.com/news/local/obituaries/hector-tahu/article_a90d5db9-843e-5700-a8bd-b3260b945449.html.

Herendeen, Charles B. "Indians," in *Pioneers of Macedon, and other papers of the Macedon Center Historical Society*, ed. Mary Louise Eldredge Macedon Center, NY: Macedon Center Historical Society, 1912.

Hickman, Jared. "The Book of Mormon as Amerindian Apocalypse." *American Literature* 80, no. 3 (2014): 429–61.

Hicks, Jack, James D. Houston, Maxine Hong Kingston, and Al Young, eds., *The Literature of California: Native American Beginnings to 1945*. Berkeley: University of California Press, 2000.

Hills, Louis E. *A Short Work on the Geography of Mexico and Central America from 2234 B.C. to 421 A. D.* Independence: Louis E. Hills, 1917.

———. *Historical Data from Ancient Records and Ruins of Mexico and Central America*. Independence: Louis E. Hills, 1919.

Hinderaker, Eric. *The Two Hendricks: Unraveling a Mohawk Mystery*. Cambridge, MA: Harvard University Press, 2010.

Hirshon, Stanley P. *The Lion of the Lord: A Biography of Brigham Young*. New York: Knopf, 1969.

"History, Circa Summer 1832." In *Joseph Smith Papers: Histories, Vol. 1, 1832–1844*, Karen Lynn Davidson, David J. Whittaker, Mark R. Ashurst-McGee, and, Richard L. Jensen, eds. Salt Lake City: The Church Historian's Press, 2012.

Holler, Clyde. *Black Elk's Religion: The Sun Dance and Lakota Catholicism*. Syracuse, New York: Syracuse University Press, 1995.

"How Not to Go 'Native.'" *Akwesasne Notes* 2, no. 2 (May 1970): 14.

Howe, Daniel Walker. *What Hath God Wrought: The Transformation of America, 1815–1848*. New York: Oxford University Press, 2007.

Hubbard, William. *A Narrative of the Troubles with the Indians*. London: Printed for Tho. Parkhurst, 1677.

Hudson, Charles M. *The Catawba Nation*. Athens, GA: University of Georgia Press, 1970.

Hundley, Norris Jr. *The Great Thirst: Californians and Water, 1770s–1990s*. Berkley: University of California Press, 1992.

Hunter, Margaret L. *Race, Gender, and the Politics of Skin Tone*. New York: Routledge, 2005.

Hyde, Anne. *Empires, Nations, Families: A History of the North American West, 1800–1860*. Lincoln: University of Nebraska Press, 2012.

Hyde, Orson. "Minutes, 12 March 1835." In *The Joseph Smith Papers Documents*, edited by Mathew C. Godfrey, Brenden W. Rensink, Alex D. Smith, Max H. Parkin and Alexander L. Baugh, 287–89. Salt Lake City, UT: The Church Historian's Press, 2016.

Iese, Zenobia Kapahulehua. Interview by Farina King, July 6, 2013, telephone communication, recording of interview in possession of Farina King.

Imada, Adria. "Aloha 'Oe:" Settler-Colonial Nostalgia and the Genealogy of a Love Song." *American Indian Culture and Research Journal* 37, no. 2 (2014): 35–52.

Indian Child Welfare Act of 1978, Pub. L. No. 95-608, 92 Stat. 3069 (1978).

"Indian Letter." *Palmyra Register*, March 24, 1818, 2.

"Indian Student Placement Policy Changed." *Ensign*, May 1984.

Indian Student Placement Program. "Foster Parent Guide." April 1965. Brigham Young University Library, Provo, Utah.

Indian Student Placement Service. "Cultural Contrast: A Hand Out, February 1968." Unpublished manuscript. 1970. Brigham Young University Library, Provo, Utah.

"Is the Placement Program Legal? Doing the LDS Sidestep." *Akwesasne Notes* 10, no. 5 (Winter 1978): 16–17.

Iverson, Peter. *Diné: A History of the Navajos*. Albuquerque: University of New Mexico Press, 2002.

Jacket, Red. "Reply to Rev. Jacob Cram, November 1805." In *The Collected Speeches of Sagoyewatha, or Red Jacket*, edited by Granville Ganter, 138–43. Syracuse, NY: Syracuse University Press, 2006 [1809].

Jackman, Levi. *Journal*, July 28, 1847. LDS Church History Archive.

Jackson, Donald C. *Big Dams of the New Deal Era: A Confluence of Engineering and Politics*. Norman: University of Oklahoma Press, 2006.

Jacob Hamblin Papers, Huntington Library, San Marino, California.

Jacobs, Margaret D. *A Generation Removed: The Fostering and Adoption of Indigenous Children in the Postwar World.* Lincoln: University of Nebraska Press, 2014.

———. *White Mother to a Dark Race: Settler Colonialism, Maternalism, and the Removal of Indigenous Children in the American West and Australia, 1880–1940.* Lincoln: University of Nebraska Press, 2009.

Jemison, Pete. "Mother of Nations—the Peace Queen, a Neglected Tradition." *Northeast Indian Quarterly* (1988): 68–70.

Jennings, Francis, ed. *Iroquois Indians: A Documentary History of the Diplomacy of the Six Nations and their League. Guide to the Microfilm.* Woodbridge, CT: Research Publications, 1985.

Jennings, Warren A. "The First Mormon Mission to the Indians." *Kansas Historical Quarterly* 37 (August 1971): 288–99.

Jessee, Dean C., ed. *The Personal Writings of Joseph Smith.* Salt Lake City: Deseret Book, 1984.

Johansen, Bruce E. *Forgotten Founders: Benjamin Franklin, the Iroqouis and the Rationale for the American Revolution.* Ipswich, MA: Gambit Publishers, 1982.

Johansen, Bruce E., ed. *Debating Democracy: Native American Legacy of Freedom.* Santa Fe, NM: Clear Light Publishers, 1998.

John H. Morgan papers. Marriott Library Special Collections, University of Utah, Salt Lake City, Utah.

Johnson, Broderick H., ed. *Stories of Traditional Navajo Life and Culture/ Ałk'idą́ą́'yę́ę́k'ehgo Diné Kéédahahat'íné̜e̜ Baa Nahane'.* Tsaile, Arizona: Navajo Community College Press, 1977.

Johnson, Lady Bird. "Glen Canyon Dam Dedication Ceremony," item display 75982, Cline Library, Northern Arizona University.

Johnson, Lane. "Who and Where are the Lamanites? Worldwide Distribution of Lamanites." *Ensign*, December 1975.

Johnson, Scott, and Joel Kramer. "The Bible vs. The Book of Mormon." Brigham City, Utah: Living Hope Ministries, 2005.

Johnston, Jerry. "LDS Shoshone Is a Visionary of 2 Cultures." *Deseret News*, July 24, 1999.

Jones, Daniel. *Forty Years among the Indians.* Salt Lake City: Juvenile Instructor's Office, 1890.

Jones, Paul. "Reclamation and the Indian." *Utah Historical Quarterly* (January 1959): 51–58.

Jones, Sondra. *The Trial of Don Pedro León Luján.* Salt Lake City: The University of Utah Press, 1999.

Jorgensen, Danny L. "Building the Kingdom of God: Alpheus Cutler and the Second Mormon Mission to the Indians, 1846–1853." *Kansas History* 15 (Autumn 1992): 192–209.

Journals of the Military Expedition of Major General John Sullivan against the Six Nations of Indians in 1779. Glendale, NY: Benchmark Publishing Company, 1970 [1887].

Judge, Peter M. "Catawba Mormons hold services in new church," *Rock Hill Herald*, August 31, 1985.

Justice, Daniel Heath. "'Go Away Water!': Kinship Criticism and the Decolonization Imperative," in *Reasoning Together: The Native Critics Collective*, 147–68. Norman: University of Oklahoma Press, 2008.

Kalauli, Mitchell Davis Kapuni. Interview by Matthew Heiss, Tuba City, Arizona, April 28, 1992, OH 1524, LDS Church Archives.

Kane, Thomas. *The Mormons*. Philadelphia: King and Baird, 1850.

Kauanui, J. Kēhaulani. *Hawaiian Blood: Colonialism and the Politics of Sovereignty and Indigeneity*. Durham: Duke University Press, 2008.

Kellogg, Laura Cornelius. *Our Democracy and the American Indian and Other Works*. Edited by Kristina Ackley and Cristina Stanciu. Syracuse, NY: Syracuse University Press, 2015.

Kelly, Klara B. and Francis Harris. *Navajo Sacred Places*. Bloomington: Indiana University Press, 1994.

Kelly, William Keoniana. Interview by Rachel Nathan, Orem, Utah, February 6, 1994, LDS Polynesian American Oral History Project, MSS OH 1880, Tom Perry Special Collections and Manuscripts, Harold B. Lee Library, Brigham Young University, Provo, Utah.

Kenney, Scott. *Wilford Woodruff's Journal*, IV. Midvale, UT: Signature Books, 1983.

Kim, Harvard C.S. Email to Farina King, May 20, 2013, printout in possession of Farina King.

———. Interview by Farina King, May 27, 2013, telephone communication, recording in possession of Farina King.

Kimball, Adelia Almira Wilcox. *Memoirs of Adelia Almira Wilcox*. New York: Stanley Kimball, 1956.

Kimball, Edward L. "Spencer W. Kimball and the Lamanite Cause." *Brigham Young University Studies* 25, no. 4 (Fall 1985): 73–76.

Kimball, Edward L. and Andrew E. Kimball Jr. "Apostle to the Indians." In *Spencer W. Kimball: The Early and Apostolic Years*. Salt Lake City: Deseret Book, 1977.

———. *Spencer W. Kimball: The Early and Apostolic Years*. 1977; Salt Lake City: Deseret Book, 2006.

Kimball, Edward. *Spencer W. Kimball: Twelfth President of the Church of Jesus Christ of Latter-day Saints*. Salt Lake City: Bookcraft, Inc., 1977.

Kimball, Spencer W. Talk, October 6, 1956. In "One Hundred Twenty-seventh Semi-Annual Conference of The Church of Jesus Christ of Latter-day Saints, Held in the Tabernacle, Salt Lake City, Utah, October 5, 6 and 7, 1956, With Report of Discourses." Salt Lake City: The Church of Jesus Christ of Latter-day Saints, 1956: 52–58.

———. Talk, September 30, 1950. In "One Hundred Twenty-first Semi-Annual Conference of the Church of Jesus Christ of Latter-day Saints, Held in the Tabernacle, Salt Lake City, Utah, September 29, 30, and October 1, 1950, With Report of Discourses." Salt Lake City: Church of Jesus Christ of Latter-day Saints, 1950: 63–69.

———. "Of Royal Blood," *Ensign*, July 1971, 7.

———. "Our Paths Have Met Again." *Ensign*, December 1975, 2.

———. "The Day of the Lamanites," *Improvement Era*, December 1960, 922–25.

———. "The Lamanite: Their Burden, Our Burden." In *The Lamanites: In the Words of the Prophets*. Edited by John R. Maestes and Jeff Simons. Provo: Brigham Young University, 1980.

———. "The Navajo . . . His Predicament: Part II." *The Improvement Era* 51, no. 4 (April 1948): 210–12, 252, 253, 255.

———. "The Navajo . . . His Predicament: The First of Two Articles." *The Improvement Era* 51, no. 2 (February 1948): 67–78.

King, Farina. "Miss Indian BYU: Contestation over the Crown and Indian Identity." *Journal of the West* 52 (Summer 2013): 11.

Kipling, Rudyard. "The White Man's Burden," in *The White Man's Burdens: An Anthology of British Poetry of the Empire*, edited by Chris Brooks and Peter Faulkner, 307–8. Exeter: The University of Exeter Press, 1996.

Kirsch, Stuart. 1997. "Lost Tribes: Indigenous People and the Social Imaginary." *Anthropological Quarterly* 70: 58–67.

Knack, Martha C. *Boundaries Between: The Southern Paiutes, 1775–1995*. Reno: University of Nevada Press, 2004.

Korevaar, Hannah. "This is the Place: Race, Space, Religion and Law in Salt Lake City." BA honors thesis, Wesleyan University, 2014.

Kovach, Margaret E. *Indigenous Methodologies: Characteristics, Conversations, and Contexts*. Toronto: University of Toronto Press, 2010.

Kramer, Joel, and Jeremy Reyes. "DNA vs. The Book of Mormon." Brigham City, Utah: Living Hope Ministries, 2003.

Kruckenberg, R. Janet. "The Church in the Dakotas." *Church News*, November 30, 1996.

Laidlaw, Zoe and Alan Lester, eds. *Indigenous Communities and Settler Colonialism: Land Holding, Loss and Survival in an Interconnected World*. New York: Palgrave Macmillan, 2015.

Lamanite Handbook of the Church of Jesus Christ of Latter-day Saints. Salt Lake City, UT: Church of Jesus Christ of Latter-day Saints, 1968.

Lamanite Israel, February 1966, Southwest Indian Mission Papers, 1961–1965, John Edwin Baird (1908–2003), MS 20569, LDS Church Archives, Salt Lake City, Utah.

Larsen, John, and Christopher Smith. *The Iroquois as the Lamanite: An Argument for a Contemporary Reading of the* Book of Mormon. Podcast audio, 2012. https://www.sunstonemagazine.com/the-iroquois-as-the-lamanite-an-argument-for-a-contemporary-reading-of-the-book-of-mormon/.

Lauter, Paul, ed. *Heath Anthology of American Literature*. 7. Boston: Wadsworth Publishing, 2013.

LDS Native American Oral History Project. MSS OH 1180, Tom Perry Special Collections and Manuscripts, Harold B. Lee Library, Brigham Young University, Provo, Utah.

———, MSS 7752, Series 20, Brigham Young University Harold B. Lee Library Special Collections, Provo, UT.

Lee, George P. "My Heritage Is My Choice." *Ensign*, November 1975.

———. *Silent Courage: An Indian Story, The Autobiography of George P. Lee, a Navajo.* Salt Lake City: Deseret Book Company, 1987.

Lee, Jerry D. "A Study of the Influence of the Mormon Church on the Catawba Indians of South Carolina, 1882–1975." MA thesis, Brigham Young University, 1976.

Lee, Lloyd L. ed. *Diné Perspectives: Revitalizing and Reclaiming Navajo Thought.* Tucson: University of Arizona Press, 2014.

———. *Navajo Sovereignty: Understandings and Visions of the Diné People.* Tucson: University of Arizona Press, 2017.

Lepore, Jill. *The Name of War: King Philip's War and the Origins of American Identity.* New York: Vintage, 1999.

Lesson 151: The Utah War and the Mountain Meadows Massacre." In Doctrine and Covenants and Church History Seminary Teacher Manual. Salt Lake City, UT: The Church of Jesus Christ of Latter-day Saints, 2013. Accessed April 18, 2016. https://www.lds.org/manual/doctrine-and-covenants-and-church-history -seminary-teacher-manual-2014/section-7/lesson-151-the-utah-war-and-the -mountain-meadows-massacre?lang=eng.

"Let's Give Indians a Bill of Rights," *Deseret News*, February 6, 1952, Church News Section, 10.

Little, Dennis. Personal telephone conversation with Farina King, October 12, 2016.

Livingstone, John P. "Chapter 6: American Indian Services," in *Same Drum, Different Beat: The Story of Dale T. Tingey and American Indian Services* (Provo, Utah: Religious Studies Center, Brigham Young University, 2003), 79–92, accessed October 13, 2016. https://rsc.byu.edu/archived/same-drum-different-beat-story-dale-t -tingey-and-american-indian-services/chapter-6#_ednref19.

———. "Establishing the Church Simply." *BYU Studies* 39, no. 4 (2000): 127–60.

———. *Same Drum, Different Beat: The Story of Dale T. Tingey and American Indian Services.* Provo: Religious Studies Center, Brigham Young University, 2003.

Lopenzina, Drew. *Through an Indian's Looking-Glass: A Cultural Biography of William Apess, Pequot.* Amherst: University of Massachusetts Press, 2017.

Luckert, Karl W. *Navajo Mountain and Rainbow Bridge Religion.* Flagstaff, AZ: Museum of Northern Arizona, 1977.

———. "Rainbow Mountain and Rainbow Bridge Religion." *American Tribal Religions*, Volume One. Flagstaff: Museum of Northern Arizona, 1977.

Lyman, Albert R. *A Voice Calling: From the Hills of America to the Children of its Ancient People.* Salt Lake City: The Church of Jesus Christ of Latter-day Saints, 1947.

Lyman, Melvin A. *Out of Obscurity into Light.* Salt Lake City: Albany Book, 1985.

Lynch, Ernesteen B. Oral history interview, conducted by Jesse Embry, May 17, 1990. Harold B. Lee Library (HBLL) Special Collections, Brigham Young University, Provo, Utah.

Lyon, William. "The Navajos in the Anglo-American Historical Imagination, 1807–1870." *Ethnohistory* (Summer 1996): 483–509.

MacKay, Michael H. and Grant Underwood, et al., eds. *The Joseph Smith Papers: Documents, vol. 1 (July 1828–June 1831).* Salt Lake City: The Church Historian's Press, 2013.

Mangum, Garth L. and Bruce D. Blumell. *The Mormons' War on Poverty: A History of LDS Welfare, 1830–1990*. Salt Lake City: University of Utah Press, 1993.

Mann, Barbara Alice, and Jerry L. Fields. "A Sign in the Sky: Dating the League of the Haudenosaunee." *American Indian Culture and Research Journal* 21, no. 2 (1997): 105–63.

Mann, Barbara Alice. "Epilogue: Euro-Forming the Data." In *Debating Democracy: Native American Legacy of Freedom*, edited by Bruce E. Johansen, 159–90. Santa Fe, NM: Clear Light Publishers, 1998.

———. *Iroquoian Women: The Gantowisas*. New York: Peter Lang, 2011.

———. *Native Americans, Archaeologists, and the Mounds*. New York, NY: Peter Lang, 2003.

Manseau, Peter. *One Nation under Gods: A New American History*. New York: Little, Brown, and Company, 2015.

Martin, Judy Canty. *Genealogy of the Western Catawba*. N.p., 1998.

———. *My Father's People: A Complete Genealogy of the Catawba Nation*. Self-published, 1999.

Martin, Russell. *A Story that Stands like a Dam: Glen Canyon and the Soul of the West*. Salt Lake City: UT, University of Utah Press, 2017.

Mason, Patrick. *The Mormon Menace: Violence and Anti-Mormonism in the Postbellum South*. New York: Oxford University Press, 2011.

Mauss, Armand L. *All Abraham's Children: Changing Mormon Conceptions of Race and Lineage*. Urbana: University of Illinois Press, 2003.

———. "Mormonism's Worldwide Aspirations and its Changing Conceptions of Race and Lineage." *Dialogue: A Journal of Mormon Thought*, 34, no. 3 and 4 (Fall-Winter 2001), 116.

May, Jon D. "Catawba," Encyclopedia of Oklahoma History and Culture, accessed April 7, 2016, www.okhistory.org.

McCarty-Stonex, Farina. Personal conversations with Farina King, October 2016.

McCombs, Ruth Ann Brown. Chinle Stake Annual Report, 1992, LDS Church History Library.

McDonald, Lucinda. Oral history interview, conducted by Jim M. Dandy, March 19, 1991. Harold B. Lee Library Special Collections, Brigham Young University.

McGregor, Davianna Pomoaikai. "Recognizing Native Hawaiians: A Quest for Sovereignty," in *Pacific Diaspora: Island Peoples in the United States and Across the Pacific*, ed. Paul R. Spickard, Joanne L. Rondilla, and Debbie Hippolite Wright. Honolulu: University of Hawaii Press, 2002.

McIntosh, W. H. *History of Wayne County, New York*. Philadelphia: Everts, Ensign & Everts, 1877.

Meldrum, D. Jeffrey, and Trent D. Stephens. *Who Are the Children of Lehi? DNA and the Book of Mormon*. Salt Lake City, UT: Greg Kofford Books, 2007.

Meriam, Lewis, et al. *The Problem of Indian Administration*. Baltimore: Johns Hopkins Press, 1928.

Merrell, James H. *The Indians' New World: Catawbas and Their Neighbors from European Contact through the Era of Removal*. Chapel Hill: University of North Carolina Press, 2009.

Message from the President of the United States Transmitting a Report of the Secretary of War, Containing the Information Required by the Resolution of the House, Respecting the Negotiations with the Six Nations of Indians in the State of New York. Washington, DC: Gales and Seaton, 1821.

Metcalf, R. Warren. *Termination's Legacy: The Discarded Indians of Utah.* Lincoln, NE: University of Nebraska Press, 2002.

Metcalfe, Brent L. "Reinventing Lamanite Identity." *Sunstone* 131 (March 2004): 20–25.

Mihesuah, Devon, ed. *Repatriation Reader Who Owns American Indian Remains?* Lincoln: University of Nebraska Press, 2000.

Miller, Henry W. "Missionaries of the Latter-day Saints Church in Indian Territory." *Chronicles of Oklahoma* 13 (June 1935): 196–213.

Miller, Scott K. "Undamming Glen Canyon: Lunacy, Rationality, or Prophecy?" *Stanford Environmental Law Journal*, 19 (January 2000): 121–205.

Miller, Susan A., and James Riding In. *Native Historians Write Back: Decolonizing American Indian History.* Lubbock, TX: Texas Tech University Press, 2011.

Milliken, Charles F. *History of Ontario County, New York, and Its People.* New York: Lewis Historical Publishing, 1911.

"Miss Indian America Begay travels extensively, seeks unity." *Eagle's Eye*, January 1972.

Mix, Tamara and Kirsten Waldo. "Knowing your Power: Risk Society, Astroturf Campaigns, and the Battle over Red Rock Coal-Fired Plant." *The Sociological Quarterly* 56: (2015): 125–26.

Mohawk, John C. "Indians and Democracy: No One Ever Told Us," in *Exiled in the Land of the Free: Democracy, Indian Nations, and the U.S. Constitution*, ed., Oren Lyons, et al. Santa Fe: Clear Light Press, 1992.

Moore, Carrie A. "Debate renewed with change in Book of Mormon introduction." *Deseret News*, November 8, 2007.

Moorehead, Warren K. *Stone Ornaments Used by Indians in the United States and Canada.* Andover, MA: The Andover Press, 1917.

Morais, Sara. "Archive Practice and Digital Humanities," The Centre for the Internet & Society, http://cis-india.org/raw/digital-humanities/archive-practice-and -digital-humanities.

Morgan, Brandon. "Educating the Lamanites: A Brief History of the LDS Indian Student Placement Program." *Journal of Mormon History* 35, no. 4 (Fall 2009): 191–217.

Morgan, Lewis H. *League of the Ho-de'-no-sau-nee, Iroquois.* Rochester, NY: Sage & Brothers, 1851.

"Mormons Assure Indian Militants On Aid by Church." *New York Times*, April 9, 1973.

Morrison, Toni. *Playing in the Dark.* New York: Random House, 2007.

Morse, Jedediah. *A Report to the Secretary of War of the United States, on Indian Affairs.* New Haven, CT: S. Converse, 1822.

Mueller, Max Perry. "Playing Jane," *Journal of Africana Religions* 1, no. 4 (2013): 513–61.

———. *Race and the Making of the Mormon People.* Chapel Hill: University of North Carolina Press, 2017.

———. "Review: The Columbia Sourcebook on Mormons in the United States," *Mormon Studies Review* (forthcoming).

Murphy, Thomas W. "Decolonization on the Salish Sea: A Tribal Journey Back to Mormon Studies." In *Towards a Post-Colonial Mormonism*, edited by Joanna Brooks and Gina Colvin, 47–66. Salt Lake City: University of Utah Press, 2018.

———. "From Racist Stereotype to Ethnic Identity: Instrumental Uses of Mormon Racial Doctrine." *Ethnohistory* 46, no. 3 (Summer 1999): 451–80.

———. "Guatemalan Hot/Cold Medicine and Mormon Words of Wisdom: Intercultural Negotiation of Meaning." *Journal for the Scientific Study of Religion* 36, no. 2 (1997): 297–308.

———. "Imagining Lamanites: Native Americans and the Book of Mormon." PhD dissertation, University of Washington, 2003.

———. "Lamanite Genesis, Genealogy, and Genetics." In *American Apocrypha: Essays on the* Book of Mormon, edited by Dan Vogel and Brent Lee Metcalfe. Salt Lake City: Signature Books, 2002.

———. "Other Mormon Histories: Lamanite Subjectivity in Mexico." *Journal of Mormon History* 26, no. 2 (Fall 2000): 179–214.

———. "Other Scriptures: Restoring Voices of Gantowisas to an Open Canon," Chapter herein.

———. "Reinventing Mormonism: Guatemala as a Harbinger of the Future?" *Dialogue: A Journal of Mormon Thought* 29, no. 1 (1996): 177–92.

———. "Simply Implausible: DNA and a Mesoamerican Setting for the Book of Mormon." *Dialogue: A Journal of Mormon Thought* (2003): 109–31.

———. "Sin, Skin, and Seed: Mistakes of Men in the Book of Mormon." *Journal of the John Whitmer Historical Association* 25 (2004): 36–51.

Murphy, Thomas W. and Angelo Baca. "Rejecting Racism in Any Form: Latter-Day Saint Rhetoric, Religion, and Repatriation." *Open Theology*, no. 2 (2016): 700–725.

———. "Science, Settlers, and Scripture: Native Perspectives on DNA and the Book of Mormon." In *The Mormon Church and Its Gospel Topics Essays: The Scholarly Community Responds*, edited by Matthew L. Harris and Newell G. Bringhurst. Salt Lake City, UT: University of Utah Press, In Press.

Murphy, Thomas W., Jessyca B. Murphy, and Kerrie S. Murphy. "An Indian Princess and a Mormon Sacagawea: Decolonizing Memories of Our Grandmothers." In *Race, Gender, and Power on the Mormon Borderlands*, edited by Andrea Radke-Moss Dee Garceau, and Sujey Vega, manuscript under review.

Nabokov, Peter. *Where Lightening Strikes: The Lives of American Indian Sacred Places*. London: Penguin Book, 2006.

Nakai, Raymond. "Dedication of Glen Canyon Dam," "Equality of Opportunity," item display 77978, Cline Library, Northern Arizona University.

———. "Glen Canyon (Lake Powell) Speech," Nakai Papers, Cline Library, Northern Arizona University.

Nash, Gerald. *The Federal Landscape: An Economic History of the Twentieth Century West*. Tucson: University of Arizona Press, 1999.

Nauvoo Legion Papers, July-August 1853, MS 17208, LDS Church History Library.

"Navajo Nation Judge Weighs Jurisdiction of Mormon Church." *Navajo-Hopi Observer*, April 17, 2018.

Navajo Tribal Council. "Tribal Policy on Adoption of Navajo Orphans and Abandoned or Neglected Children." In *The Destruction of American Indian Families*, edited by Steven Unger (New York: Association on American Indian Affairs, 1977), 85–86.

"Ned Kaili Aikau." Obituaries. *Daily Herald*, June 28, 2010, accessed May 3, 2016. http://www.heraldextra.com/lifestyles/announcements/obituaries/ned-kaili -aikau/article_8f94384d-3b40-5e69-81b7-813850b90074.html.

Neihardt, John G. *Black Elk Speaks: Being the Life Story of a Holy Man of the Oglala Sioux*. Lincoln, NE: Bison Books, 1988 [1932].

Newton, Marjorie. *Tiki and Temple: The Mormon Mission in New Zealand, 1854–1958*. Draper, Utah: Greg Kofford Books, 2012.

Nielson, Parker M. *Cultural Genocide of the Mixed-Blood Utes: An Advocate's Chronicle*. Norman: University of Oklahoma Press, 1982.

Nihipali, Elizabeth, Lessa Kanani'opua Pelayo, Christian Hanz Lozada, Lorelie San-tonil Olaes, and Cheryl Villareal Roberts. *Hawaiians in Los Angeles*. Charleston, South Carolina: Arcadia Publishing, 2012.

Norton, John. "The Creation of the World." In *Early American Writings*, edited by Carla Mulford, 7–8. New York: Oxford University Press, 2002[1816].

Norwood, Kimberly Jade, ed. *Color Matters: Skin Tone Bias and the Myth of a Postra-cial America*. New York: Routledge, 2013.

Nosmelone. "Black Elk's Vision and Lehi's Dream." http://inthecavityofarock .blogspot.com/2015/05/black-elks-vision-and-lehis-dream.html.

Notes, Akwesasne, ed. *Basic Call to Consciousness*. Summertown, TN: Native Voices, 2005.

O'Grady, Deborah. "Navajo Code Talkers." *Deborah O'Grady*, accessed September 24, 2016. http://www.deborahogrady.com/portfolio-items/navajo-code-talkers/.

O'Reilly, Henry. *Settlement in the West. Sketches of Rochester; with incidental notices of western New-York*. Rochester, NY: William Alling, 1838.

Oaks, Dallin H. "Teaching and Learning by the Spirit." *Ensign*, March 1997.

——. "The Special Language of Prayer." *New Era* (January 2006).

Obituary: "Mrs. Martha Head Dead at Age 102," clipping in private collection.

Olsen, Emma R., compiler. "Mission to the Indians." *An Enduring Legacy* 12 (1989): 353–400.

Omi, Michael and Howard Winant, *Racial Formations in the United States: From the 1960s to the 1980s*. New York: Routledge & Kegan Paul, 1986.

Oral History Transcript. Charles Redd Center for Western Studies, L. Tom Perry Spe-cial Collections, Harold B. Lee Library, Provo, Utah.

Osborne, Virgus C. "An Appraisal of the Education Program for Native Americans at Brigham Young University, 1966–1974." PhD diss., University of Utah, 1975.

——. "Indian Education at Brigham Young University, 1965–1985." Unpublished mss., 1993. L. Tom Perry Special Collections, Harold B. Lee Library, Provo, Utah.

Oskison, John Milton. *The Tales of the Old Indian Territory*, edited by Lionel Larré. Lincoln: University of Nebraska Press, 2012.

Packer, Boyd K. "Manual of Policies and Procedures for the Administration of the Indian Seminaries of the Church of Jesus Christ of Latter-day Saints." PhD diss., Brigham Young University, 1962.

———. Untitled address to Indians students during BYU Indian Week, February 1979. *Eagle's Eye* 11 [3]: 2–3.

Parfitt, June S. *A Genealogy of the Walter Family.* Self-published. Manchester, NH, 1986.

Parins, James W. *John Rollin Ridge: His Life and Works.* Lincoln: University of Nebraska Press, 1991.

Park, Lindsay Hansen, Gina Colvin, and Thomas W. Murphy. *Lamanite DNA with Thomas Murphy.* Color of Heaven, Podcast audio. 2016.

———. "Code of Handsome Lake, the Seneca Prophet." In *Parker on the Iroquois,* edited by William N. Fenton. Syracuse, NY: Syracuse University Press, 1968.

Parker, Arthur C. *An Analytical History of the Seneca Indians.* Researches and Transactions of the New York State Archaeological Association. Rochester, NY: Lewis H. Morgan Chapter, 1926.

———. "Ancient Land of the Genesee," in *History of the Genesee Country,* ed. Lockwood R. Doty. Chicago: S. J. Clarke Publishing, 1925.

———. *Red Jacket: Seneca Chief.* Lincoln, NE: University of Nebraska Press, 1998 [1952].

———. *The Code of Handsome Lake, the Seneca Prophet. New York State Museum Bulletin 163.* Albany, New York, 1912: 5–148.

Parker, Stuart. "Queso y gusanos: The Cosmos of Indigenous Mormon Intellectual Margarito Bautista," in *Just South of Zion: The Mormons in Mexico and Its Borderlands,* ed. Jason H. Dormady and Jared M. Tamez. Albuquerque: University of New Mexico Press, 2015.

Parkin, Max H. "Lamanite Mission of 1830–31." *Encyclopedia of Mormonism,* 802–804.

Parry, Keith. "Joseph Smith and the Clash of Sacred Cultures." *Dialogue: A Journal of Mormon Thought* 18 (Winter 1985): 65–80.

———. "'To Raise These People Up': An Examination of a Mormon Mission to an Indian Community as an Agent of Social Change." Ph.D. diss., University of Rochester, 1972.

Pascoe, Peggy. *What Comes Naturally: Miscegenation Law and the Making of Race in America.* New York: Oxford University Press, 2009.

Paul, Erich Robert. *Science, Religion, and Mormon Cosmology.* Urbana: University of Illinois Press, 1992.

Pavlik, Steve. "Of Saints and Lamanites: An Analysis of Navajo Mormons." *Wicazo Sa Review* 8, no. 1 (Spring 1992): 21–30.

Pearce, Roy Harvey. *Savagism and Civilization: A Study of the Indian and the American Mind.* Berkeley: University of California Press, 1988.

Pearl of Great Price. 2018. The Church of Jesus Christ of Latter-day Saints.

Perego, Ugo A. "The Book of Mormon and the Origin of Native Americans from a Maternally Inherited DNA Standpoint." *The FARMS Review* 22, no. 1 (2010): 191–227.

Peters, Charles S. *Take up your Mission: Mormon Colonizing Along the Little Colorado River, 1870–1900*. Tucson: The University of Arizona Press, 1973.

Petersen, Mark E. *Children of the Promise: The Lamanites, Yesterday and Today*. Salt Lake City: Bookcraft, 1981.

Peterson, Charles S. and Brian Q. Cannon. *The Awkward State of Utah: Coming of Age in the Nation, 1896–1945*. Salt Lake City: University of Utah Press/Utah State Historical Society, 2016.

Phelps, W. W. "O stop and tell me, Red Man." In *A Collection of Sacred Hymns, for The Church of the Latter Day Saints*, edited by Emma Smith, 83–84. Kirtland, OH: F. G. Williams & co., 1835.

Philp, Kenneth R. "Dillion S. Meyer and the Advent of Termination, 1950–1953." *Western Historical Quarterly* (January 1988): 37–59

Pine, Mary. Informal conversation with Farina King, Fort Wingate, New Mexico, June 3, 2018.

Pokagon, Simon. "The Future of the Red Man." *Forum* 23 (1897): 698–708.

Porter, Larry. "The Church in New York and Pennsylvania, 1816–1831," in *The Restoration Movement: Essays in Mormon History*, eds F. Mark McKiernan, Alma R. Blair, and Paul M. Edwards. Rev. eds. Independence, MO: Herald Publishing House, 1992.

Porter, Tom. *And Grandma Said . . . Iroquois Teachings as Passed Down through the Oral Tradition*. Bloomington, IN: Xlibris Corporation, 2008.

———. *Kanatsiohareke: Traditional Mohawk Indians Return to Their Ancestral Homeland*. Greenfield Center, New York: Bowman Books, 2006.

Posey, Alexander. *The Fus Fixico Letters*. Lincoln: University of Nebraska Press, 1993.

Powers, William. "When Black Elk Speaks, Everybody Listens." *Social Text*, no. 24 (1990): 43–56.

Pratt, Mary Louise. "Arts of the Contact Zone," *Profession* 91 (1991): 33–40.

Pratt, Parley P. *Autobiography of Parley P. Pratt*. Salt Lake City: Deseret Book, 1963.

Preece, Edward B. "Mormon Missionary Work among the Indians of North America in the Twentieth Century." L. Tom Perry Special Collections, Harold B. Lee Library, Provo, Utah, 1965.

"Press Coverage of Lee's Excommunication Ambivalent." *Sunstone* 13, no. 4 (August 1989): 47–49.

Price, John A. "The Book of Mormon vs. Anthropological Prehistory." *Indian Historian* 7, no. Summer (1974): 35–40.

"Prophet of the Alleghany." *Portfolio* 5, no. 1 (1811): 58–64.

Prucha, Francis P. *Atlas of American Indian Affairs*. Lincoln: University of Nebraska Press, 1990.

———. *The Great Father: The United States Government and the American Indians*, 2 vols. Lincoln: University of Nebraska Press, 1984.

"Quarterly Historical Report for the Northern Indian Mission." *Manuscript History and Historical Reports*. Microfilm, Church History Library, Salt Lake City.

Quinn, D. Michael. *Early Mormonism and the Magic World View, Revised and Enlarged*. Salt Lake City: Signature Books, 1998.

Raff, Jennifer A., and Deborah A. Bolnick. "Does Mitochondrial Haplogroup X Indicate Ancient Trans-Atlantic Migration to the Americas? A Critical Re-Evaluation." *PaleoAmerica* 1, no. 4 (2015): 297–304.

Rainer, Howard, "The Realities of Today's Indian Leadership." *Indian Liahona* 7, no. 5 (September-October 1970): 30.

Raleigh, Robert. "Elder George P. Lee: Navajo General Authority Speaks on Self-Image, Discipline." *Eagle's Eye* 18, no. 2 (Winter 1985–1986): 20–21.

Rasmussen, Birgit Brander. *Queequeg's Coffin: Indigenous Literacies & Early American Literature.* Durham: Duke University Press, 2012.

"Red and Delightful." *Time* 74, no. 16 (September 7, 1959).

Reed, Christopher. "Samuel Billison: Navajo Code Talker Whose Complex Native Language Baffled Wartime Japanese Cryptographers." Obituary. *Guardian*, December 6, 2004.

Reed, Rachel. "Tiyarra Roanhorse: Bringing Native American Culture to Hawaii." *Ke Alaka'i* (Fall 2016): 63.

Reeve, Rex C., Jr. "Northern Indian Mission Scrapbook, 1964–1972." Microfilm, Church History Library, Salt Lake City.

———. Northern Indian Mission Collection, MSS 8816. L. Tom Perry Special Collections, Harold B. Lee Library, Brigham Young University, Provo, Utah.

Reeve, W. Paul. *Religion of a Different Color: Race and the Mormon Struggle for Whiteness.* New York: Oxford University Press, 2015.

Reisner, Mark. *Cadillac Desert: The American West and its Disappearing Water.* New York: Penguin Books, 1993.

"Remarks by President Brigham Young, Tabernacle, January 12, 1862." *The Deseret News,* February 12, 1862.

Reséndez, Andres. *The Other Slavery: The Uncovered Story of Indian Enslavement in America.* New York: Houghton Mifflin Harcourt, 2016.

Rice, Brian. *The Rotinonshonni: A Traditional Iroquoian History through the Eyes of Teharonhhia:Wako and Sawiskera.* Syracuse, NY: Syracuse University Press, 2013.

Richter, Daniel K. *The Ordeal of the Longhouse: The Peoples of the Iroquois League in the Era of European Colonization.* Chapel Hill, NC: University of North Carolina Press, 1992.

Ridge, John Rollin. "John Rollin Ridge Goes West." *Northwest Arkansas Times,* March 11–14, 1973. Accessed May 2, 2016, http://www.fayettevillehistory.com/primary/2009/06/john-rollin-ridge-goes-west.html.

Riding In, James and Susan A. Miller. *Native Historians Write Back: Decolonizing American Indian History.* Lubbock: Texas Tech University Press, 2011.

Riess, Jana. "New Theory Connects a Native American Prophet with Joseph Smith and the Book of Mormon." *Flunking Sainthood, Religion News Service,* February 5, 2015.

Riggs, Lynette A. "The Church of Jesus Christ of Latter-day Saints' Indian Student Placement Service: A History." PhD diss., Utah State University, 2008.

Ripley, Dorothy. *The Bank of Faith of Works United.* Philadelphia: J.H. Cunningham, 1819.

Roberts, B. H. *New Witnesses for God Vol. II.* Salt Lake City: Deseret News, 1909.

Roberts, B.H., ed. *The History of the Church of Jesus Christ of Latter-day Saints: Period I. History of Joseph Smith the Prophet.* Salt Lake City, Utah: Deseret Press, 1902–1912.

Rogers, Brent. "A 'Distinction Between Mormons and American: Mormon Indian Missionaries, Federal Indian Policies, and the Utah War." *Utah Historical Quarterly* 82:4 (2014): 251–72

Rogers, Jedediah S. and Matthew C. Godfrey, eds. *The Earth Will Appear as the Garden of Eden: Essays on Mormon Environmental History.* Salt Lake City: The University of Utah Press, 2018.

Rogers, Will. *More Letters of a Self-Made Diplomat.* Edited by Steven K. Gragert. Stillwater: Oklahoma State University Press, 1982.

———. *Radio Broadcasts of Will Rogers.* Edited by Steven K. Gragert. Stillwater: Oklahoma State University Press, 1983.

———. *Will Rogers' Daily Telegrams.* Edited by James M. Smallwood. Vols. 1–5. Stillwater: Oklahoma State University Press, 1978–1982.

Romig, Ronald E. "The [1831] Lamanite Mission." *John Whitmer Historical Association Journal* 14 (1994): 25–33.

Romney, Marion G. *The Power of God unto Salvation,* Brigham Young University Speeches of the Year, Provo, February 3, 1960.

Rosier, Paul. "They Are Ancestral Homelands: Race, Place, and Politics in Cold War Native America, 1945–1961." *Journal of American History* (March 2006), pp. 1300–1326

Round, Phillip H. *Removable Type: Histories of the Book in Indian Country, 1663–1880.* Chapel Hill: University of North Carolina Press, 2010.

Rust, Richard Dilworth. "A Mission to the Lamanites." In *Revelations in Context.* Salt Lake City: Church of Jesus Christ of Latter-day Saints, 2013. Accessed May 13, 2016. https://history.lds.org/article/doctrine-and-covenants-lamanite-mission ?lang=eng.

Select Comm. on Indian Affairs, Senate. *Indian Child Welfare Act of 1977: Hearings on S. 1214,* 95th Cong. (1977).

"Senate Child Welfare Hearings." *Indian Family Defense* 8 (November 1977): 1–2.

"Seneca Indians." *Palmyra Herald,* July 31, 1822.

Shannon, Don. "River Storage Project Lobbyists Get Top Fee." *Los Angeles Times,* January 13, 1957, p. 27.

Shreve, Bradley G. *Red Power Rising: The National Indian Youth Council and the Origins of Native Activism.* Norman: University of Oklahoma Press, 2011.

Shumway, Dale and Margene Shumway, eds. *The Blossoming: Dramatic Accounts of the Lives of Native Americans in the Foster Care Program of The Church of Jesus Christ of Latter-day Saints.* Published by the authors, 2002.

———. *The Blossoming II: Dramatic Accounts in the Lives of Native Americans.* Dale and Margene Shumway, 2007.

Shupe, Barbara, Janet Steins, and Jyoti Pandit, eds. *New York State Population: A Compilation of Federal Census Data.* New York: Neal-Schuman Publishers, 1987.

Silko, Leslie Marmon. *Gardens in the Dunes*. New York: Simon & Shuster, 1999.

Sillitoe, Linda. "Who We Are, Where We Come From." *Dialogue: A Journal of Mormon Thought* 25 no. 3 (1992): 9–18.

Silva, Noenoe K. *Aloha Betrayed: Native Hawaiian Resistance to American Colonialism*. Durham: Duke University Press, 2004.

Silverberg, Robert. *Mound Builders of Ancient America: The Archaeology of a Myth*. Greenwich: New York Graphic Society, 1968.

Simon, Jerald F. "Thomas Bullock as an Early Mormon Historian, *BYU Studies* 30 no. 1 (Winter 1990): 71–88.

Simpson, Audra. *Mohawk Interruptus: Political Life across the Borders of Settler States*. Durham, NC: Duke University Press, 2014.

Simpson, Robert L. "Help Available Here: A Conversation with Elder Robert L. Simpson about LDS Social Services." *Ensign*, December 1973.

Smith, Dan K. Interview by Matthew Heiss, Chinle, Arizona, April 30, 1992, OH 1609, LDS Church Archives.

Smith, Ethan. *View of the Hebrews: Or the Tribes of Israel in America*. 2nd ed. Poultney: Smith and Smith, 1825.

Smith, JoAnn. Personal conversation with Farina King, September 16, 2016.

Smith, Joseph, Jr. *American Revivalist and Rochester Observer* 7/6, February 2, 1833.

———. Book of Mormon. Palmyra: E. B. Grandin, 1830.

———. "The Articles of Faith of the Church of Jesus Christ of Latter-day Saints." Accessed September 16, 2016. https://www.lds.org/scriptures/pgp/a-of-f/1.10?lang=eng#9.

———. *The Doctrine and Covenants*. Salt Lake City: The Deseret News Office, 1876.

Smith, Linda Tuihiwai. *Decolonizing Methodologies: Research and Indigenous Peoples*. 2nd ed. New York: Zed Books, 2012.

Smith, Lucy Mack. *Biographical Sketches of Joseph Smith, the Prophet, and His Progenitors for Many Generations*. Liverpool: S.W. Richards, 1853.

Smith, Phillip L. Personal telecommunication conversation with Farina King, September 28, 2016.

Smith, Samuel. Diary, July 10, 1832. MS 4213. LDS Church History Library, Salt Lake City.

Snow, Dean R. *The Iroquois*. Cambridge, MA: Blackwell, 1996.

Snyder, Charles M. ed., *Red and White on the New York Frontier: A Struggle for Survival. Insights from the Papers of Erastus Granger, Indian Agent, 1807–1819*. Harrison, NY: Harbor Hill Books, 1978.

Southerton, Simon G. *Losing a Lost Tribe: Native Americans, DNA, and the Mormon Church*. Salt Lake City: Signature, 2004.

"Southwest Indian Mission Youth Conference." *Indian Liahona* 7, no. 6 (November-December 1970): 32.

Special Subcommittee on Indian Education. "Indian Education: A National Tragedy—A National Challenge." S. Rep. No. P-91-501. Washington, DC: US Government Printing Office, 1969.

Speck, Frank. "Catawba Religious Beliefs, Mortuary Customs, and Dances," *Primitive Man* 12.2 (April 1939): 21–28.

Sproul, David Kent. *A Bridge Between Cultures: An Administrative History of Rainbow Bridge National Monument.* Washington: GPO, 2001.

Stack, Peggy Fletcher. "New Mormon Scriptures Tweak Race, Polygamy References." *Salt Lake Tribune,* March 19, 2013.

———. "Single Word Change in Book of Mormon Speaks Volumes." *Salt Lake Tribune,* November 8, 2007.

Stambor, Howard. "Manifest Destiny and American Indian Religious Freedom: Sequoya, Badoni, and Drowned Gods," *American Indian Law Review,* 10:1 (1982): 59–89.

Stanciu, Cristina. 2013. "An Indian Woman of Many Hats: Laura Cornelius Kellogg's Embattled Search for an Indigenous Voice." *American Indian Quarterly* 37. (The Society of American Indians and Its Legacies: A Special Combined Issue of SAIL and AIQ,): 87–115.

Stanton, Megan. "The Indian Student Placement Program and Native Direction." Herein.

Stewart, Jon and Peter Wiley. "Cultural Genocide: The American Indians' Two Greatest Resources—Their Children and Their Land—Are Threatened by the Mormon Church." *Penthouse* 12 (June 1981): 80–84, 152–54, 163–64.

Stoffle, Richard W., Kristine L. Jones and Henry F. Dobyns. "Direct European Immigrant Transmission of Old World Pathogens to Numic Indians during the Nineteenth Century." *American Indian Quarterly* 19, no. 2 (Spring, 1995): 181–203.

Stoler, Ann Laura. *Along the Archival Grain: Epistemic Anxieties and Colonial Common Sense.* Princeton, NJ: Princeton University Press, 2010.

Stone, William L. *The Life and Times of Red Jacket, or Sa-go-ye-wat-ha; being the sequel to the history of the Six Nations.* New York: Wiley and Putnam, 1841.

Ström, Åke B. "Red Indian Elements in Early Mormonism," *Temenos: Studies in Comparative Religion* 5 (1969): 120–68.

Subcommittee on Indian Affairs and Public Lands of the Committee on Interior and Insular Affairs, House of Representatives. *Indian Child Welfare Act of 1977: Hearings on S. 1214.* 95th Cong. (1978).

Swatzler, David. *A Friend among the Seneca: The Quaker Mission to Cornplanter's People.* Mechanicsburg, PA: Stackpole Books, 2000.

T'hohahoken. "Organizing Indigenous Governance to Invent the Future." In *For Indigenous Eyes Only: A Decolonization Handbook,* edited by Waziyatawin Angela Wilson and Michael Yellow Bird, 157–77. Santa Fe, NM: School of American Research, 2005.

Talker, Fred. Public talk, Church of Jesus Christ of Latter-day Saints chapel, Monument Valley, Utah, February 14, 2016. Farina King in attendance of this talk and took personal notes.

Tanner, Helen Hornbeck, ed., *Atlas of Great Lakes Indian History.* Norman: University of Oklahoma Press for the Newberry Library, 1987.

Tano, Edwin I. Interview by Farina King, January 13, 2013, telephone communication, transcription in Farina King's possession.

———. Interview by Matthew Heiss, Kayenta, Arizona, May 4, 1991, OH 1073, LDS Church Archives.

Taosoga, Helan Wells Grady. Oral history interview, conducted by Jesse Embry, May 17, 1990. Harold B. Lee Library Special Collections, Brigham Young University.

Tate, Lucile C. *LeGrand Richards: Beloved Apostle*. Salt Lake City: Bookcraft, 1982.

Taylor, Alan. *William Cooper's Town: Power and Persuasion on the Frontier of the Early American Republic*. New York: Vintage Books, 1995.

Taylor, Lori Elaine. "Elder Nigeajasha and Other Mormon Indians Moving Westward." *The John Whitmer Historical Association Journal*. Vol. 24 (2004), pp. 111–24.

———. "Joseph Smith in Iroquois Country: The Handsome Lake Story." *The Juvenile Instructor*, June 30, 2010.

———. "Telling Stories about Mormons and Indians." PhD diss., University at Buffalo, State University of New York, 2000.

Tedlock, Dennis. *Popol Vuh: The Definitive Edition of the Mayan Book of the Dawn of Life and the Glories of Gods and Kings*. Translated by Dennis Tedlock. revised and expanded ed. New York: Touchstone, 1996.

Thayne, Stanley. "Wandering Significance: Hagoth and the Many Migrations of Latter-day Lamanite/Nephite Identity," *Juvenile Instructor Blog*, December 5, 2013, accessed September 12, 2016, http://www.juvenileinstructor.org/wandering-significance-hagoth-and-the-many-migrations-of-latter-day-lamanitenephite-identity/.

Thayne, Stanley. "The Blood of Father Lehi: The Book of Mormon and Indigenous Peoples." PhD diss., University of North Carolina at Chapel Hill, 2016.

"Termination of Federal Supervision Over Certain Tribes of Indians," *Joint Hearing before the Subcommittees of the Committees on Interior and Insular Affairs Congress of the United States*, 83rd Cong., second sess. on S. 2670 and H.R. 7674 (Washington: Government Printing Office, 1954), 45.

The Book of Mormon. 1981. The Church of Jesus Christ of Latter-day Saints.

The Book of Mormon. 2018. The Church of Jesus Christ of Latter-day Saints.

The Church of Jesus Christ of Latter-day Saints Indian Seminary Program, Manual of Instructions. Provo: Department of Education, Brigham Young University, 1961.

The Church of Jesus Christ of Latter-day Saints. "Culture for Missionaries: Sioux Indian." Salt Lake City: Church of Jesus Christ of Latter-day Saints, 1984.

"The Guide to the Scriptures." Church of Jesus Christ of Latter-day Saints, https://www.lds.org/scriptures/gs/laman.p2.

"The Lee Letters." *Sunstone* 13, no. 4 (August 1989): 50–55.

The U. S. Army/Marine Corps Counterinsurgency Field Manual. Chicago: University of Chicago Press, 2006.

Thomas, Cyrus. "Report on the Mound Explorations of the Bureau of Ethnology." Washington, DC: Government Printing Office, 1985 [1894].

Thomas, Jacob, and Terry Boyle. *Teachings from the Longhouse*. Toronto: Stoddart, 1994.

Thomasson, Gordon C. "What exactly does the word Lamanite mean?" *Ensign*, September 1977, 39.

Timberlake, Henry. *Memoirs of Lieut. Henry Timberlake*. London: J. Ridley, W. Nicoll, and C. Henderson, 1765.

Tooker, Elisabeth. "Cayuga," in *Handbook of North American Indians*, vol. 15, Northeast, ed. Bruce G. Trigger, Washington, DC: Smithsonian Institution, 1978.

Topper, Martin D. "Mormon Placement: Survival Strategy or a Finger in the Dyke?"
    In "Supportive Care, Custody, Placement and Adoption of American Indian Chil-
    dren: Special Questions and New Answers." American Academy of Child Psychi-
    atry conference proceedings, April 19–22, 1977, Bottle Hollow, UT, edited by
    Janet P. Swenson.

———. "'Mormon Placement': The Effects of Missionary Foster Families on Navajo
    Adolescents." *Ethos* 7, no. 2 (Summer 1979): 142–60.

Tsinnijinnie, Deborah Pe'a. Interview by Farina King, Salt River Pima-Maricopa
    Indian Community, Arizona, January 23, 2013.

Tsinnijinnie, Thomas. Interview by Farina King, LDS Papago Ward building, Salt
    River Pima-Maricopa Indian Community, Arizona, September 12, 2012, recording
    in Farina King's possession.

Turner, D. L. "Akimel Au-Authm, Xalychidom Piipaash, and the LDS Papago Ward,"
    Journal of Mormon History 39.1 (Winter 2013): 158–180.

Turner, Orasmus. *History of the Pioneer Settlement of Phelps and Gorham's Purchase,
    and Morris' Reserve.* Rochester, NY: William Alling, 1851.

Tvedtnes, John A. "Reinventing the Book of Mormon." Mormon *Studies Review* 16,
    no. 2 (2004): 91–106.

———. "The Charge of 'Racism' in the Book of Mormon." *FARMS Review* 15/2
    (2003): 183–197.

Twiss, Richard. *Rescuing the Gospel from the Cowboys: A Native American Expression
    of the Jesus Way.* Downers Grove, IL: IVP Books, 2015.

Tyler, S. Lyman. *Modern Results of the Lamanite Dispersion: The Indians of the Ameri-
    cas.* Provo, Utah: Extension Publications, Division of Continuing Education,
    Brigham Young University, 1965.

Udall, Stewart. "Glen Canyon Dam Dedication Ceremony," item display 75977, Cline
    Library, Northern Arizona University.

Underwood, Grant. "The Mission to the Lamanites." In *Joseph: Exploring the Life and
    Ministry of the Prophet,* 144–55. Edited by Susan Easton Black and Andrew Skin-
    ner. Salt Lake City: Deseret Book, 2005.

Unger, Steven. "The Indian Child Welfare Act of 1978: A Case Study." DPA diss.,
    University of Southern California, 2004.

US Congress. House Concurrent Resolution 108, 83rd Cong., 1st sess. 1953.

US Statutes at Large, Public Law, 485, 70 Stat 106, April 11, 1956.

Utah Territorial Militia Records, 1849–1877, Utah State Archives and Records, Series
    2210, https://familysearch.org/pal:/MM9.3.1/TH-1951-22024-3922-55?cc=
    1462415&wc=14229733.

Vigil, Kiara M. 2015. *Indigenous Intellectuals: Sovereignty, Citizenship, and the American
    Imagination, 1880–1930.* New York: Cambridge University Press.

Vogel, Dan. *Religious Seekers and the Advent of Mormonism.* Salt Lake City: Signature
    Books, 1988.

Vogt, Evon Z. with Malcolm J. Arth. "Intercultural Relations." In *People of Rimrock:
    A Study of Values in Five Cultures,* edited by Evon Z. Vogt and Ethel M. Albert,
    46–82. Cambridge: Harvard University Press, 1966.

Vrooman, Nicholas. *"The Whole Country was ... 'One Robe'": The Little Shell Tribe's America*. Helena, MT: Drumlummon Institute, 2012.

W. A. Dawson Collection, A. V. Watkins, "The Last Water Hole," Box 5, book 2, section 20. Marriott Library, University of Utah.

Walker, John Phillip, ed. *Dale Morgan on Early Mormonism: Correspondence and a New History*. Salt Lake City: Signature Books, 1986.

Walker, Ronald. "Seeking the 'Remnant': The Native American during the Joseph Smith Period." *Journal of Mormon History* 19, no. 1 (Spring 1993): 1–33.

———. "Wakara Meets the Mormons, 1848–52: A Case Study in Native American Accommodation," *Utah Historical Quarterly* 70 (Summer 2002): 215–37

Wallace, Anthony F.C. *The Death and Rebirth of the Seneca*. New York: Vintage Books, 1972.

Wallace, Paul A. W. *White Roots of Peace*. Philadelphia: University of Pennsylvania Press, 1946.

Warner, Ted J. "Nevada, Pioneer Settlements in." In *Encyclopedia of Mormonism*, edited by Daniel H. Ludlow, 1006–1007. New York: Macmillan Publishing Company, 1992.

Warrior, Robert ed. *The World of Indigenous North America*. New York: Routledge, 2014.

Watkins, Arthur V. Interview, January 4, 1968, p.10, Eisenhower *Administration Project*, Oral History Research Office, Columbia University, 1970.

———. "Speech to President given by Watkins," File 4/9/1951, Watkins Papers, Brigham Young University.

Wauchope, Robert. *Lost Tribes and Sunken Continents: Myth and Method in the Study of American Indians* Chicago: University of Chicago Press, 1962.

Weaver, Jace. "Missions and Missionaries." Chap. 346–49 In *Native America in the Twentieth Century: An Encyclopedia*. New York: Garland Publishing, 1994.

Webb, L. Robert. "An Examination of Certain Aspects of the American Indian Education Program at Brigham Young University." Provo: Brigham Young University, February 1972.

———. "The American Indian Education Program at Brigham Young University: a Report to Interested Publics." Provo, UT: Brigham Young University, 1972.

Weisiger, Marsha. *Dreaming in Sheep in Navajo Country*. Seattle, WA: University of Washington Press, 2008.

Welch, John W. and Tim Rathbone, "The Translation of the Book of Mormon: Preliminary Report on the Basic Historical Information" Paper & Reprint WRR-86. Provo, UT: F.A.R.M.S., 1986.

Westerman, Gwen and Bruce White. *Mni Sota Makoce: The Land of the Dakota*. Minneapolis: Minnesota State Historical Society Press, 2012.

Wetmore, Ruth Y. *First on the Land: The North Carolina Indians*. Winston-Salem, NC: John F. Blair, 1975.

White, Richard. "Frederick Jackson Turner and Buffalo Bill," in *The Frontier in American Culture*, edited by James R. Grossman. Berkeley: University of California Press, 1994.

———. *The Roots of Dependency: Subsistence, Environment, and Social Change among the Choctaws, Pawnee, and Navajos.* Lincoln: University of Nebraska Press, 1983.

Whittaker, David J. "Mormons and Native Americans: A Historical and Bibliographical Introduction." *Dialogue: A Journal of Mormon Thought* 18 (Winter 1985): 33–64.

Wilford, John Noble. "Pacific Islanders' Ancestry Emerges in Genetic Study," *The New York Times*, January 18, 2008.

Wilkenson, Charles F. and Eric Biggs. "The Evolution of the Termination Policy." *American Indian Law Review,* Vol. 5, No. 1 (1977): 139–84.

Wilkinson, Charles. *Blood Struggle: The Rise of Modern Indian Nations.* New York: W. W. Norton, 2005.

Wilkinson, Ernest L. and Lenard J. Arrington, eds. "Education of Native Americans." In *Brigham Young University: The First One Hundred Years,* 3:503–35. Provo: Brigham Young University Press, 1976.

Williams, Arlene Nofchissey and Carnes Burson. *Go My Son.* Audio recording. Provo, Utah: Blue Eagle Records, 1970.

Willis, Koko and Pali Jae Lee. *Tales from the Night Rainbow.* Honolulu: Night Rainbow Publishing, 1990.

Wilson, Waziyatawin Angela, and Michael Yellow Bird. *For Indigenous Eyes Only: A Decolonization Handbook.* Santa Fe, NM: School of American Research, 2005.

Wilson, Edmund. *Apologies to the Iroquois.* Syracuse, NY: Syracuse University Press, 1992[1959].

Wilson, Shawn. *Research Is Ceremony: Indigenous Research Methods.* Winnipeg, Manitoba: Fernwood Publishing, 2008.

Wilson, Waziyatawin Angela and Michael Yellowbird, eds. *For Indigenous Eyes Only: A Decolonization Handbook.* Santa Fe, NM: School of American Research, 2005.

Winnemucca, Sarah. *Life among the Piutes; Their Wrongs and Claims.* New York: G. P. Putnam's Sons, 1883.

Winslow, Ben. "Judge Quashes Deposition Subpoena of LDS Church President Thomas S. Monson." *Fox13 Salt Lake City,* February 25, 2017.

———. "Judge Won't Dismiss Lawsuit against LDS Church over Sex Abuse Claims." *Fox13 Salt Lake City,* May 31, 2018.

Wolfe, Patrick. "Settler Colonialism and the Elimination of the Native." *Journal of Genocide Research* 8, no. 4 (2006): 387–409.

Wood, Beth. "LDS Indian Placement Program: To Whose Advantage?" *Akwesasne Notes* 10, no. 5 (Winter 1978): 16–18.

———. "The LDS Indian Placement Program: An Educational System that Works." *Navajo Times,* September 28, 1978: B6-B10.

Woodruff, Wilford. "Preaching the Gospel to, and Helping the Lamanites," July 15, 1855, *Journal of Discourses* IX: 227, http://jod.mrm.org/9/221.

Woods Susan E. and Robert S. McPherson, eds. *Along Navajo Trails: Recollections of a Trader.* Logan, UT: Utah State University Press, 2005.

Worster, Donald. *Rivers of Empire.* Seattle: University of Washington Press, 2000.

Yarrow, Henry C. "A Further Contribution to the Study of the Mortuary Customs of the North American Indians," *First Annual Report of the Bureau of Ethnology*. Washington, DC: Government Printing Office, 1881.

Yellowjohn, Carletta O. Interview by Odessa Neaman, July 10, 1990, transcript. LDS Native American Oral History Project. Brigham Young University Library, Provo, Utah.

Yellowjohn, Ione. Interview by Odessa Neaman, March 1, 1990, transcript. LDS Native American Oral History Project. Brigham Young University Library, Provo, Utah.Young, Brigham. "Indian Hostilities," July 31, 1853, *Journal of Discourses* I: 171, http://jod.mrm.org/1/162.

Zitkala-Ša. *American Indian Stories, Legends, and Other Writings*. Eds. Cathy N. Davidson and Ada Norris. New York: Penguin Classics, 2003.

———. *Dreams and Thunder: Stories, Poems, and the Sun Dance Opera*. Ed. P. Jane Hafen. Lincoln, NE: Bison Books, 2005.

Zolbrod, Paul G. *Diné Bahane': The Navajo Creation Story*. Albuquerque: University of New Mexico Press, 1987.

List of Contributors

P. Jane Hafen (Taos Pueblo) is professor emerita of English at the University of Nevada, Las Vegas (UNLV). She serves as an advisory editor of *Great Plains Quarterly*; on the editorial board of Michigan State University Press, American Indian Series; on the board of the Charles Redd Center for Western Studies; and is associate fellow at the Center for Great Plains Studies. She is a Frances C. Allen Fellow, D'Arcy McNickle Center for the History of the American Indian, the Newberry Library, and was a founding clan mother of the Native American Literature Symposium. She received the William H. Morris Teaching Award for the College of Liberal Arts, UNLV, and the UNLV Foundation Award for Distinguished Teaching. She edited *Dreams and Thunder: Stories, Poems and The Sun Dance Opera* by Zitkala-Ša (University of Nebraska Press, 2001), coedited *The Great Plains Reader*, and is author of *Reading Louise Erdrich's* Love Medicine (Boise State University, 2003), and articles and book chapters about Indigenous literatures, including a collection of essays, *Critical Insights: Louise Erdrich*.

Brenden W. Rensink (PhD, University of Nebraska, 2010) is assistant director of the Charles Redd Center for Western Studies and assistant professor of History at Brigham Young University. He specializes in North American West and Borderlands History, Comparative Genocide Studies, Native Peoples, Wilderness and the Environment, and Public History. Digital copies of some of his publications may be downloaded at www.bwrensink.org. Most recently, he authored *Native but Foreign: Indigenous Immigrants and Refugees in the North American Borderlands* (Texas A&M University Press, 2018). He is co-author of the *Historical Dictionary of the American Frontier* (Rowman & Littlefield, 2015), coeditor of Documents Volume 4 and Volume 6 of the Joseph Smith Papers (Church Historian's Press, 2016 and 2017). He is also project manager and general editor of the Intermountain Histories digital public history website and mobile app project, and the host and producer of the Writing Westward Podcast.

Tacey M. Atsitty is Tsénahabiłnii (Sleep Rock People) and born for Taʼneeszahnii (Tangle People). She is a recipient of the Truman Capote Creative Writing Fellowship, the Corson-Browning Poetry Prize, Morning Star Creative Writing Award, and the Philip Freund Prize. She holds BAs from Brigham Young University and the Institute of American Indian Arts, and an MFA in Creative Writing from Cornell University. Her work has appeared or is forthcoming in POETRY, Crab Orchard Review, Kenyon Review Online, Prairie Schooner, Crazyhorse, New Poets of Native Nations, and other publications. Her first book is Rain Scald (University of New Mexico Press, 2018).

Michalyn Steele graduated from the Georgetown University Law Center in 2001 and, following graduation, worked at a law firm specializing in representing Indian tribes. She has also worked at the Civil Rights Division of the U.S. Department of Justice and as counsel to the assistant secretary for Indian Affairs at the U.S. Department of the Interior. She has been a member of the faculty at Brigham Young University Law since 2014 and teaches Federal Indian Law, Constitutional Law, Civil Rights, and Evidence. Her work has been published in journals such as the UCLA Law Review, the Colorado Law Review, and the Yale Law and Policy Review, among others.

Darren Parry is chairman of the Northwestern Band of the Shoshone Nation. Darren serves on the Board of Directors for the American West Heritage Center, in Wellsville, Utah; the Utah State Museum board; and the Advisory Board of the Huntsman Cancer Institute. His passions in life are his family, which includes his wife, Melody; nine children and thirteen grandchildren; and his tribal family. Darren wants to ensure that those who have gone before him are not forgotten.

Elise Boxer is an enrolled citizen of the Fort Peck Assiniboine and Sioux tribe. She is currently assistant professor in History and Native American Studies at the University of South Dakota. She also serves as Program Coordinator for the Native American Studies program. She received her PhD in History from Arizona State University in December, 2009, under the direction of Peter Iverson. Her publications include "'This is the Place!': Disrupting Mormon Settler Colonialism" in Joanna Brooks and Gina Colvin's *Decolonizing Mormonism: Approaching Postcolonial Zion* (University of Utah Press, 2018); "'The Lamanites Shall Blossom as a Rose:' The Indian Student Placement Program, Mormon Whiteness and Indigenous Identity" in the *Journal of Mormon History*; and "Advocacy and Indigenous Resistance: The Ongoing Assault against Indigenous Sovereignty, Community and Land" in the *Wicazo Sa Review*. She is currently working on her manuscript, *To Become White and Delightsome: Mormons and the Construction of Indigenous Identity*.

Thomas W. Murphy has a PhD in anthropology from the University of Washington (2003). He is Anthropology Department head at Edmonds Community College in Lynnwood, WA, and affiliate faculty in Canadian Studies at UW. He leads a community-based field school focused on the combination of traditional and scientific knowledge. He and his students travel on Tribal Canoe Journeys in the U.S. and Canada each summer and paddle with Samish, Stillaguamish, Blue Heron, and G'ana'k'w canoe families. He received the 2005 Outstanding Faculty Award from the Associated Students at Edmonds Community College and was named the 2011 Washington State Conservation Educator of the Year. The field school he leads won the VISION 2040 award from the Puget Sound Regional Council in 2012 for their help repatriating salmon to the site of the Point Elliot Treaty. He is the author of "Other Mormon Histories: Lamanite Subjectivity in Mexico," published in *Journal of Mormon History*.

Lori Elaine Taylor is an independent scholar with a specialization in propaganda, persuasion, and the slippery stories people tell themselves about their collective pasts. Her work includes religion and racism, music and music communities, and labor history. Lori completed her PhD at the University at Buffalo and her MA at The George Washington University. The John Whitmer Historical Association awarded her Best Dissertation for "Telling Stories about Mormons and Indians." She recently published flash fiction, "Latter-day Confederacy of Many Nations," in the alternate history anthology, *States of Deseret* (Peculiar Pages, 2017). Her superpowers are writing Python and speaking Finnish.

Max Perry Mueller (PhD, Harvard, 2015) is the author of *Race and the Making of the Mormon People* (The University of North Carolina Press, 2017) and the forthcoming *Wakara's America: A Native and American History of the West*. He is assistant professor of Religious Studies at the University of Nebraska–Lincoln.

Michael P. Taylor is assistant professor of English and associate director of American Indian Studies at Brigham Young University. He holds an MA in American Studies from Ruprecht-Karls-Universität Heidelberg and a PhD in English from the University of British Columbia. His research focuses on Indigenous North American and Pacific literatures and is grounded in archive-based Indigenous literary histories.

Stanley Thayne is visiting assistant professor of Anthropology and Religion at Whitman College in Walla Walla, Washington. He received his PhD in Religious Studies from the University of North Carolina at Chapel Hill.

Erika Marie Bsumek earned her BA in history from the University of Utah and her PhD from Rutgers University. She is author of the award winning *Indian-made: Navajo Culture in the Marketplace, 1848–1860* (University Press of Kansas, 2008) and the coeditor of a collection of essays on global environmental history titled *Nation States and the Global Environment: New Approaches to International Environmental History* (Oxford University Press, 2013). Her current research explores the social and environmental history of the area surrounding Glen Canyon on the Utah-Arizona border from the 1840s to the present. The working title of the book is *Damming Zion: Race, Religion, and the Fight for Resources on the Colorado Plateau, 1800 to the Present*. She is also working on a larger project that examines the impact that large public works had on the American West, tentatively titled *The Concrete West: Engineering Society and Culture in the Arid West, 1900–1970*. In addition to other projects, she has developed software called ClioVis for use in history courses.

Bilagáanaa niliigo' dóó Kinyaa'áanii yásh'chíín. Bilagáanaa dabicheii dóó Tsinaajinii dabinálí. Ákót'éego diné asdzáá nilí. Farina King is a Bilagáanaa Diné historian. She is assistant professor of History and an affiliate of the Cherokee and Indigenous Studies Department at Northeastern State University in Tahlequah, Oklahoma. Her first book is *The Earth Memory Compass: Diné Landscapes and Education in the Twentieth Century* (University Press of Kansas, 2018). She received her PhD in U.S. History at Arizona State University. To learn more about her work and background, visit her website at farinaking.com.

Jay H. Buckley (PhD, Nebraska) is associate professor of History at Brigham Young University, where he teaches United States, American West, and American Indian history courses. Buckley directs the American Indian Studies Minor and is director of the Charles Redd Center for Western Studies. Buckley is the author of the award-winning *William Clark: Indian Diplomat* (University of Oklahoma Press, 2008). He is co-author of *By His Own Hand?: The Mysterious Death of Meriwether Lewis* (University of Oklahoma Press, 2006); *Zebulon Pike, Thomas Jefferson, and the Opening of the American West* (University of Oklahoma Press, 2012); *Historical Dictionary of the American Frontier* (Rowman and Littlefield, 2015); *Explorers of the American West: Mapping the World through Primary Documents* (ABC-CLIO, 2016); and *Explorers of the American East: Mapping the World through Primary Documents* (ABC-CLIO, 2018). Current book projects include *Great Plains Forts* and *A Fur Trade History of the Great Plains and Canadian Prairies*. Coauthors Taylor Brooks, Kathryn Cochran, and Krisent Hollist were all undergraduate students of Buckley at Brigham Young University.

Megan Ann Stanton is a historian of American religion and kinship. She received a PhD in History from the University of Wisconsin–Madison, an MA from the University of Wisconsin-Madison, and a BA from Arizona State University. Her dissertation, "All in the Family: Ecclesiastical Authority and Family Theology in The Church of Jesus Christ of Latter-day Saints," examines interactions between nineteenth-century LDS leadership and kinship doctrine. Fellowships and grants from the Newberry Library, the Charles Redd Center for Western Studies, the John Whitmer Historical Association, and the University of Wisconsin–Madison have supported her research.

R. Warren Metcalf is associate professor of History at the University of Oklahoma and author of *Termination's Legacy: The Discarded Indians of Utah* (University of Nebraska Press, 2002). He is currently engaged in writing a general history of Mormon-Indian relations.

Index